e3 Chemistry

Review Book

High School Chemistry

with

NYS Chemistry Regents Exams
The Physical Setting

2018

E3 Chemistry Books
Student and teacher-friendly High School books 1

✓ **Excite** students to study
✓ **Engage** students in learning
✓ **Enhance** students' understanding

E3 Chemistry
Review Book 2018

ISBN-13: 978-1978362291

ISBN-10: 1978362293

Printed in the United States of America

E3Chemistry.com

(877) 224 – 0484

info@e3chemistry.com

E3 Scholastic Publishing

Acknowledgement

Many thanks go to Mr. Stephen Costanza, chemistry teacher at Whitesboro High School in Marcy, New York. His superb editing has made this book better.

Table of Contents

E3chemistry.com

Lesson 1: Types of Matter

Chemistry is the study of matter: its composition, structures, properties, changes it undergoes, and energy accompanying these changes.

Matter is anything that has mass and takes up space. Matter, in other words, is "stuff." Matter can be grouped and classified as pure substances or mixtures.

In this lesson, you will learn about the different types of matter.

Types of Matter: *Elements, Compounds, Mixtures*

Pure Substances: *Elements and Compounds*
Pure substances are types of matter composed (made up) of particles that are the same. The composition and properties of a pure substance are uniform and definite in every sample. Elements and compounds are classified as pure substances.

Elements: *Composed of the Same Atom. Cannot be Broken Down.*
An atom is the most basic unit of matter. Elements are pure substances that are composed of identical atoms with the same atomic number. Elements cannot be decomposed or broken down into simpler substances by physical nor chemical methods. Calcium (Ca) and bromine (Br_2) are examples of elements. All known elements are listed on the Periodic Table. The structure of an atom is covered in Topic 3.

Compounds: *Different Atoms Chemically Bonded. Fixed Composition. Chemically Separated.*
Compounds are pure substances composed of two or more different elements that are *chemically* combined in a fixed ratio. The properties and composition of a compound are definite or the same in all samples of the compound. Compounds can be decomposed or broken down into simpler substances by *chemical methods* only. Properties of a compound are different from those of the elements found in the compound. Calcium bromide ($CaBr_2$), water (H_2O), and ammonia (NH_3) are examples of compounds.

The Law of definite proportions states that elements in a compound are combined in a *fixed ratio* by mass. For example, the composition in every sample of water is always 89% O to 11% H. That means any 10-gram sample of water will always contain 8.9 grams of oxygen and 1.1 grams of hydrogen.

Mixtures: *Different Substances Physically Combined. Variable Composition. Physically Separated.*
Mixtures are types of matter that are composed of two or more different substances that are *physically* combined. The proportion of the substances in a mixture may vary or can change from one sample to another. A mixture retains the properties of the individual substances. A mixture can be separated into its components only by *physical methods*. A mixture can be classified as homogeneous or heterogeneous.

Particle Diagrams of Matter

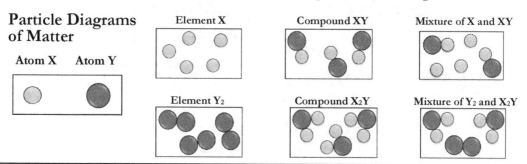

Atom X   Atom Y

Element X

Compound XY

Mixture of X and XY

Element Y_2

Compound X_2Y

Mixture of Y_2 and X_2Y

Homogeneous and Heterogeneous Mixtures

Homogeneous mixtures are mixtures that are uniformly and evenly mixed throughout so the individual substances are not easy to tell apart. Samples taken within the same homogeneous mixture have the exact same composition and characteristics. Aqueous solutions are homogeneous mixtures that are made with water. Salt water, NaCl*(aq)*, is an example of an aqueous solution.

Heterogeneous mixtures are mixtures that are not evenly mixed throughout. The individual substances in a heterogeneous mixture can be identified. Samples taken within the same mixture have different compositions and characteristics. A mixture of oil and water is a heterogeneous mixture.

Separation of Mixtures: *By Physical Methods*

A mixture can be separated using one or more *physical methods*. The separation method or technique depends on the type of mixture and differences in the physical properties of the substances in the mixture.

Separation of Homogeneous Mixtures

Evaporation: *boiling point difference*
The process of heating a soluble salt solution to boil off the solvent and leave behind the solute.

Distillation: *boiling point difference*
The process of boiling off and collecting each liquid of a mixture from the lowest to the highest boiling point.

Crystallization: *solubility difference*
The process of recovering the solid of an aqueous mixture by evaporating off the water or cooling the solution.

Chromatography: *polarity difference*
The process of separating and analyzing the components of an ink or a pigment by how far they travel with the solvent.

Separation of Heterogeneous Mixtures

Filtration: *particle size or solubility difference*
The process of separating a solid from a liquid through a filter setup.

Decantation/Funnel Separation: *density difference*
The process of removing layers of liquids that do not dissolve well in each other.

Paper Chromatography

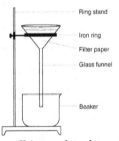

Filtration Apparatus

Classification of Matter: Summary Diagram

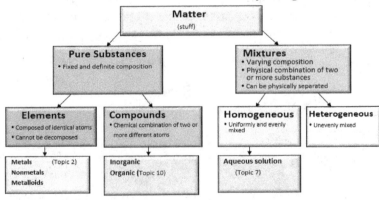

Review Questions: Types of Matter

Vocabulary: Briefly define each of the following terms.
1. Pure substance 2. Mixture 3. Element 4. Compound
5. Aqueous solution 6. Law of definite proportions 7. Homogeneous mixture
8. Heterogeneous mixture 9. Crystallization 10. Distillation. 11. Chromatography

12. Which property correctly describes all compounds?
   (1) They are always homogeneous
   (2) They are always heterogeneous
   (3) They can be physically separated
   (4) They cannot be decomposed

13. Bronze contains 90 to 95 percent copper and 5 to 10 percent tin. Because these percentages can vary, bronze is classified as
   (1) a compound
   (2) a mixture
   (3) an element
   (4) a substance

14. When sample X is passed through a filter a white residue, Y, remains on the filter paper and a clear liquid, Z, passes through. When liquid Z is vaporized, another white residue remains. Sample X is best classified as
   (1) an element
   (2) a heterogeneous mixture
   (3) a compound
   (4) a homogeneous mixture

15. Which is a formula of a mixture of substances?
   (1) $Cl_2(g)$
   (2) $MgCl_2(s)$
   (3) $H_2O(\ell)$
   (4) $HF(aq)$

16. The formula $N_2(g)$ is best classified as
   (1) a compound
   (2) a mixture
   (3) an element
   (4) a solution

17. A mixture of crystals of salt and sugar is added to water and stirred until all solids have dissolved. Which statement best describes the resulting mixture?
   (1) The mixture is homogeneous and can be separated by filtration.
   (2) The mixture is homogeneous and cannot be separated by filtration.
   (3) The mixture is heterogeneous and can be separated by filtration.
   (4) The mixture is heterogeneous and cannot be separated by filtration.

18. Given diagrams A, B, and C below:

● = particle X
○ = particle Y

Which diagrams represent pure substances?
   (1) A and B
   (2) B and C
   (3) A and C
   (4) A, B and C

Base your answers to questions 19 through 21 on the information below.

A student prepares two 141-gram mixtures, *A* and *B*. Each mixture consists of NH_4Cl, sand, and H_2O at 15°C. Both mixtures are thoroughly stirred and allowed to stand. The mass of each component used to make the mixtures is listed in the data table below.

Mass of the Components in Each Mixture

Component	Mixture A (g)	Mixture B (g)
NH_4Cl	40.	10.
sand	1	31
H_2O	100.	100.

19. Describe *one* property of sand that would enable the student to separate the sand from the other components in mixture *B*.

20. Which type of mixture is mixture *B*?

21. State evidence from the table indicating that the proportion of the components in a mixture can vary.

Lesson 2: Phases of Matter, Energy and Temperature

Matter can exist in one of three main states or phases; *solid, liquid,* or *gas.* The nature of a substance determines the phase of the substance under normal conditions. Most substances can change from one phase to another. The nature of a substance also determines conditions necessary for the substance to change from one phase to another.

In this lesson, you will learn about the three phases of matter. You will also learn about phase changes of matter and the relationship to temperature and energy.

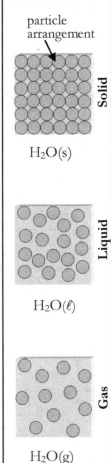

particle arrangement

Solid: *Definite Shape and Volume. Rigid. Crystalline Structure.*

A substance in the solid phase is relatively rigid, and has a definite volume and shape. Particles (atoms, molecules, or ions) of a substance in the solid state are orderly arranged in a *crystalline geometric structure.* Very strong attractive forces hold the particles close together and keep them in fixed positions. The particles vibrate but will not flow pass each other. *(s)* is used to indicate that a substance is in the solid state. Most substances are solids at standard conditions of temperature and pressure, STP. Aluminum (Al), gold (Au), and salt (NaCl) are solids at STP.

$H_2O(s)$

Solid

Liquid: *Definite Volume. No Definite Shape. Free Flowing.*
A substance in the liquid phase has a definite volume but not a definite shape. Particles are still close together, but they move more freely than those in the solid state. It is this free movement of particles that allows a contained liquid to take the shape of its container. *(ℓ)* is used to indicate that a substance is in the liquid state. At STP, bromine (Br_2), water, (H_2O), and ammonia (NH_3) are liquids.

$H_2O(\ell)$

Liquid

Gas: *No Definite Shape nor Volume. Fast Moving. Weak Forces.*
A substance in the gas phase has no definite volume nor shape. Particles move very freely because the attractive forces between them are very weak. If a gas is not contained, the particles will move indefinitely. If a gas is contained, the particles will move about to take the shape and volume of the container. At STP, oxygen (O_2), helium (He), and carbon dioxide (CO_2) are gases.

$H_2O(g)$

Gas

Physical Property Differences: *Different Volumes and Densities.*
A solid, liquid and gas sample of the same substance have different physical properties such as density, volume and heat capacity. Equal masses of the samples have different volumes, therefore different densities. For example, at standard pressure, the density of ice is 0.934 g/cm³ and that of liquid water is 1.0 g/cm³. The difference is due to the different arrangements of the particles in each phase. **As temperature and /or pressure changes, volume and density of a substance change.** However, the chemical composition always stays the same.

Phase Change: *A Physical Change. No Change in Composition.*

A **phase change** is a physical change. During a phase change, a substance changes its form (or state) without changing its chemical composition. Any substance can change from one phase to another given the right conditions of temperature and/or pressure. Most substances require a large change in temperature to go through one phase change. Water is one of a few chemical substances that can change through all three phases within a narrow range of temperature change. The six phase changes and their examples are given below.

Melting is a change from *solid* to *liquid*. $H_2O(s) \rightarrow H_2O(\ell)$

Freezing is a change from *liquid* to *solid*. $H_2O(\ell) \rightarrow H_2O(s)$

Evaporation is a change from *liquid* to *gas*. $C_2H_5OH(\ell) \rightarrow C_2H_5OH(g)$

Condensation is a change from *gas* to *liquid*. $C_2H_5OH(g) \rightarrow C_2H_5OH(\ell)$

Deposition is a change from *gas* to *solid*. $CO_2(g) \rightarrow CO_2(s)$

Sublimation is a change from *solid* to *gas*. $CO_2(s) \rightarrow CO_2(g)$

$I_2(s)$ (Iodine) and $CO_2(s)$ (dry ice) are two substances that readily sublime at normal conditions. Most solids do not sublime.

Phase Changes and Energy

A substance changes phase when it has absorbed or released enough heat energy to rearrange its particles (atoms, molecules, or ions) from one form to another. Some phase changes require a release of heat by the substance, while others require heat to be absorbed.

Endothermic describes a process that absorbs heat energy.
Melting, evaporation and *sublimation* are endothermic phase changes.

Exothermic describes a process that releases heat energy.
Freezing, condensation and *deposition* are exothermic phase changes.

The diagram below summarizes phase changes and the relationship to energy.

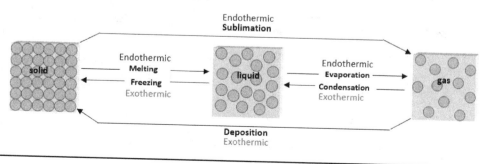

Temperature: *A Measure of the Average Kinetic Energy*

A phase change of a substance occurs at a specific temperature. Every substance has its own melting point and boiling point.

Temperature is a measure of the average kinetic energy of particles in matter.

Kinetic energy is the energy due to the movement of particles in matter. The higher the temperature of a substance, the greater its kinetic energy. As temperature increases, the average kinetic energy also increases.

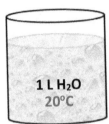

Molecules of water in container B have a greater kinetic energy than those in container A because B is at a higher temperature.

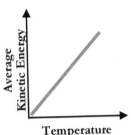

Graph of temperature versus average kinetic energy.

A **thermometer** is a piece of equipment that is used for measuring temperature.

Degree Celsius (ºC) and **Kelvin (K)** are the two most common units for measuring temperature. **Two fixed reference points** are needed to create a thermometer scale. The *freezing point (0ºC, 273K)* and the *boiling point (100ºC, 373K)* of water are often used as the two reference points in creating a thermometer scale.

The temperature conversion between Celsius and Kelvin is given below.

$$K = ºC + 273$$ *Table T equation*

According to this equation, the Kelvin temperature value is always 273 units higher than the same temperature in Celsius.

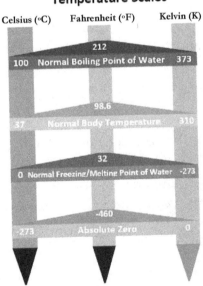

Temperature Scales

Celsius (ºC)   Fahrenheit (ºF)   Kelvin (K)

100	Normal Boiling Point of Water 212	373
37	Normal Body Temperature 98.6	310
0	Normal Freezing/Melting Point of Water 32	-273
-273	Absolute Zero -460	0

Absolute zero is the temperature at which all particles stop moving.

Example 1: *Temperature Unit Conversion*
What Celsius temperature is equivalent to 175 K?

ºC = K − 273

ºC = 175 − 273 = **-98.0 ºC**

E3chemistry.com

Phase Change Diagrams: *Heating and Cooling Curves*

A **phase change diagram** shows the relationship between temperature and phase changes of a substance over time as the substance is heating or cooling.

A **heating curve** shows a change of a substance starting with the substance as a solid. Changes represented on a heating curve are endothermic because heat is being absorbed by the substance.

A **cooling curve** shows a change of a substance starting with the substance as a gas. Changes represented on a cooling curve are exothermic because heat is being released by the substance.

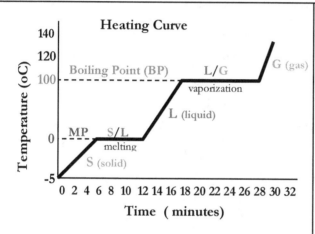

Heating Curve

During segment S, L, or G.
• One phase is present
• Temperature increases
• Kinetic energy increases
• Potential energy stays the same

During segment S/L or L/G
• Two phases are present
• Temperature stays the same
• Kinetic energy stays the same
• Potential energy increases

The substance represented by this curve is likely water.

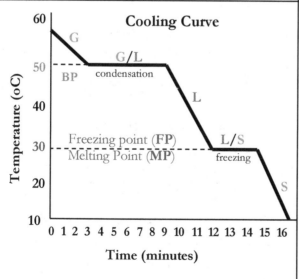

Cooling Curve

During segment G, L, or S.
• One phase is present
• Temperature decreases
• Kinetic energy decreases
• Potential energy stays the same

During segment G/L or L/S
• Two phases are present
• Temperature stays the same
• Kinetic energy stays the same
• Potential energy decreases

The substance represented by this curve is not water

Review Questions: Phases of Matter and Temperature

Vocabulary: Briefly define each of the following terms
22. Solid   23. Liquid   24. Gas   25. Condensation   26. Evaporation
27. Sublimation   28. Deposition   29. Exothermic   30. Endothermic   31. Temperature
32. Kinetic energy 33. Phase change diagram   34. Absolute zero

35. Substance X is a gas and substance Y is a liquid. One similarity between substance X and substance Y is that
    (1) both have definite shape
    (2) both have definite volume
    (3) both are compressible
    (4) both take the shapes of their containers

36. What is the equivalent of 546 K on a Celsius scale?
    (1) 273 °C
    (2) 818 °C
    (3) -273 °C
    (4) 546 °C

37. Which of the following substances has particles that are arranged in a regular geometric pattern?
    (1) $CCl_4(\ell)$
    (2) $Ar(g)$
    (3) $Al(s)$
    (4) $NH_3(aq)$

38. A sample of $CO_2(s)$ and a sample of $CO_2(g)$ differ in their
    (1) chemical compositions
    (2) molecular structures
    (3) empirical formulas
    (4) physical properties

39. Which formula correctly represents a substance that has a definite volume but no definite shape?
    (1) $Hg(\ell)$
    (2) $HCl(g)$
    (3) $Na(s)$
    (4) $H_2(g)$

40. Which equation is showing sublimation of iodine?
    (1) $I_2(g) \rightarrow I_2(s)$
    (2) $I_2(s) \rightarrow I_2(g)$
    (3) $I_2(s) \rightarrow I_2(\ell)$
    (4) $I_2(g) \rightarrow I_2(\ell)$

41. Which sample has the highest kinetic energy?
    (1) 20 mL of $H_2O(\ell)$ at 35°C
    (2) 40 ml of $H_2O(\ell)$ at 25°C
    (3) 20 mL of $C_2H_5OH(\ell)$ at 55°C
    (4) 40 mL of $C_2H_5OH(\ell)$ at 45°C

42. Which change in temperature of a sample of water would result in the smallest decrease in the average kinetic energy of its molecules?
    (1) 25°C to 32°C
    (2) 25°C to 29°C
    (3) 15°C to 9°C
    (4) 12°C to 2°C

Base your answers to questions 43 through 45 on the information below.

Starting as a gas at 206°C, a sample of a substance is allowed to cool for 16 minutes. This process is represented by the cooling curve below.

43. At what time do the particles of this sample have the *highest* average kinetic energy?

44. What is the boiling point of this substance?

45. Using the key below, draw *two* particle diagrams to represent the *two* phases of the sample at minute 4. Your response must include *at least six* particles for *each* diagram.

Cooling Curve for a Substance

Temperature (°C)
240
220
200
180
160
140
120
100
80
60
40
0 2 4 6 8 10 12 14 16
Time (min)

| Key |
| O = particle of the substance |

one phase at minute 4   another phase at minute 4

Lesson 3: Thermal Energy and Heat Calculations

Thermal Energy is the energy produced by the random motion of particles (atoms, molecules, or ions) in a sample of matter. Thermal energy, therefore, is a type of kinetic energy. **Heat** is the flow or transfer of thermal energy between two objects or areas. The direction of heat flow depends on the *temperature difference*. Heat always flows from an area or object of *high* temperature (metal at 65°C) to an area or object of *low* temperature (water at 25°C) until an equilibrium temperature is reached. The equilibrium temperature in the above diagram is 45°C (the sum of 65°C and 25°C divided by 2).

 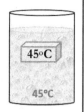

During a chemical or physical change, heat is either absorbed or released. **Exothermic** describes a process that releases (emits or loses) heat.

Endothermic describes a process that absorbs (gains) heat.

Joules and *calories* are units for measuring thermal energy. **See Table D** A **calorimeter** is a device that is used for measuring heat during physical and chemical changes.

J	joule	energy, work, quantity of heat

Heat Constants and Heat Equations: *Use Both to Calculate Heat*

Table B: Physical Constants for Water

Heat of Fusion	334 J/g
Heat of Vaporization	2260 J/g
Specific Heat Capacity of $H_2O(\ell)$	4.18 J/g•K

Table T: Important Formulas and Equations

Heat	$q = mC\Delta T$	q = heat	H_f = heat of fustion
	$q = mH_f$	m = mass	H_v = heat of vaporization
	$q = mH_v$	C = specific heat capacity	
		ΔT = change in temperature	

Specific Heat Capacity (C): *Heat absorbed to warm up or released to cool down*

The **specific heat capacity** of a substance is the amount of heat needed to change the temperature of a one-gram sample of the substance by just one Kelvin. The specific heat capacity is different for each substance.

The specific heat capacity (C) of water is 4.18 J/g•K **(See Table B)**. In other words, a one-gram sample of water will absorb 4.18 Joules of heat to increase its temperature by one Kelvin, or release 4.18 Joules of heat to decrease its temperature by one Kelvin. When the mass and specific heat capacity of a substance are known, the amount of heat absorbed or released by that substance to change between any two temperatures can be calculated using

Table T equation below.

Heat(q) = mCΔT

m = mass of substance e

C = specific heat capacity (J/g•K)

ΔT = difference in temp (K or °C)

ΔT = high temp - low temp

Example 2: *Heat Calculation During Temp Change*
How much heat is released by a 7-gram sample of water to change its temperature from 15°C to 10°C?

q = (m)(C)(ΔT)

q = (7)(4.18)(5)   *numerical setup*

q = **146.3 J**   *calculated result*

Heat of Fusion (H_f): *Heat absorbed to melt or released to freeze*

The **heat of fusion** of a substance is the amount of heat needed to melt a one-gram sample of the substance at its melting point. The heat of fusion of water is 334 J/g **(See Table B)**. In other words, a one-gram sample of water will absorb 334 joules of heat to melt, or release 334 joules of heat to freeze.

When the mass and heat of fusion of a substance are known, the amount of heat absorbed or released by the substance to change between the solid and liquid states can be calculated using

Table T equation below.

$$Heat(q) = mH_f$$

m = mass of substance (g)

H_f = heat of fusion (J/g)

Example 3: *Heat Calculation During Melting*
What is the number of joules needed to melt a 16-g sample of ice to water at 0°C?

q = $(m)(H_f)$
q = $(16)(334)$ *numerical setup*
q = **5344 J**   *calculated result*

Heat of Vaporization (H_v): *Heat absorbed to evaporate or released to condense*

The **heat of vaporization** of a substance is the amount of heat needed to vaporize a one-gram sample of the substance at its boiling point.

The heat of vaporization of water is 2260 J/g. In other words, a one-gram sample of water will absorb 2260 joules of heat to vaporize, or release 2260 joules of heat to condense.

When the mass and heat of vaporization of a substance are known, the amount of heat absorbed or released by the substance to change between the liquid and gas states can be calculated using

Table T equation below:

$$Heat(q) = mH_v$$

m = mass of substance (g)

H_v = heat of vaporization (J/g)

Example 4: *Heat Calculation During Evaporation*
Liquid ammonia has a heat of vaporization of 1.35 kJ/g. How many kilojoules of heat are needed to evaporate a 5-gram sample of ammonia at its boiling point?

q = $(m)(H_v)$
q = $(5)(1.35)$ *numerical setup*
q = **6.75 kJ**   *calculated result*

Other Types of Energy

Although thermal energy is the only type of energy discussed in this topic, there are many other types and forms of energy. Some of them are discussed in different topics of this book. Examples of other types of energy are given below:

Potential (stored) energy: Chemical, nuclear, gravitational, and elastic energy.

Kinetic (motion) energy: Thermal, sound, electromagnetic, and electric energy.

Both potential and kinetic: Mechanical energy

Review Questions: Thermal Energy and Heat Calculations

Vocabulary: Briefly define each of the following terms
46. Thermal energy   47. Heat   48. Joules   49. Specific heat capacity
50. Heat of fusion   51. Heat of vaporization   52. Calorimeter

53. Three forms of energy are
    (1) chemical, exothermic, and temperature
    (2) chemical, thermal, and electromagnetic
    (3) electrical, nuclear, and temperature
    (4) electrical, mechanical, and endothermic

54. The heat of fusion of ice is 334 Joules per gram. Adding 334 Joules to one gram of ice at STP will cause the ice to
    (1) increase in temperature
    (2) decrease in temperature
    (3) change to water at a higher temperature
    (4) change to water at the same temperature

55. A beaker with water and the surrounding air are all at 24°C. After ice cubes are placed in the water, heat is transferred from
    (1) the water to the ice cubes
    (2) the water to the beaker
    (3) the ice cubes to the air
    (4) the beaker to the air

56. What is the minimum amount of heat required to completely melt 20.0 grams of ice at its melting point?
    (1) 20.0 J
    (2) 83.6 J
    (3) 6,680 J
    (4) 45,200 J

57. A 10.0-gram sample of $H_2O(\ell)$ at 23.0°C absorbs 209 joules of heat. What is the final temperature of the sample?
    (1) 5.0°C
    (2) 18.0°C
    (3) 28.0°C
    (4) 50.0°C

Base your answers to questions 58 through 60 on the information below.

A student investigated heat transfer using a bottle of water. The student placed the bottle in a room at 20.5°C. The student measured the temperature of the water in the bottle at 7 a.m. and again at 3 p.m. The data from the investigation are shown in the table to the right.

Water Bottle Investigation Data

7 a.m.		3 p.m.	
Mass of Water (g)	Temperature (°C)	Mass of Water (g)	Temperature (°C)
800.	12.5	800.	20.5

58. Compare the average kinetic energy of the water molecules in the bottle at 7 a.m. to the average kinetic energy of the water molecules in the bottle at 3 p.m.

59. State the direction of heat transfer between the surroundings and the water in the bottle from 7 a.m. to 3 p.m.

60. Show a numerical setup for calculating the change in the thermal energy of the water in the bottle from 7 a.m. to 3 p.m.

Base your answers to questions 61 through 63 on the information below.

Heat is added to a 200.-gram sample of $H_2O(s)$ to melt the sample at 0°C. Then the resulting $H_2O(\ell)$ is heated to a final temperature of 65°C.

61. Compare the amount of heat required to vaporize a 200.-gram sample of $H_2O(\ell)$ at its boiling point to the amount of heat required to melt a 200.-gram sample of $H_2O(s)$ at its melting point.

62. In the space below, show a numerical setup for calculating the total amount of heat required to raise the temperature of the $H_2O(\ell)$ from 0°C to its final temperature.

63. Determine the total amount of heat required to completely melt the sample.

Lesson 4: Gas Characteristics and Gas Laws

Gas behavior is influenced by three key factors; volume (space of container), pressure and temperature. The relationships between these three factors are the basis for gas laws and gas theories. These laws and theories attempt to explain how gases behave.

In this lesson, you will learn about gas theories, gas laws and gas law calculations.

Kinetic Molecular Theory: *Describes ideal gas behavior*

The **kinetic molecular theory** of an ideal gas is a model that is often used to explain the behavior of gases. This theory is summarized below.

- Gases are composed of individual particles.
- Distances between gas particles are far apart.
- Gas particles are in continuous, random, straight-line motion.
- When two particles of a gas collide, energy is transferred from one particle to another.
- Particles of a gas have no attraction to each other.
- Individual gas particles have no volume. Volume is negligible or insignificant.

An **ideal gas** is a theoretical gas that has all the properties summarized above.

A **real gas** is a gas that does exist. Examples of real gases are *oxygen, carbon dioxide, hydrogen, helium, etc.*

Since the kinetic molecular theory (summarized above) applies mainly to an ideal gas, the model cannot be used to predict an exact behavior of real gases. Therefore, real gases *deviate* from or do not behave exactly as an ideal gas for the following two reasons.

- Real gas particles do attract each other.
  Ideal gas particles are assumed to have no attraction to each other.
- Real gas particles do have volume.
  Ideal gases are assumed to have no volume.

Real gases with small molecular masses behave the most like an ideal gas. Hydrogen (H) and helium (He), the two smallest real gases by mass, behave the most like an ideal gas in comparison to all other real gases.

Real gases behave more like an ideal gas under conditions of **high temperature** and **low pressure.**

For example: Oxygen, a real gas, will deviate less from an ideal gas at **300 K and 0.5 atm** (in container A) than at 273 K and 1 atm (in container B).

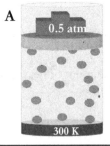

A
0.5 atm
300 K

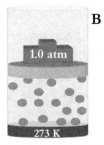

B
1.0 atm
273 K

Volume, Pressure and Temperature of a Gas

Volume

The volume of a confined gas is the of amount space in the container in which it is placed.

Units: *milliliters (mL) or liters (L)*   1 L = 1000 mL

Pressure

The pressure of a gas is the amount of force the gas particles exert on the walls of the container. This pressure is equal, but opposite in magnitude, to the external pressure exerted on the gas.

Units: *atmosphere (atm) or Kilopascal (kPa)*   1 atm = 101.3 kPa

Temperature

The temperature of a gas is a measure of the average kinetic energy of the gas particles. As temperature increases, the gas particles move faster, and their average kinetic energy increases.

Units: *degree Celsius (°C) or Kelvin (K)*   K = °C + 273

TABLE A: Standard Temperature and Pressure (STP)

Name	Value	Unit
Standard Pressure	101.3 kPa 1 atm	kilopascal atmosphere
Standard Temperature	273 K 0°C	kelvin degree Celsius

Avogadro's Law: *Equal Number of Molecules.*

Avogadro's Law states that under the same temperature and pressure, gases of equal volume contain **equal number of molecules or particles.**

Containers A and B below contain the same number of molecules because they have the same volume (2 L), temperature (290 K) and pressure (0.5 atm).

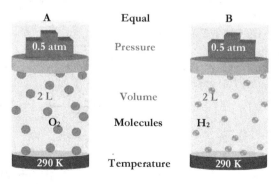

Gas Laws

Boyle's Law: At constant temperature, the volume of a set mass of a confined gas is inversely proportional to the pressure of the gas.
- As pressure increases, volume of the gas decreases.
  Doubling pressure cuts the volume in half.
  Reducing pressure in half doubles the volume.

Charles' Law: At constant pressure, the volume of a set mass of a confined gas is directly proportional to the Kelvin temperature.
- As temperature increases, volume of the gas increases.
  Doubling temperature doubles the volume of the gas.
  Reducing temperature in half cuts the volume in half.

Gay-Lussac's Law: At constant volume, the pressure of a set mass of a confined gas is directly proportional to the Kelvin temperature.
- As temperature increases, pressure of the gas increases.
  Doubling temperature doubles the pressure on the gas.
  Reducing temperature in half cuts the pressure in half.

Combined Gas Law Equation: *Use for Gas Law Calculations*

There are several gas law calculations that relate volume, pressure and temperature. Most of these calculations include other factors such as moles of the gas and a gas constant. Gas law calculations in this book focus on the **combined gas law**, which relates volume, pressure, and temperature, only. The combined gas law equation is the combination of the three laws described above. In all gas law problems, the *total number of moles (number of particles) of the gas sample stays the same.* The combined gas law equation can be found on *Reference Table T.*

TABLE T: Table of Equations and Formulas

Combined Gas Law	$\dfrac{P_1 V_1}{T_1} = \dfrac{P_2 V_2}{T_2}$	P = pressure V = volume T = temperature

V_1 = Initial volume (mL or L)
V_1 = New volume (mL or L)
P_1 = Initial pressure (atm or kPa)
P_2 = New pressure (atm or kPa)
T_1 = Initial Kelvin temperature (K)
T_2 = New Kelvin temperature (K)

Example 5: *Combined Gas Law Problem*

Hydrogen gas has a volume of 100 mL at STP. If temperature and pressure are changed to 546 K and 0.5 atm respectively, what will be the new volume of the gas?

$V_1 = 100$ mL $\qquad V_2 = ?$

STP $\begin{cases} T_1 = 273 \text{ K} & T_2 = 546 \text{ K} \\ P_1 = 1 \text{ atm} & P_2 = 0.5 \text{ atm} \end{cases}$

$$\frac{P_1 V_1}{T_1} = \frac{P_2 V_2}{T_2}$$

$$\left. \frac{(1)(100)}{273} = \frac{(0.5)(V_2)}{546} \atop (136.5)V_2 = 54600 \right\} \begin{array}{l} \textit{numerical} \\ \textit{setup} \end{array}$$

$$V_2 = 400 \text{ mL} \qquad \textit{result}$$

When one of the factors in a gas law problem is held constant, eliminating the constant from the combined gas law equation will yield the equation needed to set up and solve the problem. Three example problems with a constant are given and solved below.

Example 6: *Constant Temperature Problem*
At constant temperature, what is the new volume of a 3.0-L sample of oxygen gas if the pressure is changed from 0.50 atm to 0.25 atm?

$$V_1 = 3.0 \text{ L} \qquad V_2 = ? \text{ (unknown)}$$
$$P_1 = 0.50 \text{ atm} \qquad P_2 = 0.25 \text{ atm}$$

Eliminate T, the constant, from the combined gas law equation, set up, and solve.

$$P_1 V_1 = P_2 V_2$$
$$(0.50)(3.0) = (0.25)(V_2)$$
$$\frac{1.5}{0.25} = V_2 \qquad \text{\textit{numerical setup}}$$
$$\textbf{6.0 L} = \textbf{V}_2 \quad \text{\textit{result}}$$

Example 7: *Constant Pressure Problem*
The volume of a gas is 25 mL at 280 K. If the pressure is held constant, what will be the temperature of the gas when the volume is 75 mL?

$$V_1 = 25 \text{ mL} \qquad V_2 = 75 \text{ mL}$$
$$T_1 = 280 \text{ K} \qquad T_2 = ?$$

Eliminate P, the constant, from the combined gas law equation, set up, and solve.

$$\frac{V_1}{T_1} = \frac{V_2}{T_2}$$
$$\frac{25}{280} = \frac{75}{T_2} \qquad \text{\textit{numerical setup}}$$
$$\textbf{T}_2 = \textbf{840 K} \quad \text{\textit{result}}$$

Example 8: *Constant Volume Problem*
At constant volume, the pressure on a gas changes from 20 kPa to 50 kPa when the temperature of the gas is changed to 303K. What was the initial temperature of the gas?

$$P_1 = 20 \text{ kPa} \qquad P_2 = 50 \text{ kPa}$$
$$T_1 = ? \qquad T_2 = 303 \text{ K}$$

Eliminate V, the constant, from the combined gas law equation, set up, and solve.

$$\frac{P_1}{T_1} = \frac{P_2}{T_2}$$
$$\frac{20}{T_1} = \frac{50}{303} \qquad \text{\textit{numerical setup}}$$
$$\textbf{T}_1 = \textbf{121 K} \quad \text{\textit{result}}$$

Review Questions: Gas Laws and Gas Law Calculations

Vocabulary: Briefly define each of the following terms
64. Ideal gas   65. Kinetic molecular theory   66. Avogadro's law   67. Boyle's law
68. Charles' law   69. Gay-Lussac's law   70. Dalton's law of partial pressure

71. The kinetic molecular theory assumes that the particles of an ideal gas
    (1) are in random, constant, straight-line motion
    (2) are arranged in a regular geometric pattern
    (3) have strong attractive forces between them
    (4) have collisions that result in the system losing energy

72. Under which two conditions do real gases behave least like an ideal gas?
    (1) Low pressure and low temperature   (3) High pressure and low temperature
    (2) Low pressure and high temperature   (4) High pressure and high temperature

73. Which graph best illustrates the relationship between the Kelvin temperature of a
    gas and its volume when the pressure on the gas is held constant?

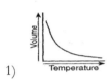 1) (2) (3) (4)

74. Which gas is least likely to obey the ideal gas model under the same temperature
    and pressure?
    (1) Xe   (3) Ne
    (2) Kr   (4) He

75. A real gas will behave most like an ideal gas under which conditions of temperature
    and pressure?
    (1) 273 K and 1 atm   (3) 546 K and 2 atm
    (2) 273 K and 2 atm   (4) 546 K and 1 atm

76. Under which conditions would a 2 L sample of O_2 have the same number of molecules
    as a 2 L sample of N_2 that is at STP?
    (1) 0 K and 1 atm   (3) 0 K and 2 atm
    (2) 273 K and 1 atm   (4) 273 K and 2 atm

77. A cylinder with a movable piston contains a sample of gas having a volume of 6.0 liters
    at 293 K and 1.0 atmosphere. What is the volume of the sample after the gas is heated
    to 303 K, while the pressure is held at 1.0 atmosphere?
    (1) 9.0 L   (3) 5.8 L
    (2) 6.2 L   (4) 4.0 L

Base your answers to questions 78 through 80 on the information below.
    A sample of helium gas is in a closed system with a movable piston. The volume of the
gas sample is changed when both the temperature and the pressure of the sample are
increased. The table below shows the initial temperature, pressure, and volume of the gas
sample, as well as the final temperature and pressure of the sample.

Helium Gas in a Closed System			
Condition	Temperature (K)	Pressure (atm)	Volume (mL)
Initial	200.	2.0	500.
final	300.	7.0	?

79. Compare the total number of gas particles in
    the sample under the initial conditions to the
    total number of gas particles in the sample
    under the final conditions.

80. In the space below, show a correct numerical
    setup for calculating the final volume of the
    helium gas sample.

78. Convert the final pressure of the
    helium gas sample to kilopascals.

Lesson 5: Physical and Chemical Properties and Changes

Properties are characteristics of a substance that can be used to identify and classify that substance. Two types of properties of matter are physical and chemical properties.

Physical Properties: *Phase Change, Solubility, Density, Boiling Point, Melting Point*

A **physical property** is a characteristic of a substance that can be observed or measured without changing the chemical composition of the substance. Some physical properties of a substance depend on the sample size or amount, while others do not.

Extensive properties depend on the sample size or amount present. Mass, weight and volume are examples of *extensive physical properties*.

Intensive properties do not depend on the sample size or amount. Melting, freezing and boiling points, density, solubility, color, odor, conductivity, luster, and hardness are *intensive physical properties*.

• The difference in physical properties of substances make it possible to separate one substance from the others in a mixture.

Physical Change: *No Change in Chemical Composition*

A **physical change** is the change of a substance from one form to another without altering its chemical composition. Examples of physical changes are listed below.

Phase Change   Size Change   Dissolving (forming a solution)

  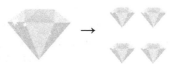

$H_2O(s) \rightarrow H_2O(l)$ $NaCl(s) \rightarrow Na^+(aq) + Cl^-(aq)$

Chemical Properties: *It Burns, Reacts, Combines With, Decomposes Into*

A **chemical property** is a characteristic of a substance that is observed or measured through interaction with other substances.

Examples:
It burns, it combusts, it decomposes, it reacts with, it combines with, or it rusts are some of the phrases that can be used to describe the chemical property of a substance.

Chemical Change: *A Change in Chemical Composition*

A chemical change is the change in composition and properties of one substance to those of other substances. A **chemical reaction** is the way a chemical change occurs. Compounds are formed or broken down through chemical reactions.

Types of chemical reactions include *synthesis, decomposition, replacement, and combustion*. These reactions and others are discussed in Topics 5, 8, 9, 10 and 11.

Particle Arrangements After Physical and Chemical Changes

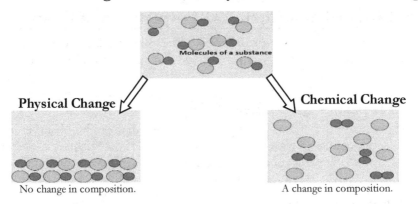

Review Questions: Physical and Chemical Properties and Changes

Vocabulary: Briefly define each of the following terms

81. Physical property
82. Physical change

83. Chemical property
84. Chemical change

85. Which best describes a chemical property of sodium?
    (1) It is a shiny metal.
    (2) It is smooth.
    (3) It reacts vigorously with water.
    (4) It is a hard solid.

86. A large sample of solid calcium sulfate is crushed into smaller pieces. Which two physical properties are the same for both the large sample and one of the smaller pieces?
    (1) Mass and density
    (2) Mass and volume
    (3) Solubility and density
    (4) Solubility and volume

87. During a chemical change, a substance changes its
    (1) density
    (2) composition
    (3) solubility
    (4) phase

88. An example of a physical property of an element is the element's ability to
    (1) form a compound
    (2) react with oxygen
    (3) react with an acid
    (4) form an aqueous solution

Base your answer to the following question on the information below.

The reaction between aluminum and an aqueous solution of copper(II) sulfate is represented by the unbalanced equation below.

$Al(s) + CuSO_4(aq) \rightarrow Al_2(SO_4)_3(aq) + Cu(s)$

89. Explain why the equation represents a chemical change.

Base your answer to the following question on the information below.

Heat is added to a sample of liquid water, starting at 80.°C, until the entire sample is a gas at 120.°C. This process, occurring at standard pressure, is represented by the balanced equation below.

$H_2O(\ell) + heat \rightarrow H_2O(g)$

90. In the box, using the key, draw a particle diagram to represent *at least five* molecules of the product of this physical change at 120.°C.

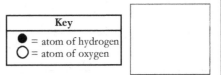

Key	
● = atom of hydrogen	
○ = atom of oxygen	

E3chemistry.com

Additional Materials

Ideal Gas Equation

The **ideal gas equation** relates all three factors (pressure, volume, and temperature) of a gas, as well as the number of moles, n, of the gas. When any three variables of a gas are known, the ideal gas equation below can be used to calculate the fourth variable.

$$PV = nRT$$

n = the number of moles of the gas
R = the universal gas constant, 0.0821 L · atm /(mol·K)
T must always be in Kelvin

Example 9: *Ideal gas problem*
A 5.0 L sample of an ideal gas at 310 K exerts a pressure of 2.0 atm on the walls of its container. What is the number of moles of the gas?

$$n = \frac{PV}{RT} = \frac{(2.0)(5.0)}{(0.0821)(310)}$$

n = moles = **0.39 moles**

Graham's Law of Effusion

When speeds of two gases are compared, the lighter gas will diffuse (spread out) faster than the heavier gas. But how much faster? **Graham's Law** states that under the same conditions of temperature and pressure, the rate (speed) at which gases effuse (escape through a pinhole) is inversely proportional to the square root of their molecular masses.

$$\frac{r_1}{r_2} = \sqrt{\frac{M_2}{M_1}}$$

r_1 = rate (speed) of Gas 1
r_2 = rate (speed) of Gas 2
M_1 = molecular mass of Gas 1
M_2 = molecular mass of Gas 2

The calculated result shows how much faster (or slower) one gas travels relatively to another gas.

Example 10: *Graham's Law Problem*
How much faster does hydrogen gas, H_2, escape through a hole of a container than sulfur dioxide, SO_2 ?

$$\frac{r_{H2}}{r_{SO2}} = \sqrt{\frac{\text{mass of } SO_2}{\text{mass of } H_2}}$$

$$\frac{r_{H2}}{r_{SO2}} = \sqrt{\frac{64 \text{ g}}{2 \text{ g}}} = \textbf{5.63 times}$$

H_2 travels 5.63 times faster than SO_2.

91. A 35-liter sample of an ideal gas is at 25°C and 1.5 atm. Calculate the number of moles of the gas.

92. 2.39 moles of an ideal gas occupy a volume of 29.0 liters at 300 K.. What is the pressure of the gas?

93. 0.105 moles of an ideal gas occupy 5.00 L at a pressure of 0.975 atm. What is the temperature of the gas in Kelvin?

94. Of these gases; SO_2, CO, HCl, and NO_2 .
    a) Which will travel the fastest?

    b) Which will travel the slowest?

    c) Calculate the rate of effusion of NO_2 in comparison to SO_2 at the same temperature and pressure.

95. An unknown gas effuses 1.66 times more rapidly than CO_2. What is the molar mass of the unknown gas?

96. A sample of hydrogen gas effuses through a porous container 9 times faster than an unknown gas. Estimate the molar mass of the unknown gas.

Dalton's Law of Partial Pressure

Dalton's Law of partial pressure states that the total pressure (P_{total}) of a mixture of gases is equal to the sum of their partial pressures. Partial pressure is the pressure exerted by individual gases in a gas mixture. The examples below show how to solve three different partial pressure problems.

Example 11: Total Pressure from Partial Pressures

What is the total pressure of the three-gas mixture to the right.

$P_{total} = P_{gasA} + P_{gasB} + P_{gasC}$

P_{total} = .2 atm + .4 atm + .5 atm = **1.1 atm**

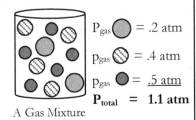

A Gas Mixture

Example 12: Partial Pressure of Gas X When Collected Over Water

Oxygen gas is collected over water at 45°C in a test tube. If the total pressure of the gas mixture in the test tube is 26 kPa, what is the partial pressure of the oxygen gas?

$P_{total} = P_{gasX} + VP_{H_2O}$

26 kPa = $P_{gas}O$ + VP_{H_2O} at 45°C

26 kPa = $P_{gas}O$ + 10

16 kPa = $P_{gas}O$

> VP_{H_2O} is the vapor pressure of water at the given water temperature. ***Reference Table H*** gives vapor pressure of water at different temperatures.

Example 13: Partial Pressure of Gas X from Mole Fraction

A gas mixture contains 0.8 moles of O_2 and 1.2 moles of N_2. If the total pressure of the mixture is 0.5 atm, what is the partial pressure of N_2 in this mixture?

$$P_{gas\ X} = \frac{\text{moles of gas X}}{\text{total moles}} (P_{total})$$

$$P_{gas\ N_2} = \frac{1.2 \text{ moles}}{2.0 \text{ moles}} \text{ x } 0.5 \text{ atm} = \boxed{0.3 \text{ atm}}$$

---

97. What is the pressure of a mixture of CO_2, SO_2, and H_2O gases, if each gas has a partial pressure of 25 kPa?

98. When 7.00 moles of gas *A* and 3.00 moles of gas *B* are combined, the total pressure exerted by the gas mixture is 76.0 kPa. What is the partial pressure exerted by gas *A* in this mixture?

99. A mixture of oxygen, nitrogen, and hydrogen gases exerts a total pressure of 74 kPa at 0°C. The partial pressure of the oxygen is 20 kPa and the partial pressure of the nitrogen is 40 kPa. What is the partial pressure of the hydrogen gas in this mixture?

100. A sealed container has 1 mole of helium and 2 moles of nitrogen at 30°C. When the total pressure of the mixture is 60 kPa, what is the partial pressure of the nitrogen?

101. If 4.00 moles of oxygen gas, 3.00 moles of hydrogen gas, and 1.00 mole of nitrogen gas are combined in a closed container at standard pressure, what is the partial pressure exerted by the hydrogen gas?

Lesson 1: Arrangement of the Elements

There are more than 100 known elements. Most of the elements are naturally occurring, while a few are artificially produced. The modern Periodic Table lists all known elements. The elements are arranged on the Periodic Table in order of increasing atomic number. Important information about an element can be found in the box of the element on the Periodic Table.

In this lesson, you will learn about the arrangement of the elements on the Periodic Table.

The Modern Periodic Table: *Elements Arranged by Increasing Atomic Number*

The modern Periodic Table, which is based on the work of Dmitri Mendeleev, has the following properties:

• The elements are arranged in the order of increasing atomic number.

• The three types of elements found on the Periodic Table are metals, nonmetals, and metalloids.

• More than two thirds (majority) of the elements are metals.

• The Periodic Table contains elements that are in all three phases (solid, liquid, and gas) at STP.

• Of more than 100 known elements at STP:
    Two (bromine and mercury) are liquids.
    Eleven are gases.
    The rest are solids.

• An element's symbol can be one (O), two (Au), or three (Uub) letters.
  The first letter of a symbol is always a capital letter.
  The second and third letters, if present, are lowercase.

Information listed in the box of each element reveals a lot about the atomic structure of the element. Atomic structure is discussed in Topic 3.

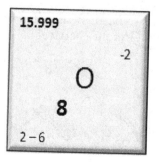

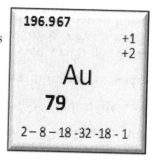

Atomic mass

Selected oxidation states
(charges)

Element's symbol

Atomic number

Electron configuration

Groups and Periods

Groups: *Same Valence Electrons, Similar Chemical Properties*

Groups are the vertical arrangements of the elements.
There are 18 groups of elements on the Periodic Table.
Group names are listed below.

	Group	
	1	2

6.941 +1 **Li** 3 2-1 | 9.01218 +2 **Be** 4 2-2

22.98977 +1 **Na** 11 2-8-1 | 24.305 +2 **Mg** 12 2-8-2

39.0983 +1 **K** 19 2-8-8-1 | 40.08 +2 **Ca** 20 2-8-8-2

85.4678 +1 **Rb** 37 2-8-18-8-1 | 87.62 +2 **Sr** 38 2-8-18-8-2

132.905 +1 **Cs** 55 2-8-18-18-8-1 | 137.33 +2 **Ba** 56 2-8-18-18-8-2

(223) +1 **Fr** 87 -18-32-18-8-1 | (226) +2 **Ra** 88 -18-32-18-8-2

    Group 1:   Alkali metals

    Group 2:   Alkaline earth metals

    Group 3 – 12: Transition metals

    Group 17:   Halogens

    Group 18:   Noble gases

Elements in the same group have the same number of valence electrons. Valence electrons are electrons in the outermost energy level of an atom. Elements in the same group have similar chemical properties and reactivity because they have the same number of valence electrons.

Periods: *Same Electron Shells (Energy Levels)*

Periods are the horizontal rows of the Periodic Table. Elements in the same period have the same number of occupied electron shells. There are seven (7) periods of elements.

Period 4

39.0983 +1 **K** 19 2-8-8-1	40.08 +2 **Ca** 20 2-8-8-2	44.9559 +3 **Sc** 21 2-8-9-2

Period 5

85.4678 +1 **Rb** 37 2-8-18-8-1	87.62 +2 **Sr** 38 2-8-18-8-2	88.9059 +3 **Y** 39 2-8-18-9-2

The **periodic law** states that the properties of the elements are a periodic function of their atomic numbers. In other words, by arranging the elements in order of increasing atomic number, a new period of elements is formed so that elements with similar chemical properties fall in the same group.

Allotropes: *Same Element, Different Structural Forms, Different Properties*

Allotropes are different molecular or crystalline forms of the same element in the same state. Allotropes of the same element have different molecular or crystal structures. Differences in structures give allotropes of the same element different physical properties (color, shape, density, mass, etc.) and different chemical properties and reactivities.

Examples of Common Allotropes:

Oxygen allotropes: oxygen gas (O_2) and ozone (O_3)

Carbon allotropes: carbon, diamond, and graphite

Phosphorus allotropes: red, black, and white

Atomic oxygen
O

O_2
oxygen

O_3
ozone

Two molecuar structures
of oxygen.

Review Questions: Arrangements of the Elements

Vocabulary: Briefly define each of the following terms

1. Periodic law   2. Group   3. Period   4. Allotrope

5. The observed regularities in the properties of the elements are periodic functions of their
   (1) oxidation state
   (2) atomic number
   (3) atomic mass
   (4) reactivity

6. Which of the following information cannot be found in the box of elements on the Periodic Table?
   (1) Oxidation state
   (2) Atomic number
   (3) Atomic mass
   (4) Phase

7. In general, elements within each group of the Periodic Table share similar
   (1) chemical properties
   (2) electron configurations
   (3) mass numbers
   (4) numbers of occupied energy levels

8. The Periodic Table of the Elements contains elements that are
   (1) solids only
   (2) solids and liquids only
   (3) liquids and gases only
   (4) solids, liquids and gases

9. Which list contains elements with the greatest variation in chemical properties?
   (1) O, S and Se
   (2) N, P and As
   (3) Be, N and O
   (4) Ba, Sr and Ca

10. Which element has similar chemical reactivity to the element chlorine?
    (1) Bromine
    (2) Sulfur
    (3) Argon
    (4) Calcium

11. Oxygen and sulfur can both form a bond with sodium with similar chemical formulas. The similarity in their formulas is due to
    (1) Oxygen and sulfur having the same number of kernel electrons.
    (2) Oxygen and sulfur having the same number of valence electrons.
    (3) Oxygen and sulfur having the same number of protons.
    (4) Oxygen and sulfur having the same molecular structure.

12. Which statement describes oxygen gas, $O_2(g)$, and ozone gas, $O_3(g)$?
    (1) They have different molecular structures, only.
    (2) They have different properties, only.
    (3) They have different molecular structures and different properties.
    (4) They have the same molecular structure and the same properties.

Base your answers to questions 13 through 15 on the information below.

Before atomic numbers were known, Mendeleev developed a classification system for the 63 elements known in 1872, using oxide formulas and atomic masses. He used an R in the oxide formulas to represent any element in each group. The atomic mass was listed in parentheses after the symbol of each element. A modified version of Mendeleev's classification system is shown in the table below.

Modified Version of Mendeleev's Table

Group →	I	II	III	IV	V	VI	VII
Oxide formulas	R_2O	RO	R_2O_3	RO_2	R_2O_5	RO_3	R_2O_7
1	H(1)						
2	Li(7)	Be(9.4)	B(11)	C(12)	N(14)	O(16)	F(19)
3	Na(23)	Mg(24)	Al(27.3)	Si(28)	P(31)	S(32)	Cl(35.5)
4	K(39)	Ca(40)		Ti(48)	V(51)	Cr(52)	Mn(55)
5	Cu(63)	Zn(65)			As(75)	Se(78)	Br(80)
6	Rb(85)	Sr(87)	Yt(88)	Zr(90)	Nb(94)	Mo(96)	
7	Ag(108)	Cd(112)	In(113)	Sn(118)	Sb(122)	Te(125)	I(127)
8	Cs(133)	Ba(137)	Di(138)	Ce(140)			

(Series)

13. Identify two elements on Mendeleev's table that combines with oxygen in the same ratio as magnesium.

14. Identify *one* characteristic used by Mendeleev to develop his classification system of the elements.

15. State one difference between Mendeleev's Table and the Modern Periodic Table.

Lesson 2: Types of Elements and their Properties

There are three general categories of elements: metals, nonmetals and metalloids. Elements in each category have a set of physical and chemical properties that can be used to distinguish them from elements in other categories.

In this lesson, you will learn about different types of elements, their locations in the Periodic Table, and their properties.

Locations of Metals, Metalloids, and Nonmetals

Properties of the Elements

There are several physical properties that are used to describe or identify the elements. Below are terms and definitions of these properties.

Malleable describes a solid that is easily hammered into a thin sheet. *ex. aluminum (Al)*

Ductile describes a solid that is easily drawn into a thin wire. *ex. copper (Cu)*

Brittle describes a solid that is easily broken into pieces when struck. *ex. sulfur (S)*

Luster describes the shininess of a substance. *ex. silver (Ag) or gold (Au)*

Conductivity describes how well heat or electricity can flow through the material.

Ionization energy is the energy needed to remove the most loosely bound valence electrons from an atom.

Electronegativity describes an atom's ability to attract electrons from another atom during bonding.

Melting point is the temperature at which a solid becomes a liquid.

Boiling point is the temperature at which a liquid becomes a gas (vapor).

Density describes the mass per volume ratio of an element.

Atomic radius describes the size of the atom of an element.

Ionic radius describes the size of an atom after losing or gaining an electron to form an ion.

Use Table S to find and compare values for these six properties of the elements.

Metals: *Luster, Ductile, Malleable, Conductors, Low Electronegativity and Low Ionization Energy*

Metal elements are located on the left side of the Periodic Table.
All elements in Groups 1 through 12 (except for hydrogen) are classified as a metal.
The rest of the metal elements are found near the bottom of Groups 13, 14 and 15.
The majority (about 75%) of the elements are metals.

General properties of metals are listed below.
- All metals (except Hg) exist as a solid at STP. Mercury (Hg) is the only liquid metal.
- Metallic solids are malleable, ductile, and have luster.
- Metals have high thermal (heat) conductivity and high electrical conductivity. Electrical conductivity is due to mobile or free moving electrons in metal atoms.
- Metals have low electronegativity values; they do not easily attract electrons.
- Metals have low ionization energy values; they lose electrons easily.
- Metals lose electrons and form a positive ion during chemical bonding.

Nonmetals: *Brittle, Dull, No Conductivity, High Electronegativity and Ionization Energy*

Nonmetal elements are located to the right of the Periodic Table.
All elements in Groups 17 and 18 (except astatine, At) are classified as nonmetals.
The rest of the nonmetals are found near the top of Groups 14, 15, and 16. Hydrogen is also a nonmetal.

General properties of nonmetals are listed below.
- Nonmetals are found in all three phases: solid, liquid, and gas.
- Most nonmetals are either a gas or solid at STP. Bromine is the only liquid nonmetal.
- Solid nonmetals are generally brittle and dull (lack luster, not shiny).
- Nonmetals have low heat (thermal) and low electrical conductivity.
- Nonmetals have high electronegativity values; they attract electrons easily.
- Nonmetals have high ionization energy values; they do not lose electrons easily.
- Nonmetals generally gain electrons and form a negative ion during bonding.

Metalloids: *Have Metallic and Nonmetallic Properties*

Metalloids are the elements located between the metals and nonmetals along the thick zigzag line of the Periodic Table.

General properties of metalloids are listed below.
- Metalloids tend to have properties of both the metals and nonmetals.
- Their properties are more like those of metals and less like nonmetals.
- Metalloids exist only as solids at STP.

Summary of Types of Elements and Properties

	Phases at STP	Physical Properties	Conduc-tivity	Electrone-gativity	Ionization Energy	During Bonding	Common Ion	Ionic Size (Radius)
Metals	solid liquid	malleable luster ductile	high	low	low	lose electrons	+ (positive)	smaller than atom
Nonmetals	solid liquid gas	brittle dull	low	high	high	gain electrons	- (negative)	bigger than atom
Metalloids	solid only	properties of metals and nonmetals	low	varies	varies	lose electrons	+ (positive)	smaller than atom

Properties of Groups: Summary Table

Elements with similar chemical properties belong in the same group.
Below is a table summarizing group names and general characteristics of each group.

Group number	Group name	Types of elements in the group	Phases (at STP)	Valence electrons (during bonding)	Common oxidation number (charge)	Chemical bonding (general formula)
1	Alkali metals	Metal	Solid (all)	1 (lose)	+1	XY with halogens (17) X_2O with oxygen (16)
2	Alkaline earth	Metal	Solid (all)	2 (lose)	+2	MY_2 with halogens (17) MO with oxygen (16)
3-12	Transition metals	Metal	Liquid (Hg) Solid (the rest)	(lose)	Multiple +charges	varies (form colorful compounds)
13	-	Metalloid Metal	Solid (all)	3 (lose)	+3	LY_3 with halogens (17) L_2O_3 with oxygen (16)
14	-	Nonmetal Metalloid Metal	Solid (all)	4 (some share) (some lose)	varies	varies
15	-	Nonmetal Metalloid Metal	Gas (N) Solid (the rest)	5 (gain or share)	-3	varies
16	Oxygen group	Nonmetal Metalloid	Gas (O) Solid (the rest)	6 (gain or share)	-2	X_2O with alkali metals (1) MO with alkaline earth (2)
17	Halogens (Diatomic)	Nonmetal	Gas (F and Cl) Liquid (Br) Solid (I)	7 (gain or share)	-1	XY with alkali metals (1) MY with alkaline earth (2)
18	Noble gases (Monatomic)	Nonmetal	Gas (all)	8 (neither gain, lose, nor share)	0	Form very few compounds. XeF_4 is the most common.

Periodic Table of the Elements

KEY

Atomic Mass → 12.011

Symbol → **C**

Atomic Number → 6

Electron Configuration → 2-4

-4
+2
+4 → Selected Oxidation States

Relative atomic masses are based on $^{12}C = 12$ (exact)

Note: Numbers in parentheses are mass numbers of the most stable or common isotope.

Group

Group 1	Group 2	3	4	5	6	7	8	9	10	11	12	13	14	15	16	17	18

Period

Period 1: H (1.00794), He (4.00260)

Period 2: Li, Be, B, C, N, O, F, Ne

Period 3: Na, Mg, Al, Si, P, S, Cl, Ar

Period 4: K, Ca, Sc, Ti, V, Cr, Mn, Fe, Co, Ni, Cu, Zn, Ga, Ge, As, Se, Br, Kr

Period 5: Rb, Sr, Y, Zr, Nb, Mo, Tc, Ru, Rh, Pd, Ag, Cd, In, Sn, Sb, Te, I, Xe

Period 6: Cs, Ba, La, Hf, Ta, W, Re, Os, Ir, Pt, Au, Hg, Tl, Pb, Bi, Po, At, Rn

Period 7: Fr, Ra, Ac, Rf, Db, Sg, Bh, Hs, Mt, Ds, Rg, Cn, Uut**, Uuq, Uup, Uuh, Uus, Uuo

Lanthanides: Ce, Pr, Nd, Pm, Sm, Eu, Gd, Tb, Dy, Ho, Er, Tm, Yb, Lu

Actinides: Th, Pa, U, Np, Pu, Am, Cm, Bk, Cf, Es, Fm, Md, No, Lr

* denotes the presence of (2-8-) for elements 72 and above

** The systematic names and symbols for elements of atomic numbers 113 and above will be used until the approval of trivial names by IUPAC.

Source: *CRC Handbook of Chemistry and Physics*, 91st ed., 2010–2011, CRC Press

27

Group Names and Characteristics

Group 1 - Alkali Metals: *One Valence Electron, +1 Charge, Very Reactive*

- Found in nature as compounds, not as free elements, due to high reactivity.
- Are obtained from electrolytic reduction of fused salts (NaCl, KBr, etc.).
- Francium (Fr), a radioactive element, is the most reactive of all metals.
- All alkali metals exist as solids at room temperature.

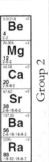

Group 2 - Alkaline Earth Metals: *Two Valence Electrons, +2 Charge*

- Found in nature as compounds, not as free elements, due to high reactivity.
- Are obtained from fused salt compounds ($MgCl_2$, $CaBr_2$, etc.).
- All alkaline earth metals exist as solids at room temperature.
- Radium (Ra), a radioactive element, is the most reactive metal in this group.

Groups 3 to 12 - Transition Metals: *Multiple +charges, Colored Compounds*

- The properties of these elements vary widely.
- They tend to form multiple positive oxidation numbers.
- Most can lose electrons in two or more different sublevels of their atoms.
- Their ions usually form colorful compounds.

Group 17 - Halogens: *Seven Valence Electrons, -1 Charge, Highly Reactive*

- Exist as diatomic (two-atom) molecules (F_2, Br_2, etc.).
- The only group with elements in all three phases at STP.
- Fluorine (F) is the most reactive of the group, and of all nonmetals.
- Halogens are obtained from halide salt compounds (NaF, NaCl, etc.).
- Astatine (At) in this group is a metalloid.

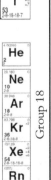

Group 18 - Noble gases: *Two or Eight Valence Electrons, Non-reactive*

- Exist as monatomic (one-atom) molecules (Ne, He, Kr, etc.)
- They all have full and stable valence shells with 8 electrons, except for He. Helium (He) has a full and stable valence shell with just 2 electrons.
- Noble gases are non-reactive, so they do not form many compounds.
- Argon (Ar) and Xenon (Xe) have been found to produce a few stable compounds with fluorine.
    Example: **XeF**$_4$ (xenon tetrafluoride)

Review Questions: Types and Properties of the Elements

Vocabulary: Briefly define each of the following terms

16. Malleable   17. Luster   18. Brittleness   19. Ductile   20. Ionization energy
21. Electronegativity   22. Density   23. Atomic radius   24. Alkali metal
25. Alkaline earth metal   26. Transition metal   27. Halogen   28. Noble gas

29. Solid nonmetal elements tend to be
    (1) malleable   (3) ductile
    (2) brittle   (4) shiny

30. Which two characteristics are associated with metals?
    (1) low first ionization energy and low electronegativity
    (2) low first ionization energy and high electronegativity
    (3) high first ionization energy and low electronegativity
    (4) high first ionization energy and high electronegativity

31. At STP, which element is solid, brittle, and a poor conductor of electricity?
    (1) Al   (2) K   (3) Ne   (4) S

32. Which list of elements contains a metal, a metalloid, a nonmetal, and a noble gas?
    (1) C, N, Ne, Ar   (3) K, Fe, B, F
    (2) Be, Si, Cl, Kr   (4) Na, Zn, As, Sb

33. Element X is a solid that is brittle, lacks luster, and has six valence electrons. In which group on the Periodic Table would element X be found?
    (1) 1   (2) 2   (3) 15   (4) 16

34. If an element, X, can form an oxide that has the formula X_2O_3, then element X would most likely be located on the Periodic Table in the same group as
    (1) Ba   (2) Cd   (3) In   (4) Na

35. Pure silicon is chemically classified as a metalloid because silicon
    (1) is malleable and ductile
    (2) is an excellent conductor of heat and electricity
    (3) exhibits metallic and nonmetallic properties
    (4) none of the above

Base your answers to questions 36 and 37 on the information below.

    Three elements, represented by D, E, and Q, are located in Period 3. Some properties of these elements are listed in the table below.

Properties of Samples of Three Elements at Room Temperature and Standard Pressure

Element	Phase	Mass (g)	Density (g/cm³)	Oxide Formula
D	solid	50.0	0.97	D_2O
E	solid	50.0	1.74	EO
Q	solid	50.0	2.00	QO_2 or QO_3

36. Identify the group on the Periodic Table to which element D belongs.

37. Using Table S, identify element Q.

Base your answers to questions 38 and 39 on the information below.

    There are six elements in Group 14 on the Periodic Table. One of these elements has the symbol Uuq, which is a temporary, systematic symbol. This element is now known as flerovium.

38. State the expected number of valence electrons in an atom of the element flerovium in the ground state.

39. Identify an element in Group 14 that is classified as a metalloid.

Lesson 3: Periodic Trends

Periodic trends are specific patterns in properties of the elements that exist on the Periodic Table. Certain properties of the elements change orderly within a group or period as the elements are considered one after the other. The trend in atomic number is an example of a periodic trend found on the Periodic Table.

As elements are considered one after the other from:

Left to **Right** across a Period: Atomic number of the elements increases.

Top to **Bottom** down a Group: Atomic number of the elements increases.

Many other trends exist on the Periodic Table even though they may not be as obvious.

In this lesson, you will learn of the following trends:

       Trends in atomic radius (size).

       Trends in metallic and nonmetallic properties.

       Trends in electronegativity and ionization energy.

Summary of Periodic Trends

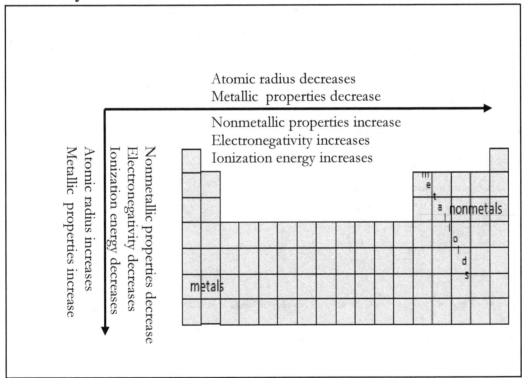

Trends in Atomic Radius: *Increases Top to Bottom, and Right to Left*

Atomic radius is defined as half the distance between two nuclei of the same atom when they are joined together.

Atomic radius gives a good approximation of the size of an atom. Trend in atomic radius is as follows.

Top to Bottom down a Group:
Atomic size (radius) increases due to an increase in the number of *electron shells*. (see diagram to the right)

Left to Right across a Period:
Atomic size (radius) decreases due to an increase in *nuclear charge*. (see diagram below)

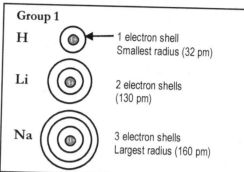

Group 1

H — 1 electron shell
Smallest radius (32 pm)

Li — 2 electron shells (130 pm)

Na — 3 electron shells
Largest radius (160 pm)

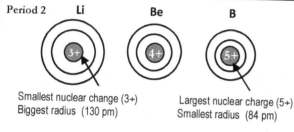

Period 2   Li   Be   B

Smallest nuclear change (3+)
Biggest radius (130 pm)

Largest nuclear charge (5+)
Smallest radius (84 pm)

Use Reference Table S to identify and compare atomic radii (sizes) for any set of elements.

Atomic Number	Symbol	Name	Atomic Radius (pm)
1	H	hydrogen	32
2	He	helium	37
3	Li	lithium	130
4	Be	beryllium	99
5	B	boron	84
6	C	carbon	75
7	N	nitrogen	71
8	O	oxygen	64
9	F	fluorine	60.
10	Ne	neon	62
11	Na	sodium	160
12	Mg	magnesium	140.
13	Al	aluminum	124

Trends in Metallic and Nonmetallic Properties
Metallic Increases Top to Bottom and Right to Left. Nonmetallic Increases Bottom to Top and Left to Right.

Trends in metallic and nonmetallic properties vary.
For metals, the most reactive metals are on the bottom left corner of the table. **Francium** is the most reactive of all metals.

For nonmetals, the most reactive nonmetals are on the top right corner of the table. **Fluorine** is the most reactive of all nonmetals.

Trends in metallic and nonmetallic properties are summarized below:

Top to **Bottom** down a **Group**:
Metallic properties and reactivity increase *(ex. K is more reactive than Na)*
Nonmetallic properties and reactivity decrease *(ex. Br is less reactive than Cl)*

Group 1   Group 17

Na 11	Cl 17
K 19	Br 35

LEFT to **Right** across a **Period**:
Metallic properties and reactivity decrease. *(ex. Mg is less reactive than Na)*
Nonmetallic properties and reactivity increase. *(ex. Cl is more reactive than S)*

Na 11	Mg 12	Period 3
S 16	Cl 17	Period 3

Trends in Electronegativity and Ionization Energy
Both Increase Bottom to Top, and Left to Right

Electronegativity: *Tendency to Attract or Gain Electrons*
Electronegativity defines an atom's tendency to attract (or gain) electrons from another atom during chemical bonding. The electronegativity value assigned to each element is relative to one another. The higher the electronegativity value, the more likely it is for the atom to attract electrons during bonding.
Fluorine (F) is assigned the highest electronegativity value of 4.0.
Francium (Fr) is assigned the lowest electronegativity value of 0.7.
This means that of all the elements:
Fluorine has the greatest ability or tendency to attract electrons during bonding.
Francium has the least ability or tendency to attract electrons during bonding.

Ionization Energy: *Energy to Remove or Tendency to Lose Electrons.*
Ionization energy is the amount of energy needed to remove an electron from an atom. The ***first ionization energy*** is the energy to remove the most loosely bound electron from an atom. Ionization energy measures the tendency of an atom to lose electrons and form a positive ion. The lower the first ionization energy of an atom, the easier or the more likely it is for that atom to lose its most loosely bound valence electron and form a positive ion.
Metals lose electrons because of their low ionization energies.
The *alkali metals* in Group 1 generally have the lowest ionization energies, which is why they readily lose electrons and react very easily.

Nonmetals have a low tendency to lose electrons because of their high ionization energies. The *noble gases* in Group 18 tend to have the highest ionization energy values. Since these elements already have a full valence shell of electrons, a high amount of energy is required to remove any electron from their atoms.

Trends in electronegativity and ionization energy are as follows:

Top to Bottom down a Group:

Electronegativity (attraction to electrons) *decreases* due to increasing atomic size.
Ex. Carbon (2.6) has a stronger attraction to electrons than silicon (1.9).

Ionization energy (tendency to lose electrons) *decreases* due to increasing atomic size.

Left to Right across a Period:

Electronegativity (attraction to electrons) *increases* due to decreasing atomic size.

Ionization energy (tendency to lose electrons) *increases* due to decreasing atomic size.

Ex. Aluminum (578 kJ) has a lower tendency to lose electrons than sodium (496 kJ).

Use Reference Table S: Properties of Selected Elements to identify and compare electronegativity and ionization energy values

Atomic Number	Symbol	Name	First Ionization Energy (kJ/mol)	Electro- negativity
1	H	hydrogen	1312	2.2
2	He	helium	2372	—
3	Li	lithium	520.	1.0
4	Be	beryllium	900.	1.6
5	B	boron	801	2.0
6	C	carbon	1086	2.6
7	N	nitrogen	1402	3.0
8	O	oxygen	1314	3.4
9	F	fluorine	1681	4.0
10	Ne	neon	2081	—
11	Na	sodium	496	0.9
12	Mg	magnesium	738	1.3
13	Al	aluminum	578	1.6
14	Si	silicon	787	1.9
15	P	phosphorus (white)	1012	2.2

E3chemistry.com

Melting Point, Boiling Point, and Density

Reference Table S contains other physical properties of the elements. These properties are melting point, boiling point, and density. Periodic trends exist for some of these properties within Groups 1, 2, 17 and 18.

For example:

Melting and boiling points of the elements in Groups 1 and 2 tend to decrease from top to bottom.

Density of the elements in Groups 17 and 18 tends to increase from top to bottom. These trends are not consistent across a period because each period contains a variety of elements. Comparison questions for these properties can be answered by using Reference Table S to locate and compare values for any given set of elements.

Reference Table S

Atomic Number	Symbol	Name	Melting Point (K)	Boiling* Point (K)	Density** (g/cm^3)
1	H	hydrogen	14	20.	0.000082
2	He	helium	—	4	0.000164
3	Li	lithium	454	1615	0.534
4	Be	beryllium	1560.	2744	1.85
5	B	boron	2348	4273	2.34
6	C	carbon	—	—	—
7	N	nitrogen	63	77	0.001145
8	O	oxygen	54	90.	0.001308
9	F	fluorine	53	85	0.001553
10	Ne	neon	24	27	0.000825
11	Na	sodium	371	1156	0.97
12	Mg	magnesium	923	1363	1.74
13	Al	aluminum	933	2792	2.70
14	Si	silicon	1687	3538	2.3296

Melting point is the temperature at which a solid turns to a liquid.

Solid lithium will melt to a liquid at 454 K (181°C).

Boiling point is the temperature at which a liquid turns to a gas or vapor.

Liquid nitrogen will boil to a gas at only 77 K (-196°C).

Density of a substance measures how much mass is within a given volume (space) of the substance. Density, the mass per volume ratio, for any substance can be calculated using the **Table T** equation:

$$\text{Density} = \frac{\text{mass (g)}}{\text{volume (cm}^3\text{)}}$$

Since the density values of the elements are listed on Table S, students are often asked to set up and calculate the volume or mass of a given sample of an element. An example problem is shown on the right.

Example 1: *Calculation Using Density from Table S.*

What is the volume of an aluminum block that has a mass of 43.5 grams at STP?

$$\text{Volume} = \frac{\text{mass}}{\text{density}} = \frac{43.5 \text{ g}}{2.70 \text{ g/cm}^3} = \textbf{16.1 cm}^3$$

setup   *result*

Review Questions: Periodic Trends

40. As the elements in Group 1 of the Periodic Table are considered in order of increasing atomic number, the atomic radius of each successive element increases. This is primarily due to an increase in the number of
    (1) neutrons in the nucleus
    (2) unpaired electrons
    (3) valence electrons
    (4) electron shells

41. In the ground state, each atom of an element has two valence electrons. This element has a lower first ionization energy than calcium. Where is this element located on the Periodic Table?
    (1) Group 1, Period 4
    (2) Group 2, Period 5
    (3) Group 2, Period 3
    (4) Group 3, Period 4

42. Which statement describes the general trends in electronegativity and first ionization energy as the elements in Period 3 are considered in order from Na to Cl?
    (1) Electronegativity increases, and first ionization energy decreases.
    (2) Electronegativity decreases, and first ionization energy increases.
    (3) Electronegativity and first ionization energy both increase.
    (4) Electronegativity and first ionization energy both decrease.

43. Which list of elements is arranged in order of increasing atomic radii?
    (1) Li, Be, B, C
    (2) Sr, Ca, Mg, Be
    (3) Sc, Ti, V, Cr
    (4) F, Cl, Br, I

44. Which atom has the weakest attraction for electrons in a chemical bond?
    (1) a boron atom
    (2) a calcium atom
    (3) a fluorine atom
    (4) a nitrogen atom

45. The atom of which element is bigger than an atom of calcium?
    (1) Sr   (2) Sc   (3) Mg   (4) Be

46. Which of these elements is most likely to attract electrons from another atom during chemical bonding?
    (1) Fe   (2) C   (3) Al   (4) Cs

47. Samples of four Group 15 elements, antimony, arsenic, bismuth, and phosphorus, are in the gaseous phase. An atom in the ground state of which element requires the least amount of energy to remove its most loosely held electron?
    (1) As   (2) Bi   (3) P   (4) Sb

48. Which of the following elements has the most pronounced metallic characteristics?
    (1) C   (2) Co   (3) Al   (4) Rb

49. Which of these halogens is the least reactive on the Period Table?
    (1) I   (2) Br   (3) Cl   (4) F

50. Which element has the highest melting point?
    (1) tantalum
    (2) rhenium
    (3) osmium
    (4) hafnium

51. Which element has the greatest density at STP?
    (1) scandium
    (2) selenium
    (3) silicon
    (4) sodium

52. At STP, a 7.49-gram sample of an element has a volume of 1.65 cubic centimeters. The sample is most likely
    (1) Ta
    (2) Tc
    (3) Te
    (4) Ti

Base your answers to questions 53 through 56 on the information below.

The atomic number and corresponding atomic radius of the Period 3 elements are shown in the data table below.

Data Table

Atomic Number	Atomic Radius (pm)
11	160.
12	140.
13	124
14	114
15	109
16	104
17	100.
18	101

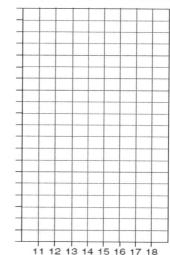

Atomic Radius Versus Atomic Number

53. On the grid, mark an appropriate scale on the axis labeled "Atomic Radius (pm)."

54. On the grid, plot the data from the data table. Circle and connect the points.

55. State the general relationship between the atomic number and the atomic radius for the Period 3 elements.

56. Explain, in terms of atomic structure, why the atomic radius of the element with atomic number 13 is greater than the atomic radius of the element with atomic number 15.

Base your answers to questions 57 through 59 on the information below.

The table below lists physical and chemical properties of six elements at standard pressure that correspond to known elements on the Periodic Table. The elements are identified by the code letters, D, E, G, J, L, and Q.

Properties of Six Elements at Standard Pressure

Element D	Element E	Element G
Density 0.00018 g/cm³	Density 1.82 g/cm³	Density 0.53 g/cm³
Melting point −272°C	Melting point 44°C	Melting point 181°C
Boiling point −269°C	Boiling point 280°C	Boiling point 1347°C
Oxide formula (none)	Oxide formula E_2O_5	Oxide formula G_2O
Element J	Element L	Element Q
Density 0.0013 g/cm³	Density 0.86 g/cm³	Density 0.97 g/cm³
Melting point −210°C	Melting point 64°C	Melting point 98°C
Boiling point −196°C	Boiling point 774°C	Boiling point 883°C
Oxide formula J_2O_5	Oxide formula L_2O	Oxide formula Q_2O

57. Identify, by code letter, the element that is a noble gas in the "Properties of Six Elements at Standard Pressure" table.

58. Letter Z corresponds to an element on the Periodic Table other than the six listed elements. Elements G, Q, L, and Z are in the same group, as shown in the diagram below.

G
Q
L
Z

Based on the trend in the melting points for elements G, Q, and L listed in the "Properties of Six Elements at Standard Pressure" table, estimate the melting point of element Z, in degrees Celsius.

59. What is the total number of elements in the "Properties of Six Elements at Standard Pressure" table that are solids at STP?

Lesson 1: History of the Atomic Model

The **atom** is the most basic unit of matter. Since atoms are very small and cannot be seen with the most sophisticated equipment, many scientists for hundreds of years have proposed different models of the atom to help explain the nature and behavior of matter.

In this lesson, you will learn about these historical scientists, their experiments and their proposed models of the atom.

Atomic Theories and Models of Atoms

Some of the atomic theories and models proposed by scientists over the years are briefly described below. On the next page, the work of two of these scientists is further explained.

John Dalton: Hard-sphere (Cannonball) Model
- All matter is composed of atoms.
- Atoms are indivisible and indestructible building blocks of matter.
- Atoms of the same element are the same. Atoms of different elements are different.
- Atoms have no internal structures.

J.J. Thomson: Plum-pudding Model
- An atom is composed of negative electrons.
- The electrons are surrounded by positive charges to balance out.

Ernest Rutherford: Empty-space Model
- An atom has a small, positive, high-mass center, the nucleus.
- Most of an atom is empty space.

Niels Bohr: Electron-shell (Planetary) Model
- Electrons in atoms go around the nucleus in orbit.
- Electrons have fixed energy in specific orbits.
- Electrons can gain or lose energy only by jumping from one orbit to another.
- Atoms absorb and release energy as an electron changes levels.

Many Scientists: Wave Mechanical (Electron-cloud) Model
- An atom has a small, dense, positive nucleus.
- Protons and neutrons are in the nucleus.
- Electrons are in **orbitals** outside the nucleus.

orbital ⟶

The **wave-mechanical model** is the currently accepted model of the atom. In the wave-mechanical model, electrons are found outside the nucleus in regions called orbitals. **Orbitals** are the most probable location of finding an electron with a certain amount of energy in an atom.

The wave-mechanical model brought together the work and discoveries of many scientists over a long period of time.

Two Atomic Model Experiments

Cathode Ray Experiment (J.J. Thomson)

Led to the discovery of electrons.

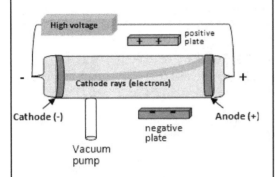

The Setup
A tube with a metal disk at each end was set up to trace a beam from an electrical source. The metals were connected to the electrical source.
Anode: The metal disk that is +.
Cathode: The metal disk that is −.

Results
A beam of light (ray) traveled from the cathode end to the anode end of the tube. When electrically charged + and - plates were brought near the tube, the beam was deflected toward and attracted the positive plate. The beam was repelled by the negative plate.

Conclusion
The beam was composed of negatively charged particles. The term "electron" was later used to describe the negative particles of an atom.

Gold Foil Experiment (Rutherford)
Led to the discovery of the nucleus, and the proposed "empty space theory."

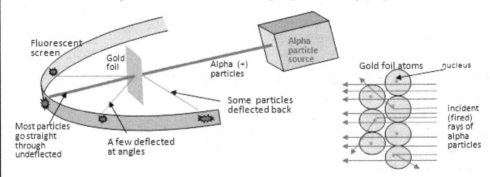

The Setup
Alpha particles (α) were fired at gold foil. A fluorescent screen was set up   around the foil to detect paths of the particles after hitting the gold foil.

Result 1
Most of the alpha particles went straight through the gold foil undeflected.

Conclusion 1
An atom is mostly empty space (Empty Space Theory)

Result 2
A few of the particles were deflected back or hit the screen at angles.

Conclusion 2
The center of the atom is dense, positive, and very small.

Review Questions: History of Atomic Models

Vocabulary: Briefly define the following terms.
1. Wave-mechanical model   2. Orbital

3. The modern model of an atom shows that electrons are
   (1) orbiting the nucleus in fixed paths.
   (2) found in regions called orbital.
   (3) combined with neutrons in the nucleus.
   (4) located in a solid sphere covering the nucleus.

4. In the wave-mechanical model, the orbital is a region in space of an atom where there is a
   (1) high probability of finding an electron.   (3) circular path in which electrons are found
   (2) high probability of finding a neutron.   (4) circular path in which neutrons are found

5. The modern model of the atom is based on the work of
   (1) one scientist over a short period of time   (3) many scientists over a short period of time.
   (2) one scientist over a long period of time   (4) many scientists over a long period of time.

6. Which group of atomic models is listed in order from the earliest to the most recent?
   (1) Hard-sphere model, wave-mechanical model, electron-shell model.
   (2) Hard-sphere model, electron-shell model, wave-mechanical model.
   (3) Electron-shell model, wave-mechanical model, hard-sphere model.
   (4) Electron-shell model, hard-sphere model, wave-mechanical model.

7. An experiment in which alpha particles were used to bombard thin sheets of gold foil led to the conclusion that an atom is composed mostly of
   (1) a large, dense, positively charged nucleus
   (2) a large, dense, negatively charged nucleus
   (3) empty space and has a small, positively charged nucleus
   (4) empty space and has a small, negatively charged nucleus

Base your answers to questions 8 through 11 on the information below and on your knowledge of chemistry.

A student compares some models of the atom. These models are listed in the table below in order of development from top to bottom.

Models of the Atom

Model	Observation	Conclusion
Dalton model	Matter is conserved during a chemical reaction.	Atoms are hard, indivisible spheres of different sizes.
Thomson model	Cathode rays are deflected by magnetic/electric fields.	Atoms have small, negatively charged particles as part of their internal structure.
Rutherford model	Most alpha particles pass straight through gold foil but a few are deflected.	An atom is mostly empty space with a small, dense, positively charged nucleus.
Bohr model	Unique spectral lines are emitted by excited gaseous elements.	Packets of energy are absorbed or emitted by atoms when an electron changes shells.

8. State *one* conclusion about the internal structure of the atom that resulted from the gold foil experiment.

9. State *one* way in which the Bohr model agrees with the Thomson model.

10. Using the conclusion from the Rutherford model, identify the charged subatomic particle that is located in the nucleus.

11. State the model that first included electrons as subatomic particles.

Lesson 2: The Atom

Although the atom is described as the smallest unit of matter, it is also composed of much smaller particles called **subatomic particles**.
The three subatomic particles are protons, electrons, and neutrons.

In this lesson, you will learn more about the modern atom and the subatomic particles. You will also learn the relationships between the subatomic particles, atomic number, and mass number of an atom.

Structure of the Atom

Atom: *Smallest Unit of Matter*
The atom is the basic unit of matter. Atoms are composed of protons, electrons and neutrons. Hydrogen-1 (hydrogen with 1 atomic mass unit) is the only atom without a neutron. According to the modern atomic theory:
- An atom is mostly empty space.
- An atom has a small dense positive core (nucleus), and negative electron cloud surrounding the nucleus.
- Elements are composed of atoms with the same atomic number.
- Atoms of the same element are similar.
- Atoms of different elements are different.

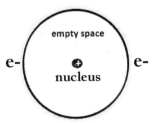
An Atom

Nucleus: *Center of an Atom. Contains Protons and Neutrons*
The nucleus is the center (core) of an atom.
- The nucleus contains protons(+) and neutrons (no charge).
- The overall charge of the nucleus is positive due to the protons.
- The nucleus is much smaller and denser in comparison to the rest of the atom.
- Most of an atom's mass (over 99%) is found within the nucleus.

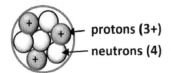
A nucleus of a lithium atom
— protons (3+)
— neutrons (4)

Protons: *Positive Charge, 1 Atomic Mass Unit, Found in Nucleus*
Protons are positively charged subatomic particles found in the nucleus of an atom.
- A proton has a mass of 1 atomic mass unit (u) and a +1 charge.
- A proton is about 1836 times more massive (heavier) than an electron.
- The number of protons is the atomic number of an element.
- All atoms of the same element have the same number of protons.
- The number of protons in the nucleus is also the nuclear charge of the element.

The number of protons (3+) in the nucleus of an atom. = The atomic number (3) given on the Periodic Table for that element.

E3chemistry.com

Electrons: *Negative Charge, Zero Mass. Found in Orbitals.*
Electrons are negatively charged subatomic particles found in orbitals outside the nucleus of an atom.
- An electron has insignificant mass (zero) and a -1 charge.
- Mass is $1/1836^{th}$ that of a proton (or neutron).
- The arrangement of electrons determines the chemical properties of an element.
- The number of electrons is the same as the number of protons in a neutral atom.

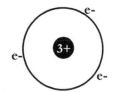

A lithium atom

A lithium atom is neutral because it contains
3+ protons and **3-** electrons.

Neutrons: *Zero Charge. 1 Atomic Mass Unit. Found in Nucleus.*
Neutrons are neutral (no charge) subatomic particles located inside the nucleus of an atom.

- A neutron has a mass of 1 atomic mass unit and zero charge.
- A neutron has approximately the same mass as a proton.
- Atoms of the same element have different numbers of neutrons.

The diagrams below show two different nuclei of lithium.

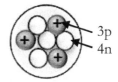

3p
4n

For this Li atom:

Atomic number = **3**
Nucleons   = **7** (3p + 4n)
Mass number = **7 u** (3 u + 5 u)

Nucleons: *Protons and Neutrons*
Nucleons are particles in the nucleus of an atom (protons and neutrons).
- Nucleons account for the total mass of an atom.
- The total number of nucleons in an atom is equal to the sum of the protons *and* neutrons.

Atomic Number: *Number of Protons*
Atomic number identifies the element.
- Atomic number is equal to the number of protons.
- Elements are made of atoms with the same atomic number.

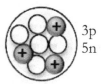

3p
5n

Mass Number: *Mass of Protons and Neutrons*
Mass number identifies an isotope of a given element.
- Atoms of the same element differ in mass numbers due to *different numbers of neutrons.*
- The mass number is equal to the mass of protons *plus* neutrons.

For this Li atom:

Atomic number = **3**
Nucleons   = **8** (3p + 5n)
Mass number = **8 u** (3 u + 5 u)

Summary of Subatomic Particles (Also see Reference Table O)

Subatomic Particle	Symbol	Mass	Charge	Location
Proton	1 *mass* p $+1$ *charge*	1	+1	Nucleus
Neutron	1 n 0	1	0	Nucleus
Electron	0 e -1	0	-1	Orbital (outside the nucleus)

Summary of Relationships Between the Atomic Particles

Number of protons	= the atomic number of the element = electrons (for neutral atoms) = nuclear charge = nucleons − neutrons = mass number − neutrons
Number of electrons (in neutral atoms)	= protons = atomic number = nuclear charge = mass number − neutrons
Number of electrons (in ions)	= atomic number − charge of ion = protons − charge of ion = nuclear charge − charge of ion
Number of neutrons	= mass number − protons = mass number − atomic number = mass number − electrons (for neutral atoms) = nucleons − protons
Atomic number (Nuclear charge)	= protons = electrons (for neutral atoms) = mass number - neutrons
Mass number	= neutrons + protons = neutrons + electrons (for neutral atoms) = neutrons + nuclear charge = nucleons
Number of nucleons	= mass number = neutrons + protons = neutrons + electrons (for neutral atoms) = neutrons + nuclear charge

E3chemistry.com

Isotopes: *Same Protons. Same Atomic Number. Different Neutrons. Different Mass Numbers.*

Isotopes are atoms of the same element with the same number of protons but different amounts of neutrons.

For example: There are a few different atoms of the element lithium. The nucleus of all atoms of lithium contains the same number of protons. The difference between these atoms is the number of neutrons in the nucleus. Since all lithium atoms have the same number of protons (3), they all have the same atomic number of 3. Since they have different numbers of neutrons, they have different mass numbers.

These different atoms of lithium are referred to as isotopes of lithium.

Isotopes of the same element must have:

- **Different** mass numbers
- **Different** amounts of nucleons

- **Same** atomic number
- **Same** amounts of protons
- **Same** amounts of electrons
- **Same** chemical reactivity

. **Different** amounts of neutrons

$$^{7}_{3}\text{Li} \qquad\qquad ^{8}_{3}\text{Li}$$

4   (mass – protons)   5

Isotope Names and Notations

Isotopes of an element have different mass numbers. The mass number of an isotope is written next to the element's name or symbol to distinguish it from the other isotopes.

The notations below show how to represent two isotopes of lithium.

Element – **mass number** (nuclide name)	*Lithium* – 7	*Lithium* – 8
Symbol – **mass number**	*Li* – 7	*Li* – 8
Common isotope notation	$^{7}_{3}\text{Li}$	$^{8}_{3}\text{Li}$
Nuclear diagram	4 n 3 p	5 n 3 p

Atomic Mass Unit: *Based on Carbon-12*

An **atomic mass unit (amu or u)** is the unit for measuring the mass of an atom or a particle by comparing it to the mass of carbon – 12.

$$1 \text{ u } = {}^{1}/_{12}{}^{th} \text{ the mass of } {}^{12}C$$

This means:
Hydrogen–1 (^{1}H) has a mass that is $1/12^{th}$ the mass of ^{12}C.
Lithium–6 (^{6}Li) has a mass that is $6/12^{th}$ or half the mass of ^{12}C.
Magnesium–24 (^{24}Mg) has a mass that is $24/12^{th}$ or 2 times the mass of ^{12}C.

Atomic Mass: *Average Mass of an Atom's Natural Stable Isotopes*

The **atomic mass** of an element is the weighted average mass of all the naturally occurring stable isotopes of that element. Natural samples of an element consist of a mix of two or more isotopes (different atoms). Usually, there is a lot of one isotope and very little of the others. The atomic mass of an element given on the Periodic Table is calculated from both the *masses* and the *relative abundances* (percentages) of the *individual naturally occurring isotopes* of that element.

Atomic mass

Atomic Mass Calculations: *Using Masses and Relative Abundances*

Example 1: *Show a setup and the calculated result.*
A natural sample of chlorine contains 75.76% of ^{35}Cl (atomic mass = 34.97 u) and 24.24% of ^{37}Cl (atomic mass = 36.97 u). Calculate the atomic mass of chlorine.

	^{35}Cl	^{37}Cl	*isotopes given in the question.*
Step 1:	.7576	.2424	*change % to decimal*
Step 2:	x 34.97 u	x 36.97 u	*multiply by atomic mass of the isotope*
Step 3:	(.7576 x 34.97 u) +	(.2424 x 36.97 u)	**numerical setup** *(combine both)*
	26.493 +	8.961 = **35.454 u**	*result (add both products to get mass of Cl)*

Example 2: *Show a setup and the calculated result.*

The data table to the right shows three isotopes of neon. Calculate the atomic mass of neon.

Isotope	Atomic Mass (atomic mass units)	Percent Natural Abundance
^{20}Ne	19.99	90.9%
^{21}Ne	20.99	0.3%
^{22}Ne	21.99	8.8%

	Ne-20	Ne-21	Ne-22	*isotopes given on the table.*
Step 1:	.909	.003	.088	*change % to decimal*
Step 2:	x 19.99 u	x 20.99 u	x 21.99 u	*multiply by atomic mass*
Step 3:	(.909 x 19.99 u) +	(.003 x 20.99 u) +	(.088 x 21.99 u)	**numerical setup**
	18.171 u +	.063 u +	1.935 u = **20.169 u**	**result**

E3chemistry.com

Review Questions: Structure of an Atom

Vocabulary: Briefly define each of the following terms.
12. Nucleus   13. Neutron   14. Proton   15. Electron   16. Nucleons   17. Isotope
18. Atomic number 19. Mass number   20. Atomic mass   21. Atomic mass unit

22. What is the charge and mass of an electron?
    (1) Charge of +1 and a mass of 1 amu
    (2) Charge of +1 and a mass of 1/1836 amu
    (3) Charge of -1 and a mass of 1 amu
    (4) Charge of -1 and a mass of 1/1836 amu

23. Which particle has approximately the same mass as a proton?
    (1) Alpha
    (2) Beta
    (3) Electron
    (4) Neutron

24. The atomic mass of titanium is 47.88 atomic mass units. This atomic mass represents the
    (1) total mass of all the protons and neutrons in an atom of Ti.
    (2) total mass of all the protons, neutrons, and electrons in an atom of Ti.
    (3) weighted average mass of all the naturally occurring isotopes of Ti.
    (4) weighted average mass of the most abundant isotope of Ti.

25. What is the structure of krypton - 85?
    (1) 49 electrons, 49 protons, and 85 neutrons
    (2) 49 electrons, 49 protons, and 49 neutrons
    (3) 36 electrons, 36 protons, and 85 neutrons
    (4) 36 electrons, 36 protons, and 49 neutrons

26. All isotopes of a given atom have
    (1) different mass numbers but the same atomic number.
    (2) different mass numbers and different atomic numbers.
    (3) the same mass number and the same atomic number.
    (4) the same mass number but different atomic numbers

27. Which pair of atoms are isotopes of the same element X?
    (1) $^{226}_{91}X$ and $^{226}_{90}X$
    (2) $^{227}_{91}X$ and $^{227}_{91}X$
    (3) $^{226}_{90}X$ and $^{227}_{91}X$
    (4) $^{226}_{91}X$ and $^{227}_{91}X$

28. A sample of naturally occurring boron contains 19.78% of boron-10 (atomic mass =10.01 u) and 80.22% of boron-11 (atomic mass = 11.01 u). Which numerical setup can be used to determine the atomic mass of naturally occurring boron?
    (1) (0.1978)(10.01) + (0.8022)(11.01)
    (2) (0.8022)(10.01) + (0.1978)(11.01)
    (3) (0.1978)(10.01)/(0.8022)(11.01)
    (4) (0.8022)(10.01)/(0.1978)(11.01)

29. The diagram below represents the nucleus of an atom.

What are the atomic number and mass number of this atom?
    (1) The atomic number is 9 and the mass number is 19.
    (2) The atomic number is 9 and the mass number is 20.
    (3) The atomic number is 11 and the mass number is 19.
    (4) The atomic number is 11 and the mass number is 20.

30. Two isotopes of potassium are K-37 and K-42. Explain, in terms of subatomic particles, why K-37 and K-42 are isotopes of potassium.

31. State, in terms of subatomic particles, *one* difference between the nucleus of a carbon-11 atom and the nucleus of a boron-11 atom.

32. Show a numerical setup and the calculated atomic mass of silicon given the following three natural isotopes.
    92.23% of ^{28}Si (atomic mass = 27.98 u)
    4.67% of ^{29}Si (atomic mass = 28.98 u)
    3.10% of ^{30}Si (atomic mass = 29.97 u)

Lesson 3: Location and Arrangement of Electrons

According to the wave-mechanical model of atoms, electrons are found in orbitals outside the nucleus. An **orbital** describes the most probable or likely region outside the nucleus where an electron can be found. The orbital of an electron depends on the energy of the electron. While one electron of an atom may have enough energy to occupy an orbital far from the nucleus, another electron of that same atom may have just enough energy to occupy a region closer to the nucleus. The result is the formation of energy levels or electron shells around the nucleus of the atom.

The arrangement of electrons in atoms is complex. In this lesson, you will learn the basic and simplified arrangement of electrons in electron shells. You will also learn of electron transition or movement from one shell to another, and the production of bright-line spectra of colors.

Electron Shell, Electron Configuration, and Bohr's Diagram

Electron shells refer to the orbits of electrons around the nucleus of an atom.
• The electron shell (1st) closest to the nucleus contains electrons with the least amount of energy.
• The electron shell farthest from the nucleus contains electrons with the most amount of energy.
• On the Periodic Table, the period or horizontal row number of an element indicates the total number of electron shells in the atom of that element.

Electron configurations show the arrangement of electrons in an atom. Electron configurations can be found in the box of each element on the Periodic Table.

Bohr's (shell) diagram can be drawn to show electrons in the electron shells of an atom.

Periodic Table for Phosphorus   **Bohr's (Shell) Diagram for P**

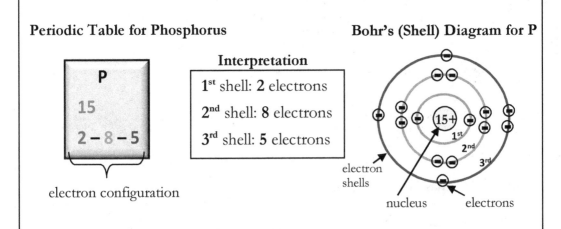

Interpretation

1st shell: 2 electrons
2nd shell: 8 electrons
3rd shell: 5 electrons

electron configuration

electron shells

nucleus   electrons

Maximum Number of Electrons in an Electron Shell

Each electron shell has a maximum number of electrons that can occupy that shell. A full understanding of this concept requires lessons on quantum numbers, which is briefly discussed on pages 55 and 56.

Maximum Number of Electrons: *2(electron shell)²*

The maximum number of electrons in any electron shell can be determined using the formula: $2n^2$ **n** represents the electron shell in question.

For example: n = 1 means 1st shell, n = 3 means 3rd shell, etc.

Maximum electrons in the **1st** shell = $2(n^2)$ = $2(1^2)$ = **2** electrons
Maximum electrons in the **2nd** shell = $2(n^2)$ = $2(2^2)$ = **8** electrons
Maximum electrons in the **3rd** shell = $2(n^2)$ = $2(3^2)$ = **18** electrons

Completely and Partially Filled Electron Shells

An electron shell is completely filled if it has the maximum number of electrons according to the equation $2n^2$.

The electron configuration given on the Periodic Table for phosphorus is shown below. According to this configuration:

$$2 - 8 - 5$$
 1st shell of P is completely filled with electrons.
 2nd shell of P is completely filled with electrons.
 3rd shell of P is partially filled with electrons.

Valence Electrons: *Electrons in the Outer (Last) Shell*

Valence electrons are the electrons in the outermost electron shell of an atom. The valence shell of an atom is the outermost shell that contains electrons. The number of valence electrons in an atom is always the last number in the configuration.

• Elements in the same group or vertical column of the Periodic Table have the *same number of valence electrons,* therefore, *similar chemical reactivity.*

A Lewis electron-dot diagram is a notation that shows the symbol of an atom and dots equal to the number of valence electrons. Lewis electron-dot diagrams can be drawn for neutral atoms, ions and compounds. A Lewis electron-dot diagram for a phosphorus atom is shown on the right.
In topic 4 you'll learn to draw and recognize dot diagrams for ions, ionic compounds, and molecular substances.

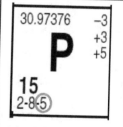

Phosphorus has
5 valence electrons.
Its valence shell is the 3rd shell.

**Electron-dot
diagram for P**

Phosphorus has
5 valence electrons.
Its valence shell is the 3rd shell.

**Electron-dot
diagram for P**

5 dots = 5 valence
electrons

Ground and Excited State Atoms

An atom is most stable when its electrons occupy the lowest available electron shells. When this is the case, the atom is said to be in the ground state. When an electron of an atom occupies a higher energy level than it should, the atom is said to be in the excited state. Facts related to ground and excited state atoms are summarized below.

Ground State Atom: *Low Energy, Normal Configuration*
When an atom is in the ground state:

- The electron configuration is the same as given on the Periodic Table.

- Electrons are filled in order from the lowest to highest energy shell.

- Energy of the atom is at its lowest, and the atom is stable.

- A ground state electron must absorb energy to go from a low shell to a higher shell. *Ex.* from 2nd to 3rd.

14.0067
N
7
2-5

Ground state configuration for nitrogen **(2 – 5)**

Same as given on the Periodic Table

Excited State Atom: *High Energy State*
When an atom is in the excited state:

- The electron configuration is different from that on the Periodic Table.

- The energy of the atom is at its highest, and the atom is unstable.

- An excited state electron must release energy to return from the high level to a lower level. *Ex.* From 3rd to 2nd.

- A spectrum of colors is produced when an excited electron releases energy and returns to the ground state.

N
7
1 – 6
2 – 4 – 1

Two possible **excited state** configurations for nitrogen.

These configurations are different from that of the Periodic Table for nitrogen, *but* the total number of electrons is still **7**.

Electron Transition Between Shells.
Electrons absorb and release a *specific amount* of energy to go between two shells of an atom.

  From a **low** to a **higher** shell
  Ex. 5th shell to 6th shell
  - Energy is *absorbed* or gained by the electron.

  From a **high** to a **lower** shell
  Ex. 6th shell to 5th shell
  - Energy is *released* or emitted by the electron.
  - A bright-line spectrum is produced.

Bright-line Spectrum: *Energy Released by Excited Electrons Returning to Ground State*

A **bright-line spectrum** is produced when an electron in an excited state releases or emits energy as it returns to the ground state. When viewed through a *spectroscope,* the light energy released by the electrons separates into bright, colored lines. Just like a *"fingerprint,"* each element produces a unique pattern of lines. Each colored line corresponds to a specific wavelength in the visible light part of the spectrum.

Spectral lines (bright-line spectra)

The chart below shows the bright-line spectra for hydrogen, lithium, sodium and potassium. A bright-line spectrum of an unknown mixture is compared to those of H, Li, Na and K. The elements in the unknown mixture can be identified by matching the lines in the unknown to those for H, Li, Na and K.

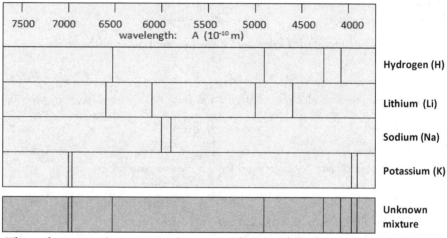

The unknown mixture contains **potassium** and **hydrogen**.
Lines in the spectrum of the unknown match all the lines
in the spectra for potassium and hydrogen.

Flame Test: *Identification of Metallic Ions*

A **flame test** is a lab procedure in which compounds of metallic ions are heated over a Bunsen burner to produce different flame colors.
• The flame color that is produced is the light energy released by an excited electron returning to the ground or low state of the atom.

The color of the flame that is observed can be used to identify the metal ion that's in the substance. However, since two or more metallic ions can produce similar colors, flame test results are not very reliable for identification.

A **spectroscope** is a device that is used to separate light into color patterns (spectra) at different wavelengths. When a flame color produced during a flame test procedure is viewed through a spectroscope, it is separated into bright-line spectra. Each flame color will produce a unique bright-line spectrum, which provides a more reliable result for identification of the metal ion in each compound.

Review Questions: Location and Arrangement of Electrons

33. How do the energy and the most probable location of an electron in the third shell of an atom compare to the energy and the most probable location of an electron in the first shell of the same atom?
    (1) In the third shell, an electron has more energy and is closer to the nucleus.
    (2) In the third shell, an electron has more energy and is farther from the nucleus.
    (3) In the third shell, an electron has less energy and is closer to the nucleus.
    (4) In the third shell, an electron has less energy and is farther from the nucleus.

34. In the electron configuration $2 - 8 - 3 - 1$, which shell contains electrons with the greatest energy?
    (1) 1st   (3) 3rd
    (2) 2nd   (4) 4th

35. Which set of symbols represents atoms with valence electrons in the same electron shell?
    (1) Ba, Br, Bi   (3) O, S, Te
    (2) Sr, Sn, I   (4) Mn, Hg, Cu

36. Which of these atoms in the ground state has the most number of electron shells containing electrons?
    (1) Cs–132   (3) Xe–134
    (2) I–127   (4) Na–23

37. Which element has a total of 5 valence electrons present in the fifth shell?
    (1) Sb   (3) I
    (2) Bi   (4) Br

38. Which is an excited state electron configuration for a neutral atom with 16 protons and 18 neutrons?
    (1) $2 - 8 - 5 - 1$ (3) $2 - 8 - 6 - 2$
    (2) $2 - 8 - 8$ (4) $2 - 8 - 6$

39. Which is the ground state configuration for a potassium atom?
    (1) $2 - 8 - 7 - 1$ (3) $2 - 8 - 8 - 7$
    (2) $2 - 8 - 8 - 1$ (4) $2 - 8 - 6 - 1$

40. The electron configuration 2–8–18–5–1 could be of
    (1) an arsenic atom in the ground state
    (2) an arsenic atom in the excited state
    (3) a selenium atom in the ground state
    (4) a selenium atom in the excited state

41. As an electron moves from the 3rd electron shell to the 4th electron shell, the energy of the atom
    (1) increases as the electron absorbs energy
    (2) increases as the electron releases energy
    (3) decreases as the electron absorbs energy
    (4) decreases as the electron releases energy

42. The electron transition between which two electron shells will produce a bright-line spectrum of colors?
    (1) 2nd to 3rd   (3) 1st to 4th
    (2) 3rd to 4th   (4) 2nd to 1st

43. As an electron in an atom moves between electron shells, which transition would cause the electron to absorb the most energy?
    (1) 1st to 2nd   (3) 2nd to 4th
    (2) 2nd to 1st   (4) 4th to 2nd

E3chemistry.com

Base your answers to questions 44 and 45 on the information below and on your knowledge of chemistry.

The Bohr model of the atom was developed in the early part of the twentieth century. A diagram of the Bohr model for one atom, in the ground state of a specific element, is shown below. The nucleus of this atom contains 4 protons and 5 neutrons.

Bohr Model

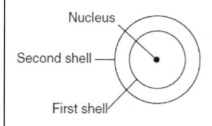

44. State the number of electrons in each shell in this atom in the ground state.

   Number of electrons in first shell:

   Number of electrons in second shell:

45. State the atomic number and the mass number of this element.

   Atomic number:

   Mass number:

Base your answers to questions 46 through 48 on the information below.

The bright-line spectra for three elements and a mixture of elements are shown below.

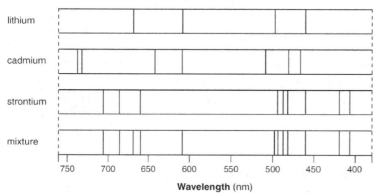

46. State the total number of valence electrons in a cadmium atom in the ground state.

47. Identify all the elements in the mixture.

48. Explain, in terms of both electrons and energy, how the bright-line spectrum of an element is produced.

Base your answers to questions 49 and 50 on the information below.

An atom in an excited state has an electron configuration of 2-7-2.

49. Write the electron configuration of this atom in the ground state.

50. Identify the element that this atom represents.

Lesson 4: Neutral Atoms and Ions

Other than the noble gases in group 18, elements have incomplete valence or outermost electron shells. For this reason, most elements need to lose, gain or share electrons when bonding to get a full valence shell and become more stable. A neutral atom may lose all its valence electrons to form a new valence shell that is completely filled. A neutral atom may also gain or share electrons to fill its valence shell. An ion is formed when a neutral atom loses or gains electrons.

In this lesson, you will learn similarities and differences between neutral atoms and ions.

Neutral Atoms: *Equal Numbers of Electrons and Protons*
A neutral atom has an equal number of protons and electrons.
The electron configuration given on the Periodic Table for each element is for the neutral atom in the ground state.

Ions: *Unequal Numbers of Electrons and Protons*
An ion is a charged atom with unequal numbers of electrons and protons.
An ion is formed when a neutral atom loses or gains electrons.
An ion has a different chemical property and reactivity from the neutral atom.

A **positive ion** is a charged atom with **fewer electrons(-)** than protons(+).
- A positive ion is formed when a neutral atom loses one or more electrons.
- Metals and metalloids tend to lose electrons and form positive ions.
- As a neutral atom loses electrons, its size decreases.
- Ionic radius (size) of a positive ion is always smaller than the atomic radius because the ion has one *less electron shell.*

A **negative ion** is a charged atom with **more electrons(-)** than protons(+).
- A negative ion is formed when a neutral atom gains one or more electrons.
- Nonmetals tend to gain electrons and form negative ions.
- As a neutral atom gains electrons, its size increases.
- The ionic radius (size) of a negative ion is always larger than the atomic radius because the ion has *more electrons.*

Number of Electrons in an Ion = atomic number or protons − charge

Charge of an Ion = atomic number or protons − electrons

Example 3: *Number of Electrons in Ions*
How many electrons are in a sodium ion (Na^+) and in a sulfur ion (S^{2-})?

$Na^+ = 11 - (+1) =$ **10** electrons

$S^{2-} = 16 - (-2) =$ **18** electrons

Example 4: *Charge of an Ion*
What is the charge of a manganese ion with 21 electrons?

Charge = atomic number − electrons
Charge = $24 - 21 =$ **+3**

Comparing Ions to Neutral Atoms

When electrons are lost or gained by a neutral atom, the ion formed will be different in many ways from the neutral atom. Number of electrons, electron configuration, properties, and size of the ion will all be different from those of the neutral atom. Below are diagrams and tables showing comparisons between two atoms and their ions.

Comparing a Positive Ion to the Neutral Atom

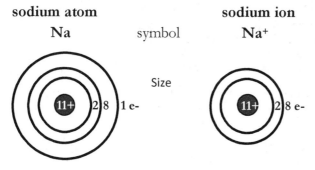

sodium atom		sodium ion
Na	symbol	**Na⁺**

| | Size | |

11	protons (atomic number)	11
11	electrons	10
2 – 8 – 1	configuration	2 – 8

Comparing a Negative Ion to the Neutral Atom

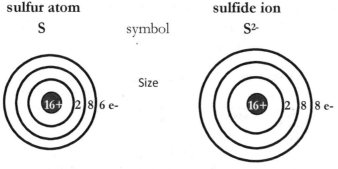

sulfur atom		sulfide ion
S	symbol	**S²⁻**

| | Size | |

16	protons (atomic number)	16
16	electrons	18
2 – 8 – 6	configuration	2 – 8 – 8

Review Questions: Neutral Atoms and Ions

Vocabulary: Briefly define each of the following terms.

51. Neutral atom   52. Ion   53. Positive ion   54. Negative ion

55. Which changes occur as an atom becomes a positively charged ion?
    (1) The atom gains electrons, and the number of protons increases.
    (2) The atom gains electrons, and the number of protons remains the same.
    (3) The atom loses electrons, and the number of protons decreases.
    (4) The atom loses electrons, and the number of protons remains the same.

56. A neutral oxygen atom (O) differs from an ion of oxygen (O^{2-}) in that the atom has
    (1) more protons   (3) fewer protons
    (2) more electrons   (4) fewer electrons

57. How does the size of an N^{3-} ion compare to the size of an N atom?
    (1) N^{3-} is bigger than N because N^{3-} has 3 more electrons.
    (2) N^{3-} is bigger than N because N^{3-} has 3 fewer electrons.
    (3) N^{3-} is smaller than N because N^{3-} has 3 more electrons.
    (4) N^{3-} is smaller than N because N^{3-} has 3 fewer electrons.

58. An ion of which element has a larger radius than an atom of the same element?
    (1) aluminum   (3) magnesium
    (2) chlorine   (4) lithium

59. The total number of electrons in a Br^- ion is
    (1) 36   (2) 35   (3) 34   (4) 54

60. What is the total number of electrons in a Cr^{3+} ion?
    (1) 3   (2) 21   (3) 24   (4) 27

61. An atom has a nuclear charge of +50 and 46 electrons. The net ionic charge of this atom is
    (1) +46   (2) -46   (3) -4   (4) +4

62. The electron configuration for As^{3-} is
    (1) $2 - 8 - 18 - 5$ (3) $2 - 8 - 17 - 6$
    (2) $2 - 8 - 18 - 8$ (4) $2 - 8 - 18 - 5 - 3$

Base your answers to questions 63 through 65 on the information below.

The atomic radius and the ionic radius for some Group 1 and some Group 17 elements are given in the tables below.

Atomic and Ionic Radii of Some Elements

Group 1		Group 17	
Particle	Radius (pm)	Particle	Radius (pm)
Li atom	130.	F atom	60.
Li+ ion	78	F- ion	133
Na atom	160.	Cl atom	100.
Na+ ion	98	Cl- ion	181
K atom	200.	Br atom	117
K+ ion	133	Br- ion	?
Rb atom	215	I atom	136
Rb+ ion	148	I- ion	220.

63. Write both the name and the charge of the particle that is gained by an F atom when the atom becomes an F- ion.

64. Explain, in terms of electron shells, why the radius of a K^+ ion is greater than the radius of an Na^+ ion.

65. Estimate the radius of a Br^- ion.

Quantum Numbers

In lesson 3, you learned the basic arrangement of electrons in an atom. A better understanding of electron configurations requires a brief lesson in quantum chemistry.

Quantum theory uses mathematical equations to describe location, as well as behavior of electrons in an atom. This theory uses a set of four quantum numbers to describe location of an electron in atoms.

The principal energy levels

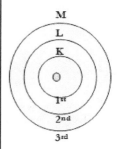

First quantum number: *Principal energy level (electron shell).*
The first quantum number is designated with a letter (K, L, M) or a number (1, 2, 3..) to show the major energy level of an electron. For example, an electron with a principal quantum number of L or 2 is in the second energy level. On the Periodic Table, the period number of an element indicates how many principal energy levels are in the atoms of that element.

Second quantum number: *Sublevel of an electron.*
The second quantum number is designated with s, p, d, f, g, h, and i to indicate the sublevel of an electron within the principal energy level. The s sublevel is always the first sublevel in any principal energy level. The next sublevel is always the p. The number of sublevels in an atom is equal to the principal energy level number. For example:
The 1st principal energy has 1 sublevel (1s).
The 3rd principal energy level has three sublevels (3s, 3p, and 3d). The difference between the sublevels is the shape of their orbitals. The s orbitals are spherically shaped. The p orbitals are dumbbell shaped. The shapes of d, f, g, h, and i orbitals are too complex to be discussed here.

spherical shapes of s orbitals

Size of an orbital varies depending on the principal energy level

Third quantum number: *Orbital of an electron.*
The third quantum number is designated with an x, y or z to describe the *orbital,* which is the *probable location of an electron* within a sublevel. For example, $2p_x$, $2p_y$, and $2p_z$ describe the three p orbitals of the second energy level. Each sublevel has a set number of orbitals that can have electrons All s sublevels, regardless of the energy level, have just 1 orbital. All p sublevels have 3 orbitals. The d sublevels have 5 orbitals. Each orbital, regardless of the sublevel, can hold a maximum of two electrons.

dumbbell shapes of 2p orbitals

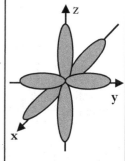

Fourth quantum number: *Spin of an electron.*
The fourth quantum number describes the spin direction of an electron in orbitals. An orbital with 2 electrons must have the electrons spinning in opposite directions to overcome repulsion of the same charge.

Summary of Principal Quantum Numbers

Principal Energy Level (n)	Number of Sublevels	Types and Available Sublevels	Number of Available Orbitals	Maximum Number of Electrons in Energy Level ($2n^2$)
1	1	1s	1	2
2	2	2s	1	8
		2p	3	
3	3	3s	1	18
		3p	3	
		3d	5	
4	4	4s	1	32
		4p	3	
		4d	5	
		4f	7	

Note: Each orbital can hold a maximum of 2 electrons.

Electron Configurations and Orbital Notations

The **electron configuration** shows the arrangement of electrons in the energy levels and sublevels of an atom. Electrons in a ground state atom must always occupy the lowest available levels. The order in which electrons must fill in the energy levels is given below:

1s 2s 2p 3s 3p 4s 3d 4p 5s 4d 5p ......
lowest energy ——— increasing energy ——→

Orbital notation shows distribution of electrons in the orbitals. When placing electrons in orbitals, keep the following in mind:
- No more than two electrons in an orbital.
- Each orbital in p, d, f.. must have an electron before pairing.
- Two electrons in an orbital must show opposite spins (↑↓).
- Valence e- are *only* the electrons in the s and p sublevels of the highest level

Ground state for fluorine

$1s^2 2s^2 2p^5$

Excited state for fluorine

$1s^2 2s^2 2p^4 3s^1$

Examples of configurations and orbital notations for four elements.

	H 1e-	He 2e-	N 7e -	Na 11e-
e- config.	$1s^1$	$1s^2$	$1s^2$ $2s^2$ $2p^3$	$1s^2$ $2s^2$ $2p^6$ $3s^1$
orbital notation	↑	↑↓	↑↓ ↑↓ ↑ ↑ ↑	↑↓ ↑↓ ↑↓ ↑↓ ↑↓ ↑
e- config	1	2	2 – 5	2 – 8 – 1
valence e-	1	2	5	1

66. Which is the correct electron configuration of a magnesium atom in the ground state?
    (1) $1s^2 2s^2 2p^6 3s^1 3p^1$ (3) $1s^2 2s^2 2p^6 3s^2$
    (2) $1s^2 2s^2 2p^6$ (4) $1s^2 2s^2 2p^6 3s^2 3p^1$

67. Which electron configuration represents an atom of sodium in the ground state?
    (1) $1s^2 2s^2 2p^6 3p^1$ (3) $1s^2 2s^2 2p^6 3s^2 3p^6 4s^1$
    (2) $1s^2 2s^2 2p^5 3s^1$ (4) $1s^2 2s^2 2p^6 3s^1 4s^1$

68. An atom in the excited state can have an electron configuration of
    (1) $1s^2 2p^1$ (2) $1s^2 2s^2$ (3) $1s^2 2s^2 2p^5$ (4) $1s^2 2s^2 2p^6$

69. What is the electron configuration of an Mn atom in the excited state?
    (1) $1s^2 2s^2 2p^6 3s^2$ (3) $1s^2 2s^2 2p^6 3s^2 3p^6 3d^5 4s^2$
    (2) $1s^2 2s^2 2p^6 3s^2 3p^6 3d^6 4s^1$ (4) $1s^2 2s^2 2p^6 3s^2 3p^6 3d^5$

70. Which atom in the ground state has only three electrons in the 3p sublevel?
    (1) Phosphorus   (2) Potassium   (3) Argon   (4) Aluminum

71. Which atom in the ground state has two half-filled orbitals?
    (1) P   (2) N   (3) Li   (4) Si

72. What is the total number of completely filled principal energy levels in an atom with a configuration of $1s^2 2s^2 2p^6 3s^2 3p^6 3d^{10} 4s^2 4p^1$?
    (1) 1   (2) 2   (3) 3   (4) 4

73. Using quantum chemistry(s, p, d.), write electron configurations and draw orbital notations for the following atoms and ions.

atoms:

C

Al

S

Ar

Ca

Se

ions:

Li$^+$

Mg^{2+}

K$^+$

F$^-$

S^{2-}

As^{3-}

Lesson 1: Stability and Energy in Bonding

Chemical bonding is the simultaneous attraction of two positive nuclei to negative electrons. Chemical bonding is the "glue" that holds particles (atoms, ions, or molecules) together in matter. Since most atoms do not have full valence shells, they must bond with other atoms. When atoms bond, energy of the atoms decreases as they become more stable.

In this lesson, you will learn about stability and energy in bonding.

Bonding and Stability: *A Bonded Atom is More Stable.*

Atoms bond so they can attain full valence shells and become stable.

The **octet rule** states that a stable valence shell configuration must have eight electrons.

• An atom can get a full and stable valence shell configuration by

        transferring or **accepting electrons** (during ionic bonding)

        or

        sharing electrons (during covalent bonding)

• The ground state electron configuration of a bonded atom is similar to that of the nearest noble gas (Group 18) atom.

Electron Configuration of an Atom in a Bond: *Similar to Nearest Noble Gas*

Each atom in a bond has an electron configuration that is similar to its nearest noble gas atom.

For example, in a bond between sodium and chlorine in the compound NaCl:
Na (atomic number 11) resembles Ne (atomic number 10).
Cl (atomic number 17) resembles Ar (atomic number 18).

In **NaCl**, **Na** is the **Na⁺** ion (10 electrons).
The Na⁺ configuration is 2–8, which is the same as that of Ne, 2–8.

In NaCl, **Cl** is the **Cl⁻** ion (18 electrons).
The Cl⁻ configuration is 2–8–8, which is the same as that of Ar, 2–8–8.

Use the Periodic Table to figure out which noble gas (group 18 element) is the closest to each element in a formula.

Bonding and Energy

All chemical substances contain potential energy.

Potential energy is the *stored energy in the bonds* holding particles of a substance together. The amount of potential energy depends on *composition and structure* of the substance.

Forming a Bond: *Exothermic Process*

Bond formation between two atoms is an exothermic process. Exothermic processes release heat energy. When two atoms come together to form a bond, heat energy is always released. Since energy is released, the energy of the atoms decreases. The atoms are now more stable than they were before bonding.
As energy is released during bond formation:

- Potential energy of the atoms decreases.
- Stability of the atoms increases.
- Stability of the chemical system increases.

A **bond formation equation** has the energy released to the right of the arrow.

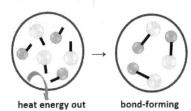

heat energy out   **bond-forming**

$$H \ + \ Cl \ \longrightarrow \ H - Cl \ + \ \textbf{\textit{energy}}$$

A chemical bond
that is formed.

Breaking a Bond: *Endothermic Process*

The breaking of a bond in chemical substances is an endothermic process. Endothermic processes absorb heat energy. When a bond between two atoms of a substance is to be broken, energy must be absorbed by the substance. Since energy is absorbed, the energy of the atoms increases. The free atoms are now less stable than when they were bonded together.

As energy is absorbed during bond-breaking:

- Potential energy of the atoms increases.
- Stability of the atoms decreases.
- Stability of the chemical system decreases.

A **bond breakage equation** has energy absorbed to the left of the arrow.

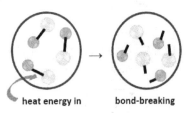

heat energy in   **bond-breaking**

$$H - Cl \ + \ \textbf{\textit{energy}} \ \longrightarrow \ H \ + \ Cl$$

A chemical bond
to be broken.

Review Questions: Stability and Energy in Bonding

Vocabulary: Briefly define each of the following terms.

1. Chemical bond   2. Octet rule   3. Exothermic   4. Endothermic

5. When a sulfur atom bonds with sodium atoms to form the compound Na_2S, the configuration of sulfur in the compound is similar to
   (1) Na   (2) O   (3) Ne   (4) Ar

6. The electron configuration of Sr and H ions in the formula SrH_2 are similar to those of elements
   (1) Kr and He   (3) Ar and Ne
   (2) Rb and He   (4) Ca and Li

7. Atom X and atom Y bond to form a compound. The electron configuration of X in the bond is $2 - 8 - 8$. The electron configuration of Y in the compound is $2 - 8$. Which two atoms could be X and Y?
   (1) X could be magnesium and Y could be sulfur.
   (2) X could be calcium and Y could be sulfur.
   (3) X could be magnesium and Y could be nitrogen.
   (4) X could be calcium and Y could be nitrogen.

8. When two atoms form a bond to produce a chemical substance, the stability of the chemical system
   (1) decreases as energy is absorbed.   (3) decreases as energy is released.
   (2) increases as energy is absorbed.   (4) increases as energy is released.

9. Given the balanced equation:

   $$I_2 + energy \rightarrow I + I$$

   Which statement describes the process represented by this equation?
   (1) A bond is formed, and energy is absorbed
   (2) A bond is formed, and energy is released
   (3) A bond is broken, and energy is absorbed
   (4) A bond is broken, and energy is released

10. Given the equation

    $$2H_2 + O_2 \rightarrow 2H_2O$$

    Which statement best describes the process taking place as bonds are broken and formed?
    (1) The breaking of the O–O bond releases energy.
    (2) The breaking of the H–H bond releases energy.
    (3) The forming of the H–O bond absorbs energy.
    (4) The forming of the H–O bond releases energy.

11. When two fluorine atoms combine to form a molecule of fluorine, energy is
    (1) always absorbed   (3) sometimes absorbed
    (2) always released   (4) sometimes released

Base your answers to questions 12 and 13 on the information below.

Ozone, $O_3(g)$, is produced from oxygen, $O_2(g)$, by electrical discharge during thunderstorms. The unbalanced equation below represents the reaction that forms ozone.

$$O_2(g) \xrightarrow{\text{electricity}} O_3(g)$$

12. Explain, in terms of electron configurations, why an oxygen molecule is more stable than an oxygen atom.

13. Explain why the equation represents a chemical change.

Lesson 2: Types of Bonding and Substances

Intramolecular forces are bonds that hold atoms together to create molecules and compounds. **Ionic, covalent,** *and* **metallic** are types of bonding between the atoms of a substance. Bonding between atoms is a result of atoms competing for electrons to fill their valence shells.

In this lesson, you will learn about the types of bonding between atoms, and types of substances and their properties.

Ionic Bonds: *Transfer of Electrons from Metal to Nonmetal*
Ionic bonds are forces holding charged particles together in ionic compounds. Ionic bonds are formed by the transfer of one or more electrons from a metal to nonmetal.
• The metal atom always loses (or transfers) electrons and becomes a positively charged ion.
• The nonmetal atom always gains (or accepts) electrons and becomes a negatively charged ion.
• An ionic bond is formed by the electrostatic attraction between the +metal ions and the -nonmetal ions.
• The electronegativity difference between the nonmetal and metal atoms in an ionic bond is usually 1.7 or greater.

metal   nonmetal

22.98977 +1	35.453 −1
Na	**Cl** +1 +5 +7
11 2-8-1	17 2-8-7

loses ↓ e-   gains ↓ e-

Na^+ Cl^-

Na^+Cl^-

Ionic bond
Electrostatic attraction between the positive and negative ions.

Opposites attract.

Ionic compounds are formed by positively and negatively charged particles. There are two categories of ionic compounds.

Ionic Compounds with Only Ionic Bonds: *Composed of Two Elements*
These compounds are composed of two different atoms. They are *binary* ionic compounds composed of positively charged metal and negatively charged nonmetal atoms. Example compounds in this category are given below.

| **NaCl** | **K₂O** | **LiBr** |
| *sodium chloride* | *potassium oxide* | *lithium bromide* |

Ionic Compounds with Both Ionic and Covalent Bonds: *Composed of Three Elements*
These compounds usually have three or more different atoms because they contain a polyatomic ion. Polyatomic ions (**See Table E**) are ions usually containing two or more nonmetal atoms with an excess charge. Bonding within most polyatomic ions is *covalent*. Compounds of this category are generally formed by the electrostatic attraction (*ionic bond*) between a positive metal (or NH_4^+) and a negative polyatomic ion. Example compounds in this category are given below.

| **NaNO₃** | **CaSO₄** | **(NH₄)₂O** |
| *sodium nitrate* | *calcium sulfate* | *ammonium oxide* |

Physical Properties of Ionic Substances
• Hard, brittle, crystalline *solid* at STP • High melting points • Soluble in water
• Electrolytes; good electrical conductivity as a *liquid* or in *aqueous* solution. Conductivity is due to *mobile (free moving) ions* in liquid and aqueous forms.

Covalent Bonds and Molecular Substances

Covalent Bonds: *Sharing of Electrons by Two Nonmetals*
Covalent bonds are forces holding nonmetal atoms together in covalent and molecular substances.

- Covalent bonding occurs between two nonmetal atoms that are sharing electrons.
- The electronegativity difference between the two nonmetals in a covalent bond is usually less than 1.7.
- A single or multiple (double or triple) covalent bond can form between two nonmetal atoms depending on the number of electrons they share.
- Sharing in a covalent bond could be equal or unequal.

Polar Covalent: *Unequal Sharing by Two Different Nonmetals*
Polar covalent bonds are formed by unequal sharing of electrons between two different nonmetal atoms. A polar covalent bond is the most common type of bond between atoms of molecular substances. *Examples:* HCl and CO

Nonpolar Covalent: *Equal Sharing by the Same Nonmetal*
Nonpolar covalent bonds are formed by equal sharing of electrons between two of the same nonmetal atoms. Nonpolar bonds are commonly found in diatomic (two-atom) elements. *Examples:* fluorine, F_2, and nitrogen, N_2.

Molecular compounds are substances containing molecules. A **molecule** is a group of covalently bonded atoms. A molecular substance is classified as polar or nonpolar depending on the symmetry of its molecules.

Polar Substances: *Asymmetrically Shaped Molecules*
Polar molecular substances contain molecules that have asymmetrical structures. A molecule has an asymmetrical structure when charges are unevenly distributed within the molecule. A polar molecule is only formed by polar covalently bonded atoms (as in HBr and NH_3).

Nonpolar Substances: *Symmetrically Shaped Molecules*
Nonpolar molecular substances contain molecules that have symmetrical structures. A molecule has a symmetrical structure when charges are evenly distributed within the molecule. Even charge distribution means that a molecule does not have positive and negative poles. Nonpolar means no poles. A nonpolar molecule can be formed by nonpolar covalently bonded atoms (as in O_2) or by polar covalently bonded atoms (as in CH_4).

Physical Properties of Molecular Substances
- Could be a *solid, liquid* or *gas* at STP • Low melting points
- Low solubility in water • Nonelectrolytes (except for acids)

---

nonmetal   nonmetal

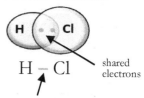

H – Cl ← shared electrons

A **covalent bond** $(-)$

Single covalent: H – Cl (HCl) contains two (one pair of) **shared electrons.**

Multiple Covalent Bonds

Double covalent: O=O (O_2) contains four (two pairs of) shared electrons.

Triple covalent: N≡N (N_2) contains six (three pairs of) shared electrons.

---

polar covalent bond (different atoms)

H — Cl   C = O

nonpolar covalent bond (same atom)

F — F   N ≡ N

Polar substances (asymmetrical)

hydrogen bromide (HBr)

H – Br

ammonia (NH_3)

$$H - \underset{\underset{H}{|}}{N} - H$$

Nonpolar substances (symmetrical)

oxygen (O_2)

O = O

methane (CH_4)

$$H - \overset{\overset{H}{|}}{\underset{\underset{H}{|}}{C}} - H$$

Other Types of Covalent Bonds

Coordinate Covalent Bonds: *Found in Polyatomic Ions*
A coordinate covalent bond is formed when both shared electrons are provided by only one of the atoms in the bond.
- The bond is formed when H^+ (hydrogen ion, proton), which does not have an electron, bonds with a molecule such as NH_3 (ammonia) or H_2O (water).
- NH_3 and H_2O molecules have lone pairs of electrons that they can share with an H^+ (hydrogen ion, proton) that has no electrons.
Two polyatomic ions containing coordinate covalent bonds are given below.

H_3O^+ (hydronium ion) *forms from* H_2O (water) and H^+ (hydrogen ion).

NH_4^+ (ammonium ion) *forms from* NH_3 (ammonia) and H^+ (hydrogen ion).

Network Covalent Bonds: *No Discrete Particles*
A network covalent bond holds the nonmetal atoms of a network solid compound together. Compounds formed by network covalent bonding cannot exist as discrete individual molecules. Below are three network solid compounds.

C	**SiO$_2$**	**SiC**
(Diamond)	*(Silicon dioxide)*	*(Silicon carbide)*

Physical Properties of Network Solids
- Very hard *solids* at STP
- Insoluble in water
- Extremely high melting points
- No electrical conductivity

Metallic Bonds and Substances: *Positive Metal Ions in Sea of Electrons*
A metallic bond is the force that holds metal atoms together in metallic substances.
- Metallic bonding is described as *positive metal ions (Cu^{2+}) immersed in a sea of mobile valence electrons(–).* See diagram to the right.
- Substances containing metallic bonds are metallic elements.

  Ca (calcium)   **Au** (Gold)   **Fe** (iron) *(see Periodic Table)*

Physical Properties of Metallic Substances
- Hard *solids* at STP (except for mercury, Hg, a *liquid*) • High melting points
- Insoluble in water • Electrical conductivity due to *mobile (free moving) electrons*

Melting Point Comparison for the Four Types of Substances

Melting points for four types of solids are given below.

Note the big difference in temperature at which each solid will melt at STP.

Type of substance	Molecular	Ionic	Metallic	Network Solid
Example solid:	Ice (H$_2$O)	Salt (NaCl)	Gold (Au)	Diamond (C)
Melting point	0°C	801°C	1065°C	3550°C

Summary Table: Types of Substances and Properties

Type of Substance	Phase at room temperature	Physical Properties (characteristics)		
		Melting point	Conductivity	Solubility (in water)
Metallic	Solid (except Hg - liquid)	Very High	Good (High) (in Solid and Liquid phases) (due to mobile electrons)	No (insoluble)
Ionic	Solid only	High	Good (High) (in Liquid and Aqueous phases) (due to mobile ions)	Yes (soluble)
Molecular	solid, liquid, gas	Low	Poor (low) (in all phases)	Yes (slightly soluble)
Network solid	Solid only	Extremely high	Very poor (in all phases)	No (insoluble)

Bond Types: Summary of Facts and Examples

Bond Type	Types of Elements in the Bond	Bond Description	Electronegativity Difference	Types of Substances Containing Bond	Example Substance Containing Bond
Metallic	metal atoms of the same element	positive ions in sea of electrons	-------------	metallic substances	Ag K
Ionic	metal & nonmetal	transfer of electrons	1.7 or greater	ionic substances	NaCl Li$_2$O
Covalent	nonmetals only	sharing of electrons	less than 1.7	molecular and network solids	HCl
Polar covalent	two different nonmetals	unequal sharing of electrons	greater than 0 but less than 1.7	polar and nonpolar	H$_2$O CH$_4$
Nonpolar covalent	same nonmetal (or nonmetal atoms with the same electronegativity)	equal sharing of electrons	zero (0)	diatomic nonpolar substances	H$_2$ O$_2$
Coordinate covalent	two different nonmetals	One atom provides both shared electrons	-------------	polyatomic ions	NH$_4^+$ H$_3$O$^+$
Network solid covalent	nonmetals only	No discrete particles	-------------	network solids	C, SiC, SiO$_2$

                                      65

Review Questions: Types of Bonds and Substances

Vocabulary: Briefly define each of the following terms.

14. Intramolecular force 15. Ionic bond 16. Covalent bond 17. Polar covalent
18. Nonpolar covalent 19. Network solid covalent 20. Coordinate covalent
21. Metallic bond 22. Molecule 23. Polar substance 24. Nonpolar substance

25. When combining with a metallic atom, a nonmetallic atom tends to
    (1) lose electrons and form a negative ion   (3) gain electrons and form a negative ion
    (2) lose electrons and form a positive ion   (4) gain electrons and form a positive ion

26. The sharing of electrons in covalent bonding
    (1) must always be equal   (3) is neither equal nor unequal
    (2) must always be unequal   (4) can be equal or unequal

27. The ability to conduct electricity in the solid state is a characteristic of metallic
    substances. This characteristic is best explained by the presence of
    (1) mobile neutrons   (3) mobile protons
    (2) mobile ions   (4) mobile electrons

28. Which pair of elements forms a bond that is mostly ionic?
    (1) $CaCl_2$ (3) HCl
    (2) CCl_4 (4) PCl_5

29. Element X combines with rubidium to form an ionic bond. In which group of the
    Periodic Table could element X be found?
    (1) Group 1   (3) Group 13
    (2) Group 2   (4) Group 16

30. Which compound contains atoms held together by covalent bonds?
    (1) Sodium chloride   (3) Aluminum oxide
    (2) Calcium hydride   (4) Nitrogen oxide

31. Which electron configuration belongs to a substance whose atoms are held together
    by metallic bonds?
    (1) $2 - 8 - 8$ (3) 1
    (2) $2 - 8 - 18 - 18$ (4) $2 - 8 - 18 - 3$

32. Which formula contains both ionic and covalent bonds?
    (1) MgS   (3) $C_6H_{12}O_6$
    (2) NaBr   (4) $MgSO_4$

33. The structure of which molecule is nonpolar with polar covalent bonds?

$$\begin{array}{ccccc}
 & & Cl & & \\
 & & | & & \\
(1)\ \ H-S & (2)\ Cl-C-Cl & (3)\ \ O=O & (4)\ Na-F \\
 & | & | & & \\
 & H & Cl & &
\end{array}$$

34. Which two substances are covalent compounds?
    (1) $C_6H_{12}O_6(s)$ and KI(s)   (3) KI(s) and NaCl(s)
    (2) $C_6H_{12}O_6(s)$ and HCl(g)   (4) NaCl(s) and HCl(g)

35. A solid substance was tested in the laboratory. The test results are listed below.
    • Dissolves in water   • Is an electrolyte   • Melts at a high temperature
    Based on these results, the solid substance could be
    (1) Cu   (3) $CuBr_2$
    (2) C   (4) $C_6H_{12}O_6$

36. Which set of properties best describes $NH_4Cl(s)$?
    (1) It is a good electrolyte with a high melting point.
    (2) It is a poor electrolyte with a high melting point.
    (3) It is a good electrolyte with a low melting point.
    (4) It is a poor electrolyte with a low melting point.

37. Which diagram best represents a polar molecule?

1) Br_2 (2) HBr (3) CH_4 (4) $Li\,Br$

38. Which pair of electron configurations belongs to atoms that will share electrons when they bond with each other?
    (1) $2 - 8 - 2$ and $2 - 8 - 1$
    (2) $2 - 8 - 6$ and $2 - 8 - 18 - 7$
    (3) $2 - 8 - 18 - 8$ and $2 - 8 - 13 - 1$
    (4) $2 - 8 - 5$ and $2 - 8 - 18 - 8 - 1$

39. A solid substance is an excellent conductor of electricity. The chemical bonds in this substance are most likely
    (1) ionic, because the valence electrons are shared between atoms
    (2) ionic, because the valence electrons are mobile
    (3) metallic, because the valence electrons are stationary
    (4) metallic, because the valence electrons are mobile

40. Given the balanced equation below.

    $$2Na(s) + Cl_2 \rightarrow 2NaCl(s)$$

    Explain, in terms of electrons, why the bonding in NaCl is ionic.

41. Explain, in terms of valence electrons, why the bonding in magnesium oxide, MgO, is similar to the bonding in barium chloride, $BaCl_2$.

Base your answers to questions 42 and 43 on the information below.

In 1864, the Solvay process was developed to make soda ash. One step in the process is represented by the balanced equation below.

$$NaCl + NH_3 + CO_2 + H_2O \rightarrow NaHCO_3 + NH_4Cl$$

42. Write the chemical formula for one compound in the equation that contains both ionic bonds and covalent bonds.

43. Write the chemical formula for one compound with bonding similar to NH_3.

Base your answers to questions 44 and 45 on the information below.

A student tested the conductivity of three magnesium substances and noted the following observations.

Magnesium strip, Mg(s) .... Conducts electrical current
Magnesium nitrate solid, $Mg(NO_3)_2(s)$............ No electrical conductivity
Magnesium nitrate solution, $Mg(NO_3)_2(aq)$ .... Conducts electrical current

44. Explain, in terms of atomic particles, why the magnesium strip conducts electrical current.

45. Explain why the solution of magnesium nitrate conducts electrical current but the solid magnesium nitrate did not. Include both the solid and solution in your answer.

Lesson 3: Molecular Polarity and Intermolecular Forces

Bond polarity of a substance refers to the extent of the positive and negative charges on the two bonded atoms. Polarity of a bond depends largely on the electronegativity difference (ED) between the two atoms.

- The bigger the difference in electronegativity, the greater the ionic and polar characteristics of the bond.
- The smaller the difference in electronegativity, the greater the covalent characteristics of the bond.

Molecular polarity refers to the extent of the overall positive and negative charges on a molecule. Molecular polarity of a substance depends largely on the electronegativity difference between the bonded atoms, the number of atoms, and the symmetry of its structure.

Degree of Polarity: *Depends on the Electronegativity Difference*

Comparing degree of polarity between two or more substances can be done by determining and comparing the electronegativity difference (ED) of the bonded atoms. Electronegativity values for the elements can be found on *Reference Table S.*

To calculate the electronegativity difference between two atoms in a bond:

Step 1: Use Table S to get electronegativity values for the atoms in each formula

Step 2: Determine ED: High electronegativity – Low electronegativity

To determine which formula is most or least ionic or polar, use the information below.

The formula with the **highest ED** is the **most ionic, most polar,** and **least covalent.**

The formula with the **lowest ED** is the **least ionic, least polar,** and **most covalent.**

The note below shows how to calculate electronegativity difference (ED) and compare degree of polarity for $MgCl_2$, LiCl, and KCl.

Use Table S		
Atomic Number	Symbol	Electro-negativity
3	Li	1.0
12	Mg	1.3
17	Cl	3.2
19	K	0.8

$MgCl_2$
Cl = 3.2
Mg = 1.3
ED   1.9
(Lowest ED)

LiCl
Cl = 3.2
Li = 1.0
       2.2

KCl
Cl = 3.2
K = 0.8
      2.4
(Highest ED)

$MgCl_2$
Least ionic
Least polar
Most covalent

KCl
Most ionic
Most polar
Least covalent

Intermolecular Forces

Intermolecular forces are forces that exist between molecules in molecular substances. Intermolecular forces hold molecules of molecular substances together in liquid and solid states. These forces exist in molecular substances because of unequal charge distribution within molecules. Intermolecular forces are generally weaker than the intramolecular forces (bonding between atoms) of the substance.

Many physical properties of a substance depend on the strength of the intermolecular forces (IMFs) holding particles of the substance together. These properties include melting point, boiling point, and vapor pressure.

The stronger the intermolecular forces of a substance:
• The higher the melting and boiling points of the substance.
• The lower the vapor pressure of the substance.

The Strength of intermolecular forces depends on the following three factors.

1. Polarity of the Molecules: *Most Polar, Highest Boiling and Melting Points*

Polar substances generally have stronger intermolecular forces than nonpolar substances. Therefore, polar substances tend to have higher boiling points, higher melting points, and lower vapor pressures when compared to nonpolar substances. An example comparison is shown below.

Molecular Substance	Relative Strength of Intermolecular Forces	Relative Boiling Point
CH_4 (nonpolar)	Weaker	Lower (-161°C)
H_2O (polar)	Stronger	Higher (100°C)

2. Size of Molecules: *Biggest Size, Highest Boiling and Melting Points*

The strength of intermolecular forces among similar nonpolar substances varies depending on the size of their molecules. In general, intermolecular forces (IMF) are stronger in a nonpolar substance with a large molecular mass when compared to a similar substance of a smaller molecular mass.

The relative comparison of molecular size, IMF strength, and boiling point for three groups of nonpolar substances are shown below.

Nonpolar Substances			Relative size of Molecule	Relative IMF Strength	Relative Boiling point
Halogens	Noble gases	Hydrocarbons			
F_2	He	CH_4	Smallest	Weakest	Lowest
Cl_2	Ne	C_2H_6			
Br_2	Ar	C_3H_8	Biggest	Strongest	Highest

3. Phase of a Substance/Distance Between the Molecules

The strength of intermolecular forces of a substance varies depending on the phase of the substance. In general, intermolecular forces are stronger between molecules of a substance in the solid phase. The force is weaker when the substance is in the gas phase. This is best observed among the Group 17 halogens.

Halogen	Phase at STP	Relative Strength of IMFs
F_2 and Cl_2	Gas	Weakest
Br_2	Liquid	A little stronger
I_2	Solid	Strongest

At STP, iodine is a solid and fluorine is a gas because iodine has stronger intermolecular forces than fluorine.

Hydrogen Bonding: *Gives Water High Boiling and Melting Points*

Hydrogen bonding is a type of intermolecular force that exists in certain polar substances. Among similar polar substances, the degree of polarity varies. Because of the difference in degree of polarity, the strength of intermolecular forces also varies among similar polar substances.

Hydrogen bonding is a strong intermolecular force that exists in the following three polar substances:

H_2O (water), NH_3 (ammonia) and HF (hydrogen fluoride).

Hydrogen bonding exists in these substances because H in each formula is bonded to an atom (O, F, or N) of small radius and high electronegativity.

When H_2O is compared to similar substances (such as H_2S and H_2Te), H_2O will always have the strongest intermolecular forces (hydrogen bonding).

As a result, the boiling point and the melting point of H_2O are higher than those of H_2S or H_2Te.

Bonding in Water

In a molecular substance, such as water, there are two forces holding particles of the substance together in the liquid or solid state.

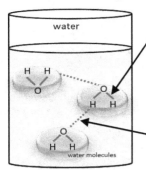

water

water molecules

Hydrogen Bonding:
the O end of one molecule attracts the H end of another molecule.

Intramolecular (polar covalent bond)
• Holds O and H atoms to make water molecules.
• Chemical properties (or reactions) of water require the breaking of this bond.
• A stronger bond than the intermolecular forces.

Intermolecular (hydrogen bonding)
• Holds the molecules together in solid and liquid phases.
• Physical properties (such as vapor pressure, boiling and melting points) depend on the strength of this force.
• A weaker force than the intramolecular bond.

Review Questions: Molecular Polarity and Intermolecular Forces

Vocabulary: Briefly define each of the following terms.

46. Intermolecular forces   47. Hydrogen bonding

48. The degree of polarity of a chemical bond in a molecule of a compound can be predicted by determining the difference in the
    (1) melting points of the elements in the compound
    (2) densities of the elements in the compound
    (3) electronegativities of the bonded atoms in a molecule of the compound
    (4) atomic masses of the bonded atoms in a molecule of the compound

49. Which bond is the least ionic?
    (1) Al – O   (2) N – O   (3) Li – O   (4) S – O

50. The bonding in which compound has the greatest degree of ionic character?
    (1) KBr   (2) BeO   (3) HF   (4) PCl_3

51. Which molecule is the least polar?
    (1) H – Br   (2) H – F   (3) H – Cl   (4) H – I

52. Which set of properties are due to the strength of intermolecular forces between molecules?
    (1) Vapor pressure and boiling point   (3) Molar mass and vapor pressure
    (2) Boiling point and molar density   (4) Vapor pressure and molar density

53. Which kind of attractive forces are found in a sample of $H_2O(l)$?
    (1) Covalent bonds, only   (3) Both covalent and hydrogen bonds
    (2) Hydrogen bonds, only   (4) Both ionic and hydrogen bonds

54. In which substance would the force of attraction between the molecules be considered hydrogen bonding?
    (1) $O_2(g)$ (2) $NH_3(l)$ (3) NaCl(s)   (4) $CO_2(g)$

55. The abnormally high boiling point of HF as compared to HCl is primarily due to intermolecular forces of attraction called
    (1) network bonds   (3) electrovalent forces
    (2) Van der Waals forces   (4) hydrogen bonding

56. At 298 K, the vapor pressure of H_2O is less than the vapor pressure of CH_3OH because H_2O has
    (1) larger molecules   (3) stronger intermolecular forces
    (2) smaller molecules   (4) weaker intermolecular forces

Base your answers to questions 57 through 59 on the table below.

Physical Properties of Four Gasses				
Name of Gas	hydrogen	hydrogen chloride	hydrogen bromide	hydrogen iodide
Molecular Structure	H-H	H-Cl	H-Br	H-I
Boiling Point (K) at 1 Atm	20.	188	207	237
Density (g/L) at STP	0.0899	1.64	?	5.66

57. Explain, in terms of intermolecular forces, why hydrogen has a *lower* boiling point than hydrogen bromide.

58. Explain, in terms of electronegativity difference, why the bond in H – Cl is more polar than the bond in H – I.

59. Identify the bonding in H – H.

Lesson 4: Valence Electrons and Lewis Electron-dot Diagrams

Valence electrons are the electrons in the outermost electron shell of an atom. During ionic bonding, valence electrons are lost by a metal to form a positive ion, and are gained by a nonmetal to form a negative ion. During covalent bonding, nonmetal atoms share their valence electrons.

In this lesson, you will learn how to show different types of bonds using Lewis electron-dot diagrams.

Lewis Electron–dot Diagrams for Neutral Atoms and Ions

A **Lewis electron-dot diagram** is a notation that shows the symbol of an atom and dots to represent valence electrons of the atom. Lewis electron-dot diagrams can be drawn for neutral atoms, ions and compounds.

Neutral Atoms: *Dots Equal to Valence Electrons*

A Lewis electron-dot diagram for a neutral atom is the symbol of the atom surrounded with dots equal to the number of its valence electrons. Examples are given below.

	e- configuration	valence electrons	dot diagram
Sodium atom (Na)	2 – 8 – 1	1	Na ·
Phosphorus atom (P)	2 – 8 – 5	5	· P :

Positive Ions: *Symbol of the Positive Ion*

A Lewis dot-diagram for a positive ion is just the symbol of the positive ion, which can be determined from the Periodic Table.

	e- configuration	valence electrons	dot diagram
Sodium ion (Na⁺)	2 – 8	8	Na^+
Beryllium ion (Be²⁺)	2	2	Be^{2+}

Negative Ions: *Symbol of the Negative Ion with 8 Dots*

A Lewis electron-dot diagram for a negative ion is the symbol of the ion and 8 dots around it. A bracket often surrounds the atom's symbol and the dots.

Note: A Lewis electron-dot diagram for a negative hydrogen ion (H⁻) has just 2 dots as shown below. Hydrogen has only one occupied electron shell (the 1st), which has enough orbitals for just two electrons.

	e- configuration	valence electrons	dot diagram
Phosphide ion (P³⁻)	2 – 8 – 8	8	$\left(: \overset{\cdot\cdot}{\underset{\cdot\cdot}{P}} : \right)^{3-}$
Hydride ion (H⁻)	2	2	$\left[H : \right]^-$

TIP: Use the Periodic Table to get the correct ion symbol.

Lewis Electron-dot Diagrams for Ionic Compounds

Ionic compounds are composed of positive and negative ions. The positive ion is formed by a metal transferring (losing) its valence electrons to a nonmetal. The nonmetal accepts (gains) the electrons to become a negative ion.

Lewis electron-dot diagrams for an ionic substance must show the Lewis electron-dot symbols for both the positive and negative ions of the substance.

A Lewis electron-dot diagram for a given ionic substance is correct when it contains the following:

The correct symbol and charge of the positive and negative ions in the formula.

The correct number of each ion in the formula.

The correct number of dots around the negative ion of the formula.
A bracket should surround the dot diagram of the negative ion.

Follow the four examples below to learn to recognize and draw Lewis electron-dot diagrams for other ionic compounds.

Lewis Electron-dot Diagram for Ionic Compounds

Name of Compound	Chemical Formula	Electron-dot Diagram
Sodium chloride	NaCl	$Na^+ \left[:\ddot{Cl}: \right]^-$
Calcium bromide	CaBr$_2$	$Ca^{2+} 2\left[:\ddot{Br}: \right]^-$
Potassium oxide	K$_2$O	$2K^+ \left[:\ddot{O}: \right]^{2-}$
Magnesium hydride	MgH$_2$	$^-[H:]Mg^{2+}[:H]^-$

Note: o represents the valence electron transferred from the metal atom.

The Importance of Having the Correct Number of Each Ion.
Compounds are neutral; the sum of charges in compound formulas must equal zero.

In calcium bromide, 2 bromide ions (each with -1 charge) are needed to equalize 1 calcium ion (a +2 charge).

In potassium oxide, 2 potassium ions (each with +1 charge) are needed to equalize 1 oxide ion (a -2 charge).

Lewis Electron-dot Diagrams for Molecular Substances

Lewis electron-dot diagrams for covalently bonded atoms of molecule must show the sharing of valence electrons by the nonmetal atoms. Each pair of electrons (2 electrons) shared between two atoms forms a single covalent bond. The Lewis electron-dot diagram for a molecular substance must have the following:

> The correct symbols and correct number of each nonmetal atom.
> The correct number of shared electrons between the atoms.
> The correct number of valence electrons around each atom.

Follow the examples below to learn to recognize and draw Lewis electron-dot diagrams for polar and nonpolar molecular substances.

Polar Substances: *Diagrams Have Asymmetrical Shapes.*

Substance Name	Formula	Lewis Electron-dot Diagrams
Hydrogen chloride	HCl	H ∘ • C̈l̤: or H – C̈l̤:
Water	H_2O	:Ö: / H∘ ∘H or H⌃H
Ammonia	NH_3	H∘•N̈•∘H or H–N̈–H with H below

Nonpolar Substances: *Diagrams Have Symmetrical Shapes.*

Substance Name	Formula	Lewis Electron-dot Diagrams
Chlorine	Cl_2	⸬C̈l∘•C̈l̤: or ⸬C̈l–C̈l̤:
Carbon dioxide	CO_2	Ö⸬:C:⸬Ö or Ö=C=Ö
Methane	CH_4	H∘•Ċ•∘H or H–C–H (with H above and below)
Carbon tetrachloride	CCl_4	C̈l∘•Ċ•∘C̈l or C̈l–C–C̈l (with C̈l above and below)

Review Questions: Lewis Electron-dot Diagrams in Bonding

60. In the Lewis electron-dot diagram $H:\overset{..}{\underset{..}{Cl}}:$, the dots represent
    (1) valence electrons of H only
    (2) valence electrons for both the H and C atom
    (3) valence electrons of Cl only
    (4) all the electrons found in H and C atoms

61. Which electron-dot symbol is correctly drawn for the atom it represents?

    (1) $:\overset{..}{N}$ (2) $:\overset{..}{\underset{..}{F}}:$ (3) $:\overset{..}{\underset{.}{O}}:$ (4) $:\overset{..}{\underset{..}{Ne}}:$

62. Which Lewis electron-dot diagram represents a fluoride ion?

    (1) $\left[:\overset{..}{\underset{..}{F}}:\right]^-$ (2) $\left[:\overset{..}{F}:\right]^-$ (3) $:\overset{..}{\underset{..}{F}}:$ (4) $:\overset{..}{\underset{.}{F}}:$

63. Which electron-dot formula represents ionic bonding between two atoms?

    (1) $\overset{xx}{\underset{xx}{x}}Br\overset{x}{:}\overset{..}{\underset{..}{Br}}:$ (2) $H\overset{x}{:}\overset{..}{\underset{..}{Br}}:$ (3) $Na^+\left[\overset{xx}{\underset{xx}{x}}F\overset{x}{x}\right]^-$ (4) $H\overset{x}{:}\overset{xx}{\underset{xx}{F}}\overset{x}{x}$

64. Which Lewis electron-dot diagram represents calcium oxide?

    (1) $Ca\overset{x}{\underset{x}{:}}\overset{..}{\underset{..}{O}}:$ (2) $\overset{x}{\underset{x}{:}}Ca\overset{.}{\underset{.}{:}}\overset{..}{\underset{..}{O}}:$ (3) $\left[:\overset{.x}{\underset{..}{Ca}}\overset{x}{:}\right]^{2+}O^{2-}$ (4) $Ca^{2+}\left[\overset{..}{\underset{x.}{:}}O\overset{..}{:}\right]^{2-}$

Base your answers to questions 65 through 67 on the information below.

The Lewis electron-dot diagrams for three substances are shown below.

$K^+\left[:\overset{..}{\underset{..}{Br}}:\right]^-$ $H:\overset{..}{\underset{\underset{H}{H}}{N}}:H$ $H:\overset{\overset{H}{x}}{\underset{\underset{H}{x}}{C}}:H$

Diagram 1   Diagram 2   Diagram 3

65. Determine the total number of electrons in the bonds between the nitrogen atom and the three hydrogen atoms represented in diagram 2.

66. Explain, in terms of distribution of charge, why a molecule of the substance represented in diagram 3 is nonpolar.

67. Identify the noble gas that has atoms with the same electron configuration as the positive ion represented in diagram 1, when both the atoms and the ion are in the ground state.

Lesson 1: Types of Chemical Formulas

Chemical formulas are used to represent the compositions of elements and compounds (pure substances). A chemical formula expresses the *qualitative* and *quantitative* compositions of a substance.

Qualitative information of a formula shows the types of atoms (or ions) that make up the substance.

Quantitative information of a formula shows how many of each atom (or ion) is in the formula. The number of each atom in a formula is shown with a subscript. A **subscript** in a chemical formula is the whole number written to the bottom right of each atom in the formula.

$$H_2SO_4$$

subscripts

Counting Atoms in Formulas

Qualitative and quantitative information of a formula can be determined by counting how many of each atom is in the formula. Three examples are given below.

Type of Formula	Example Formula	Number of Atoms	Total Atoms
Simple formula	H_2SO_4	2 **H** atoms 1 **S** atom 4 **O** atoms	**Three** different atoms. **7** total atoms.
Formula with parentheses	$(NH_4)_2O$	2 **N** atoms (2 x 1) 8 **H** atoms (4 x 2) 1 **O** atom	**Three** different atoms. **11** total atoms.
Formula of hydrates	$CuSO_4 \cdot 5H_2O$	1 **Cu** atom 1 **S** atom 9 **O** atoms (4 + 5) 10 **H** atoms (5 x 2)	**Four** different atoms. **21** total atoms.

Counting Ratio of Ions in Formulas

Another way of expressing the qualitative and quantitative compositions of a substance is to determine the ratio of ions in the formula.

Type of Formula	Example Formula	Ions in Formula	Ratio of Ions
Binary ionic	$CaCl_2$ calcium chloride	Ca^{2+} Cl^- calcium ion chloride ion	1 Ca^{2+} : 2 Cl^-
Polyatomic formula (with parentheses)	$Al_2(SO_4)_3$ aluminum sulfate	Al^{3+} SO_4^{2-} aluminum ion sulfate ion	2 Al^{3+} : 3 SO_4^{2-}
Polyatomic formula (without parentheses)	KNO_3 potassium nitrate	K^+ NO_3^- potassium ion nitrate ion	1 K^+ : 1 NO_3^-

Types of Chemical Formulas: *Molecular, Structural, Empirical*

There are three types of chemical formulas that can be used to show the composition of a substance.

A **molecular formula** shows the true composition of a known substance.

A **structural formula** is a formula that shows how the atoms in a substance are bonded together.

An **empirical formula** shows the simplest or smallest whole-number ratio in which the atoms of a substance are combined.

Examples of the three formulas are shown below:

	water	ethane	glucose
Molecular	H_2O	C_2H_6	$C_6H_{12}O_6$
Structural			
Empirical	H_2O	CH_3	CH_2O

H_2O is a molecular formula, as well as an empirical formula. Subscripts in H_2O can't be reduced to a simpler form.

C_2H_6 is reduced to CH_3 by dividing each subscript of the formula by 2 (the Greatest Common Factor).

$C_6H_{12}O_6$ is reduced to CH_2O by dividing each subscript of the formula by 6 (the Greatest Common Factor).

Review Questions: Types of Chemical Formulas

Vocabulary: Briefly define each of the following terms.

1. Chemical formula
2. Qualitative
3. Quantitative
4. Subscript
5. Molecular formula
6. Empirical formula
7. Binary compound

8. Which list includes only types of chemical formulas?
   (1) Combustion, synthesis, and decomposition
   (2) Empirical, molecular, and substitution
   (3) Empirical, molecular, and structural
   (4) Structural, combustion, and synthesis

9. A type of formula showing the simplest ratio in which atoms are combined is
   (1) a molecular formula
   (3) a structural formula
   (2) an empirical formula
   (4) a condensed formula

10. What is the total number of moles of sulfur atoms in 1 mole of $Fe_2(SO_4)_3$?
    (1) 1
    (2) 12
    (3) 3
    (4) 4

11. What is the total number of nitrate ions found in sodium nitrate, $NaNO_3$?
    (1) 1
    (2) 2
    (3) 3
    (4) 4

12. What is the total number of atoms in one formula unit of $MgSO_4 \cdot 7H_2O$?
    (1) 27
    (2) 13
    (3) 16
    (4) 20

13. What is the ratio of sodium ions to phosphate ions in the formula Na_3PO_4?
    (1) 4 : 3
    (2) 3 : 4
    (3) 1 : 3
    (4) 3 : 1

14. An example of an empirical formula is
    (1) C_4H_{10}
    (3) $HC_2H_3O_2$
    (2) $C_6H_{12}O_6$
    (4) CH_2O

15. Which represents both an empirical formula and a molecular formula?
    (1) P_2O_5
    (3) C_3H_6
    (2) N_2O_4
    (4) $C_6H_{12}O_6$

16. What is the empirical formula of $C_{12}H_{22}O_{11}$?
    (1) $C_{12}H_{22}O_{11}$
    (3) $C_3H_6O_3$
    (2) $C_6H_{11}O_{11}$
    (4) $C_{22}H_{48}H_{22}$

17. Which molecular formula is correctly paired with its empirical formula?
    (1) CO_2 and CO
    (3) C_4H_4 and C_2H_2
    (2) P_2O_4 and PO_2
    (4) P_4O_{10} and PO_5

18. What is the empirical formula for the structure shown below?

```
    H   H   H   H   H   H
    |   |   |   |   |   |
H – C – C – C – C – C – C – H
    |   |   |   |   |   |
    H   F   F   F   F   H
```

   (1) $C_6H_{10}F_4$
   (3) $C_3H_2F_2$
   (2) $C_3H_5F_2$
   (4) CHF

19. The reaction between 1-butene, C_4H_8, and bromine, Br_2, forms the compound 1,2-dibromobutane, $C_4H_8Br_2$. Write the empirical formula for the product.

Lesson 2 – Chemical Nomenclature

There are millions of known chemical substances, with many more being discovered yearly.

Chemical nomenclature refers to the systematic rules for naming and writing formulas of chemical substances. The International Union of Pure and Applied Chemistry (IUPAC) is an organization that makes recommendations as to how chemical substances are named.

In this lesson, you will learn how to apply IUPAC rules to writing formulas and names for compounds in different classes of *inorganic* compounds.

Chemical Formulas: *Sum of Charges Must Equal Zero*

A chemical formula is correctly written for a known substance when both the qualitative and quantitative information of the formula are correct. This means:
• Element or ion symbols in a formula must be correct for the substance.
• Subscripts of the elements or ions in a formula must be in the correct ratio so that the sum of the charges is equal to zero.
  All compounds are electrically neutral.

Steps to Writing Chemical Formulas for Ionic Compounds

When the IUPAC name for an ionic compound is given, the steps below can be used to write its correct formula.

Step 1:　　**Write** the correct ion symbols for the chemical name.

　　　　　　Use the Periodic Table to get the correct ion symbol for an element.

　　　　　　Use Table E to get the correct polyatomic ion symbol.

　　　　　　At first, put parentheses around the polyatomic ion. Ex. $(SO_4)^{2-}$

Step 2:　　**Criss-cross** charge values so one becomes the subscript for the other.

Step 3:　　**Clean up** formula after criss-crossing by:

　　　　　　Reducing subscripts that are reducible to empirical form.

　　　　　　For polyatomic ion compounds:
　　　　　　Do not change subscripts of the polyatomic ion.

　　　　　　Remove the parentheses if subscript outside the parentheses is a 1.

　　　　　　Keep parentheses if subscript outside the parentheses is greater than 1.

Steps shown above and on the next pages are to ensure that your final (correct) formula has the correct element symbols and correct subscripts for the compound name that is given. If you can write a correct formula without going through all these steps, you should do so.

Writing Chemical Formulas

Binary Ionic Compounds have formulas that are composed of two different elements: a metal and a nonmetal. IUPAC names of binary compounds always end with *–ide*. Examples: Calcium brom*ide*, Aluminum sulf*ide*, and Zinc ox*ide*

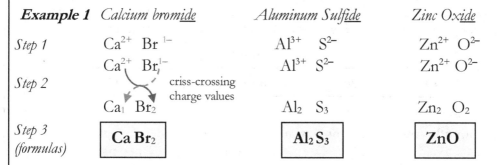

	Example 1 *Calcium bromide*	*Aluminum Sulfide*	*Zinc Oxide*
Step 1	Ca^{2+} Br^{1-}	Al^{3+} S^{2-}	Zn^{2+} O^{2-}
Step 2	Ca^{2+} Br_j^{1-} criss-crossing charge values Ca_1 Br_2	Al^{3+} S^{2-} Al_2 S_3	Zn^{2+} O^{2-} Zn_2 O_2
Step 3 (formulas)	$Ca\,Br_2$	Al_2S_3	ZnO

Ionic Compounds Containing a Polyatomic Ion

A polyatomic ion is composed of two or more atoms with an excess charge. *Reference Table E lists some common polyatomic ions*. IUPAC names of polyatomic ions typically end with *-ate* or *–ite*. Examples of compounds containing a polyatomic ion are: sodium *nitrate*, calcium *sulfite*, and *ammonium* oxide.

	Example 2 *Sodium Nitrate*	*Calcium Sulfite*	*Ammonium Oxide*
Step 1	Na^{+1} $(NO_3)^{1-}$	Ca^{2+} $(SO_3)^{2-}$	$(NH_4)^{1+}$ O^{2-}
Step 2	Na^{+1} $(NO_3)^{1-}$	Ca^{2+} $(SO_3)^{2-}$	$(NH_4)^{1+}$ O^{2-}
Step 3 (formulas)	Na_1 $(NO_3)_1$ $NaNO_3$	Ca_2 $(SO_3)_2$ $CaSO_3$	$(NH_4)_2$ O_1 $(NH_4)_2O$

Ionic Compounds Containing an Atom with Multiple Oxidation States

The **stock system** nomenclature uses Roman numerals in parentheses to distinguish names of compounds produced by different positive oxidation states of an atom. Examples of Stock system naming and the interpretation of a Roman numeral in names are given below.

Iron(II) chloride   **(II)** indicates a compound of a **+2** iron.

Iron(III) chloride   **(III)** indicates a compound of a **+3** iron.

Nitrogen(IV) oxide   **(IV)** indicates a compound of a **+4** nitrogen.

Example 3 Iron(II) chloride	Iron(III) chloride	Nitrogen(IV) oxide
↓	↓	↓
Fe^{2+} Cl^{1-}	Fe^{3+} Cl^{1-}	N^{4+} O^{2-}
$FeCl_2$	$FeCl_3$	NO_2

Writing IUPAC Names for Ionic Compounds

A name is correctly written for a given formula when all of the following are represented correctly.

• Atoms and/or ions in the formula are named correctly.
• Name ending, if necessary, is applied correctly.
• Roman numeral, if necessary, is correctly used.

Binary ionic compounds contain just two elements: a metal and a nonmetal. *Examples* are $ZnCl_2$, CaO and Li_3N. IUPAC naming of binary compounds involves changing the nonmetal ending to *–ide*. The metal name is never changed.

Example 4 $ZnCl_2$ CaO Li_3N

| Zinc Chlor*ide* | Calcium ox*ide* | Lithium nitr*ide* |

Compounds containing a polyatomic ion generally contain three or more elements. Examples are $Mg_3(PO_4)_2$, NH_4NO_3, and NH_4Cl. When naming compounds containing a polyatomic ion, no change should be made to the name of the polyatomic ion or to the name of the metal. *See Table E for polyatomic ions.*

Example 5 $Mg_3(PO_4)_2$ NH_4NO_3 NH_4Cl

| Magnesium phosphate | Ammonium nitrate | Ammonium chlor*ide* |

Compounds containing an element with multiple oxidation numbers must be named using the Stock system. In each of the three formulas below, the first element has multiple positive oxidation numbers (Look on the Periodic Table to confirm). A Roman numeral (in parentheses) is used in naming to identify which positive charge of the element formed the compound.

SnF_4 N_2O $Fe_3(PO_4)_2$

| Tin(IV) fluor*ide* | Nitrogen(I) ox*ide* | Iron(II) phosphate |

In some formulas, like the three above, the *subscript* of the second symbol in each formula is used as the Roman numeral value in parentheses. In other formulas, like the two below, the +charge value or Roman numeral must be determined mathematically by following the steps below for example 6 or setting up a simple algebraic equation as in example 7. The key in both methods is to determine the correct positive charge to be used in parentheses to correctly name the formula.

	Example 6 CrN_2	***Example 7*** $MnSO_4$
Assign $(-)$ charge value to N.	$Cr\ N_2^{3-}$	$1Mn + 1SO_4$ $\quad$ (Table E) charge of SO_4
Multiply $(-)$ charge by **subscript of N** to get total $(-)$ in the formula.	$2 \times 3- = -6$	$Mn + 1(-2) = 0$
Determine the **total (+)** needed to make charges equal to zero.	**+6**	$Mn = +2$
Use **+charge** as **Roman numeral** in ( ) to name the formula·	Chromium(VI) nitr*ide*	Manganese(II) sulfate

E3chemistry.com

Writing Formulas and Naming Covalent and Molecular Substances

Molecular and covalent compounds are composed only of nonmetal atoms. **Binary covalent** compounds, which contain two different nonmetals, are commonly named with IUPAC recommended prefixes. A **prefix** in a chemical name indicates how many of the nonmetal atom is in the given compound. The table below lists prefixes for naming covalent compounds.

Table of IUPAC Prefixes

Number of Atom	Prefix	Number of Atom	Prefix
1	mono-	6	hexa-
2	di-	7	hepta-
3	tri-	8	octa-
4	tetra-	9	nona-
5	penta-	10	deca-

To write a formula for a covalent substance, follow rules and examples below.
- Prefixes are interpreted into subscripts for the elements.
- Absence of a prefix indicates that there is just one of that atom.
- No criss-crossing or reducing of the formula into an empirical form.

Example 8: Write Formulas to These Three Covalent Substances

Molecular name	Carbon **di**oxide	Carbon **mono**xide	**di**nitrogen **mono**xide
Interpretation	1C 2 O	1C 1 O	2 N 1 O
Formula	CO_2	CO	N_2O

To name a given covalent substance, follow rules and examples below.
- Subscripts are interpreted into prefixes for the elements
- No prefix is used when there is just one of the first nonmetal atom (see PCl_3).
- The "a" or "o" of a prefix is dropped if the addition of the prefix resulted in a name having two vowels next to each other (see N_2O_5).
  In N_2O_5, the **a** in pent**ao**xide is dropped, and the formula is correctly named. *pentoxide*.
- Name ending for the second nonmetal atom must be changed to *-ide*.

Example 9: Name These Three Covalent Substances

PCl_3	N_2O_5	H_2S
1 phosphorus **3** chlorine	**2** nitrogen **5** oxygen	**2** hydrogen **1** sulfur
Phosphorus **tri**chlor<u>ide</u>	**di**nitrogen **pent**ox<u>ide</u>	**di**hydrogen **mono**sulf<u>ide</u>

Review Questions: Chemical Nomenclature

Vocabulary: Briefly define each of the following terms.

20. Chemical nomenclature   21. Binary compound   22. Stock system

23. The correct formula for potassium oxide is
    (1) PO_2 (3) K_2O
    (2) P_2O (4) KO_2

24. The correct formula for a compound with an IUPAC name of nickel(III) hypochlorite is
    (1) $NiCl_3$ (3) $NiClO_3$
    (2) Ni_3ClO (4) $Ni(ClO)_3$

25. The correct formula for manganese(VII) oxide is
    (1) Mg_7O_2 (3) Mn_7O_2
    (2) Mg_2O_7 (4) Mn_2O_7

26. Which formula is correct for antimony(III) nitride?
    (1) SbN (3) SbN_3
    (2) Sb_3N (4) Sb_6O_3

27. Which formula correctly represents lead(II) thiosulfate?
    (1) PbS_2O_3 (3) $Pb_2(S_2O_3)_2$
    (2) $Pb_2S_4O_6$ (4) $PbSO_3$

28. The compound with the formula of $Cu(ClO_2)_2$ is
    (1) Copper(I) chlorite   (3) Copper(I) chlorate
    (2) Copper(II) chlorite   (4) Copper(II) chlorate

29. The correct name for $NaClO_4$ is sodium
    (1) chlorate   (3) perchlorate
    (2) chloride   (4) chlorite

30. Which formula is correct for $V(NO_3)_2$?
    (1) Vanadium(I) nitrate   (3) Vanadium(III) nitrate
    (2) Vanadium(II) nitrate   (4) Vanadium(IV) nitrate

31. .Which of the following compounds is composed of just two elements?
    (1) Lithium hydroxide   (3) Aluminum oxide
    (2) Magnesium sulfate   (4) Ammonium chloride

Base your answers to questions 32 through 36 on the information given in each question.

32. Buildings and statues are often made of limestone which is composed of calcium carbonate. Write the chemical formula for calcium carbonate.

33. Te_3Cl_2 is a gray semiconductor solid. Its structure consists of a long chain of Te atoms, with every third Te center carrying two chlorine atoms. What is the IUPAC name for Te_3Cl_2?

34. Some antacids contain the acid-neutralizing agent sodium hydrogen carbonate. Write the chemical formula for sodium hydrogen carbonate.

35. Element X reacts with iron to form two different compounds with formulas Fe_3X_2 and FeX. In which group on the Periodic Table does element X belong?

36. A compound is made up of iron and oxygen only. The ratio of iron ions to oxide ions is 2 : 3 in this compound. What is the IUPAC name for this compound?

E3chemistry.com

Lesson 4: Chemical Reactions and Equations

An **equation** shows changes that are taking place in substances. There are three major types of changes, and each can be represented with an equation.

Chemical equations show changes in chemical compositions of one or more substances to other substances.

Example Equations

$$H_2(g) + O_2(g) \rightarrow H_2O(\ell)$$

Physical change equations show a change of a substance from one form to a different form without a change in the chemical composition.

$$H_2O(s) \rightarrow H_2O(\ell)$$

Nuclear equations show changes in the nucleus contents of one or more atoms to those of different atoms.

$$^{220}_{87}Fr \rightarrow \, ^{4}_{2}He + \, ^{216}_{85}At$$

In this lesson, you will learn only of chemical changes and equations.

Interpreting Chemical Equations

A chemical equation uses symbols to show changes in the chemical compositions of one or more substances during a chemical reaction.
A **chemical reaction** is the process that leads to a chemical change.

Reactants are the starting substances that are present before a chemical reaction. Reactants are shown to the *left* of the arrow in an equation.

Products are the substances that remain at the end of a chemical reaction. Products are shown to the *right* of the arrow in an equation.

A **coefficient** is a whole number in front of a substance to show the number of moles or how many of that substance is taking part in the reaction.

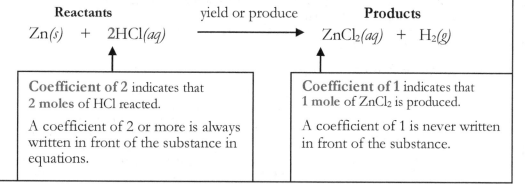

Reactants	yield or produce	Products
$Zn(s) + 2HCl(aq)$		$ZnCl_2(aq) + H_2(g)$

Coefficient of 2 indicates that 2 moles of HCl reacted.

A coefficient of 2 or more is always written in front of the substance in equations.

Coefficient of 1 indicates that 1 mole of $ZnCl_2$ is produced.

A coefficient of 1 is never written in front of the substance.

Types of Reactions: *Synthesis, Decomposition, Replacements, Combustion*

There are many types of chemical reactions. Five of them are defined and explained below. Diagrams and example equations representing each type of reaction are given to the right of each reaction. Many other types of chemical reactions are discussed in topics 8 through 11 of this book.

reactants yield **products**

Synthesis reactions always involve two or more substances as reactants. During a synthesis reaction, reactants combine to form one compound product.

$$2H_2 + O_2 \rightarrow 2H_2O$$

Decomposition reactions always involve one single substance as a reactant. During a decomposition reaction, the reactant breaks down or decomposes into two or more products.

$$2H_2O \rightarrow 2H_2 + O_2$$

Single replacement reactions typically involve a compound and a free element as reactants. During a single replacement reaction, the free element replaces one of the elements in the compound. This reaction only occurs when the free element reactant is more reactive than the similar element in the compound it is replacing.

$$Zn + 2HCl \rightarrow ZnCl_2 + H_2$$

Double replacement reactions usually involve two compounds in aqueous phase. During a double replacement reaction, the ions of the compounds switch partners. This reaction is also called a metathesis.

$$NaCl + AgNO_3 \rightarrow NaNO_3 + AgCl$$

Combustion reactions typically involve the burning of an organic substance in the presence of oxygen. Water and carbon dioxide are produced in combustion reactions.

$$CH_4 + 2O_2 \rightarrow CO_2 + H_2O$$
organic substance

Balanced Equations: *Gives Relative Moles of Substances in a Reaction*

A balanced chemical equation gives the correct mole proportion of substances reacting and being produced in the reaction. The correct set of coefficients (moles) in an equation is a way of showing conservation of matter and energy in the reaction. **Law of Conservation** states that neither atoms nor energy is created or destroyed during a chemical reaction. In other words, atoms, mass, charge and energy before and after a reaction are equal.

Conservation of Atoms: *Equal Number of Atoms on Both Sides*

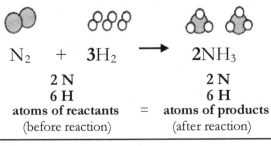

$$N_2 + 3H_2 \rightarrow 2NH_3$$

2 N	2 N
6 H	6 H
atoms of reactants	=	**atoms of products**
(before reaction)		(after reaction)

The equation to the left is balanced because it has the correct combination of smallest *whole-number coefficients* needed to make the number of atoms on both sides equal. In other words, the substances in the reaction are represented in the correct *mole proportion* to show conservation.

Conservation of Mass: *Equal Mass on Both Sides*

During a chemical reaction, mass of substances before and after the reaction is the same. Conservation of mass is shown in the reaction below.

$$3Fe \; + \; 2O_2 \; \rightarrow \; Fe_3O_4 :$$

$$20.9 \, g \qquad 8.0 \, g \;\; = \;\; 28.9 \, g$$

The total mass of Fe and O_2 before reaction is the same as the total mass of Fe_3O_4 after reaction.

Balancing Equations: *Only the Coefficients (Moles) Should Be Changed*

An equation is balanced when it contains the correct combination of smallest whole-number coefficients. Correct coefficients allow the number of each atom on both sides of an equation to be the same.

To Balance an Equation
One or more coefficients in front of the substances must be changed in the equation so atoms are equal on both sides.

Suggestions for Balancing Equations
- Make a table to keep track of the number of atoms as coefficients are changed.
- Try balancing one atom at a time.
- Every time a coefficient is changed, *recount* and note the number of each atom affected by the change. Be sure to count atoms correctly.
- Always change the coefficients of free elements last. (ex. Li, O_2 are free elements)
- Always put parentheses around a polyatomic ion and count it as one unit.
- Be sure that your final coefficients are in the *smallest whole-number ratio*.

Examples of Unbalanced and Balanced Equations

Unbalanced $\qquad\qquad Li_3N \; \rightarrow \; Li \; + \; N_2$

Balanced $\qquad\qquad 2Li_3N \; \rightarrow \; 6Li \; + \; N_2$

Sum of Coefficients = 2 $\qquad$ + 6 $\quad$ + 1 = 9

Unbalanced $\qquad\qquad Ca(OH)_2 \; + \; H_3PO_4 \rightarrow Ca_3(PO_4)_2 \; + \; H_2O$

Balanced $\qquad\qquad 3Ca(OH)_2 \; + \; 2H_3PO_4 \rightarrow Ca_3(PO_4)_2 \; + \; 6H_2O$

Sum of Coefficients = $\quad$ 3 $\qquad$ + 2 $\qquad$ + 1 $\qquad$ + 6 = 12

Unbalanced $\qquad\qquad C_3H_4 \; + \; O_2 \; \rightarrow \; CO_2 \; + \; H_2O$

Balanced $\qquad\qquad C_3H_4 \; + \; 4O_2 \; \rightarrow \; 3CO_2 \; + \; 2H_2O$

Sum of Coefficients = $\quad$ 1 $\quad$ + 4 $\quad$ + 3 $\qquad$ + 2 = 10

When determining the sum of coefficients, remember to add all coefficients of 1 (as in N_2, $Ca_3(PO_4)_2$, and C_3H_4). A coefficient of 1 may not be written in front of the substance.

Review Questions: Chemical Equations

Vocabulary: Briefly define each of the following terms.

37. Coefficient   38. Reactant   39. Product   40. Yield   41. Synthesis
42. Decomposition   43. Single replacement   44. Double replacement   45. Combustion

46. What is conserved during chemical reactions?
    (1) Energy, only
    (2) Matter, only
    (3) Both matter and energy
    (4) Neither matter nor energy

47. If equations are balanced properly, both sides of the equation must have the same number of
    (1) atoms
    (2) coefficients
    (3) molecules
    (4) moles of molecules

48. Given a balanced chemical equation, it is always possible to determine
    (1) whether a reaction will or will not take place
    (2) the conditions necessary for the reaction to take place
    (3) the relative number of moles taking place in the reaction
    (4) the physical state of the products and reactants

49. Which list is composed only of types of chemical reactions?
    (1) Synthesis, decomposition, single replacement
    (2) Synthesis, decomposition, freezing
    (3) Decomposition, evaporation, and double replacement
    (4) Decomposition, melting, combustion

50. Given the equation:

$$C_3H_8 \ + \ 5O_2 \ \rightarrow \ 3CO_2 \ + \ 4H_2O$$

This reaction represents

    (1) combustion
    (2) synthesis
    (3) single replacement
    (4) double replacement

51. Given the chemical equation:

$$2KClO_3(s) \ \rightarrow \ 2KCl(s) \ + \ 3O_2(g)$$

What type of reaction is represented by the above equation?

    (1) Combustion
    (2) Neutralization
    (3) Synthesis
    (4) Decomposition

52. Which equation represents a double replacement reaction?
    (1) $2Na \ + \ 2H_2O \ \rightarrow \ 2NaOH \ + \ H_2$
    (2) $CaCO_3 \ \rightarrow CaO \ + \ CO_2$
    (3) $LiOH \ + \ HCl \ \rightarrow \ LiCl \ + \ H_2O$
    (4) $CH_4 \ + \ 2O_2 \ \rightarrow \ CO_2 \ + \ 2H_2O$

53. Which of these equations is correctly balanced?
    (1) $Fe(s) \ + \ O_2(g) \ \rightarrow \ Fe_2O_3(s)$
    (2) $Fe(s) \ + \ O_2(g) \ \rightarrow \ 2Fe_2O_3(s)$
    (3) $2Fe(s) \ + \ 2O_2(g) \ \rightarrow \ Fe_2O_3(s)$
    (4) $4Fe(s) \ + \ 3O_2(g) \ \rightarrow \ 2Fe_2O_3(s)$

54. Which equation is correctly balanced?
    (1) $CaO \ + \ 2H_2O \ \rightarrow \ Ca(OH)_2$
    (2) $NH_3 \ + \ 2O_2 \ \rightarrow \ HNO_3 \ + \ H_2O$
    (3) $Ca(OH)_2 \ + \ 2H_2PO_4 \ \rightarrow \ Ca_3(PO_4)_2 \ + \ 3H_2O$
    (4) $Cu \ + \ H_2SO_4 \ \rightarrow \ CuSO_4 \ + \ H_2O \ + \ SO_2$

55. Given the equation for the reaction:

  ___Na + ___H_2O → __ H_2 + __NaOH

  When the equation is correctly balanced using the smallest whole-number coefficients, what is the coefficient of H_2O?

  (1) 1   (3) 3
  (2) 2   (4) 4

56. Given the equation for the reaction:

  ___SiO_2 + ___ C → ___SiC + ___CO

  When the equation is correctly balanced using the smallest whole-number coefficients, the sum of all coefficients is

  (1) 6   (3) 8
  (2) 7   (4) 9

57. Given the balanced equation for the reaction:

  $2NaCl(\ell)$ → $2Na(s)$ + $Cl_2(g)$

  A 1170.-gram sample of $NaCl(\ell)$ completely reacts, producing 460. grams of Na(s). What is the total mass of $Cl_2(g)$ produced?

  (1) 355 g   (3) 1420. g
  (2) 710. g   (4) 1630. g

58. Given the incomplete equation below:

  $3Ca(OH)_2$ + $2H_3PO_4$ → $Ca_3(PO_4)_2$ + X

  Which correctly represents X?

  (1) $3H_2$ (3) $3H_2O$
  (2) $6H_2$ (4) $6H_2O$

59. Balance each of the following equations using the smallest whole-number coefficients.

  __Al(s) + __ $CuSO_4(aq)$ → __$Al_2(SO_4)_3(aq)$ + __Cu(s)

  __$Ca(OH)_2$ + __ $(NH_4)_2SO_4$ → __$CaSO_4$ + __NH_3 + __H_2O

  __C_5H_{12} + __O_2 → __CO_2 + __H_2O

Base your answers to questions 60 and 61 on the information below.

A tablet of one antacid contains citric acid, $H_3C_6H_5O_7$, and sodium hydrogen carbonate, $NaHCO_3$. When the tablet dissolves in water, bubbles of CO_2 are produced. This reaction is represented by the incomplete equation below.

  $H_3C_6H_5O_7(aq)$ + $3NaHCO_3(aq)$ → $Na_3C_6H_5O_7(aq)$ + $3CO_2(g)$ + 3 _____ ( )

60. Write the formula of the missing product.

61. Write the formula of the negative ion in the aqueous sodium hydrogen carbonate.

Base your answers to questions 62 through 64 on the information below.

In an experiment, 2.54 grams of copper completely react with sulfur, producing 3.18 grams of copper(I) sulfide as the only product.

62. Write the chemical formula of the compound produced.

63. Determine the total mass of sulfur consumed.

64. Identify the type of chemical reaction that took place in the experiment.

Lesson 1: Mole Calculations in Formulas

A **mole** is a unit that describes the quantity of 6.02×10^{23}. A mole is a unit of quantity in the same sense that a dozen refers to the quantity of 12.
The following are examples of units of quantities:

> **1 dozen** eggs   = **12** eggs
> **1 gross** of apples = **144** apples.
> **1 mole** of atoms   = **602000000000000000000000** atoms.

A mole is a very large unit of quantity that is only used to represent the number of particles (atoms, molecules, ions, or electrons, etc.) in chemical substances.
The number, **602000000000000000000000**, is called **Avogadro's number**. It is always written in its scientific notation form of **6.02×10^{23}** .

Stoichiometry involves calculating the relative quantities of substances in chemical formulas (composition stoichiometry) and in chemical equations (reaction stoichiometry).
In this lesson, you will learn to interpret and calculate molar quantities in formulas.

Moles of Atoms in Formulas

The number of moles of an atom in a given formula can be determined by counting how many of that atom are in the formula and then multiplying that by the number of moles of the substance.

moles of atom = given mole x how many of the atom in the formula

Example 1
1 mole of HNO_3 can be represented as HNO_3. This formula consists of:

1 x 1 H = **1** mole of H atoms	Total moles of atoms in 1 mole
1 x 1 N = **1** mole of N atoms	of HNO_3 = **5** moles of atoms
1 x 3 O = **3** moles of O atoms	

Example 2
2 moles of HNO_3 can be represented as $2HNO_3$. This formula consists of:

2 x 1 H = **2** moles of H atoms	Total moles of atoms in 2 moles
2 x 1 N = **2** moles of N atoms	of HNO_3 = **10** moles of atoms
2 x 3 O = **6** moles of O atoms	

Example 3
0.5 moles of $Al_2(SO_4)_3$ can be represented as ½ $Al_2(SO_4)_3$. This consists of :

0.5 x 2 Al = **1.0** mole of Al atoms	Total moles of atoms in 0.5 moles
0.5 x 3 S = **1.5** moles of S atoms	of $Al_2(SO_4)_3$ = **8.5** moles of atoms
0.5 x 12 O = **6.0** moles of O atoms	

Molar Mass: *Mass of 1 Mole of a Substance*

The **molar mass** of a substance is the mass, in grams, of 1 mole of that substance. One mole of a substance contains 6.02×10^{23} particles (atoms, molecules, or ions) found in that substance. For example, water is composed of water molecules. One mole of water contains 6.02×10^{23} (60200000000000000000000) molecules of water. The molar mass of water, which is 18 g, is the mass of 6.02×10^{23} molecules of water.

Below are different variations of molar mass.

Atomic mass specifically refers to the average mass of an element. The atomic mass of an element can be found on the Periodic Table.

Atomic mass

15.9994	-2
O	
8	
2-6	

Formula mass is commonly used when referring to the sum of the atomic masses of all the elements in a substance.

Molecular mass is commonly used when referring to the mass of 1 mole of a molecular substance such as H_2O (water) and CO_2 (carbon dioxide).

Regardless of the formula, the mass of one mole of a substance is the sum of the masses of all the atoms in the formula.

Gram-formula mass = Sum of all the Atomic Masses
expressed in grams

There are different methods of setting up and calculating the gram-formula mass of a substance. Three examples are shown below.

Example 4: *Calculation of Formula Mass*
What is the gram-formula mass of H_2O?

$2 H + 1 O$ — rounded atomic mass from the Periodic Table

$2(1) + 1(16)$ } *numerical setup*

$2 + 16$

Formula mass = **18 g/mol** *calculated result*

Example 5: *Calculation of Formula Mass*
What is the formula mass of $(NH_4)_2SO_4$?

$2 N + 8 H + 1 S + 4 O$

$2(14) + 8(1) + 1(32) + 4(16)$ } *numerical setup*

$28 + 8 + 32 + 64$

Formula mass = 132 g/mol *calculated result*

Example 6: *Calculation of Formula Mass*
What is the gram-formula mass of $NaNO_3 \cdot 4H_2O$?

Atoms	Atomic Mass	x How Many	= Total Mass
Na	23.989 g	1	23.989 g
N	14.007 g	1	14.007 g
H	1.008 g	8	8.064 g
O	15.999 g	7	111.993 g

Formula mass = **158.053 g/mol**

E3chemistry.com

Moles and Mass Calculations in Formulas

The mass of one mole of a substance is the gram-formula mass of that substance. In other words, 6.02×10^{23} particles or one mole of a given substance has a mass equal to the calculated gram-formula mass. What if there are more than one mole (more than 6.02×10^{23} particles of that substance)? It makes sense to think that a sample containing more than one mole of a substance (more than 6.02×10^{23} particles) will have a mass that is greater than the calculated gram-formula mass. Likewise, a sample containing less than one mole of a substance (fewer than 6.02×10^{23} particles) will have a mass that is less than the calculated gram-formula mass. The mathematical relationship between moles and mass is given by the **Table T** equation.

$$\text{number of moles} = \frac{\text{given mass}}{\text{gram-formula mass}}$$

Example 7: *Moles from Mass Calculation. Table T Equation Setup*
How many moles of H_2O are in 100. grams of the substance?

$$\text{\bf Number of moles} = \frac{100.\ \text{g}}{18.0\ \text{g}} = \textbf{5.60 mol } H_2O$$

Example 8: *Moles from Mass Calculation. Factor-label Setup*
What is the number of moles of ammonium sulfate, $(NH_4)_2SO_4$, in 50 grams of the substance?

$$50\ g\ (NH_4)_2SO_4 \times \frac{1\ \text{mol } (NH_4)_2SO_4}{132\ g\ (NH_4)_2SO_4} = \textbf{0.38 mol } (NH_4)_2SO_4$$

Example 9: *Mass from Moles Calculation. Table T Equation Setup*
What is the mass of 3.0 moles of water, H_2O?

$$\textbf{Mass} = \text{given moles} \times \text{gram-formula-mass}$$
$$\textbf{Mass} = \quad 3.0 \quad \times \quad 18 \quad = \textbf{54 g } H_2O$$

Example 10: *Mass from Moles Calculation. Factor-label Setup*
What is the mass of 0.2 moles of ammonium sulfate?

$$0.2\ mol\ (NH_4)_2SO_4 \times \frac{132\ \text{g } (NH_4)_2SO_4}{1\ mol\ (NH_4)_2SO_4} = \textbf{26.4 g } (NH_4)_2SO_4$$

The gram-formula mass of H_2O (**18 g**) and of $(NH_4)_2SO_4$ (**132 g**) were calculated on page 92. *Italicized units* in factor-label setups cancel each other out.

Percent Composition

Percent composition by mass indicates the portion of a mass of a substance that is due to the mass of individual elements in a substance.

The percent composition equation is given on **Table T.**

$$\text{Percent composition} = \frac{\text{Total Mass of an Element (Part)}}{\text{Formula Mass (Whole)}} \times 100$$

Examples 11
What is the percent composition of each element in water, H_2O?

$$\% \ H = \underset{\text{setup}}{\frac{2}{18}} \times 100 = \underset{\text{calculated result}}{\textbf{11.1\%}} \qquad \% \ O = \frac{16}{18} \times 100 = \textbf{88.9\%}$$

Example 12
What is the percent composition of each element in $(NH_4)_2SO_4$?

$$\% \ N = \frac{28}{132} \times 100 = \textbf{21.2\%} \qquad \% \ H = \frac{8}{132} \times 100 = \textbf{6.0\%}$$

$$\% \ S = \frac{32}{132} \times 100 = \textbf{24.2\%} \qquad \% \ O = \frac{64}{132} \times 100 = \textbf{48.5\%}$$

Percent Composition of Hydrates
Hydrates are ionic compounds that contain water molecules within their crystalline structures. An example of a hydrate is given below.

$CuSO_4 \cdot 5H_2O$ is copper(II) sulfate pentahydrate (**penta**hydrate means $5H_2O$).
The gram-formula mass or the mass of 1 mole of a hydrate is due in part to the mass of the water. Percent by mass of water in a hydrate can be calculated in three steps as shown in the example below.

Example 13
What is the percent by mass of water in copper(II) sulfate pentahydrate?

Step 1
Mass of water, $5H_2O$ $10H + 5O = 10(1) + 5(16) = \textbf{90 g}$ or $5(18) = \textbf{\textit{90 g}}$

Step 2
Formula mass of hydrate, $CuSO_4 \cdot 5H_2O$ $1 \ Cu + 1 \ S + 10 \ H + 9 \ O$
$$1(64) + 1(32) + 10(1) + 9(16) = \textbf{250 g}$$

Step 3
$$\% \ H_2O = \frac{\text{mass of } H_2O}{\text{formula mass of hydrate}} \times 100$$

$$\% \ H_2O = \underset{\text{numerical setup}}{\frac{90 \text{ g}}{250 \text{ g}}} \times 100 = \underset{\text{calculated result}}{\textbf{36\%}}$$

Percent Composition of Hydrates from Lab Data

When a hydrate is heated, the water in its crystal structure will evaporate out. The substance that remained after all the water of hydration is driven off is the **anhydrous** solid.
If the mass of a hydrate and of the anhydrous solid are known, the mass of water that was in the hydrate can be determined. From this mass, the percent of water in the hydrate can be calculated.

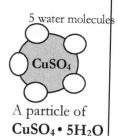

5 water molecules

A particle of
$CuSO_4 \cdot 5H_2O$

hydrate

+   heat   →

water (removed)

+

anhydrous

5 g

1.5 g

3.5 g

Example 14

What is the percent of water from the information given above.

$$\% \textbf{ water} = \frac{\text{mass of water}}{\text{mass of hydrate}} \times 100 = \frac{1.5 \text{ g}}{5 \text{ g}} \times 100 = \textbf{30\% } H_2O$$

Molecular Formula from Molecular Mass and Empirical Formula.

The **molecular formula** of a substance shows the true composition of the substance. The molecular mass (mass of 1 mole) of water (18 grams) is calculated from its molecular formula. An **empirical formula** shows the simplest ratio that the atoms of a substance are combined. If the empirical formula and molecular mass of a substance are known, the molecular formula of the substance can be determined.

Example 15

A substance has a molecular mass of 116 grams and an empirical formula of C_2H_5. What is the molecular formula of this substance?

Step 1: Find **mass** of empirical formula $= C_2H_5 = 2C + 5H = 2(1) + 5(1) = 29$ g

Step 2: Find **number of units** of empirical formula $= \dfrac{\text{molecular mass}}{\text{empirical mass}} = \dfrac{116 \text{ g}}{29 \text{ g}} = 4$

Step 3: Find **molecular formula** $= 4 (C_2H_5) = \boxed{\textbf{C}_8\textbf{H}_{20}}$
       (Multiply units, *step 2*, by subscripts)

Moles and Avogadro's Number Calculations

As mentioned at the beginning of this topic, one mole of a substance contains 6.02×10^{23} particles of that substance.

$$1 \text{ mole} = 6.02 \times 10^{23}$$

The relationship between moles and number of particles is given below.

$$\text{moles} = \frac{\text{given number of particles}}{6.02 \times 10^{23}}$$

Example 16: *Moles from Number of Particles. Equation Setup*
How many moles of water contain 2.30×10^{24} molecules of water?

$$\text{moles} = \frac{2.30 \times 10^{24}}{6.02 \times 10^{23}} = 3.80 \text{ mol}$$

Example 17: *Number of Particles from Moles. Factor-label Setup*
What is the number of gold, Au, atoms in 0.3 moles of the substance?

$$0.3 \text{ } mol \text{ } Au \text{ } \times \text{ } \frac{6.02 \times 10^{23} \text{ Au atoms}}{1 \text{ } mol \text{ } Au} = 1.86 \times 10^{23} \text{ Au atoms}$$

setup   calculated result

Moles and Volume Calculations

Molar volume describes the volume occupied by one mole of a gas at STP.

$$1 \text{ mole of a Gas} = 22.4 \text{ liters}$$
(at STP)

The mathematical relationship between moles and the volume of a gas is given below.

$$\text{moles} = \frac{\text{given volume}}{22.4 \text{ liters}}$$

Example 18: *Moles from Volume. Equation Setup*
How many moles of CO_2 gas occupy 50.8 liters at STP?

$$\text{moles} = \frac{50.8}{22.4} = 2.27 \text{ mol}$$
setup   calculated result

Example 19: *Volume from Moles. Factor-label Setup*
How much volume will 0.25 moles of hydrogen, H_2, gas occupy at STP?

$$0.25 \text{ } mol \text{ } H_2 \text{ } \times \text{ } \frac{22.4 \text{ L } H_2}{1 \text{ } mol \text{ } H_2} = 5.6 \text{ L } H_2$$

setup   calculated result

Review Questions: Mole Calculations in Formulas

Vocabulary: Briefly define each of the following terms.

1. mole   2. Avogadro's number   3. molar mass   4. gram atomic mass
5. gram-formula mass   6. percent composition   7. hydrate   8. anhydrous

9. Which quantity of particles is correctly represented by the formula "CO_2" ?
   (1) 1 mole of molecules   (3) 1 mole of atoms
   (2) 3 moles of molecules   (4) 44 moles of atoms

10. In a sample of oxygen gas at STP, which represents the greatest number of molecules?
   (1) One molecule   (3) One gram
   (2) One liter   (4) One mole

11. What is the total number of moles of hydrogen in 1 mole of $(NH_4)_2HPO_4$?
   (1) 5   (3) 8
   (2) 7   (4) 9

12. What is the total number of moles of atoms in 0.5 moles of sodium thiosulfate, $Na_2S_2O_3$?
   (1) 2.5   (3) 7.0
   (2) 3.5   (4) 14

13. How many moles of hydrogen atoms are there in 2.5 moles of $(NH_4)_2CO_3 \cdot 5H_2O$?
   (1) 8   (3) 45
   (2) 32.5   (4) 37.5

14. The gram-formula mass of $C_3H_5(OH)_3$ is
   (1) 92 g/mol   (3) 58 g/mol
   (2) 74 g /mol   (4) 48 g/mol

15. A student measured 56 grams of Fe_2O_3 for a laboratory experiment. How many moles
    of Fe_2O_3 does this mass represent?
   (1) 1.00   (3) 0.50
   (2) 0.35   (4) 2.00

16. What is the total mass in grams of 3 moles of $Al_2(CrO_4)_3$?
   (1) 134   (3) 1206
   (2) 402   (4) 1530

17. How many moles are represented by 286 grams of $Na_2CO_3 \cdot 10H_2O$?
   (1) 0.2 moles   (3) 1 mole
   (2) 0.5 moles   (4) 2 moles

18. Which setup is correct for calculating the number of moles of $Al(ClO_3)_3 \cdot 6H_2O$
    in 576 grams of the substance?
   (1) 576 x 384   (3) 6 x 576
   (2) $\dfrac{384}{576}$ (4) $\dfrac{576}{384}$

19. Which compound has the greatest composition of sulfur by mass?
   (1) $Fe_2(SO_3)_3$ (3) $FeSO_4$
   (2) $Fe_2(SO_4)_3$ (4) $FeSO_3$

20. What is the percent composition of water in the hydrate $Al(ClO_3)_3 \cdot 6H_2O$?
   (1) 56%   (3) 1.6%
   (2) 28%   (4) 60%

21. What is the total number of molecules in 0.25 mole of NO_2?
    (1) 2.5×10^{23} (3) 4.515×10^{23}
    (2) 24.08 (4) 1.5×10^{23}

22. What is the molecular formula of a compound with a molecular mass of 78 g/mol
    and an empirical formula of CH?
    (1) C_3H_3 (3) C_6H_6
    (2) C_4H_4 (4) C_4H_{10}

23. A compound has a molecular mass of 284 g and an empirical formula of P_2O_5.
    What is the molecular formula of this compound?
    (1) P_4O_{10} (3) P_2O_5
    (2) P_5O_2 (4) $P_{10}O_4$

For problems 24 through 28, show a numerical setup and the calculated result for each.

24. Calculate the molecular mass of $CH_3(CH_2)_2COOH$.

25. What is the mass of 2.3 moles of $CuSO_4 \bullet 5H_2O$?

26. A closed cylinder at STP contains 3.5 moles of CO_2. Calculate the volume of the gas.

27. A helium balloon is filled with 8.12×10^{25} molecules of helium. Calculate the number of
    moles of the gas in the balloon.

28. A hydrated salt was heated in a crucible until the anhydrous compound that remained
    has a constant mass. The following data were recorded.

Mass of crucible	17.2 g
Mass of hydrate + crucible	22.0 g
Mass of anhydrous + crucible	20.4 g

Calculate the percent composition of water in the hydrated compound?

Base your answers to questions 29 through 30 on the information below.

     Gypsum is a mineral that is used in the construction industry to make
drywall (sheetrock). The chemical formula for this hydrated compound
is $CaSO_4 \bullet 2H_2O$. A hydrated compound contains water molecules within
the crystalline structure. Gypsum contains 2 moles of water for each
1 mole of calcium sulfate.

29. What is the gram-formula mass of $CaSO_4 \bullet 2H_2O$?

30. Show a correct numerical setup for calculating the percent composition by mass of
    water in this compound and record your result.

Lesson 2: Mole Calculations in Equations

A balanced chemical equation shows the mole proportions (ratios) of reactants and products of a reaction. From these mole ratios, any number of moles of a product can be made by combining more or less of the reactants in the same proportion as given in the equation. A balanced chemical equation is like a recipe for making chemical substances.

In this lesson, you will learn how to interpret and solve problems that involve mole proportions in chemical equations.

Mole Ratio and Proportion in Equations

The coefficients in front of substances in a balanced equation indicate the number of moles of the substances. From these coefficients, mole ratios of substances can be determined as shown in the example below.

$$4NH_3 + 5O_2 \rightarrow 4NO + 6H_2O$$

Mole ratio of NH_3 to O_2 is **4 : 5**

Mole ratio of NH_3 to NO is **1 : 1**
(reduced from 4 : 4)

Mole ratio of NO to H_2O is **2 : 3**
(reduced from 4 : 6)

Mole to Mole Calculation in Equations

When the number of moles of one substance in a reaction is given, the number of moles of any other substance in the reaction can be calculated using ratios in the balanced equation. A mole to mole problem is given and solved below.

Example 20: Given the balanced equation below:

$$4NH_3 + 5O_2 \rightarrow 4NO + 6H_2O$$

How many moles of NO are produced when 12 moles of O_2 are consumed?

Proportion setup

$$\frac{5}{12} = \frac{4}{X}$$

$$5X = 48$$

$$\mathbf{X = 9.6 \text{ mol NO}}$$

Factor-label setup

given moles x mole ratio of NO/O_2
in question   in equation

$$12 \; mol \; O_2 \; \times \; \frac{4 \text{ mol NO}}{5 \; mol \; O_2} = \mathbf{9.6 \text{ mol NO}}$$

Volume to Volume Calculation in Equations

When the volume of one substance in a reaction is known, the volume of any other gaseous substance in the reaction can be calculated as shown in the example below.

Example 21: Given the balanced equation below:

$$C_3H_8 + 5O_2 \rightarrow 3CO_2 + 4H_2O$$

How many liters of propane, C_3H_8, will react to produce 9 liters of CO_2?

Proportion setup

$$\frac{1}{X} = \frac{3}{9}$$

$$3X = 9$$

$$\mathbf{X = 3\ mol\ C_3H_8}$$

Factor-label setup

given moles x mol ratio of C_3H_8/CO_2
in question   in equation

$$9\ mol\ CO_2 \ \ x\ \ \frac{1\ mol\ C_3H_8}{3\ mol\ CO_2} = \mathbf{3\ mol\ C_3H_8}$$

Mass to Mass Calculation in Equations

When the mass of one substance in a reaction is known, the mass of any other substance in the reaction can be calculated as shown in the example below.

Example 22: Given the balanced equation below:

$$2KClO_3 \rightarrow 2KCl + 3O_2$$

How many grams of KCl are produced by decomposing 100 g of $KClO_3$?

Factor-label setup

$$100\ g\ KClO_3\ x\ \frac{1\ mol\ KClO_3}{122\ g\ KClO_3}\ x\ \frac{2\ mol\ KCl}{2\ mol\ KClO_3}\ x\ \frac{74\ g\ KCl}{1\ mol\ KCl} = \mathbf{60.7\ g\ KCl}$$

Proportion setup

$$\frac{\text{Mass of } 2KClO_3}{100\ g} = \frac{\text{Mass of } 2KCl}{X}$$

$$\frac{244\ g}{100\ g} = \frac{148\ g}{X}$$

$$244X = 14800$$

$$\mathbf{X = 60.7g\ KCl}$$

These numbers are used in the setups

Molar mass of $KClO_3$	Molar mass of KCl
1 K 1(39) = 39 g	1K 1(39) = 39 g
1 Cl 1(35) = 35 g	1Cl 1(35) = 35 g
3 O 3(16) = 48 g	74 g
122 g	
Mass of 2KClO₃	**Mass of 2KCl**
2(122 g) = **244 g**	2(74 g) = **148 g**

Review Questions: Mole Interpretations in Equations

31. Given the reaction

$$2C_2H_2(g) + 5O_2(g) \rightarrow 4CO_2(g) + 2H_2O(\ell)$$

What is the mole ratio of C_2H_2 to O_2 reacted?
(1) $4:5$
(2) $1:1$
(3) $5:2$
(4) $2:5$

32. Given the reaction:

$$3Cu + 8HNO_3 \rightarrow 3Cu(NO_3)_2 + 2NO + 4H_2O$$

The mole ratio of NO produced to HNO_3 reacted is
(1) $4:1$
(2) $2:3$
(3) $1:4$
(4) $2:3$

33. In the reaction:

$$4NH_3 + 5O_2 \rightarrow 4NO + 6H_2O$$

What is the total number of moles of NO produced when 2 moles of O_2 is consumed?
(1) 2.0 moles
(2) 2.4 moles
(3) 1.6 moles
(4) 8.0 moles

34. Given the reaction:

$$6CO_2 + 6H_2O \rightarrow C_6H_{12}O_6 + 6O$$

What is the total number of moles of water needed to make 1.75 moles of $C_6H_{12}O_6$?
(1) 10.5
(2) 6
(3) 7.5
(4) 1.75

35. Given the reaction:

$$C_2H_4 + 3O_2 \rightarrow 2CO_2 + 2H_2O$$

How many liters of CO_2 are produced when 15 liters of O_2 are consumed?
(1) 10 L
(2) 15 L
(3) 30 L
(4) 45 L

36. Given the reaction:

$$4Al(s) + 3O_2(g) \rightarrow 2Al_2O_3(s)$$

What is the minimum number of grams of O_2 gas required to produce 102 grams of Al_2O_3?
(1) 32.0 g
(2) 192 g
(3) 96.0 g
(4) 48.0 g

37. Given the balanced equation representing a reaction:

$$2C_2H_6 + 7O_2 \rightarrow 4CO_2 + 6H_2O$$

Determine the total number of moles of oxygen that react completely with 8 moles of C_2H_6. Show a numerical setup and the calculated result.

Base your answers to questions 38 through 40 on the information below.

Rust on an automobile door contains $Fe_2O_3(s)$. The balanced equation representing one of the reactions between iron in the door of the automobile and oxygen in the atmosphere is given below.

$$4Fe(s) + 3O_2(g) \rightarrow 2Fe_2O_3(s)$$

38. What is the mole ratio of iron reacted to iron(III) oxide formed as rust on an automobile door?

39. Determine the gram-formula mass of the product of this reaction.

40. Identify the type of chemical reaction represented by this equation.

Additional Materials

Molecular Density

Density (D) is the mass (m) per volume (V) ratio of a substance. Molecular density of a gas is equal to the ratio of the molecular mass to molar volume of the gas at STP. Molar volume of any gas at STP is 22.4 liters.

Example 23: What is the density of oxygen, O_2, at STP ?

$$\text{Density} = \frac{\text{molecular mass of } O_2}{\text{molar volume}} = \frac{32 \text{ g}}{22.4 \text{ L}} = \textbf{1.43 g/L}$$

Mixed Unit Calculations in Formulas

Calculations that you learned in lesson 1 focus on solving formula problems in which moles of a substance are given or asked to be calculated. The example problems in this section show how to use the factor-label method to set up and solve formula related problems that involve mixed quantities.

Example 24: *Mass from Volume. Factor-label Setup*
What is the mass of a 100-liter sample of carbon dioxide, CO_2, at STP?

Mass = volume given x mole/molar volume x formula mass

$$\textbf{Mass =} \quad 100 \text{ L} \quad \text{x} \quad \frac{1 \text{ mol}}{22.4 \text{ L}} \quad \text{x} \quad \frac{44 \text{ g}}{1 \text{ mol}} = \textbf{196.4 g } CO_2$$

Example 25: *Number of Molecules from Mass. Factor-label Setup*
How many molecules of HCl are in a 10-gram sample of HCl?

number of molecules = mass given x mole/FM x number of molecules/mole

$$\textbf{number of molecules} = \quad 10 \text{ g} \quad \text{x} \quad \frac{1 \text{ mol}}{36 \text{ g}} \quad \text{x} \quad \frac{6.02 \times 10^{23} \textbf{ molecules}}{1 \text{ mol}} = \textbf{1.67} \times \textbf{10}^{23} \text{ molecules of HCl}$$

Mixed Unit Calculations in Equations

Calculations that you learned in lesson 2 focus on solving equation problems of the same quantity; mole to mole, volume to volume, and mass to mass. The example below shows how to use the factor-label method to set up and solve an equation problem involving mixed quantities.

Example 26: *Mass to Volume. Factor-label Setup*
Given the reaction;
$$2C(s) + 3H_2(g) \rightarrow C_2H_6(g) .$$
How many liters of $C_2H_6(g)$ will be produced from reacting 36 g of C at STP?

Volume = mass given x mole/mass ratio x mole ratio in equation x volume/mole ratio

$$\textbf{Volume} = 36 \text{ g } C \quad \text{x} \quad \frac{1 \text{ mol } C}{12 \text{ g } C} \quad \text{x} \quad \frac{1 \text{ mol } C_2H_6}{2 \text{ mol } C} \quad \text{x} \quad \frac{22.4 \text{ L } C_2H_6}{1 \text{ mol } C_2H_6} = \textbf{33.6 L } C_2H_6$$

E3chemistry.com

Review Questions: Molecular Density and Mixed Unit Calculations

41. What is the density of $SO_3(g)$ at STP?

42. A gas has a density of 0.71 g/L at STP? What is the molar mass of the gas?

43. What is the total volume occupied by 132 grams of $CO_2(g)$ at STP?

44. What is the volume, in liters, of 576 grams of SO_2 gas at STP?

45. What is the mass of a 10-liter sample of ammonia gas, $NH_3(g)$, at STP?

46. What is the total number of molecules in 50.0 grams of vinegar, CH_3COOH?

47. Given the reaction at STP:

$$2KClO_3(s) \rightarrow 2KCl(s) + 3O_2(g)$$

What is the total number of liters of $O_2(g)$ produced from the complete decomposition of 0.500 mole of $KClO_3(s)$?

48. Given the reaction

$$N_2(g) + 3H_2(g) \rightarrow 2NH_3(g)$$

How many molecules of ammonia, measured at STP, are produced when 48.0 grams of nitrogen is completely consumed?

49. Given the reaction:

$$2C_8H_{18}(g) + 25O_2(g) \rightarrow 16CO_2(g) + 18H_2O(g)$$

What volume of $C_8H_{18}(g)$ will completely react to produce exactly 36 liters of $H_2O(g)$?

50. Magnesium was reacted with an excess of dilute hydrochloric acid and the hydrogen gas produced collected in a eudiometer. The volume of hydrogen in the eudiometer was corrected to conditions of STP. If 94.1 milliliters of hydrogen was produced, how much magnesium reacted in this experiment?

Lesson 1 : Properties of Aqueous Solutions

Solutions are homogeneous mixtures. A homogeneous mixture is a type of mixture in which all components are evenly and uniformly mixed throughout the mixture. One good example of a solution is saltwater. Milk is also a homogeneous mixture. Although there are different types of solutions, the discussion in this topic will focus on aqueous solutions only.

Aqueous solutions are solutions in which the solvent is water.
In this lesson, you will learn about properties of aqueous solutions.

Components of Aqueous Solutions

LiCl*(s)*
Solute

Solute (Salt)
A solute is the substance that is being dissolved in a solution.
A solute is always present in a smaller amount than the solvent.
A solute can be a solid, liquid or gas. Dissolving of a solute in water to make a solution is a physical change.

Solvent (Water)
A solvent is the substance in which the solute is dispersed.
A solvent is always present in a greater amount relative to the solute.
In aqueous solutions, the solvent is always water.
In all solutions, the solvent is usually a liquid.

$H_2O(\ell)$
Solvent

Solution (Mixture)
An aqueous solution is a mixture of a solvent (water) and solute.
The equation below shows the dissolving of a lithium chloride salt (solute) in water.

LiCl*(aq)*
Solution

$$LiCl(s) \quad + \quad H_2O(\ell) \quad \xrightarrow{\text{dissolving}} \quad LiCl(aq)$$

    solute   **solvent**   **solution**

(s) solid   *(ℓ)* liquid   *(aq)* aqueous

Dissolving (Hydration) of a Salt

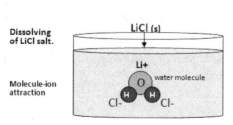

Dissolving of LiCl salt.

Molecule-ion attraction

In a solution of LiCl(aq)

Li⁺ (the +ion of the salt)
attracts
O (the -end of a water molecule)

Cl⁻ (the -ion of the salt)
attracts
H (the +ends of a water molecule)

Opposites attract.

Physical Properties of Solutions

The following are some general characteristics of properly made solutions.

• Solutions are homogenous mixtures.

• Solutions are generally clear.

• Solutions that are colorful likely contain an ion of a transition element

• Solutions are transparent and do not disperse light.

• Particles in a solution will not settle to the bottom of the container or separate into layers.

• The solute and solvent of a solution can be separated by evaporation, crystallization or distillation processes.

Crystallization is a process of recovering a salt (solute) from a mixture by evaporating (or boiling) off the water. When a solution is boiled, particles of water will evaporate out of the mixture, leaving behind ions of the solute to re-crystallize.

Filtration *cannot* be used to remove or separate the solute particles from the solvent of a solution. Both the solute and solvent particles are generally smaller than holes of a filter. As a result, both the solute and solvent will go through filtering equipment.

Examples of Solutions

A chemical formula can only be used to represent pure substances such as elements and compounds. Aqueous solutions can be represented by symbols, not by chemical formulas. A symbol for an aqueous solution is not a chemical formula of that solution.

Examples below give names and symbols of some common solutions, as well as the solute of each solution.

Solution name	Solution symbol	Solute formula
Sodium chloride solution	$NaCl(aq)$	$NaCl(s)$ or Na^+Cl^-
Potassium nitrate solution	$KNO_3(aq)$	$KNO_3(s)$ or $K^+NO_3^-$
Sugar solution	$C_6H_{12}O_6(aq)$	$C_6H_{12}O_6(s)$
Carbon dioxide solution	$CO_2(aq)$	$CO_2(g)$
Ethanol (alcohol) solution	$C_2H_5OH(aq)$	$C_2H_5OH(\ell)$

NOTE: The aqueous symbol *(aq)* next to a formula of a substance always indicates that the substance is dissolved in water.

Review Questions: Properties of Aqueous Solutions

Vocabulary: Briefly define each of the following terms.
1. Aqueous solution   2. Homogeneous mixture   3. Solute   4. Solvent
5. Crystallization   6. Filtration   7. Hydration of ions

8. All aqueous mixtures must contain
   (1) water   (3) oxygen
   (2) sodium chloride   (4) sand

9. The process of recovering a salt from a solution by evaporating the solvent is known as
   (1) decomposition   (3) reduction
   (2) crystallization   (4) filtration

10. In a true solution, the dissolved particles
   (1) are visible to the eyes   (3) are always solids
   (2) will settle out on standing   (4) cannot be removed by filtration

11. When sample X is passed through a filter paper a white residue, Y, remains on the paper and a clear liquid, Z, passes through. When Z is vaporized, another white residue remains. Z is best classified as
   (1) an element   (3) a heterogeneous mixture
   (2) a compound   (4) a homogeneous mixture

12. An aqueous solution of copper sulfate is poured into a filter paper cone. What passes through the filter paper?
   (1) Only the solvent   (3) Both solvent and solute
   (2) Only the solute   (4) Neither the solvent nor solute

13. A small amount of Na_2SO_4 is dissolved in H_2O to make a solution. In this solution
   (1) Na_2SO_4 is the solute   (3) H_2O is the solute
   (2) Na_2SO_4 is the solvent   (4) H_2O is the precipitate

14. What happens when KI(s) is dissolved in water?
   (1) I^- ions are attracted to the oxygen atoms of water
   (2) K^+ ions are attracted to the oxygen atoms of water
   (3) K^+ ions are attracted to the hydrogen atoms of water
   (4) No attractions are involved; the crystal just falls apart

Base your answer to question 15 on the information below.

     A 2.0-liter aqueous solution contains a total of 3.0 moles of dissolved NH_4Br at 25°C and standard pressure.

15. Identify the *two* ions present in the solute. Include name and symbol for both ions.

Base your answer to question 16 on the information below.
   Given the balanced equation for the dissolving of $NaNO_3(s)$ in water:

$$NaNO_3(s) \xrightarrow{H_2O(\ell)} Na^+(aq) \ + \ NO^-(aq)$$

16. Using the key to the right, draw at least two water molecules near each ion in the box. Your drawing must show the correct orientation of each water molecule when it is near the Na^+ ion or NO_3^- ion in the solution.

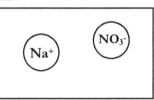

Lesson 2 : Solubility Factors

Not every substance that is put in water will dissolve. Some substances dissolve very well, others very little, and some not at all. In addition, how well a given substance dissolves in water is affected by conditions such as temperature and/or pressure.

In this lesson, you'll learn about factors that affect how well substances dissolve in water. You will also learn how to determine which substance will dissolve and which will not dissolve in water.

Solubility: *How Well a Solute Dissolves*

Solubility describes the extent to which a substance will dissolve in water under a given set of conditions.

Soluble means that a substance has *high* solubility. Soluble salts dissolve very well in water to produce a solution with a high concentration of ions.
Ex. NaCl (sodium chloride) is soluble in water.

Insoluble means that a substance has *low* solubility. Insoluble salts dissolve very little in water to produce a solution with a low concentration of ions.
Ex. AgCl (silver chloride) is insoluble in water.

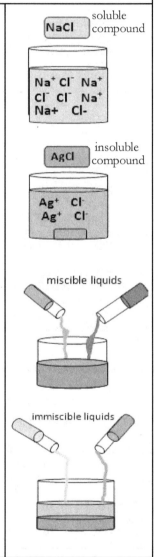

Miscibility: *How Well Liquids Mix*

Miscibility describes the extent to which two or more liquids will mix.

Miscible refers to two liquids with *high* miscibility. Two miscible liquids will mix evenly and will not form layers.
Ex. Ethanol (alcohol) and water are miscible liquids.

Immiscible refers to two liquids with *low* miscibility. Two immiscible liquids will not mix evenly and may separate into layers.
Ex. Oil and water are immiscible liquids.

E3chemistry.com

Factors that Affect Solubility: *Temperature, Pressure, Nature of Solute*

The extent to which a solute will dissolve in water depends largely on the following three factors: Temperature, pressure, and nature of the solute.

Temperature: *Affects the Solubility of Solids, Liquids, and Gases*
The effect of temperature on the solubility of a solute varies depending if the solute is a solid or gas. Table G (The Solubility Curves) shows the solubility of a few selected solutes at different water temperatures.

Solid solutes: ↑*Temperature* ↑*Solubility*
The solubility of many solids increases with increasing water temperature. $KCl(s)$ and $C_6H_{12}O_6(s)$ dissolve better in 45°C water than in 25°C water.

A greater amount of KCl(s) can be dissolved at 45°C.

Gaseous Solutes: ↓*Temperature* ↑*Solubility*
The solubility of a gas increases with decreasing water temperature. $O_2(g)$ and $CO_2(g)$ dissolve better in 25°C water than in 45°C water.

The 25°C water contains more dissolved O_2 gas.

Pressure: *Affects the Solubility of Gases only*
For a given gaseous solute, the solubility of the solute changes with a change in pressure.

Gaseous solutes: ↑*Pressure,* ↑*Solubility*
The solubility of a gas increases with increasing pressure. $O_2(g)$ and $CO_2(g)$ dissolve better in a high-pressure system than in a low-pressure system.

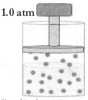

Solid solutes: *No Effect*
Pressure has no effect on the solubility of a solid. The amount of $NaNO_3(s)$ or $KCl(s)$ that dissolves in water will not be affected by a change in pressure.

A greater amount of O_2 gas is dissolved at 1.0 atm.

Nature of Solutes: *Like Dissolves Like*
"Like dissolves like" is a saying that emphasizes the fact that polar solutes and ionic solutes dissolve better in polar solvents.

Nonpolar solutes: *Higher Solubility in Polar Solvents (Water)*
$NaCl(s)$ and $LiNO_3(s)$ dissolve well in water because they are *alike in terms of polarity.*
• Water is a polar substance with positive(+) and negative(−) ends.
• Ionic solids such as $NaCl(s)$ and $LiNO_3(s)$ are composed of positive and negative ions.

Nonpolar solutes: *Higher Solubility in Nonpolar Solvents*
$I_2(s)$, iodine, which has no positive and no negative ends, has a low solubility in water.
• $I_2(s)$ dissolves much better in a solvent like $CCl_4(\ell)$, carbon tetrachloride, because they are both nonpolar substances.

Soluble and Insoluble Salts: *Reference Table F*

The solubility of an ionic solute depends on the nature of the ions it contains. The **Solubility Guidelines Table** below lists ions that form soluble and insoluble compounds.

Table F: Solubility Guidelines

Soluble ions

Ions That Form *Soluble* Compounds	Exceptions
Group 1 ions (Li^+, Na^+, etc.)	
ammonium (NH_4^+)	
nitrate (NO_3^-)	
acetate ($C_2H_3O_2^-$ or CH_3COO^-)	
hydrogen carbonate (HCO_3^-)	
chlorate (ClO_3^-)	
halides (Cl^-, Br^-, I^-)	when combined with Ag^+, Pb^{2+}, or Hg_2^{2+}
sulfates (SO_4^{2-})	when combined with Ag^+, Ca^{2+}, Sr^{2+}, Ba^{2+}, or Pb^{2+}

Insoluble ions

Ions That Form *Insoluble* Compounds*	Exceptions
carbonate (CO_3^{2-})	when combined with Group 1 ions or ammonium (NH_4^+)
chromate (CrO_4^{2-})	when combined with Group 1 ions, Ca^{2+}, Mg^{2+}, or ammonium (NH_4^+)
phosphate (PO_4^{3-})	when combined with Group 1 ions or ammonium (NH_4^+)
sulfide (S^{2-})	when combined with Group 1 ions or ammonium (NH_4^+)
hydroxide (OH^-)	when combined with Group 1 ions, Ca^{2+}, Ba^{2+}, Sr^{2+}, or ammonium (NH_4^+)

*compounds having very low solubility in H_2O

Table F is used in explaining why compounds below are soluble or insoluble.

LiCl   lithium chloride   *Soluble*
Li^+ ion (and all Group 1 ions) is listed on the soluble side.
Cl^- ion, a halide ion, is also listed on the soluble side.
Neither ion is listed as an exception for the other.
Therefore, LiCl is a soluble compound.

Ag₂SO₄   silver sulfate   *Insoluble*
SO_4^{2-} (sulfate ion) is listed on the soluble side, with exceptions.
Ag^+ (silver ion) is listed as one of the exceptions for sulfates.
Therefore, Ag_2SO_4 is an insoluble compound.

Ba(OH)₂   barium hydroxide   *Soluble*
Hydroxide ion (OH^-) is listed on the insoluble side, with exceptions.
Barium (Ba^{2+}) is listed as one of the exceptions for hydroxide (OH^-) ion.
Therefore, barium hydroxide is a soluble compound.

MgS   magnesium sulfide   *Insoluble*
Sulfide ion (S^{2-}) is listed on the insoluble side, with exceptions.
Magnesium ion (Mg^{2+}) is not listed as an exception for S^{2-} ion.
Therefore, magnesium sulfide is an insoluble compound.

Review Questions: Solubility Factors and Solubility Guidelines

Vocabulary: Briefly define each of the following terms.

17. Solubility   18. Soluble   19. Insoluble   20. Miscibility   21. Miscible   22. Immiscible

23. The solubility of a salt in a given volume of water depends largely on the
    (1) surface area of the salt crystals   (3) rate at which the salt and water are stirred
    (2) pressure on the surface of the water   (4) temperature of the water

24. A change in pressure has the greatest effect on the solubility of a solution that contains a
    (1) solid in a liquid   (3) liquid in a liquid
    (2) gas in a liquid   (4) liquid in a solid

25. Which change will increase the solubility of a gas in water?
    (1) Increase in pressure and increase in temperature.
    (2) Increase in pressure and decrease in temperature.
    (3) Decrease in pressure and increase in temperature.
    (4) Decrease in pressure and decrease in temperature.

26. As the temperature of water increases, which substance will show a decrease in solubility?
    (1) $CaBr_2$ (3) CO
    (2) KNO_3 (4) KBr

27. As the pressure of a system is changed from 1 atm to 2 atm, the solubility of which substance will not be affected by this change?
    (1) $HCl(\ell)$ (3) LiCl(s)
    (2) HCl(g)   (4) $LiCl(\ell)$

28. Under which conditions would carbon dioxide be most soluble in water?
    (1) 10°C and 1 atm   (3) 20°C and 1 atm
    (2) 10°C and 2 atm   (4) 20°C and 2 atm

29. Based on Reference Table F, which substance is most soluble?
    (1) AgI   (3) $CaSO_4$
    (2) $PbCl_2$ (4) $(NH_4)_3PO_4$

30. Which of these saturated solutions has the lowest concentration of dissolved ions?
    (1) NaCl(aq)   (3) $NiCl_2$(aq)
    (2) $MgCl_2$(aq)   (4) AgCl(aq)

31. Which ion, when combined with bromide ions, Br^-, forms an insoluble substance in water?
    (1) Fe^{2+} (3) Pb^{2+}
    (2) Mg^{2+} (4) Zn^{2+}

32. According to Table F, which chromate salt is soluble?
    (1) Calcium chromate   (3) Cobalt(II) chromate
    (2) Zinc chromate   (4) Iron(II) chromate

33. State the relationship between the solubility of NH_3(g) in water and the temperature of the aqueous solution.

34. Explain, in terms of molecular polarity, why oxygen gas has a low solubility in water. Your response must include both oxygen and water.

35. The dissolving of solid lithium bromide in water is represented by the equation below.

$$LiBr(s) \longrightarrow Li^+(aq) + Br^-(aq)$$

Based on Table F, identify *one* ion that reacts with Br^- ions in an aqueous solution to form an insoluble compound.

Lesson 3: Descriptions of Solutions and Solubility Curves

A solution can be described as saturated, unsaturated, supersaturated, dilute, or concentrated depending on four factors of the solution: **Type of solute, amount of the solute, and amount and temperature of the water.**

Since it is difficult to classify a solution just by looking at it, a Solubility Curve Table is often used to determine and describe the type of solution that is made.

In this lesson, you will learn about types of solutions. You will also learn how to use *Reference Table G Solubility Curves* to answer questions about a solution.

Types of Solutions

Saturated solution: *Maximum Amount of Solute*
A solution containing the maximum amount of the solute that can be dissolved at a given water temperature. In a saturated solution, equilibrium exists between dissolved and undissolved particles. If additional solute is added, it will settle to the bottom as crystals.

Unsaturated solution: *Less Than the Maximum Amount of Solute*
A solution containing less than the maximum amount of the solute that can be dissolved at a given water temperature. An unsaturated solution can dissolve more solute.

Supersaturated solution: *More Than the Maximum Amount of Solute*
An unstable solution containing more than the maximum amount of the solute that can be dissolved at a given water temperature. A supersaturated solution is made by heating a saturated solution, adding more solute (which will dissolve at the new temperature) and then cooling down the solution.

Dilute solution: *Small Solute in Large Solvent*
A solution containing a smaller amount of dissolved solute relative to the amount of water (solvent).

Concentrated solution: *Large Solute in Little Solvent*
A solution containing a larger amount of dissolved solute relative to the amount of water (solvent).

Solubility Curves (Table G)

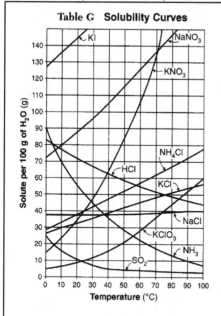

Table G   Solubility Curves

The curves on Table G show changes in the solubility of a few selected solids and gases in 100 grams of water at different temperatures.

Note the following about the curves.

- *Solid solutes (ex. KNO₃) have curves with positive slopes because the solubility of a solid increases as water temperature increases.*

- *Gaseous solutes (ex. NH₃) have curves with negative slopes because the solubility of a gas decreases as water temperature increases.*

Determining the Amount of Solute to Form a Saturated Solution

A *saturated solution* contains the maximum amount of the solute that can be dissolved in a given amount of water at a specified temperature.

Step 1: Locate the temperature on the x axis.

Step 2: Go up the temperature line to intersect the curve for the given substance.

Step 3: Go left (from intersection point) to the y axis and read the grams of solute.

Adjust saturated grams if the amount of water is different from 100 g.

If the amount of water is 200 grams:
Double the grams of solute you determined.

If the amount of water is 50 grams:
Cut the grams of solute you determined in half.

According to Table G, at 90°C.
In 100 g H_2O: **72 g of NH_4Cl** will form a saturated solution.

In 50 g H_2O: 72 ÷ 2 = **36 g of NH_4Cl** will form a saturated solution.

In 200 g H_2O: 72 x 2 = **144 g of NH_4Cl** will form a saturated solution.

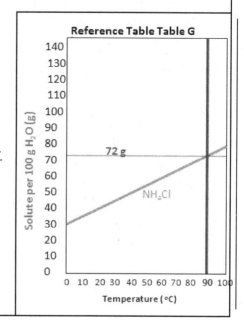

Reference Table Table G

72 g

NH_4Cl

Determining Type of Solution from Table G

A solution is described as saturated, unsaturated, or supersaturated based on how much of the solute is in the solution, the amount of water, and the temperature of the water .

Using the **Table G Solubility Curves**, you can determine the type of solution by following the steps below.

To determine type of solution from Table G

Step 1: Locate the given temperature of the solution. Go up the temperature line.

Step 2: Stop when you've gone up as high as the solute amount in the solution.

Step 3: Describe the solution as:

Supersaturated if you stop **above** the curve.(♦)
Saturated if you stop **on** the curve (x)
Unsaturated if you stop **below** the curve (•)

According to the graph on the right.

In 100 grams of water at 50°C:

22 g of $KClO_3$ forms a *saturated solution.*

10 g of $KClO_3$ forms an *unsaturated solution.*

50 g of $KClO_3$ forms a *supersaturated solution.*

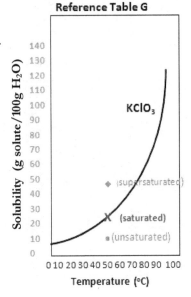

If the amount of water is 200 g at 50°C

44 g of $KClO_3$ will form a *saturated solution.*

22 g of $KClO_3$ will now be an *unsaturated solution.*

50 g of $KClO_3$ will still be a *supersaturated solution.*

Concentrated and Dilute Solutions

A **concentrated solution** contains a large amount of solute relative to the amount of water.

A **dilute solution** contains a small amount of solute relative to the amount of water.

The solubility curve to the right shows four different solutions of KNO_3 at 10°C and 60°C in 100 g of H_2O. Each solution is described below.

Solution A: saturated and dilute
Solution B: supersaturated and dilute
Solution C: saturated and concentrated
Solution D: unsaturated and concentrated

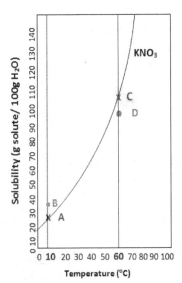

Adding Solute to an Unsaturated Solution.

A solution that is unsaturated can dissolve more solute. How many more grams of a solute that should be added to bring an unsaturated solution to saturation can be determined as shown below.

- **Determine saturated grams** of the solute at the given temperature (use Table G)
- Make note of grams of the solute in the question.
- **Determining how much more solute to** add = Saturated amount - Amount in question

Example 1

An unsaturated solution of $KClO_3$ contains 10 grams of the salt in 100 g of H_2O at 50^0C. How many more grams are needed to make this a saturated solution ?

Saturated amount = **22 g**

Amount in question = **10 g**

Amount needed = **22 – 10**

   = **12 g $KClO_3$**

See the top graph on previous page

Crystallization of Salt (Precipitate)

When a salt solution that is saturated at one temperature is cooled to a lower temperature, a smaller amount of the solute will be soluble. As a result, the ions of the solute will re-crystallize and precipitate (settle out) from solution. A **precipitate** is a solid that forms out of a solution. The amount of the solute that precipitated at the lower temperature can be determined as shown below.

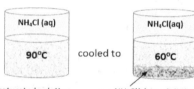

NH₄Cl (aq)   cooled to   NH₄Cl(aq)

90°C   **60°C**

A saturated solution   NH₄Cl(s) precipitate at the
of NH₄Cl at 90°C   lower temperature of 60°C.

Amount precipitated = saturation *at higher temp* – saturation *at lower temp*

Example 2

A saturated solution of NH_4Cl solution at $90^\circ C$ is cooled to $60^\circ C$. How much of the NH_4Cl will precipitate?

Saturation grams at $60^\circ C$ = 72 g

Saturation grams at $10^\circ C$ = 57 g

Grams of NH_4Cl = 72 – 57 = **15 g NH_4Cl**
Precipitated

Determining Most and Least Soluble Salts

The Solubility Curves Table can be used to determine which solute is most or least soluble at any given temperature. The graph to the right marks and compares the saturation points of four solutes at 60°C.

Highest point: NaNO₃ is the **most soluble** of the salts. The NaNO₃ solution will be the **most concentrated** or the **least dilute** at this temperature.

Lowest point: KCl is the **least soluble** of the four salts. The KCl solution will be the **least concentrated** or the **most dilute** at this temperature.

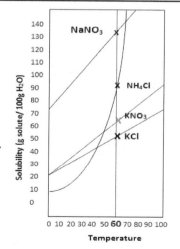

Review Questions: Types of Solutions

Vocabulary: Briefly define each of the following terms.

36. Saturated   37. Supersaturated   38. Unsaturated   39. Concentrated   40. Dilute

41. According to Reference Table G, approximately how many grams of HCl are needed to saturate 100 grams of H_2O at 50°C?
   (1) 50
   (2) 116
   (3) 58
   (4) 42

42. What is the amount of $NaNO_3$ needed to saturate 50 grams of water that is at 10°C?
   (1) 80 grams
   (2) 100 grams
   (3) 40 grams
   (4) 50 grams

43. How many grams of KCl must be dissolved in 200 g of H_2O to make a saturated solution at 60°C?
   (1) 30 g
   (2) 45 g
   (3) 56 g
   (4) 90 g

44. According to Reference Table G, which solution is a saturated solution at 30°C?
   (1) 12 g of $KClO_3$ in 100 g of water
   (2) 12 g of $KClO_3$ in 200 g of water
   (3) 30 g of NaCl in 100 g of water
   (4) 30 g of NaCl in 200 g of water

45. An unsaturated solution of $NaNO_3$ contains 70 g of $NaNO_3$ dissolved in 100 g of water at 20°C. How many more grams of $NaNO_3$ are needed to make this a saturated solution?
   (1) 30 g
   (2) 18 g
   (3) 70 g
   (4) 95 g

46. A student dissolved 40 grams of NaCl in 80 grams of water that is at 90°C. To make this a saturated solution, the student must add to the solution
   (1) 10 g of NaCl
   (2) 10 g of H_2O
   (3) 20 g of NaCl
   (4) 20 g of H_2O

47. When the temperature of a saturated solution of $KClO_3$ that is made with 100 g of H_2O is cooled from 25° C to 10°C, some salt crystals reformed at the bottom of the beaker. How many grams of the $KClO_3$ salt are at the bottom of the beaker?
   (1) 5 g
   (2) 10 g
   (3) 15 g
   (4) 20 g

48. A test tube contains a saturated solution of KNO_3 that was prepared with 100 grams of H_2O at 60°C. If the test tube is cooled to 30°C, what will be found at the bottom of the test tube?
   (1) 30 g of KNO_3
   (2) 30 g of H_2O
   (3) 57 g of KNO_3
   (4) 57 g of H_2O

49. Based on Reference Table G, a solution of SO_2 that contains 15 grams of the solute dissolved in 100 g of H_2O at 10°C is best described as
   (1) saturated and dilute
   (2) saturated and concentrated
   (3) unsaturated and concentrated
   (4) supersaturated and concentrated

50. Which of these saturated solution is the most dilute at 20°C?
   (1) KI(aq)
   (2) KCl(aq)
   (3) $NaNO_3$(aq)
   (4) NaCl(aq)

51. According to Table G, which of these substances is most soluble at 60°C?
   (1) NaCl
   (2) KCl
   (3) $KClO_3$
   (4) NH_4Cl

52. 100 g of H_2O at 40°C contains 80 g of $KNO_3(s)$. Use the solubility curve (Table G) to describe two specific ways that this solution can be made saturated.

Base your answers to questions 53 and 54 on the information below.

Scientists who study aquatic ecosystems are often interested in the concentration of dissolved oxygen in water. Oxygen, O_2, has a very low solubility in water, and therefore its solubility is usually expressed in units of milligrams per 1000. grams of water at 1.0 atmosphere pressure. The graph below shows a solubility curve of oxygen in water.

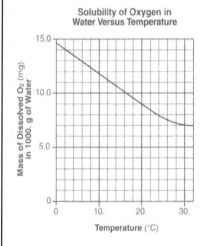

Solubility of Oxygen in Water Versus Temperature

53. A student determines that 8.2 milligrams of oxygen is dissolved in a 1000-gram sample of water at 15°C and 1.0 atmosphere of pressure. In terms of saturation, what type of solution is this sample?

54. A student prepared a solution of oxygen by dissolving 6.0 mg of oxygen in 1000 grams of water at 20°C. Determine how many more milligrams of oxygen must be added to the solution to make it a saturated solution.

Base your answers to questions 55 through 57 on the information below.

A student uses 200 grams of water at 60°C to prepare a saturated solution of potassium chloride, KCl.

55. According to reference Table G, how many grams of KCl must be used to create this saturated solution?

56. This solution is cooled to 10°C and the excess precipitates or settles out. The resulting solution is saturated at 10°C. How many grams of KCl precipitated out of the original solution?

57. Identify the solute in this solution.

Base your answers to questions 58 and 59 on the information below.

Consider the following data of solubility of $Na_2SO_4(s)$

Temperature (°C)	0	20	50	100
Solubility (g/100 g H_2O)	4.76	62	50.	41

58. What is the relationship between the temperature and the amount of dissolved materials?

59. Given the nature of $Na_2SO_4(s)$, what is unusual about the data given on the table?

Lesson 4: Expressions of Concentration of Solutions

Concentration of a solution indicates how much dissolved solute is in a given amount of the solution or the solvent. In this lesson, you will learn two expressions of concentration; parts per million and molarity. Most questions dealing with concentration involve calculations. Equations for calculating the concentration of a solution can be found on **Reference Table T**.

Parts Per Million: *ppm*

Parts per million expresses the concentration of a solution in number of grams of solute that is in every one million parts of the solution.

Concentration in parts per million can be calculated using Table T equation below.

$$\text{parts per million} = \frac{\text{mass of solute}}{\text{mass of solution}} \times 1\,000\,000$$

Table T

Example 3

A solution of carbon dioxide contains 0.5 gram of the solute in 500 grams of the solution. What is the concentration of the solution in parts per million?

$$\text{parts per million} = \frac{0.5\,g}{500\,g} \times 1000000 \quad \textit{numerical setup}$$

parts per million = 1000 ppm *calculated result*

1000 ppm means that every one million parts of the solution contains 1000 grams of carbon dioxide.

Molarity: *moles per liter*

Molarity (M) expresses the concentration of a solution in number of moles of solute per liter (volume) of the solution. Molarity, moles of solute, or volume of a solution can be calculated using Table T equation below.

$$\text{molarity} = \frac{\text{moles of solute}}{\text{liter of solution}}$$

Table T

Example 4: *Molarity from Moles and Liter*
What is the concentration of a solution that contains 1.4 moles of solute in 2.0 liters of the solution?

$$\text{Molarity} = \frac{\text{moles}}{\text{liter}} = \frac{1.4}{2.0} \quad \textit{setup}$$

Molarity = 0.70 M or 0.70 mol/L

calculated result

Example 5: *Moles from Molarity and Liter*
The concentration of a 2.0-liter NH_4Cl solution is 0.35 M. How many moles of the solute is in the solution.

$$\text{moles} = \text{molarity} \times \text{liter}$$

$$\text{moles} = 0.35 \times 2.0 \quad \textit{setup}$$

moles = 0.75 moles NH_4Cl

calculated result

Review Questions: Expressions of Concentration

Vocabulary: Briefly define each of the following terms.

60. Concentration   61. Parts per million   62 Molarity

63. Which unit can be used to express solution concentration?
    (1) J/mol   (3) mol/L
    (2) L/mol   (4) mol/s

64. A 0.25 liter of potassium chloride solution contains 0.75 moles of KCl. What is the concentration of this solution?
    (1) 0.33 M   (3) 3.0 M
    (2) 0.75 M   (4) 6.0 M

65. What is the concentration of a solution of KNO_3 (molecular mass = 101 g/mole) that contains 50.5 g of KNO_3 in 2.00 liters of the solution?
    (1) 25.25 M   (3) 2.00 M
    (2) 0.500 M   (4) 0.25 M

66. What is the total number of moles of solute in 2230 mL of 3.0 M NaOH solution?
    (1) 1.5 moles   (3) 3.0 moles
    (2) 6.7 moles   (4) 0.743 moles

67. How many milliliters of a 0.1 M KNO_3 solution would contain .02 moles of the solute?
    (1) 2000 mL   (3) 5000 mL
    (2) 200 mL   (4) 500 mL

68. What is the concentration in parts per million of a solution containing 333 grams of $NaNO_3$ in 700 grams of H_2O?
    (1) 2.10×10^6 ppm   (3) 4.75×10^5 ppm
    (2) 3.10×10^6 ppm   (4) 3.22×10^5 ppm

69. What is the total mass of solute in 1000 grams of a solution having a concentration of 5 parts per million?
    (1) 0.005 g   (3) 0.5 g
    (2) 0.05 g   (4) 5 g

For problems 70 through 72, show a numerical setup and the calculated result for each.

70. What is the total number of moles in 500 mL of a 3.0 M KI solution?

71. What is the total volume of a 2.0 molar HCl solution that contains 45 grams of HCl?

72. An aqueous solution has 0.007 grams of oxygen dissolved in 1000 grams of water. Calculate the dissolved oxygen concentration of this solution in parts per million. Your response should include both a correct numerical setup and calculated result.

Base your answers to questions 73 and 74 on the information below.
A student is instructed to make 0.250 liter of a 0.200 M aqueous solution of $Ca(NO_3)_2$.

73. In order to prepare the described solution in the laboratory, two quantities must be measured accurately. One of these quantities is the volume of the solution. What other quantity must be measured to prepare this solution?

74. Show a correct numerical setup for calculating the total number of moles of $Ca(NO_3)_2$ needed to make 0.250 liter of the 0.200 M calcium nitrate solution.

Lesson 5: Vapor Pressure and Effects of Solute on Properties of Water

A **vapor** is a gas form of a substance that is normally a liquid at STP. For example, water is normally a liquid at STP. Water vapor is the evaporated molecules of water in the gas phase. **Vaporization** is the process by which a liquid moves into the gas phase. Vaporization occurs at any temperature at the surface of the liquid.
Vapor pressure is the pressure exerted by evaporated particles of a liquid on the surface of the liquid.

- Vapor pressure of a liquid depends on the temperature of the liquid.

- The higher the temperature of a liquid, the higher its vapor pressure.

- Different substances have different vapor pressures at a given temperature.

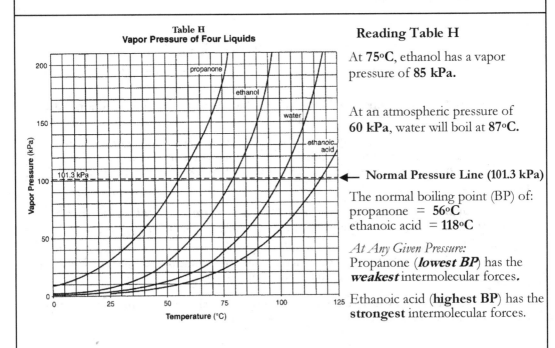

lower temp
less vapor
lower vapor
pressure

higher temp
more vapor
higher vapor
pressure

Table H shows the relationship between temperature and vapor pressure of four liquids.

Boiling Point: *Temperature that Vapor Pressure Equals Atmospheric Pressure*

Boiling is a rapid phase change of a liquid to the vapor phase.
- A liquid will boil when its vapor pressure is equal to the atmospheric pressure.

The **boiling point** of a liquid is the temperature of the liquid that will produce a vapor pressure that is the same as the atmospheric pressure. The normal atmospheric pressure is 101.3 kPa or 1 atm. The **normal boiling point** of a liquid is the temperature of the liquid that will have a vapor pressure of 101.3 kPa or 1 atm.
Table H is used to determine the boiling point of the four liquids at different pressures.

Table H
Vapor Pressure of Four Liquids

Reading Table H

At **75°C**, ethanol has a vapor pressure of **85 kPa.**

At an atmospheric pressure of **60 kPa**, water will boil at **87°C.**

◄── **Normal Pressure Line (101.3 kPa)**

The normal boiling point (BP) of:
propanone = **56°C**
ethanoic acid = **118°C**

At Any Given Pressure:
Propanone (*lowest BP*) has the **weakest** intermolecular forces.

Ethanoic acid (**highest BP**) has the **strongest** intermolecular forces.

Effects of Solutes on the Physical Properties of Water

When a solute is dissolved in water to make a solution, the physical properties of the solution will be different from those of water. In general, *a solution has a higher boiling point and a lower freezing point than pure water.*

Properties of Pure Water
Physical properties of pure water are listed below:
- Boiling point (BP) at 100°C ⎱ at standard pressure
- Freezing point (FP) at 0°C ⎰
- Vapor pressure (VP) of 101.3 kPa (at 100°C)
- No electrical conductivity (EC)

Pure water:
No dissolved particles

Changes to Physical Properties of Water
When a solute is dissolved in water to make a solution:
- The number of particles in the water is increased (↑)
      As a result:
- Boiling point of the water is elevated.   ↑BP
- Freezing point of the water is depressed.   ↓FP
- Vapor pressure of the water is lowered.   ↓VP
- Electrical conductivity of the water is increased. ↑EC

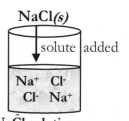

NaCl(s)

↓solute added

NaCl solution:
Contains dissolved particles

Effect of Concentration
In the diagrams below, the boiling and freezing points of three different concentrations of a KCl solution are compared.

Lowest concentration
Lowest boiling point
Highest freezing point

Highest concentration
Highest boiling point
Lowest freezing point

- **The highest concentration solution always has the highest boiling point and lowest freezing point.**

Effects of Number of Dissolved Particles
In the diagrams below, the boiling and freezing points of three different solutions are compared.

Molecular solute (CH$_3$OH)
1 dissolved particle

Lowest boiling point
Highest freezing point

Ionic solute (KCl)
2 dissolved particles

Ionic solute (CaCl$_2$)
3 dissolved particles

Highest boiling point
Lowest freezing point

- **The solution with the most dissolved particles (CaCl$_2$) always has the highest boiling point and the lowest freezing point.**

Ionic solutes will always produce more dissolved particles than molecular solutes because ionic substances are composed of two or more ions and will dissolve into those ions in water.

Molecular solutes (except for acids) only disperse in water and do not ionize.

Review Questions: Vapor Pressure and Effects of Solutes on Water

75. When the vapor pressure of a liquid equals the atmospheric pressure, the liquid will
    (1) freeze
    (2) melt
    (3) boil
    (4) condense

76. According to Reference Table H, what is the vapor pressure of propanone at 50°C?
    (1) 82 kPa
    (2) 33 KPa
    (3) 50 kPa
    (4) 101.3 kPa

77. A sample of a pure liquid is boiling at a temperature of 150°C. The atmospheric pressure is 65 kPa. The vapor pressure of the liquid is
    (1) 85 kPa
    (2) 65 kPa
    (3) 150 kPa
    (4) 101.3 kPa

78. According to Reference Table H, which sample has the highest vapor pressure?
    (1) Water at 70°C
    (2) Ethanol at 75°C
    (3) Propanone at 65°C
    (4) Ethanoic acid at 110°C

79. The normal boiling point of ethanol is closest to
    (1) 90°C
    (2) 100°C
    (3) 200°C
    (4) 80°C

80. Using your knowledge of chemistry and the information in Reference Table H, which statement concerning propanone and water at 50°C is true?
    (1) Propanone has a higher vapor pressure and stronger intermolecular forces than water.
    (2) Propanone has a higher vapor pressure and weaker intermolecular forces than water.
    (3) Propanone has a lower vapor pressure and stronger intermolecular forces than water.
    (4) Propanone has a lower vapor pressure and weaker intermolecular forces than water.

81. As a solute is added to a solvent, what happens to the freezing point and the boiling point of the solution?
    (1) The freezing point decreases and the boiling point decreases.
    (2) The freezing point decreases and the boiling point increases.
    (3) The freezing point increases and the boiling point decreases.
    (4) The freezing point increases and the boiling point increases.

82. As water is added to a 0.10 M NaCl solution, the conductivity of the solution
    (1) decreases because the concentration of the ions decreases
    (2) decreases because the concentration of the ions remains the same
    (3) increases because the concentration of the ions decreases
    (4) increases because the concentration of the ions remains the same

83. Which 1 M solution will produce the greatest increase on the boiling point of water?
    (1) $CH_3OH(aq)$
    (2) $C_2H_4(OH)_2(aq)$
    (3) $CuCl_2(aq)$
    (4) $C_6H_{12}O_6(aq)$

84. Which 0.1 M solution has the highest boiling point?
    (1) $NaCl(aq)$
    (2) $CsCl(aq)$
    (3) $LiCl(aq)$
    (4) $MgCl_2(aq)$

85. Which 1 M solution has the lowest boiling point?
    (1) $KNO_3(aq)$
    (2) $K_2SO_4(aq)$
    (3) $CaSO_4(aq)$
    (4) $C_6H_{12}O_6(aq)$

86. Which concentration of NaOH has the highest freezing temperature?
    (1) 0.1 M
    (2) 1.0 M
    (3) 1.5 M
    (4) 2.0 M

87. Which solution will freeze at the lowest temperature?
    (1) 1 M Na_2SO_4
    (2) 2 M Na_2SO_4
    (3) 1 M $NaNO_3$
    (4) 2 M $NaNO_3$

E3chemistry.com

Base your answer to the following question on the information below and on your knowledge of chemistry.

Rubbing alcohol is a product available at most pharmacies and supermarkets. One rubbing alcohol solution contains 2-propanol and water. The boiling point of 2-propanol is 82.3°C at standard pressure.

88. Determine the vapor pressure of water at a temperature equal to the boiling point of the 2-propanol.

Base your answer to the following question on the information below.

Natural gas is a mixture that includes butane, ethane, methane, and propane. Differences in boiling points can be used to separate the components of natural gas. The boiling points at standard pressure for these components are listed in the table below.

Data Table

Component of Natural Gas	Boiling Point at Standard Pressure (°C)
butane	−0.5
ethane	−88.6
methane	−161.6
propane	−42.1

89. List the four components of natural gas in order of increasing strength of intermolecular forces.

_____ _____ _____ _____
Weakest   Strongest
intermolecular   intermolecular
forces   forces

Base your answers to questions 90 through 93 on the information below.

Molar Mass and Boiling Point of Four Substances

Substance	Molar Mass (g/mol)	Boiling Point at 1 atm (K)
methane	16	112
ethane	30.	185
propane	44	231
butane	58	273

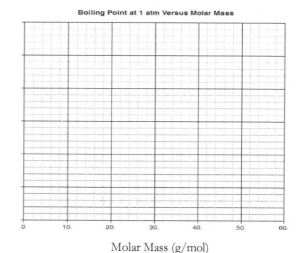

Boiling Point at 1 atm Versus Molar Mass

90. On the grid below, mark an appropriate scale on the axis labeled "Boiling Point (K)."

91. On the same grid, plot the data from the data table. Circle and connect the points.

92. Based on the data in the table, state the relationship between the boiling point at 1 atmosphere and molar mass for these four substances.

93. State, in terms of intermolecular forces, why the boiling point of propane at 1 atmosphere is lower than the boiling point of butane at 1 atmosphere.

Properties of Acids and Bases: Summary of Characteristics

Acids and bases have sets of properties that are used to identify them. Below is a summary of these properties. In the next few lessons, you will learn more about these characteristics of acids and bases.

Acids	Bases

similarities

1) Are electrolytes	1) Are electrolytes
2) Change color of indicators	2) Change color of indicators
3) React with bases in a neutralization reaction to produce water and a salt	3) React with acids in a neutralization reaction to produce water and a salt

differences

4) Produce H^+ as the only positive ion	4) Produce OH^- as the only negative ion
5) Contain more H^+ than OH^-	5) Contain more OH^- than H^+
6) When added to water, increase H^+ ion concentration of the water	6) When added to water, decrease H^+ ion concentration of the water
7) When added to water, decrease OH^- ion concentration of the water	7) When added to water, increase OH^- ion concentration of the water
8) When added to water, decrease pH	8) When added to water, increase pH
9) Have pH values less than 7	9) Have pH values greater than 7
10) Turn litmus red	10) Turn litmus blue
11) Have no effect on phenolphthalein (stays colorless)	11) Turn colorless phenolphthalein to pink
12) Taste sour	12) Taste bitter and feel slippery
13) React with certain metals to produce salt and hydrogen gas	

Neutral substances at 25°C

1) pH value of 7
2) Have equal amount of H^+ and OH^- ions

Lesson 1: Properties of Acids and Bases

What is an acid? What is a base? These questions cannot be answered with just one simple definition. Acids and bases can be defined by different theories and properties. In this lesson, you will learn how acids and bases are defined by theories and other characteristics. As you study this lesson, pay attention to similarities and differences between acids and bases.

Theories of Acids and Bases

Arrhenius Theory: *Acids Yield H⁺, Bases Yield OH⁻*

Arrhenius acids are substances that can produce H^+ (hydrogen ion or proton) as the only positive ion in solutions. Properties of acids (listed in the summary table) are due to the properties of the H^+ ions they produce. H^+ ions produced by Arrhenius acids usually combine with H_2O to become H_3O^+ in solutions. H^+ and H_3O^+ (hydronium ion) are synonymous with each other. Acids are molecular substances.

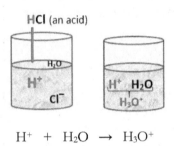

$$H^+ + H_2O \rightarrow H_3O^+$$

Formula	Name
HCl(aq)	hydrochloric acid
HNO₂(aq)	nitrous acid
HNO₃(aq)	nitric acid
H₂SO₃(aq)	sulfurous acid
H₂SO₄(aq)	sulfuric acid
H₃PO₄(aq)	phosphoric acid
H₂CO₃(aq) or CO₂(aq)	carbonic acid
CH₃COOH(aq) or HC₂H₃O₂(aq)	ethanoic acid (acetic acid)

Table K Common Acids

Arrhenius Bases are substances that can produce OH^- (hydroxide ion) as the only negative ion in solutions. Properties of bases (listed on the summary table) are due to the properties of the OH^- ions they produced. Most bases are ionic compounds.

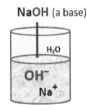

Formula	Name
NaOH(aq)	sodium hydroxide
KOH(aq)	potassium hydroxide
Ca(OH)₂(aq)	calcium hydroxide
NH₃(aq)	aqueous ammonia

Table L Common Bases

Alternate Theory: *Acids Donate H⁺, Bases Accept H⁺*

The **Brönsted-Lowry** theory defines acids and bases by their ability to donate or accept a proton (H^+, hydrogen ion) in reactions.

Brönsted-Lowry acids are substances that ***donate a proton*** in a reaction.

Brönsted-Lowry bases are substances that ***accept a proton*** in a reaction.

$H_2O \ + \ NH_3 \ \leftrightarrow \ NH_4^+ \ + \ OH^-$	H_2O is an acid because it gives up H^+ and becomes OH^- (a base).
acid base acid base	NH_3 is a base because it accepts the H^+ and becomes NH_4^+ (an acid).

         E3chemistry.com

pH Values of Acids and Bases (at 25°C): *Acids < 7, Bases > 7*

pH is a measure of the hydrogen ion (H^+) or hydronium ion (H_3O^+) concentration of a solution. A pH scale ranges in value from 0 – 14. Acids and bases can be defined by their pH values.

Acids are substances with pH values *less* than 7.

Neutral substances have pH values *equal* to 7.

Bases are substances with pH values *greater* than 7.

		Acid		**Neutral**		**Base**	
pH scale	0 --------------------------------7--------------------------------14						
		strong	weak		weak	strong	
	HCl	HNO₃	CH₃COOH	**H₂O**	NH₃	KOH	NaOH

Acid-Base Indicators: *Change Colors in an Acid or a Base*

Indicators are substances that change color in the presence of an acid or a base. Acids and bases can be defined by the changes they cause on an indicator.

Phenolphthalein is a colorless acid-base indicator.
Acids have *no effect* on phenolphthalein. It stays colorless.

Bases are substances that change colorless phenolphthalein to *pink*. Phenolphthalein is a good indicator to test for the presence of a base.

Litmus papers come in a variety of colors. When wet with an acidic or a basic solution, they will change color.
Acids are substances that will change the color of a litmus paper to *red*.

Bases are substances that will change the color of a litmus paper to *blue*.

Other common indicators are listed on **Reference Table M** shown below.

Indicator	Approximate pH Range for Color Change	Color Change
methyl orange	3.1–4.4	red to yellow
bromthymol blue	6.0–7.6	yellow to blue
phenolphthalein	8–9	colorless to pink
litmus	4.5–8.3	red to blue
bromcresol green	3.8–5.4	yellow to blue
thymol blue	8.0–9.6	yellow to blue

Reading Table M

Methyl orange will be:

Red in a solution with a pH below 3.1.

Yellow in a solution with a pH above 4.4.

Thymol blue will be:

Yellow in a solution with a pH below 8.0.

Blue in a solution with a pH above 9.6.

Relative Ion concentrations of Acids and Bases

Solutions made with water contain both H^+ and OH^- ions. A solution can be defined as acidic or basic depending on the relative amounts of H^+ and OH^- ions in the solution.

Acidic solutions contain *more* (higher concentration of) H^+ ions than OH^- ions.
The stronger the acid, the greater the H^+ ion concentration in comparison to OH^- ion concentration.

Example: HCl*(aq)*, hydrochloric acid solution, contains a higher concentration of H^+ ions than OH^- ions.

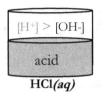

Neutral solutions and pure water contain *equal* amounts of H^+ and OH^- ions.

Example: NaCl, a neutral salt solution, and pure water contain equal concentrations of H^+ and OH^- ions.

Basic solutions contain *more* (higher concentration of) OH^- ions than H^+ ions.
The stronger the base, the greater the OH^- ion concentration in comparison to H^+ ion concentration.

Example: NaOH*(aq)*, sodium hydroxide solution, contains a higher concentration of OH^- ions than H^+ ions.

Relating pH to H^+ Concentration: *1 Value Change in pH, 10 Fold Change in H^+*

The relationship between pH and H^+ ion concentration is shown below.

$$pH = -\log [H^+]$$ or $$[H^+] = 10^{-pH}$$

When the $[H^+]$ or $[H_3O^+]$ of a solution is given as 1×10^{-x} M, the pH value = **x**

For example:

H_3O^+ Concentration	pH Value	Type of Solution
1.0×10^{-2} M	2	Acidic
1.0×10^{-8} M	8	Basic

Based on the mathematical relationship of pH to $[H^+]$, a solution with a pH of 3 has a higher concentration of H^+ ions than a solution with a pH of 4.
• The lower the pH, the greater the H^+ ion concentration of the solution.
• As H^+ ion concentration of a solution increases, pH of the solution decreases.

Difference in $[H^+]$ of two solutions = $10^{(\text{difference in pH})}$

A solution of pH 3 has 10 times more H^+ than a solution of pH 4.

Every 1 value difference in pH = 10 times (fold) difference in $[H^+]$

As the solution changes from pH 3 to pH 5, $[H^+]$ decreases 100 fold (times).

Review Questions: Properties of Acids and Bases

Vocabulary: Briefly define each of the following terms.

1. Arrhenius acid
2. Arrhenius base
3. Hydrogen ion
4. Hydronium ion
5. Hydroxide ion
6. Alternate acid theory
7. Alternate base theory
8. Acidic
9. Basic
10. Indicator
11. pH

12. Which ion is produced by all Arrhenius acids as the only positive ion in solution?
   (1) OH^+
   (2) NH_4^+
   (3) SO_4^{2+}
   (4) H_3O^+

13. Which ion is produced by a base when it is dissolved in water?
   (1) hydroxide ion
   (2) hydrogen ion
   (3) ammonium ion
   (4) hydronium ion

14. According to an "alternate theory" of acids and bases, H_2O will act as a base in a reaction if it
   (1) donates OH^- to another species in the reaction
   (2) donates H^+ to another species in the reaction
   (3) accepts OH^- from another species in the reaction
   (4) accepts H^+ from another species in the reaction

15. A solution of a base in the presence of phenolphthalein will
   (1) turn pink
   (2) turn red
   (3) turn blue
   (4) stay colorless

16. Which property do acids and bases have in common?
   (1) Both contain an equal number of OH^- ions
   (2) Both contain an equal number of H^+ ions
   (3) Both turn litmus red
   (4) Both are electrolytes

17. According to the Arrhenius theory, which list of compounds includes only acids?
   (1) HNO_3, H_2SO_4, and $C_6H_{12}O_6$
   (2) $LiOH$, HNO_3, and CH_3OH
   (3) H_2PO_4, HCO_3, and NH_4Cl
   (4) HF, H_2CO_3, and HNO_3

18. A solution of $LiOH$ is classified as
   (1) an Arrhenius base, with a pH below 7
   (2) an Arrhenius base, with a pH above 7
   (3) an Arrhenius acid, with a pH below 7
   (4) an Arrhenius acid, with a pH above 7

19. Which of these pH numbers indicates the highest level of acidity?
   (1) 7
   (2) 5
   (3) 10
   (4) 8

20. In which solution will thymol blue indicator appear blue?
   (1) 0.1 M CH_3COOH
   (2) 0.1 M HCl
   (3) 0.1 M KOH
   (4) 0.1 M H_2SO_4

21. The following results were obtained when a solution was tested with methyl orange and litmus.

   > Methyl orange......yellow
   > Litmus......... .... red

   What was the pH of the solution?
   (1) 1
   (2) 3
   (3) 5
   (4) 10

22. Which indicator, when added to a solution, changes color from yellow to blue as the pH of the solution is changed from 5.5 to 8.0?
    (1) bromcresol green   (3) methyl orange
    (2) bromthymol blue   (4) litmus

23. As NH₄OH is added to an HCl solution, the pH of the solution
    (1) decreases as the OH⁻ ion concentration increases
    (2) decreases as the OH⁻ ion concentration decreases
    (3) increases as the OH⁻ ion concentration increases
    (4) increases as the OH⁻ ion concentration decreases

24. As a solution changes from a pH of 4 to a pH of 1, there is a
    (1) 1000 fold increase in H⁺ ions   (3) 3 fold increase in H⁺ ions
    (2) 1000 fold decrease in H⁺ ions   (4) 3 fold decrease in H⁺ ions

25. Liquid A has a neutral pH and liquid B has a pH of 9. The H⁺ ion in B is
    (1) 1/10ᵗʰ as great as that of A   (3) 10 fold as great as that of A
    (2) 1/100ᵗʰ as great as that of A   (4) 100 fold as great as that of A

Base your answers to questions 26 through 28 on the information below.

Some carbonated beverages are made by forcing carbon dioxide gas into a beverage solution. When a bottle of one kind of carbonated beverage is first opened, the beverage has a pH value of 3.

26. State, in terms of the pH scale, why this beverage is classified as acidic.

27. Using Table M, identify one indicator that is yellow in a solution that has the same pH value as this beverage.

28. After the beverage bottle is left open for several hours, the hydronium ion concentration in the beverage solution decreases to 1/1000 of the original concentration. Determine the new pH of the beverage solution.

Base your answers to questions 29 through 32 on the graph below.

The graph shows the relationship between pH value and hydronium ion concentration for common aqueous solutions and mixtures.

pH Versus Hydronium Ion Concentration

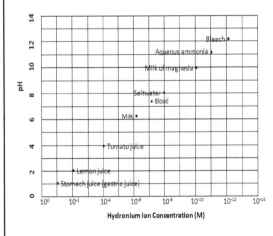

Hydronium Ion Concentration (M)

29. According to this graph, which mixture is approximately 100 times more acidic than milk of magnesia?

30. According to the graph, which mixture is approximately 10 times less acidic than aqueous ammonia?

31. What color is thymol blue when added to milk of magnesia?

32. What is the hydronium concentration of tomato juice?

Lesson 2: Reactions of Acids and Bases

Acids and bases undergo chemical reactions with other substances and with each other. In this lesson, you will learn about reactions of acids and bases.

Acid – Metal Reactions: *Produce Salt and Hydrogen Gas*

Acids react with certain metals to produce hydrogen gas and a salt.
The reaction between an acid and a metal is a single replacement reaction.

General equation: *Metal*   +   *Acid* $\rightarrow$ *Salt*   +   *Hydrogen gas*

Example reaction 1: Zn + $2HCl$ $\rightarrow$ $ZnCl_2$ + H_2

Example reaction 2: Mg + $2HNO_3$ $\rightarrow$ $Mg(NO_3)_2$ + H_2

Since the reaction is single replacement, the salt is formed by the metal replacing the hydrogen of the acid. For example, in the reaction below:

$$2Li \quad + \quad 2HBr \quad \longrightarrow \quad 2LiBr \quad + \quad H_2$$

  metal   acid   **salt**   hydrogen gas

Li (metal) replaces H of HBr (acid) to form LiBr (salt). The displaced H atoms from the acid form H_2 gas. LiBr is the correct formula for lithium bromide.

NOTE: Be sure the salt formula is correct. (Review formula writing in Topic 5).

Metals That React with Acids

Not every metal will react with acids to produce hydrogen gas and a salt. For a metal to react with an acid, the metal must be more reactive than hydrogen, H_2, on the Activity Series Table.

Metals above H_2 (Li to Pb) ***will react*** with an acid to produce H_2.

Metals below H_2 (Cu to Au) ***will not react*** with any acid.

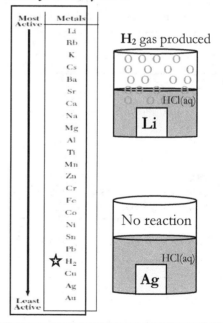

Table J – Activity Series

Neutralization Reactions: *Acid* and *Base* Produce *Salt* and *Water*

Neutralization is a chemical reaction between an acid and a base to produce *water* and a *salt.* A neutralization reaction is a double replacement reaction. During a neutralization reaction, equal moles of H^+ (of an acid) and OH^- (of a base) combine to neutralize each other.

General equation: acid   +   base $\rightarrow$ water   +   salt

Example reaction: HCl + $NaOH$ $\rightarrow$ H_2O + $NaCl$
                         hydrochloric acid   sodium hydroxide   water   sodium chloride

Net ionic equation: H^+ + OH^- $\rightarrow$ H_2O

The formula of the salt that is formed in a neutralization reaction can be determined by replacing the H of the acid with the metal of the base.
For example, in the reaction below:

$$H_2SO_4 \;\; + \;\; LiOH \;\; \rightarrow \;\; HOH \;\; + \;\; Li_2SO_4$$
             acid   base   water   salt

The **H** in H_2SO_4 is replaced by **Li** to form Li_2SO_4 salt.

Titration: *Using Solution of Known Concentration to Find Unknown Concentration*
Titration is a lab process used for determining the unknown concentration of a solution by reacting it with another solution of a known concentration. During an acid–base titration lab, a base in a buret is slowly added to an acid solution in a flask. When the number of moles of OH^- (from the base) is equal to the number of moles of H^+ (of the acid) in the flask, neutralization has occurred, and the *equivalence point* of the titration is reached. Phenolphthalein, a base indicator, is usually added to the acid beaker to indicate the endpoint. At the endpoint, the solution in the flask will turn a light-pink color indicating the acid is neutralized and the solution is slightly basic. Titration is stopped at this point. Data collected can be used to calculate the unknown concentration using one of the equations below.

Example 1: *Titration Problem When the Mole Ratio of H^+ to OH^- is 1:1*
During a titration lab, a student neutralizes 30 mL of 0.6 M HCl solution with 90 mL of NaOH solution. What is the concentration of the base?

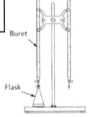

Buret

Flask

Acid – base titration set up

Table T		
$M_A \, V_A \;\; = \;\; M_B \, V_B$	Use this equation if the mole ratio of H+ (of acid) to OH- (of base) is 1:1. **For example:** A titration involving HCl and NaOH has a 1H+ : 1OH- ratio.	

$(0.6)(30) = (M_B)(90)$

$\dfrac{(0.6)(30)}{90} = M_B$ *numerical setup*

$0.2\ M \;\; = \;\; M_B$ *calculated result*

Example 2: *Titration Problem When the Ratio of H^+ to OH^- is <u>not</u> 1:1*
How many milliliters of 1.5 M H_2SO_4 are needed to exactly neutralize 20. milliliters of a 1.5 M NaOH solution?

$(M_A)(V_A)(\#H^+) = (M_B)(V_B)(\#OH^-)$	Use this equation if the mole ratio of H+ to OH- **is not** 1:1. **For examples:** A titration involving H2SO4 and NaOH has a 2H+ : 1OH- ratio. A titration involving HCl and Ca(OH)2 has a 1H+ : 2OH- ratio.

$(1.5)(V_A)(2) \;\; = \;\; (1.5)(20.)(1)$

$V_A \;\; = \;\; \dfrac{30}{3} \;\; = \;\; 3\ mL$

Review Questions: Reactions of Acids and Bases

Vocabulary: Briefly define each of the following terms.

33. Neutralization   34. Titration   35. Endpoint

36. Which substances are produced in reactions between an acid and a base?
    (1) Water and a salt
    (2) Water and hydrogen gas
    (3) A salt and hydrogen gas
    (4) A sugar and a salt

37. Which of the following metals is most likely to react with nitric acid to produce hydrogen gas?
    (1) silver
    (2) gold
    (3) chromium
    (4) copper

38. Which balanced equation represents a neutralization reaction?
    (1) $Mg + NiCl_2 \rightarrow MgCl_2 + Ni$
    (2) $2KClO_3 \rightarrow 2KCl + 3O_2$
    (3) $BaCl_2 + Cu(NO_3)_2 \rightarrow Ba(NO_3)_2 + CuCl_2$
    (4) $H_2SO_4 + 2KOH \rightarrow K_2SO_4 + 2H_2O$

39. Which equation is showing a neutralization reaction?
    (1) $H^+(aq) + OH^-(aq) \rightarrow H_2O(\ell)$
    (2) $Ag^+(aq) + I^-(aq) \rightarrow AgI(s)$
    (3) $Zn(s) + Cu^{2+}(aq) \rightarrow Zn^{2+}(aq) + Cu(s)$
    (4) $2H_2(g) + O_2(g) \rightarrow 2H_2O(\ell)$

40. In the neutralization reaction:
    $HC_2H_3O_2 + NH_4OH \rightarrow NH_4C_2H_3O_2 + H_2O$, the salt is
    (1) NH_4OH
    (2) $HC_2H_3O_2$
    (3) $NH_4C_2H_3O_2$
    (4) H_2O

41. Which two substances can react to produce H_2O and a salt with the formula K_3PO_4?
    (1) KOH and H_3PO_4
    (2) K_2O and H_3PO_4
    (3) K_3P and H_2O
    (4) KOH and H_2O

42. In a titration experiment, 20 mL of 1.0 M HCl neutralized 10 mL of NaOH solution of unknown concentration. What was the concentration of the base?
    (1) 2.5 M
    (2) 2.0 M
    (3) 1.5 M
    (4) 0.50 M

Base your answers to questions 43 and 44 on the information below.

In a titration, 3.00 M $NaOH(aq)$ was added to an Erlenmeyer flask containing 25.00 milliliters of $H_2SO_4(aq)$ and three drops of phenolphthalein until one drop of $NaOH(aq)$ turned the solution a light-pink color. The following data were collected by a student performing this titration.

Initial $NaOH(aq)$ buret reading: 14.45 milliliters
Final $NaOH(aq)$ buret reading: 32.66 milliliters

43. Show a numerical setup and the calculated result for the concentration of the acid.

44. Write a balanced equation for the neutralization reaction that occurs.

Base your answers to questions 45 through 47 on the information below.

A student titrates 60.0 mL of $HNO_3(aq)$ with 0.30 M $NaOH(aq)$. Phenolphthalein is used as the indicator. After adding 42.2 mL of $NaOH(aq)$, a color change remains for 25 seconds, and the student stops the titration.

45. What color change does phenolphthalein undergo during this titration?

46. What is the concentration of the HNO_3 that was titrated?

47. Complete the equation below for the reaction that occurs during the titration.
    $HNO_3(aq) + NaOH(aq) \rightarrow$ _____ $+$ _____

Lesson 3: Salts and Electrolytes

Salts: *Crystalline Ionic Solids*

Salts are ionic compounds composed of a positive ion (other than H^+) and a negative ion (other than OH^-).

• A salt is one of the products in acid-base neutralization reactions.

• Salts are electrolytes; they conduct electricity when liquified or dissolved in water.

• Soluble salts are better electrolytes than insoluble salts.
  Reference Table F can be used to determine soluble and insoluble salts.

Examples of some common salts are given below.

NaCl	CaSO₄	NH₄Cl
sodium chloride	*calcium sulfate*	*ammonium chloride*
metal -nonmetal	*metal - polyatomic ion*	NH_4 *- nonmetal*

Electrolytes: *Conduct Electrical Current Because of Mobile Ions. Acids, Bases and Salts.*

One property that acids, bases and salts share is that they are electrolytes.

Electrolytes are substances that can conduct electrical current when dissolved in water to make a solution.

• When dissolved, an electrolyte ionizes into its positive and negative ions.

• **Electrolytes conduct electricity because of the mobile or free moving ions in the solution**

• Acids (Table K), bases (Table L) and salts are electrolytes.

Non-electrolytes are substances that do not produce ions when dissolved, therefore they do not conduct electricity in solutions. Many molecular and organic substances (other than organic acids) are nonelectrolytes. Organic acids are discussed in Topic 10.

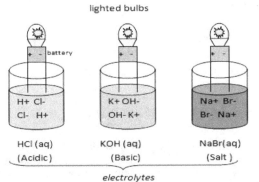

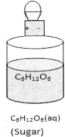

Solutions contain mobile or free-moving ions (electrical charges) that help conduct electrical current.

E3chemistry.com

Naming Acids

An acid can be classified as organic or inorganic. Inorganic acids can further be classified as binary or ternary acids.

Chemical Formulas of Acids

Inorganic acids

Chemical formulas of inorganic acids usually start with H, follow by a nonmetal or a negative polyatomic ion.

Binary acids are composed of just two nonmetal atoms: hydrogen and another nonmetal element.

Examples of binary acids: HCl   hydrochloric acid
                              H_2S hydrosulfuric acid

Ternary acids are composed of three different atoms: hydrogen and a polyatomic ion (Table E).

Examples of ternary acids: HNO_3 nitric acid
                            H_2SO_3 sulfurous acid

Organic acids

Chemical formulas of organic acids usually end with –*COOH*.

Examples of organic acids: CH_3COOH ethanoic (acetic) acid
                          $HCOOH$ methanoic acid

Chemical Names of Inorganic Acids

Chemical names of acids vary depending if an acid is a binary, ternary, or an organic acid.

Binary acids have names that begin with **hydro-** and end with –**ic**.
The name of a binary acid is formed by dropping the –gen of hydrogen and modifying the nonmetal ending to –ic.

    Ex. Hydro*gen* chlor*ide*   Hydro*gen* sul*fide*
           Hydrochlor*ic* acid   Hydrosulfur*ic* acid

Ternary acids have names that reflect only the name of the polyatomic ion (See Table E).

If an acid formula contains a polyatomic ion ending with –**ate**, the name ending of the acid is –**ic.**

$$H_2SO_4$$

ion: sulf**ate**
acid : sulfur**ic acid**

If an acid formula contains a polyatomic ion ending with –**ite**, the name ending of the acid is –**ous.**

$$H_2SO_3$$

ion: sulf**ite**
acid: sulfur**ous acid**

Review Questions: Salts and Electrolytes

Vocabulary: Briefly define each of the following terms.

48. Salt   49. Electrolyte

50. Which list of compounds includes only salts?
    (1) HNO_3, $NaNO_3$, and $Ca(NO_3)_2$
    (2) CH_3OH, $NaOH$, and $NaCl$
    (3) C_2H_5OH, CH_3COOH, and $CaCl_2$
    (4) $Ba(NO_3)_2$, Na_2SO_4, and $MgCl_2$

51. A substance that conducts electrical current when dissolved in water is called
    (1) an isotope   (3) a metalloid
    (2) a catalyst   (4) an electrolyte

52. A water solution conducts electrical current because the solution contains mobile
    (1) atoms   (3) molecules
    (2) ions   (4) electrons

53. Which list contains types of substances that are electrolytes?
    (1) Soluble salts, sugar, and acids.   (3) Soluble salts, acids and bases.
    (2) Soluble salts, alcohols, and bases.   (4) Acids, bases, and alcohols.

54. Which 0.1 M solution contains electrolytes?
    (1) $C_6H_{12}O_6(aq)$ (3) $CH_3COOH(aq)$
    (2) $CH_3OH(aq)$ (4) $CH_3OCH_3(aq)$

55. An example of a nonelectrolyte is
    (1) $C_{12}H_{22}O_{11}(aq)$ (3) $NaCl(aq)$
    (2) $K_2SO_4(aq)$ (4) $HCl(aq)$

56. According to Reference Table F, which salt solution would be the best electrolyte?
    (1) $AgCl(aq)$ (3) $NH_4Cl(aq)$
    (2) $PbCl_2(aq)$ (4) $HgCl_2(aq)$

Base your answers to questions 57 through 62 on the information and diagrams below.

Four beakers each contains 100 milliliters of aqueous solution of equal concentration at 25°C.

57. Which solutions contain electrolytes?

58. Which solution has the lowest pH?

59. Which solution is most likely to react with an Arrhenius acid to form a salt and water?

60. Which solution has the lowest freezing point?

61. What causes some aqueous solutions to have a low pH?

62. Explain how some aqueous solutions can conduct electrical current.

63. Name the following acids.

H_2Se $HClO$ HNO_2

HI $H_2C_2O_4$

Additional Materials

Salt Hydrolysis

Hydrolysis is the process of using water to break down a compound into its ions. The resulting solution can be acidic, basic, or neutral.

Salt is a product in neutralization reactions as shown below.

$$\text{Acid} + \text{Base} \rightarrow \text{Salt} + \text{water}$$

The strength of the acid and base that form the salt can be used to predict the type of solution that will form when the salt is dissolved in water.

$$\underset{\textbf{strong acid}}{\text{HBr}} + \underset{\text{weak base}}{\text{NH}_4\text{OH}} \rightarrow \underset{\textbf{\textit{acidic salt}}}{\text{NH}_4\text{Br}} + \text{H}_2\text{O}$$

A solution of **NH₄Br** will be **acidic.**

$$\underset{\text{weak acid}}{\text{H}_2\text{CO}_3} + \underset{\textbf{strong base}}{\text{NaOH}} \rightarrow \underset{\textbf{\textit{basic salt}}}{\text{Na}_2\text{CO}_3} + 2\text{H}_2\text{O}$$

A solution of **Na₂CO₃** will be **basic.**

$$\underset{\textbf{strong acid}}{\text{HCl}} + \underset{\textbf{strong base}}{\text{KOH}} \rightarrow \underset{\textbf{\textit{neutral salt}}}{\text{KCl}} + \text{H}_2\text{O}$$

A solution of **KCl** will be **neutral.**

Strong acids include: HI, HBr, HCl, HNO_3, H_2SO_4, $HClO_3$ and $HClO_4$
These acids completely dissociate (ionize) in water to produce large $[H^+]$.
All other acids are considered weak acids.

Strong bases include: $LiOH$, $NaOH$, KOH, $RbOH$, $CsOH$, $Ca(OH)_2$, and $Ba(OH)_2$.
These bases completely dissociate (ionize) in water to produce large $[OH^-$ ions$]$.
All other bases are considered weak bases.

Conjugate Acid-Base Pairs

In some acid-base reactions, protons (H^+) are donated and accepted by species in the reactions.

Brönsted-Lowry acids are species that donate protons.
Brönsted-Lowry bases are species that accept protons.

When Brönsted-Lowry acids and bases react, conjugate species are produced as shown below.

$$\underset{acid}{\text{H}_2\text{S}} + \underset{base}{\text{H}_2\text{O}} \leftrightarrow \underset{\substack{conjugate \\ acid}}{\text{H}_3\text{O}^+} + \underset{\substack{conjugate \\ base}}{\text{HS}^-}$$

In the above reaction:
H₂S is an acid because it donates (gives up) an H^+ and becomes **HS⁻ (a base).**
H₂O is a base because it accepts the H^+ and becomes **H₃O⁺ (an acid).**

Two conjugate **acid – base** pairs can be determined from the equation.

conjugate pair 1: H₂S and HS⁻

conjugate pair 2: H₃O⁺ and H₂O

TIP: Each conjugate acid-base pair contains similar species that differ only by one H+ ion. The acid in each pair contains one more H+ ion than the base.

Ionization Constant of Water at 25°C.

Water is composed of H^+ and OH^- ions. Any sample of pure water contains equal concentrations of both ions.

$[H^+] = [OH^-] = 1.0 \times 10^{-7}$ M in pure water

Ionization constant of water, K_w, is 1.0 $\times$ 10^{-14} . This value is equal to the product of the concentrations of H^+ and OH^- ions as shown below.

$$K_w = [H^+] \times [OH^-] = [1.0 \times 10^{-7}] \times [1.0 \times 10^{-7}] = \textbf{1.0 } \times \textbf{ 10}^{-14}$$

Relating H^+, OH^-, pH and pOH

The same relationship shown above for water also exists in acidic and basic solutions. However, unlike water:

> Acidic solutions have a higher concentration of H^+ than OH^- .
> Basic solutions have a higher concentration of OH^- than H^+.

If the concentration of one of the ions in a solution is known, you can calculate the concentration of the other ion using the relationship:

$$[H^+] \times [OH^-] = 1.0 \times 10^{-14} \qquad H_3O^+ \text{ is sometimes used in place of } H^+$$

The relationships between the ions and pH and pOH are as follows:

$$pH = - \log[H^+]$$
$$pOH = - \log[OH^-]$$
$$pH + pOH = 14$$

Example 3	*Example 4*
A solution has $[H^+]$ of 1.0×10^{-5} M.	A solution has $[OH^-]$ of 1.7×10^{-3} M
a) *Calculate the [OH-] of the solution.*	a) *Calculate the [H₃O⁺] of the solution*
$$[OH\text{-}] = \frac{1.0 \times 10^{-14}}{1.0 \times 10^{-5}} = \textbf{1.0} \times \textbf{10}^{-9}$$	$$[H_3O^+] = \frac{1.0 \times 10^{-14}}{1.7 \times 10^{-3}} = \textbf{5.88} \times \textbf{10}^{-12} \textbf{ M}$$
b) *Calculate the pH of the solution* $$pH = \text{-}\log[H^+] = \text{-}\log[1.0 \times 10^{-5}] = \textbf{5}$$	b) *Calculate the pH of the solution* $$pH = \text{-}\log[5.88 \times 10^{-12}] = \textbf{11.23}$$
c) *Calculate the pOH of the solution* $$pOH = 14 \text{ - } pH = 14 - 5 = \textbf{9}$$	c) *Calculate the pOH of the solution* $$pOH = \text{-}\log[1.7 \times 10^{-3}] = \textbf{2.77}$$

Practice Questions on Additional Materials

64. In the reaction: $H_2PO_4^- + H_2O \leftrightarrow H_3PO_4 + OH^-$
which pair represents an acid and its conjugate base?
(1) H_2O and $H_2PO_4^-$ (3) H_3PO_4 and OH^-
(2) H_2O and H_3PO_4 (4) H_3PO_4 and $H_2PO_4^-$

65. Given the reaction: $HSO_4^- + H_2O \leftrightarrow H_3O^+ + SO_4^{2-}$
Which is a correct conjugate acid-base pair?

(1) HSO_4^- and SO_4^{2-} (3) SO_4^{2-} and H_3O^+
(2) HSO_4^- and H_2O (4) SO_4^{2-} and H_2O

66. What is the conjugate base of NH_3?
(1) NH_4^+ (3) NO_3^-
(2) NH_2^- (4) NO_2^-

67. Hydrolysis of which salt will produce an acidic solution?
(1) $NaC_2H_3O_2$ (3) NH_4NO_3
(2) Li_2CO_3 (4) K_3PO_4

68. Hydrolysis of which salt will produce a solution with a pH close to 11.
(1) $NaNO_3$ (3) $(NH_4)_2SO_4$
(2) K_3PO_4 (4) $NaCl$

69. The $[OH^-]$ of a solution is 1.0×10^{-6} M. At 298 K and 1 atm, the product of $[H_3O^+][OH^-]$ is

(1) 1.0×10^{-2} (3) 1.0×10^{-8}
(2) 1.0×10^{-6} (4) 1.0×10^{-14}

70. A solution with a H^+ concentration of 1.0×10^{-12} M will also have a OH^- concentration of
(1) 1.0×10^{-12} M   (3) 1.0×10^{-26} M
(2) 1.0×10^{-14} M   (4) 1.0×10^{-2} M

71. What is the pH of a solution with a hydroxide concentration of 1.0×10^{-10} ?
(1) 10   (3) 14
(2) 4   (4) 1

72. Below, H^+ concentrations of three different solutions are given.
Determine pH, $[OH^-]$, and pOH of each solution.

                pH $[OH^-]$ pOH

a) 1.0×10^{-12} M H^+

b) 2.0×10^{-12} M H^+

c) 3.76×10^{-4} M H^+

73. Below, pH values of three different solutions are given.
Determine $[H_3O^+]$, $[OH^-]$, and pOH of each solution.

             $[H_3O^+]$ $[OH^-]$ pOH

a)   pH = 3

b)   pH = 5.9

c)   pH = 9.8

Lesson 1: Kinetics and Reaction Rate

Kinetics is the study of rates and mechanisms of chemical reactions.
Rate is the speed at which a reaction is taking place.
A **mechanism** is a series of steps that lead to the final products of a reaction.

In this lesson, you will learn about the rate of chemical reactions and factors that affect reaction rate.

Rate of Reaction: *Depends on Frequency of Effective Collisions*
Rate of a reaction is the speed at which a chemical reaction or physical change occurs.

In general:
• a reaction rate is increased when the number or frequency of effective collisions between reacting particles is increased.

Collision theory states that for a chemical reaction to occur between reactants, there ***must be effective collisions*** between the reacting particles.

Effective collisions occur when reacting particles collide with *sufficient kinetic energy* and at the *proper orientation or angle.*

• Rate of a reaction depends on frequency of (how often) effective collisions occur between particles.

• Any factor that can change the frequency of effective collisions between reacting particles will change the rate of that reaction.

The diagrams below show the difference between effective and ineffective collisions.

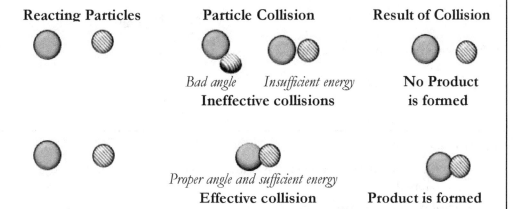

Reacting Particles	Particle Collision	Result of Collision
	Bad angle *Insufficient energy* **Ineffective collisions**	**No Product is formed**
	Proper angle and sufficient energy **Effective collision**	**Product is formed**

Activation Energy: *Energy to Start a Reaction*

Activation energy is the energy needed to start a chemical reaction. All chemical reactions, both endothermic and exothermic, require some amount of activation energy. Any factor that can change the amount of activation energy for a reaction will change the rate of that reaction.

Catalyst: *Lowers Activation Energy* and *Increases Rate*

A catalyst is any substance that increases the speed (rate) of a reaction by lowering the activation energy. A catalyst in a reaction provides an alternate (lower activation energy pathway) so a reaction can occur faster.

Factors that Increase Reaction Rate and Why

Increasing **concentration** of reactants
  ↑ number of reacting particles
  ↑ frequency of effective collisions
    between reacting particles

higher concentration, faster reaction

Increasing **pressure** on a gaseous reaction
  ↓ volume of gaseous reactants
  ↑ concentration of reactants
  ↑ frequency of effective collisions

higher pressure, faster reaction

Increasing **temperature** of reactants
  ↑ kinetic energy (speed) of particles
  ↑ frequency and effectiveness of collisions

40°C   60°C
higher temperature, faster reaction

Increasing **surface area** of a reacting solid
  ↑ in exposed area for a reaction
  ↑ frequency of effective collisions

Chunk of zinc   Pieces of zinc   Powder (ground up) zinc

least surface area slowest reaction   most surface area, fastest reaction with acid

Addition of a catalyst to a reaction
  ↓ activation energy.
    Provides alternate pathway for a
    reaction to occur faster

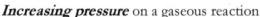

Nature of Reactants:

Reactions of ionic solutions are very fast (almost instantaneous) because no bond breaking is required.

Reactions of molecular substances are slow because reactions require breaking of strong covalent bonds. High activation energy is usually required for reactions involving molecular substances.

Some metals, because of their nature, react faster than others in solutions.

Review Questions: Kinetics and Reaction Rate

Vocabulary: Briefly define each of the following terms.
1. Kinetics   2. Rate   3. Mechanism   4. Collision theory   5. Effective collision
6. Catalyst   7. Activation energy

8. In order for any chemical reaction to occur, there must always be
   (1) a bond that breaks in a reactant particle
   (2) a reacting particle with a high charge
   (3) effective collisions between reacting particles
   (4) a catalyst

9. Two particles collide with proper orientation. The collisions will be effective if the particles have
   (1) high activation energy   (3) sufficient potential energy
   (2) high electronegativity   (4) sufficient kinetic energy

10. Which conditions will increase the rate of a chemical reaction?
   (1) Decreased temperature and decreased concentration.
   (2) Decreased temperature and increased concentration.
   (3) Increased temperature and decreased concentration.
   (4) Increased temperature and increased concentration.

11. Increasing temperature speeds up a reaction by increasing
   (1) the effectiveness of collisions, only
   (2) the frequency of collisions, only
   (3) both the effectiveness and the frequency of the collisions
   (4) neither the effectiveness nor the frequency of the collisions

12. When a catalyst is added to a reaction, the reaction rate is increased because the catalyst
   (1) increases activation energy
   (2) decreases activation energy
   (3) increases potential energy of the reactants
   (4) decreases potential energy of the reactants

13. Given the reaction:
$$Mg(s) + 2HNO_3(aq) \rightarrow Mg(NO_3)_2(aq) + H_2(g)$$
   At which temperature will the reaction occur at the greatest rate?
   (1) 10°C   (3) 50°C
   (2) 30°C   (4) 70°C

14. Given the reaction
$$CuSO_4(s) \rightarrow Cu^{2+}(aq) + SO_4^{2-}(aq)$$
   The $CuSO_4(s)$ dissolves more rapidly when it is powdered because the increase in surface area allows for
   (1) increased exposure of solute to solvent
   (2) decreased exposure of solute to solvent
   (3) increased solute solubility
   (4) decreased solute solubility

15. Based on the nature of the reactants in each equation, which reaction at 25°C will occur at the fastest rate?
   (1) $KI(aq) + AgNO_3(aq) \rightarrow AgI(s) + KNO_3(aq)$
   (2) $C(s) + O_2(g) \rightarrow CO(g)$
   (3) $2SO_2(g) + O_2(g) \rightarrow 2SO_3(g)$
   (4) $NH_3(g) + HCl(g) \rightarrow NH_4Cl(s)$

Base your answers to questions 16 through 19 on the information below.

An investigation was conducted to study the effect of the concentration of a reactant on the total time needed to complete a chemical reaction. Four trials of the same reaction were performed. In each trial, the initial concentration of the reactant was different. The time needed for the chemical reaction to be completed was measured. The data for each of the four trials are shown in the data table to the right.

Reactant Concentration and Reaction Time

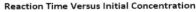

Trial	Initial Concentration (M)	Reaction Time (s)
1	0.020	11
2	0.015	14
3	0.010	23
4	0.005	58

Reaction Time Versus Initial Concentration

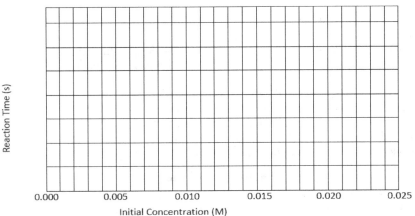

16. On the grid, mark an **appropriate scale on the axis labeled** " Reaction Time *(s)*." An appropriate scale is one that allows a trend to be seen.

17. On the same grid, plot the data from the table. Circle and connect the points.

18. State the effect of the concentration of the reactant on the rate of the chemical reaction.

19. In a different experiment involving the same reaction, it was found that an increase in temperature increased the rate of the reaction. Explain this result in terms of collision theory.

Base your answers to questions 20 through 22 on the information below.

Given the reaction:

$$Zn(s) + 2HCl(aq) \rightarrow H_2(g) + ZnCl_2(aq)$$

20. Describe the effect of increasing the concentration of HCl(aq) on the reaction rate and justify your response in terms of *collision theory*.

21. Identify one other variable that might affect the rate and should be held constant during this investigation.

22. Identify the independent variable in this investigation.

Lesson 2: Energy and Chemical Reactions

Every chemical substance contains some amount of energy that is stored within the bonds of the substance. During a chemical reaction, substances absorb and release energy as bonds are broken and formed, respectively.

In this lesson, you will learn about energy in chemical reactions.

Heat of Reaction (ΔH): *Difference in Energy of Product and Reactants*

Potential energy is the stored energy in bonds of chemical substances. The amount of potential energy in a substance depends on its *structure* and *composition*.

Potential energy of reactants is the amount of energy stored in the bonds of the reactants. Reactants are substances that are present at the start of a chemical reaction.

Potential energy of products is the amount of energy stored in the bonds of the products. Products are substances that remain at the end of a chemical reaction.

Heat of reaction (ΔH) is the overall energy absorbed or released during a reaction.
• Heat of reaction is the difference between the potential energy of the products and of the reactants.

$$\Delta H \quad = \quad \textbf{Energy of Products} \quad - \quad \textbf{Energy of Reactants}$$

The heat of reaction (ΔH) can be negative or positive.

Negative heat of reaction ($-\Delta H$) means that:

• The products of the reaction have *less energy* than the reactants.

• The reaction is exothermic, which releases heat.

Positive heat of reaction ($+\Delta H$) means that:

• The products of the reaction have *more energy* than the reactants.

• The reaction is endothermic, which absorbs heat.

Exothermic and Endothermic Reactions

Some chemical reactions absorb energy while others release energy. Reactions that release energy are exothermic. Reactions that absorb energy are endothermic. Since most chemical and physical processes occur in some form of a liquid or aqueous environment, measuring the temperature of the liquid before and after a reaction is one way to tell if a reaction is exothermic or endothermic. If heat is released during a reaction, the temperature of the liquid will be higher after the reaction.

If heat if absorbed during a reaction, the temperature of the liquid will be lower after the reaction.

Exothermic Reactions: *Release Energy*

Exothermic reactions occur when the products that are formed contain less energy than the reactants. Since the products have less energy than the reactants, the reactants lost (or released) energy during the chemical change. When heat energy is released into the liquid or aqueous surroundings, the temperature of the surroundings increases.

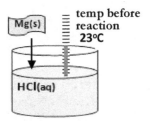

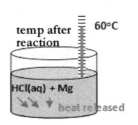

The heat of reaction is always negative (-ΔH) for all exothermic reactions.

Example equation of an exothermic reaction:

$Mg + 2HCl \rightarrow MgCl_2 + H_2 +$ **Energy**

Exothermic Reactions: *Absorb Energy*

Endothermic reactions occur when the products that are formed contain more energy than the reactants. Since the products have more energy than the reactants, the reactants gained (or absorbed) energy during the chemical change. When heat energy is absorbed from the liquid or aqueous surroundings, the temperature of the surroundings decreases.

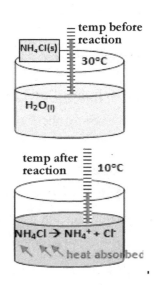

The heat of reaction is always positive (+ΔH) for all endothermic reactions.

Example equation of an endothermic reaction:

$NH_4Cl(s) +$ **Energy** $\rightarrow NH_4^+(aq) + Cl^-(aq)$

Heats of Reaction (ΔH): Reference Table I

Reference Table I (below) lists equations for selected physical and chemical changes and their heat of reaction, ΔH, values.

Reading Table I

Table I
Heats of Reaction at 101.3 kPa and 298 K

Reaction	ΔH (kJ)*
$CH_4(g) + 2O_2(g) \longrightarrow CO_2(g) + 2H_2O(\ell)$	–890.4
$C_3H_8(g) + 5O_2(g) \longrightarrow 3CO_2(g) + 4H_2O(\ell)$	–2219.2
$2C_8H_{18}(\ell) + 25O_2(g) \longrightarrow 16CO_2(g) + 18H_2O(\ell)$	–10943
$2CH_3OH(\ell) + 3O_2(g) \longrightarrow 2CO_2(g) + 4H_2O(\ell)$	–1452
$C_2H_5OH(\ell) + 3O_2(g) \longrightarrow 2CO_2(g) + 3H_2O(\ell)$	–1367
$C_6H_{12}O_6(s) + 6O_2(g) \longrightarrow 6CO_2(g) + 6H_2O(\ell)$	–2804
$2CO(g) + O_2(g) \longrightarrow 2CO_2(g)$	–566.0
$C(s) + O_2(g) \longrightarrow CO_2(g)$	–393.5
$4Al(s) + 3O_2(g) \longrightarrow 2Al_2O_3(s)$	–3351
$N_2(g) + O_2(g) \longrightarrow 2NO(g)$	+182.6
$N_2(g) + 2O_2(g) \longrightarrow 2NO_2(g)$	+66.4
$2H_2(g) + O_2(g) \longrightarrow 2H_2O(g)$	–483.6
$2H_2(g) + O_2(g) \longrightarrow 2H_2O(\ell)$	–571.6
$N_2(g) + 3H_2(g) \longrightarrow 2NH_3(g)$	–91.8
$2C(s) + 3H_2(g) \longrightarrow C_2H_6(g)$	–84.0
$2C(s) + 2H_2(g) \longrightarrow C_2H_4(g)$	+52.4
$2C(s) + H_2(g) \longrightarrow C_2H_2(g)$	+227.4
$H_2(g) + I_2(g) \longrightarrow 2HI(g)$	+53.0
$KNO_3(s) \xrightarrow{H_2O} K^+(aq) + NO_3^-(aq)$	+34.89
$NaOH(s) \xrightarrow{H_2O} Na^+(aq) + OH^-(aq)$	–44.51
$NH_4Cl(s) \xrightarrow{H_2O} NH_4^+(aq) + Cl^-(aq)$	+14.78
$NH_4NO_3(s) \xrightarrow{H_2O} NH_4^+(aq) + NO_3^-(aq)$	+25.69
$NaCl(s) \xrightarrow{H_2O} Na^+(aq) + Cl^-(aq)$	+3.88
$LiBr(s) \xrightarrow{H_2O} Li^+(aq) + Br^-(aq)$	–48.83
$H^+(aq) + OH^-(aq) \longrightarrow H_2O(\ell)$	–55.8

*Minus sign indicates an exothermic reaction.

★ **Equation with -ΔH (exothermic)**

$$2C(s) + 3H_2(g) \rightarrow C_2H_6(g)$$
$$\Delta H = -84 \text{ kJ}$$

According to the equation and ΔH:

The formation of 1 mole of C_2H_6, ethane, releases 84 kJ (kilojoules) of heat energy.

The formation of 2 moles of C_2H_6 will release 2(84 kJ) or 168 kJ of heat energy.

The product of this reaction has less energy than the reactants.

● **Equation with +ΔH (endothermic)**

$$NH_4Cl(s) \rightarrow NH_4^+(aq) + Cl^-(aq)$$
$$\Delta H = +14.78 \text{ kJ}$$

According to the equation and ΔH:

The dissolving of 1 mole of NH_4Cl, ammonium chloride, absorbs 14.78 kJ of heat energy.

The dissolving of 0.5 moles of NH_4Cl will absorb 0.5(14.78 kJ) or 7.39 kJ of heat energy.

The products of this process have more energy than the reactant.

Exothermic and Endothermic: Summary Table

Process	Potential Energy of Reactants	Potential Energy of Products	Energy Change	Temperature of Surroundings	Heat of reaction (ΔH)
Exothermic	Higher	Lower	Released	Increases	Negative (-ΔH)
Endothermic	Lower	Higher	Absorbed	Decreases	Positive (+ΔH)

Potential Energy Diagrams: *Show Energy Absorbed or Released*

A **potential energy diagram** show changes in the heat energy of substances over the course of a reaction. To understand potential energy diagrams, it is important to review components of a chemical reaction. These components are represented on all potential energy diagrams.

Consider this equation:

$$A \; + \; B_2 \longrightarrow ABB \longrightarrow AB \; + \; B$$

Reactants   *Activated*   *Products*
                           complex

Note the following three substances in the equation:

Reactants (A and B_2 are substances that are present at the beginning of the reaction.

Products (AB and B) are substances formed at the end of the reaction.

The **activated complex** (ABB) is a high energy intermediate substance that is formed during the reaction. Because of its high energy, an activated complex is very unstable and will always break down or rearrange to form more stable products. An activated complex is not usually shown in a reaction equation. However, for a potential energy diagram to be accurately drawn for any reaction, an activated complex must be represented on the diagram.

Exothermic Diagram (see above equation)

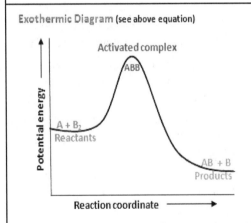

Endothermic Diagram

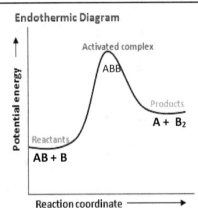

Since this is exothermic, the products are at a lower energy state than the reactants.

Since this is endothermic, the products are at a higher energy state than the reactants.

Energy Measurements on Potential Energy Diagrams

The potential energy diagrams below show the important energy measurements. The left diagram shows measurements for a reaction that is uncatalyzed. The right diagram shows energy measurements for the same reaction with a catalyst added. A catalyst speeds up a reaction by lowering the activation energy. In the diagram on the right, certain energy measurements for the reaction are lower with a catalyst.

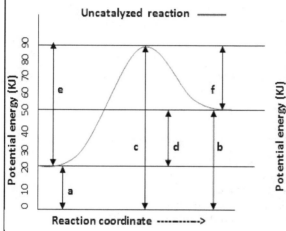
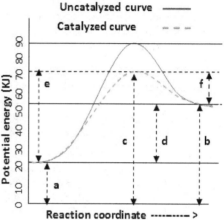

NOTE the following about each diagram:
The y axis is potential energy. The x axis is the reaction coordinate (or progress of reaction). The curves represent potential energy of substances that are present at different times over the course of the reaction, starting with reactants and ending with products.

Potential energy measurements for three substances are shown with arrows a, b and c.
These arrows are always drawn from the bottom of the diagram.

  (a) Potential energy of the reactants   (no change with catalyst)

  (b) Potential energy of the products   (no change with catalyst)

  (c) Potential energy of the activated complex   (lower with catalyst)

Differences of two potential energies are shown with arrows d, e and f.
These arrows are always drawn between two energies of the diagram.

  (d) Heat of reaction, ΔH (b – a)   (no change with catalyst)

  (e) Activation energy for forward reaction (c – a)   (lower with catalyst)

  (f) Activation energy for reverse reaction (c – b)   (lower with catalyst)

Review Questions: Energy and Chemical Reactions

Vocabulary: Briefly define each of the following terms.

23. Heat of reaction   24. Potential energy diagram

25. Which best describes all endothermic reactions?
    (1) They always release heat.   (3) They always occur spontaneously.
    (2) They always absorb heat.   (4) They never occur spontaneously.

26. The heat of reaction (ΔH) is equal to
    (1) Heat of products $-$ Heat of reactants   (3) Heat of products x Heat of reactants
    (2) Heat of products $+$ Heat of reactants   (4) Heat of products $\div$ Heat of reactants

27. When a substance is dissolved in water, the temperature of the water increases.
    This process is best described as
    (1) endothermic, with a release of energy
    (2) endothermic, with an absorption of energy
    (3) exothermic, with a release of energy
    (4) exothermic, with an absorption of energy

28. Solid X and solid Y were dissolved in separate 100 mL beakers of water. The water
    temperatures were recorded as shown in the table below.

	Salt X	Salt Y
Initial water temperature	40.3°C	40.3°C
Final water temperature	34.5°C	46.1°C

    Which statement is the best conclusion from the above information?
    (1) The dissolving of only Salt X was exothermic.
    (2) The dissolving of only Salt Y was endothermic.
    (3) The dissolving of both Salt X and Salt Y was exothermic.
    (4) The dissolving of Salt X was endothermic and the dissolving of Salt Y was exothermic.

29. A thermometer is in a beaker of water. Which statement best explains why the
    thermometer reading initially increases when LiBr(s) is dissolved in the water?
    (1) The dissolving of the LiBr(s) is endothermic, so energy is gained by the water.
    (2) The dissolving of the LiBr(s) is exothermic, so energy is gained by the water.
    (3) The dissolving of the LiBr(s) is endothermic, so energy is lost by the water.
    (4) The dissolving of the LiBr(s) is exothermic, so energy is lost by the water.

30. Given the reaction
    $$H_2 \ + \ Br_2 \ \rightarrow \ 2HBr \ + \ 73 \ kJ$$
    The heat of reaction, ΔH, is
    (1) +73, because energy is released   (3) -73, because energy is released.
    (2) +73, because energy is absorbed   (4) -73, because energy is absorbed

31. According to Reference Table I, which substance is formed by a reaction that
    absorbs heat energy?
    (1) $HI(g)$ (3) $NH_3(g)$
    (2) $H_2O(\ell)$ (4) $H_2O(g)$

32. The dissolving of which salt is accompanied by the release of heat?
    (1) Ammonium chloride   (3) Potassium nitrate
    (2) Lithium bromide   (4) Ammonium nitrate

33. In the reaction:
    $$CO(g) \ + \ O_2(g) \ \rightarrow \ 2CO_2(g) \ + \ 566 \ kJ$$
    Which is true of the heat of formation of $CO_2(g)$?
    (1) $\Delta H = \ + 283 \ kJ \ /mole$ (3) $\Delta H = \ + 566 \ kJ \ /mole$
    (2) $\Delta H = \ - 283 \ kJ \ /mole$ (4) $\Delta H = \ - 566 \ kJ \ /mole$

Answer questions 34 and 35 based on the diagram below.

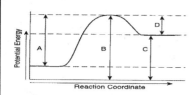

34. Energy of the activated complex is measured by which arrow in the potential energy diagram on the left?
    (1) A   (2) B   (3) C   (4) D

35. Which arrow represents the activation energy for the reverse reaction?
    (1) A   (2) B   (3) C   (4) D

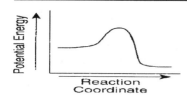

36. According to Reference Table I, which reaction could be represented by the energy diagram on the left?
    (1) $2C(s) + 3H_2(g) \rightarrow C_2H_6(g)$
    (2) $2C(s) + 2H_2(g) \rightarrow C_2H_4(g)$
    (3) $N_2(g) + O_2(g) \rightarrow 2NO(g)$
    (4) $NH_4Cl(s) \rightarrow NH_4^+(aq) + Cl^-(aq)$

37. The potential energy diagram for a chemical reaction is shown below.

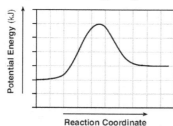

Each interval on the axis labeled "Potential Energy (kJ)" represents 40 kilojoules.
What is the activation energy for the reverse reaction?
    (1) +40 kJ   (3) +120 kJ
    (2) +60 kJ   (4) +160 kJ

Base your answers to questions 38 and 39 on the potential energy diagram below.

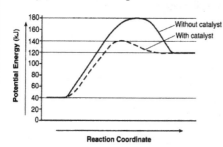

38. What is the heat of reaction with the catalyst?

39. Explain, in terms of the function of a catalyst, why the curves on the potential energy diagram for the catalyzed and uncatalyzed reactions are different.

Base your answers to questions 40 and 41 on the information below.

Given the reaction:

$$2NO_2(g) + 7H_2(g) \rightarrow 2NH_3(g) + 4H_2O(g) + 1127 \text{ kJ}$$

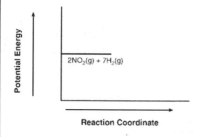

40. On the diagram to the left, complete the potential energy diagram for this reaction.

41. Determine the total amount of energy released when 0.5 moles of NO_2 is completely reacted with hydrogen.

Lesson 3: Entropy

Entropy: *Randomness and Disorder of Particles*

Particles (atoms, molecules, or ions) of a substance are arranged and organized differently in the solid, liquid, and gas states. **Entropy** is a measure of the randomness or disorder of particles in a substance or system. Entropy is relative, meaning that a disorder of one system is typically described in comparison to another system.

Comparing Entropy Between Phases

Lowest entropy: Solid or Lowest temperature
Highest entropy: Gas or Highest temperature
• Particles are more organized and less random in a solid than in a liquid, gas, or an aqueous solution.

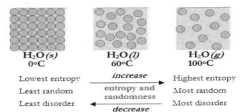

Change in Entropy

• Systems in nature tend to go in the direction of *higher entropy* and *lower energy.*

Entropy increases when a change leads to particles that are less organized or more random.

Entropy increases in each of the physical and chemical changes listed below

• A solid *melting* to liquid or liquid *evaporating* to gas. **Ex.** $Au(s) \rightarrow Au(l)$
• A solid *dissolving* in water to make a solution. **Ex:** $NaCl(s) \rightarrow NaCl(aq)$
• The temperature of a substance increasing. **Ex:** $Br_2(\ell)$ at 30°C $\rightarrow Br_2(\ell)$ at 45°C

• A solid reactant producing gaseous products. **Ex.** $2Al_2O_3(s) \rightarrow 4Al(s) + 3O_2(g)$
• A compound reactant producing free elements products.
• Fewer moles of reactants producing greater moles of products.

Entropy decreases **if any of the above changes is reversed**

42. Entropy measures which of the following about a chemical system?
    (1) Activation energy of the system.   (3) Energy change of the system.
    (2) Intermolecular forces of the system.   (4) Disorder of the system.

43. A system is most likely to undergo a reaction if the system after the reaction has
    (1) lower energy and lower entropy   (3) higher energy and higher entropy
    (2) lower energy and higher entropy   (4) higher energy and lower entropy

44. Which process is accompanied by a decrease in entropy?
    (1) Evaporation of water   (3) Melting of ice
    (2) Condensing of steam   (4) Sublimation of ice

45. Under the same temperature and pressure, which sample of carbon dioxide contains particles with the highest entropy?
    (1) $CO_2(g)$ (3) $CO_2(l)$
    (2) $CO_2(s)$ (4) $CO_2(aq)$

46. Which 1.0-mole sample at 1 atm has particles with the greatest entropy?
    (1) $CCl_4(s)$ at 250 K   (3) $CCl_4(\ell)$ at 250 K
    (2) $CCl_4(\ell)$ at 300 K   (4) $CCl_4(g)$ at 300 K

47. The compound KNO_3 is soluble in water. Compare the entropy of 30. grams of $KNO_3(s)$ at 20.°C with the entropy of 30. grams of KNO_3 dissolved in 100. grams of water at 20.°C.

Base your answer to the following question on the information below.

The balanced equation below represents the decomposition of potassium chlorate.
$$2KClO_3(s) \rightarrow 2KCl(s) + 3O_2(g)$$

48. State why the entropy of the reactant is less than the entropy of the products.

E3chemistry.com

Lesson 4: Equilibrium

Introduction

Equilibrium is the state of balance between two opposing processes taking place at the same time (simultaneously) and at equal rates. One example of two opposing processes is the freezing of water to ice and the melting of the ice back to water. Since both processes in equilibrium continue to take place, equilibrium is said to be dynamic. In this lesson, you will learn about physical and chemical equilibrium.

Equilibrium: *Equal Rates, Constant Concentrations*

Equilibrium can only occur in a *closed system* in which changes that are taking place are *reversible*. A closed system is a system in which nothing is allowed in or out.

Example of a reversible equilibrium reaction

$$N_2 \ + \ O_2 \xrightleftharpoons[\text{Reverse}]{\text{Forward}} 2NO$$

At equilibrium:

- *Rates* of forward and reverse reactions are *equal.*

- *Concentrations* or *amounts* of substances remain *constant.*

> An equation showing a reversible process at equilibrium always contains a two-headed arrow.
>
> $\leftrightarrow$ or $\rightleftarrows$

Physical Equilibrium: *Phase and Solution Equilibrium*

A **phase equilibrium** occurs in a *closed* system in which phase changes are occurring. Examples of phase equilibrium are given below.

Solid-liquid Equilibrium

Example: ***Ice-water equilibrium*** *occurs at **0°C** or **273 K** (at 1 atm pressure)*

$$H_2O(s) \xrightleftharpoons[\text{freezing}]{\text{melting}} H_2O(\ell)$$

Rates of melting and freezing are *equal.*
Amounts of ice and water stay *constant.*

Liquid-gas (vapor) Equilibrium

Example: ***Water-steam equilibrium*** occurs at **100°C or 373 K** (at 1 atm pressure)

$$H_2O(\ell) \xrightleftharpoons[\text{condensation}]{\text{evaporation}} H_2O(g)$$

Rates of evaporation and condensation are *equal.*
Amounts of water and vapor stay *constant.*

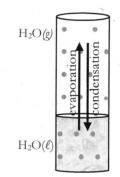

$H_2O(g)$

$H_2O(\ell)$

Solution Equilibrium

Solution equilibrium occurs in a closed system in which a substance is dissolving in a liquid. Two types of solution equilibrium are given below.

Solid in Liquid Equilibrium: Saturated Solution

• Equilibrium exists between dissolved and undissolved (crystallized) particles.

$$NaCl(s) \underset{crystallizing}{\overset{dissolving}{\rightleftarrows}} Na^+(aq) \ + \ Cl^-(aq)$$

• *Rate* of dissolving of solid is equal to *rate* of crystallization of ions.
• *Amounts* of solid and ions remain *constant* in the solution.

Gas in Liquid Equilibrium: Gaseous solution

• Equilibrium exists between dissolved gas in the liquid and undissolved gas above the liquid.

$$CO_2(g) \underset{undissolving}{\overset{dissolving}{\rightleftarrows}} CO_2(aq)$$

• *Rate* of dissolving is equal to *rate* of undissolving of the gas.
• *Amounts* of undissolved gas (above liquid) and dissolved gas (in liquid) remain *constant.*

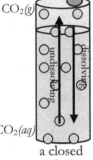

$CO_2(g)$

$CO_2(aq)$

a closed soda can

Chemical Equilibrium

Chemical equilibrium is a state of balance between the forward and reverse reactions of a chemical reaction.

$$N_2(g) \ + \ 3H_2(g) \underset{\textbf{reverse reaction}}{\overset{\textbf{forward reaction}}{\rightleftarrows}} 2NH_3(g)$$

When the above reaction has reached a state of equilibrium:
Rates of forward and reverse reactions are *equal*
Concentrations of N_2, H_2, and NH_3 remain *constant* (stay the same).

If a stress is introduced into the reaction while at equilibrium, the reaction will change or shift. A **stress** is any change in concentration, temperature or pressure to an equilibrium reaction.

Le Chatelier's Principle states that when a stress is introduced into a reaction at equilibrium, the reaction will change by speeding up in one direction while slowing down in the other direction to bring back or re-establish the reaction to a new equilibrium point. The concentrations of the substances at the new equilibrium point will be different from those of the previous equilibrium point. There will be an increase in the concentration of some substances, and a decrease in others.

Changing Concentration or Temperature

Given the reaction:

$$N_2(g) \; + \; 3H_2(g) \; \underset{\text{reverse (endothermic)}}{\overset{\text{forward (exothermic)}}{\rightleftarrows}} \; 2NH_3(g) \; + \; 92 \; KJ$$

Increasing any Reactant (Ex. ↑N₂)
- Increases forward reaction (shift right)
- Increases product concentrations (↑NH_3, ↑heat)
- Decreases reverse reaction
- Decreases the concentration of all other reactants (↓H_2)

Decreasing any Reactants
- same effect as **increasing any product.**

Increasing any Product (Ex. ↑NH₃)
- Increases reverse reaction (shift left)
- Increases reactant concentrations (↑N_2, ↑H_2)
- Decreases forward reaction
- Decreases the concentration of all other products (↓heat)

Decreasing any Products
- same effect as **increasing any reactant.**

Increasing Heat/Temperature: Favors **_Endothermic_** Reactions
- In the above reaction, similar effect as increasing any product.

Decreasing Heat/Temperature: Favors **_Exothermic_** Reactions
- In the above reaction, similar effect as increasing any reactant.

Changing Pressure: *Increasing Pressure Favors Side with Fewer Moles*

When the pressure is changed on an equilibrium reaction, **_moles_** of gaseous reactants and products determine the direction that the reaction will shift.

Given the equilibrium reaction:

$$CH_4(g) \; + \; H_2O(g) \; \underset{\text{reverse}}{\overset{\text{forward}}{\rightleftarrows}} \; 3H_2(g) \; + \; CO(g)$$

number of moles	1	1		3	1
total moles	**2 moles**			**4 moles**	

Increasing Pressure / Decreasing Volume
- Favors (speeds up) production of substances that are on the side of smaller number of moles.

In the above reaction, increasing pressure:
- increases reverse reaction (shift left)
- increases CH_4 and H_2O concentrations
- decreases forward reaction
- decreases H_2 and CO concentrations

Decreasing Pressure / Increasing Volume
- Favors (speeds up) production of substances that are on the side of greater number of moles.

In the above reaction, decreasing pressure:
- increases forward reaction (shift right)
- increases H_2 and CO concentrations
- decreases reverse reaction
- decreases CH_4 and H_2O concentrations

In reactions in which the total moles of gases on both sides of the equation are equal, a change in pressure has no effect on the equilibrium reaction. There will be no shift.

Adding a Catalyst: *No Overall Effect on Equilibrium*

When a catalyst is added to a reaction at equilibrium:
- Rates of both the forward and reverse reactions increase or speed up *equally.* As a result:
- There will be no shift to either direction of the reaction.
- There will be no change on equilibrium concentrations.

Review Questions: Equilibrium

Vocabulary: Briefly define each of the following terms.
49. Equilibrium   50. Le Chatelier's principle

51. A chemical reaction has reached equilibrium when
    (1) the forward and reverse reactions are occurring at equal rates
    (2) the forward and reversible reactions are occurring at different rates
    (3) the concentrations of the substances are equal
    (4) the concentrations of the reactants have been used up

52. Which balanced equation represents a phase equilibrium?
    (1) $H_2(g)$ + $I_2(g)$ ↔ $2HI(g)$
    (2) $2NO_2(g)$ ↔ $N_2O_4(g)$
    (3) $Cl_2(g)$ ↔ $Cl_2(l)$
    (4) $3O_2(g)$ ↔ $2O_3(g)$

53. A sample of water in a sealed flask at 298 K is in equilibrium with its vapor. This is
    an example of
    (1) chemical equilibrium   (3) solution equilibrium
    (2) energy equilibrium   (4) phase equilibrium

54. In the reaction: $Pb(NO_3)_2(s)$ ↔ $Pb^{2+}(aq)$ + $2NO_3^-(aq)$
    At equilibrium,
    (1) the rate of dissolving of the salt and the rate of crystallization of ions is constant
    (2) the concentrations of $Pb(NO_3)_2(aq)$, $Pb^{2+}(aq)$, and $NO_3^-(aq)$ are constant
    (3) the rate of dissolving of the salt is slower than the rate of crystallization of ions
    (4) the concentration of $Pb^{2+}(aq)$ is the same as the concentration of $Pb(NO_3)_2(s)$

55. Which description applies to a system in a sealed flask that is half full of water?
    (1) Only evaporation occurs, but it eventually stops.
    (2) Only condensation occurs, but it eventually stops.
    (3) Neither evaporation nor condensation occurs.
    (4) Both evaporation and condensation occur.

56. When more heat is added to an equilibrium reaction, the reaction will
    (1) shift in the direction of the exothermic reaction, and increase its rate
    (2) shift in the direction of the exothermic reaction, and decrease its rate
    (3) shift in the direction of the endothermic reaction, and increase its rate
    (4) shift in the direction of the endothermic reaction, and decrease its rate

57. Which change will have the least effect on concentration of substances in an
    equilibrium reaction?
    (1) Adding a catalyst to the reaction.   (3) Increasing temperature of the reaction.
    (2) Increasing pressure on the reaction.   (4) Increasing concentration of the reactants.

58. Given the equilibrium reaction: $N_2O_4(g)$ +   58.1 kJ ↔ $2NO_2(g)$
    If the concentration of $NO_2(g)$ is increased,
    (1) the rate of the forward reaction will increase, and equilibrium will shift right
    (2) the rate of the forward reaction will increase, and equilibrium will shift left
    (3) the rate of the reverse reaction will increase, and equilibrium will shift right
    (4) the rate of the reverse reaction will increase, and equilibrium will shift left

59. Given the equilibrium reaction

$$H_2 \quad + \quad Cl_2 \quad + \quad energy \quad \leftrightarrow \quad 2HCl$$

Which change will cause the concentration of H_2 to decrease?
(1) Decreasing Cl_2 (3) Increasing temperature
(2) Decreasing pressure   (4) Increasing HCl

60. Given the equilibrium reaction below:

$$2SO_2(g) \quad + \quad O_2(g) \quad \leftrightarrow \quad 2SO_3(g) \quad + \quad heat$$

Which change at equilibrium will cause the rate of the forward reaction to increase?
(1) Decreasing concentration of $SO_2(g)$ (3) Increasing temperature
(2) Decreasing concentration of $SO_3(g)$ (4) Decreasing pressure

61. Given the reaction at equilibrium: $\quad 2CO(g) \quad + \quad O_2(g) \quad \leftrightarrow \quad 2CO_2(g)$
If pressure is increased on this reaction, the rate of the forward reaction will
(1) decrease, and the concentration of CO_2 will also decrease
(2) decrease, and the concentration of CO_2 will increase
(3) increase, and the concentration of CO_2 will decrease
(4) increase, and the concentration of CO_2 will also increase

62. The reaction below is at equilibrium
$$2Cl_2(g) \quad + \quad 2H_2O(g) \quad + \quad 31.2 \text{ kJ} \quad \leftrightarrow \quad 4HCl(g) \quad + \quad O_2(g)$$
Which stress will cause the rate of the reverse reaction to increase?
(1) Increase in temperature   (3) Decrease in HCl(g) concentration
(2) Increase in $Cl_2(g)$ concentration   (4) Decrease in $H_2O(g)$ concentration

63. Given the equilibrium reaction below:
$$SO_2(g) \quad + \quad NO_2(g) \quad \leftrightarrow \quad SO_3(g) \quad + \quad NO(g) \quad + \quad heat$$
Which stress will NOT shift the equilibrium point of this reaction?
(1) Increasing pressure   (3) Decreasing heat
(2) Increasing $SO_2(g)$ concentration   (4) Decreasing NO(g) concentration

Base your answer to the following question on the information below.

A beaker contains 100.0 milliliters of a dilute aqueous solution of ethanoic acid at equilibrium. The equation below represents this system.

$$HC_2H_3O_2(aq) \quad \leftrightarrow \quad H^+ (aq) \quad + \quad C_2H_3O_2^- (aq)$$

64. Describe what happens to the concentration of $H^+(aq)$ when 10 drops of concentrated $HC_2H_3O_2(aq)$ are added to this system.

Base your answers to questions 65 through 67 on the information below.

At 550°C, 1.00 mole of $CO_2(g)$ and 1.00 mole of $H_2(g)$ are placed in a 1.00-liter reaction vessel. The substances react to form CO(g) and $H_2O(g)$. Changes in the concentrations of the reactants and the concentrations of the products are shown in the graph below.

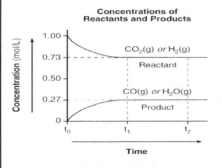

65. Determine the change in the concentration of $CO_2(g)$ between time t_0 and time t_1.

66. What can be concluded from the graph about the concentrations of the reactants and the concentrations of the products between time t_1 and time t_2?

67. Describe the change in the concentration of $H_2(g)$ if some of the CO(g) is removed at time t_2.

Additional Materials

Equilibrium Expressions: *Ratio of Products to Reactants*

An equilibrium expression shows the mathematical relationship between the concentrations (or pressures) of reactants and products of a system at equilibrium. The **equilibrium expression** is the ***ratio of the concentrations of the products to reactants.*** Each concentration in an equilibrium expression is raised to a power that is equal to the coefficient of the substance in the balanced equation. *Solids* and *liquid*s in a reaction are excluded from all equilibrium expressions because they have constant concentration. For any given reaction at a specified temperature the equilibrium expression is a constant value called the ***equilibrium constant, K_{eq}.***

In general: $$K_{eq} = \frac{[\text{Products}]^A}{[\text{Reactants}]^B}$$	***Example 1:*** What is the K_{eq} for this reaction? $$N_2(g) + 3H_2(g) \leftrightarrow 2NH_3(g)$$ $$K_{eq} = \frac{[NH_3]^2}{[N_2][H_2]^3}$$

Variations of K_{eq}

Solubility Product Constant, K_{sp} . Expresses how well a salt dissolves. . The larger the K_{sp}, the more soluble the salt is in water. $$K_{sp} = [+\text{ions}][-\text{ions}]$$	***Example 2:*** What is the K_{sp} for this reaction? $$K_2SO_4(s) \leftrightarrow 2K^+(aq) + SO_4^{2-}(aq)$$ $K_{sp} = [K^+]^2[SO_4^{2-}]$ **Note:** $K_2SO_4(s)$ is not included in the expression
Acid Dissociation Constant, K_a . Expresses how well an acid ionizes. . The larger the K_a value, the stronger the acid, and the more it ionizes in water. $$K_a = \frac{[H^+][-\text{ion}]}{[\text{Acid}]}$$	***Example 3:*** What is the K_a for this reaction? $$HCl(aq) + H_2O(\ell) \leftrightarrow H^+(aq) + Cl^-(aq)$$ $K_a = \frac{[H^+][Cl^-]}{[HCl]}$ **Note:** $H_2O(\ell)$ is not included in the expression
Base Dissociation Constant, K_b . expresses how well a base ionizes. . the larger the K_b value, the stronger. the base, and the more it ionizes in water. $$K_b = \frac{[+\text{ion}][OH^-]}{[\text{Base}]}$$	***Example 4:*** What is the K_b for this reaction? $$Ca(OH)_2(aq) \leftrightarrow Ca^{2+}(aq) + 2OH^-(aq)$$ $$K_b = \frac{[Ca^{2+}][OH^-]^2}{[Ca(OH)_2]}$$

A lot can be learned about a reaction at a given temperature from its K_{eq} value.

$K_{eq} > 1$ indicates a higher concentration of the products than the reactants.
  • Forward reaction is favored, and the equilibrium point is to the right.

$K_{eq} < 1$ indicates a higher concentration of the reactants than the products.
  • Reverse reaction is favored, and the equilibrium point is to the left.

$K_{eq} = 1$ indicates a reaction with equal amounts of products and reactants.
  • No one side is favored, and the equilibrium point is in the center.

Additional Materials

Spontaneous and Nonspontaneous Reactions.

Earlier in the topic you learned about exothermic and endothermic reactions, as well as entropy.

Exothermic reactions release energy and have $-\Delta H$ values (lower enthalpy).

Endothermic reactions absorb energy and have $+\Delta H$ values (high enthalpy).

Entropy change, ΔS, describes a change in randomness or disorder of a system.

Reactions that become more disordered (ex. solid $\rightarrow$ gas) have $+\Delta S$.

Reactions that become less disordered (ex. liquid $\rightarrow$ solid) have $-\Delta S$.

Spontaneous reactions are reactions that will occur under a specific set of conditions. Spontaneous reactions occur if the direction of the reaction leads to:

- **Lower Enthalpy** (less energy) products. This favors exothermic reactions.
- **Greater Entropy** (more random or less organized) products.

Systems in nature tend to proceed spontaneously in the direction of lower enthalpy and greater entropy.

Nonspontaneous reactions are the exact opposite.

Gibbs Free Energy

Gibbs free energy is the amount of energy available to do work. The equation for Gibbs free energy change, ΔG, relates temperature (T), enthalpy change (ΔH), and entropy change (ΔS) of a reaction.

$$\Delta G = \Delta H - T\Delta S$$

The sign of ΔG determines if a reaction is spontaneous , nonspontaneous, or at equilibrium.

- ΔG indicates a spontaneous reaction.

$+\Delta G$ indicates a nonspontaneous reaction.

$\Delta G = 0$ indicates a reaction at equilibrium.

The table to the right shows different combinations of ΔH, ΔS, and T that will lead to a reaction with $-\Delta G$ or $+\Delta G$.

ΔH	ΔS	T	ΔG
-	+	Low	-
		High	-
+	-	Low	+
		High	+
+	+	Low	+
		High	-
-	-	Low	-
		High	+

Practice Questions on Additional Materials

68. Which is the correct equilibrium expression for the reaction?

$$4NH_3(g) + 5O_2(g) \leftrightarrow 4NO(g) + 6H_2O(g)$$

(1) $K_{eq} = \dfrac{[NH_3]^4\,[O_2]^5}{[NO]^4\,[H_2O]^6}$

(3) $K_{eq} = \dfrac{[NO]^4\,[H_2O]^6}{[NH_3]^4\,[O_2]^5}$

(2) $K_{eq} = \dfrac{[4NH_3]\,[5O_2]}{[4NO]\,[6H_2O]}$

(4) $K_{eq} = \dfrac{[4NO]\,[6H_2O]}{[4NH_3]\,[5O_2]}$

69. What is the correct equilibrium expression for the reaction below?

$$Ca_3(PO_4)_2(s) \leftrightarrow 3Ca^{2+}(aq) + 2PO_4^{3-}(aq)$$

(1) $K_{sp} = [Ca^{2+}]^3\,[PO_4^{3-}]^2$

(3) $K_{sp} = [3Ca^{2+}]\,[2PO_4^{3-}]$

(2) $K_{sp} = [Ca^{2+}]^3 + [PO_4^{3-}]^2$

(4) $K_{sp} = [3Ca^{2+}] + [2PO_4^{3-}]$

70. Which equation is used to determine the free energy change of a chemical reaction?

(1) $\Delta G = \Delta H - \Delta S$

(3) $\Delta G = \Delta H - T\Delta S$

(2) $\Delta G = \Delta H + \Delta S$

(4) $\Delta G = \Delta H + T\Delta S$

71. A chemical reaction will always be spontaneous if the reaction has a negative

(1) ΔS

(3) ΔT

(2) ΔG

(4) ΔH

72. When the free energy change of a reaction is zero, the reaction is
(1) at equilibrium
(2) absorbing heat
(3) spontaneous
(4) nonspontaneous

Write equilibrium expressions for the reactions given in numbers 74 through 77.

73. $X_2(g) + 2Y_2(g) \leftrightarrow 2XY_2(g)$

74. $Pb(NO_3)_2(s) \leftrightarrow Pb^{2+}(aq) + 2NO_3^-(aq)$

75. $2Cl_2(g) + 2H_2O(\ell) \leftrightarrow 4HCl(aq) + O_2(g)$

76. $W(g) + 3X(g) \leftrightarrow 2Y(g) + 3Z(g)$

Write equilibrium expressions for the dissociation of:

77. $H_2CO_3(aq)$

78. $NH_4OH(aq)$

79. $H_2O(\ell)$

Lesson 1: Properties of Organic Compounds

Organic compounds are compounds of carbon. The chemical properties of a carbon atom make it possible for carbon to bond to each other and to other nonmetals. The result is enormous numbers of organic compounds ranging from just a few atoms to several hundred in length. Properties of organic compounds are due, in part, to the chemical properties of a carbon atom.

In this lesson, you will learn about general properties of carbon and of organic compounds.

Bonding Properties of a Carbon Atom.

A carbon atom has four valence electrons and must form 4 covalent bonds.

$$\bullet \; \underset{\bullet}{\overset{\bullet}{C}} \; \bullet \qquad -\overset{|}{\underset{|}{C}}- \qquad -\overset{|}{\underset{|}{C}}-\overset{|}{\underset{|}{C}}- \qquad -\overset{|}{C}=\overset{|}{C}- \qquad -C \equiv C-$$

electron-dot diagram for a carbon atom

All correctly drawn organic compound structures must have each C atom with exactly *four bonds* as shown above.

• Two carbon atoms can form a single (−), double (=), or triple (≡) covalent bond.

• Carbon atoms can join to form a straight chain, branched, or ring structure.

$$-C-C-C-C- \qquad -C-\overset{\overset{\displaystyle CH_3}{|}}{C}-C-C- \qquad \underset{\substack{\diagdown \\ C-C}}{\overset{\substack{C-C \\ \diagup}}{C}}\;\;C$$

straight chain   branched   ring (cyclic)

• Carbon bonds easily with other nonmetals such as H, O, N, and the halogens

Properties of Organic Compounds
Covalent, Molecular, Low Melting and Boiling Points, Slow Reactions

General properties of organic compounds are listed below.

• They are molecular (covalent) substances.

• Bonding between atoms is covalent.

• Molecules are held together by weak intermolecular forces (IMFs).

• Low melting and boiling points, and high vapor pressure due to weak IMFs

• Solids decompose easily under heat.

• Most are nonelectrolytes (except for organic acids, which are weak electrolytes).

• Reactions are slow due to strong covalent bonding between atoms.

• Solubility in water varies depending on if the compound is polar (soluble) or nonpolar (insoluble).

These properties vary within a class and between classes of organic compounds.

Names of Organic Compounds

The IUPAC (International Union of Pure and Applied Chemistry) name of an organic compound has systematic components that reveal much about the compound.

The **prefix** (beginning root) of a name indicates the number of carbon atoms. (See Reference Table P below)

The **suffix** (ending root) of a name indicates the class that the substance belongs. (See the Table below and Reference Table Q and R).

Numbers in a name indicate positions of side chains, multiple bonds, or functional groups.

di- or **tri-** in a name indicates the presence of two or three of the same side chain or functional group.

Table P- Organic Prefixes

Prefix	Number of Carbon Atoms
meth-	1
eth-	2
prop-	3
but-	4
pent-	5
hex-	6
hept-	7
oct-	8
non-	9
dec-	10

Name Endings: See Tables Q and R

Class of Compound	Name Ending
Alkanes	- ane
Alkenes	- ene
Alkynes	-yne
Alcohols	-ol
Ethers	-yl
Aldehydes	-al
Ketones	-one
Organic acids	-oic
Esters	-oate
Amines	-amine
Amides	-amide

Halides are named with a *halogen* prefix.
Ex. *Chloro*butane

Three organic substances are given below. Different parts of their IUPAC names are explained under each substance. Study this breakdown to help you understand names, formulas, and structures of substances given as examples throughout this topic.

Prop*ane*

prop-: a 3 C-atom compound

- *ane*: a compound of alkane

2-Pentan*ol*

pent-: a 5 C-atom compound

-*ol*: a compound of alcohol

2: -OH functional group on carbon number 2

2,3-dimethyl, **1**-but*ene*

but-: 4 C atoms in the main chain

-*ene*: a compound of an alkene

1: the double bond is on the 1st bond position

2,3-*dimethyl*: 2 methyl side chains on carbon 2 and 3

Review Questions: Properties of Organic Compounds

1. Which organic structure is correctly drawn?

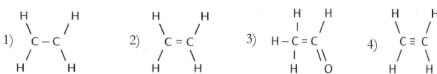

2. A compound that is classified as organic must contain the element
   (1) carbon
   (2) nitrogen
   (3) oxygen
   (4) hydrogen

3. Which type of bonds and solids are characteristics of organic compounds?
   (1) Ionic bonds and ionic solids
   (2) Ionic bonds and molecular solids
   (3) Covalent bonds and ionic solids
   (4) Covalent bonds and molecular solids

4. In general, which property do organic compounds share?
   (1) High melting points
   (2) High electrical conductivity
   (3) High solubility in water
   (4) Slow reaction rate

5. Which best explains why there are more organic compounds than inorganic compounds?
   (1) The carbon atom readily forms covalent bonds with other carbon atoms.
   (2) The carbon atom readily forms ionic bonds with other carbon atoms.
   (3) The carbon atom readily combines with oxygen.
   (4) The carbon atom readily dissolves in water.

6. A carbon atom in any organic compound can form a total of
   (1) 1 covalent bond
   (2) 2 covalent bonds
   (3) 3 covalent bonds
   (4) 4 covalent bonds

7. How many carbon atoms are in a molecule of a compound whose IUPAC name is pentanone?
   (1) 1
   (2) 5
   (3) 3
   (4) 7

8. Which is a correct name for an organic compound containing seven carbon atoms?
   (1) Butanol
   (2) Pentene
   (3) Hexanal
   (4) Heptanoic acid

9. Which compound is an organic acid?
   (1) Pentanone
   (2) Methanal
   (3) Hexanoic
   (4) Propanamide

10. The compound hexanal is classified as
    (1) an alkene
    (2) an aldehyde
    (3) an ester
    (4) a halide

11. Methyl ethanoate is classified as
    (1) an organic acid
    (2) an alcohol
    (3) a halide
    (4) an ester

Lesson 2: Classes of Organic Compounds

Homologous series are groups of related organic compounds in which each member of the class differs from the next member by a set number of atoms. Compounds belonging to the same homologous series always share the same general formula, same molecular name ending, and similar molecular structure.

In this lesson, you will learn about hydrocarbon compounds and functional group compounds.

Hydrocarbons: *Compounds of Hydrogen and Carbon*

Hydrocarbons are classes of organic compounds that are composed of just two elements: Hydrogen (H) and carbon (C). Table Q below lists three hydrocarbon classes.

Bonding between carbon atoms in a hydrocarbon molecule could be single, double or triple covalent. Depending on the bond type found between the carbon atoms, a hydrocarbon can be classified as saturated or unsaturated.

Table Q

Name	General Formula	Examples	
		Name	Structural Formula
alkanes	C_nH_{2n+2}	ethane	$H-\overset{\overset{H}{|}}{\underset{\underset{H}{|}}{C}}-\overset{\overset{H}{|}}{\underset{\underset{H}{|}}{C}}-H$
alkenes	C_nH_{2n}	ethene	$\overset{H}{\underset{H}{>}}C=C\overset{H}{\underset{H}{<}}$
alkynes	C_nH_{2n-2}	ethyne	$H-C\equiv C-H$

Saturated Hydrocarbons (Alkanes): *Single Covalent Bonds*

Saturated hydrocarbons are hydrocarbons in which the bonds between the carbon atoms are all single covalent bonds. A **single covalent** bond is formed between two C atoms when each atom shares one (1) electron.

Since each C atom contributes one electron, a single covalent bond is formed by 1 pair of (2 total) electrons

Alkanes are classified as saturated hydrocarbons.

> C ∙ ∙ C   C — C
> 2 e-   a single
> 1 e- pair   bond

Unsaturated Hydrocarbons (Alkenes and Alkynes): *Multiple Covalent Bonds*

Unsaturated hydrocarbons are hydrocarbons that contain one or more multiple (double or triple) covalent bonds between two adjacent C atoms.

A **double covalent** bond is formed between two carbon atoms when each C atom shares two (2) electrons. Since each C atom contributes two electrons, a double covalent bond contains 2 pairs of (4 total) electrons.

Alkenes are unsaturated hydrocarbons with one double bond.

> C : : C   C = C
> 4 e-   a double
> 2 e- pairs   bond

A **triple covalent** bond is formed between two carbon atoms when each C atom shares three (3) electrons. Since each C atom contributes three electrons, a triple covalent bond contains 3 pairs of (6 total) electrons.

Alkynes are unsaturated hydrocarbons with one triple bond.

> C ⦂⦂ C   C ≡ C
> 6 e-   a triple
> 3 e- pairs   bond

Topic 10   Organic Chemistry

Alkanes: *Single Bonds Between All Carbons, Saturated Hydrocarbons*

Alkanes are saturated hydrocarbons in which all members share the characteristics listed below.

molecular formula
C_nH_{2n+2}

C_3H_8

structural formula
all single bonds

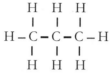

IUPAC name ending
-ane

Prop*ane*

Alkenes: *One Double Covalent Bond, Unsaturated Hydrocarbons*

Alkenes are unsaturated hydrocarbons in which all members share the characteristics listed below.

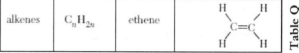

molecular formula
C_nH_{2n}

C_4H_8

structural formula
one double bond

$$H - C - C = C - C - H$$

IUPAC name ending
-ene

2-but*ene*

Alkynes: *One Triple Covalent Bond, Unsaturated Hydrocarbons*

Alkynes are unsaturated hydrocarbons in which all members share the characteristics listed below.

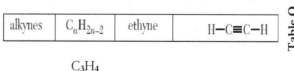

molecular formula
C_nH_{2n-2}

C_3H_4

structural formula
one triple bond

$$H - C \equiv C - C - H$$

IUPAC name ending
-yne

Prop*yne*

Functional Group Compounds

A **functional group** is an atom (other than hydrogen) or a group of atoms that replaces one or more hydrogen atoms of a hydrocarbon compound. The element commonly found in most functional groups is oxygen (O). Nitrogen (N) and halogens (F, Cl, Br, or I) are also found in functional groups. Classes of compounds containing a functional group include:

Halides, alcohols, ethers, aldehydes, ketones, organic acids, esters, amines and amides. Each class is briefly discussed below.

- Differences in physical and chemical properties between the classes is primarily due to differences in their functional groups.

Use **Reference Table R** to help you answer questions related to functional group compounds.

Halides: *Contain Halogen Atom (Group 17)*

Halides (aka halocarbons) are organic compounds in which the functional group is one or more halogen atoms (F, Cl, Br, or I).

halide (halocarbon)	—F (fluoro-) —Cl (chloro-) —Br (bromo-) —I (iodo-)	R—X (X represents any halogen)	$CH_3CHClCH_3$ 2-chloropropane	**Table R**

Molecular (condensed) formula	$CH_3CH_2\textbf{F}$	$CH_3CH_2\textbf{CHBr}CH_3$

Structural formula	H H
	  | |
	H – C – C – H
	  | |
	H **F**
		H H H H
		 | | | |
		H – C – C – **C** – C – H
		 | | | |
		H H **Br** H

IUPAC Name: *halogen* prefix	*fluoroethane*	**2-*bromo*butane**

Alcohols: *Contain –OH group*

Alcohols are organic compounds with the -OH (hydroxyl) functional group. There are a few different types of alcohols.

alcohol	—OH	R—OH	$CH_3CH_2CH_2OH$ 1-propanol	**Table R**

Note: Hydroxyl (**—OH**) is different from a hydroxide ion (OH⁻) found in bases.

Molecular (condensed) formula	CH_3CH_2OH	$CH_3\textbf{CH}(OH)CH_2CH_3$

Structural formula	H H
	  | |
	H – C – C – OH
	  | |
	H H
		H OH H H
		 | | | |
		H – C – **C** – C – C – H
		 | | | |
		H H H H

IUPAC Name: **-ol** ending	ethan*ol*	2-butan*ol*

Types of Alcohols

Monohydroxy alcohols are alcohols with just one -OH group.

Types of Monohydroxy Alcohols

Primary alcohols are alcohols in which the **C** atom with the -OH is bonded to one other C atom.
   Ex. 1-propanol

$$- \text{C} - \text{C} - \text{C} -$$
$$\overset{|}{\text{OH}} \quad \textbf{1-propanol}$$

Secondary alcohols are alcohols in which the **C** atom with the -OH is bonded to two other C atoms.
   Ex. 2 - propanol

$$- \text{C} - \text{C} - \text{C} -$$
$$\overset{|}{\text{OH}} \quad \textbf{2-propanol}$$

Tertiary alcohols are alcohols in which the **C** atom with the -OH is bonded to three other C atoms.
   Ex. 2-methyl,2-propanol

$$\overset{\displaystyle CH_3}{\underset{\displaystyle OH}{- C - \overset{|}{\underset{|}{C}} - C - C -}}$$

2-methyl,2-butanol

Dihydroxy alcohols are alcohols with two -OH groups.
   Ex. 1,3-propanediol

$$HO - C - C - C - OH$$

1,3-propanediol

Trihydroxy alcohols are alcohols with three -OH groups.
   Ex. 1,2,3-propanetriol (glycerol)

$$- \underset{\underset{\displaystyle OH}{|}}{C} - \underset{\underset{\displaystyle OH}{|}}{C} - \underset{\underset{\displaystyle OH}{|}}{C} -$$

1,2,3-propanetriol (glycerol)

Ethers: *Contain* $- O -$ *group*
Ethers are organic compounds with the $- O -$ functional group.

ether	$- O -$	$R - O - R'$	$CH_3OCH_2CH_3$ methyl ethyl ether	**Table R**

Molecular (condensed) formula $CH_3 \textbf{O} CH_3$ $CH_3CH_2CH_2 \textbf{O} CH_3$

Structural formula

$$\begin{array}{ccc} H & & H \\ | & & | \\ H - C - \textbf{O} - C - H \\ | & & | \\ H & & H \end{array}$$

$$\underbrace{}_{methyl} \quad \underbrace{}_{methyl}$$

$$\begin{array}{cccc} H & H & H & & H \\ | & | & | & & | \\ H - C - C - C - \textbf{O} - C - H \\ | & | & | & & | \\ H & H & H & & H \end{array}$$

$$\underbrace{}_{propyl} \quad \underbrace{}_{methyl}$$

IUPAC Name:
includes both
alkyl (-yl) chains.

methyl methyl ether
(*di*methyl ether)

methyl propyl ether
(The shorter alkyl chain is always named first)

Aldehydes: *Contain – CHO group*

Aldehydes are organic compounds with the -CHO functional group.

aldehyde	$\overset{\displaystyle O}{\underset{\displaystyle \|}{-C}}-H$	$R-\overset{\displaystyle O}{\underset{\displaystyle \|}{C}}-H$	$CH_3CH_2\overset{\displaystyle O}{\underset{\displaystyle \|}{C}}-H$ propanal	**Table R**

Molecular (condensed) formula   **HCHO** $CH_3\overset{\displaystyle O}{\underset{\displaystyle \|}{C}}-H$

Structural formula $H-\overset{\displaystyle O}{\underset{\displaystyle \|}{C}}-H$ $H-\overset{\displaystyle H}{\underset{\displaystyle H}{C}}-\overset{\displaystyle O}{\underset{\displaystyle \|}{C}}-H$

IUPAC Name
-al ending
     Methanal
 (formaldehyde)   ethanal

Ketones: *Contain –CO– group*

Ketones are classes of organic compounds with the – CO – functional group.

ketone	$-\overset{\displaystyle O}{\underset{\displaystyle \|}{C}}-$	$R-\overset{\displaystyle O}{\underset{\displaystyle \|}{C}}-R'$	$CH_3\overset{\displaystyle O}{\underset{\displaystyle \|}{C}}CH_2CH_2CH_3$ 2-pentanone	**Table R**

Molecular formula $CH_3\mathbf{CO}CH_3$ $CH_3CH_2\mathbf{CO}CH_3$

Structural formula $H-\overset{\displaystyle H}{\underset{\displaystyle H}{C}}-\overset{\displaystyle \mathbf{O}}{\underset{\displaystyle \|}{\mathbf{C}}}-\overset{\displaystyle H}{\underset{\displaystyle H}{C}}-H$ $H-\overset{\displaystyle H}{\underset{\displaystyle H}{C}}-\overset{\displaystyle H}{\underset{\displaystyle H}{C}}-\overset{\displaystyle \mathbf{O}}{\underset{\displaystyle \|}{\mathbf{C}}}-\overset{\displaystyle H}{\underset{\displaystyle H}{C}}-H$

IUPAC Name
-one ending
     propanone (acetone)   butanone

Amines and Amides: *Contain N atom*

methanamine

Amines are groups of organic compounds with the functional group $-\overset{\displaystyle |}{N}-$.

CH_3NH_2 $H-\overset{\displaystyle H}{\underset{\displaystyle H}{C}}-\overset{\displaystyle H}{N}-H$

Amides are groups of organic compounds with the functional group $-\overset{\displaystyle O}{\underset{\displaystyle \|}{C}}-\overset{\displaystyle |}{N}H$.

ethanamide
CH_3CONH_2 $H-\overset{\displaystyle H}{\underset{\displaystyle H}{C}}-\overset{\displaystyle O}{\underset{\displaystyle \|}{C}}-\overset{\displaystyle H}{\underset{\displaystyle H}{N}}$

amine	$-\overset{\displaystyle |}{N}-$	$R-\overset{\displaystyle R'}{\underset{\displaystyle |}{N}}-R''$	$CH_3CH_2CH_2NH_2$ 1-propanamine	
amide	$-\overset{\displaystyle O}{\underset{\displaystyle \|}{C}}-\overset{\displaystyle |}{N}H$	$R-\overset{\displaystyle O}{\underset{\displaystyle \|}{C}}-\overset{\displaystyle R'}{N}H$	$CH_3CH_2\overset{\displaystyle O}{\underset{\displaystyle \|}{C}}-NH_2$ propanamide	**Table R**

Organic Acids: *Contain –COOH group*

Organic acids are organic compounds with the -COOH functional group

organic acid	$\overset{\overset{\text{O}}{\|\|}}{-\text{C}-\text{OH}}$	$R-\overset{\overset{\text{O}}{\|\|}}{\text{C}}-\text{OH}$	$CH_3CH_2\overset{\overset{\text{O}}{\|\|}}{\text{C}}-\text{OH}$ propanoic acid	**Table R**

Molecular formula $\text{H}\textbf{COOH}$ $CH_3\textbf{COOH}$

Structural formula

$$\text{H} - \overset{\overset{\text{O}}{\|\|}}{\text{C}} - \text{OH}$$

$$\text{H} - \overset{\overset{\text{H}}{\|}}{\underset{\underset{\text{H}}{\|}}{\text{C}}} - \overset{\overset{\text{O}}{\|\|}}{\text{C}} - \text{OH}$$

IUPAC Name
-oic ending   methanoic acid   ethanoic acid

                                      (acetic acid, vinegar)

Properties of acids discussed in topic 8 also apply to organic acids. Examples:
• Organic acids ionize or dissolve in water to produce H^+ as the only positive ions.
• Organic acids are electrolytes (conduct electrical current) due to mobile ions
• Organic acids change litmus to red, and phenolphthalein will be colorless.

Esters: *Contain –COO– group*

Esters are organic compounds with the –COO– functional group.

ester	$\overset{\overset{\text{O}}{\|\|}}{-\text{C}-\text{O}-}$	$R-\overset{\overset{\text{O}}{\|\|}}{\text{C}}-\text{O}-R'$	$CH_3CH_2\overset{\overset{\text{O}}{\|\|}}{\text{C}}OCH_3$ methyl propanoate	**Table R**

Molecular formula $CH_3\textbf{COO}CH_3$ $CH_3CH_2\textbf{COO}CH_2CH_3$

Structural formula

$$\text{H} - \overset{\overset{\text{H}}{\|}}{\underset{\underset{\text{H}}{\|}}{\text{C}}} - \overset{\overset{\text{O}}{\|\|}}{\text{C}} - \text{O} - \overset{\overset{\text{H}}{\|}}{\underset{\underset{\text{H}}{\|}}{\text{C}}} - \text{H}$$

$$\text{H}-\overset{\overset{\text{H}}{\|}}{\underset{\underset{\text{H}}{\|}}{\text{C}}}-\overset{\overset{\text{H}}{\|}}{\underset{\underset{\text{H}}{\|}}{\text{C}}}-\overset{\overset{\text{O}}{\|\|}}{\text{C}}-\text{O}-\overset{\overset{\text{H}}{\|}}{\underset{\underset{\text{H}}{\|}}{\text{C}}}-\overset{\overset{\text{H}}{\|}}{\underset{\underset{\text{H}}{\|}}{\text{C}}}-\text{H}$$

            eth-   methyl   prop-   ethyl

IUPAC Name
-oate ending   methyl ethan*oate*   ethyl propan*oate*
                   (methyl acetate)   Alkyl chain after -O- is named first

Esters are found naturally in fruits and flowers and are responsible for their *odors*.
Synthetic esters are used as scents in cologne and perfume and flavoring in food.
Esters are synthesized or made by reacting an organic acid with an alcohol.

Review Questions: Classes of Organic Compounds

Vocabulary: Briefly define each of the following terms.

12. Homologous series   13. Hydrocarbon   14. Alkane   15. Alkene   16. Alkyne
17. Functional group   18. Halide   19. Alcohol   20. Ether   21. Aldehyde
22. Ketone   23. Organic acid   24. Ester   25. Amine   26. Amide

27. A series of hydrocarbons in which each member of a group differs from the preceding member by one carbon is called
    (1) a periodic series
    (2) a homologous series
    (3) an actinide series
    (4) a lanthanide series

28. Hydrocarbons are compounds that contain
    (1) carbon, only
    (2) carbon and hydrogen, only
    (3) carbon, hydrogen, and oxygen, only
    (4) carbon, hydrogen, oxygen, and nitrogen, only

29. In saturated hydrocarbons, carbon atoms are bonded to each other by
    (1) single covalent bonds, only
    (2) double covalent bonds, only
    (3) alternating single and double covalent bonds
    (4) alternating double and triple covalent bonds

30. Ethane, ethene, and ethyne are all similar in that they are
    (1) cyclic compounds
    (2) unsaturated compounds
    (3) saturated
    (4) hydrocarbons

31. The multiple covalent bond in a molecule of 1-butene is a
    (1) double covalent bond that has 6 shared electrons
    (2) double covalent bond that has 4 shared electrons
    (3) triple covalent bond that has 6 shared electrons
    (4) triple covalent bond that has 4 shared electrons

32. Butanal and butanone have different chemical and physical properties primarily because of differences in their
    (1) molecular formulas
    (2) molecular masses
    (3) functional groups
    (4) number of carbon atoms per molecule

33. What is the total number of electrons in the structure below?

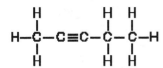

    (1) 12   (3) 14
    (2) 24   (4) 28

34. In which pair of hydrocarbons does each compound contain only one double bond per molecule?
    (1) C_2H_2 and C_2H_6
    (2) C_2H_2 and C_3H_6
    (3) C_4H_8 and C_2H_4
    (4) C_6H_6 and C_7H_8

35. Bromobutane is correctly represented by which chemical formula?
    (1) C_4H_7Br
    (2) C_4H_8Br
    (3) C_4H_9Br
    (4) $C_4H_{10}Br$

36. The condensed formula that represents methyl propanoate is
    (1) $CH_3CH_2COOCH_3$
    (2) CH_3CH_2CHO
    (3) CH_3COOH
    (4) CH_3CHO

37. Which structure represents a compound with an IUPAC name of 2-propanol?

(1)　　　　　　　(2)　　　　　　　(3)　　　　　　　4)

38. Which name represents an alkyne?
   - (1) heptanol
   - (2) pentanoic
   - (3) hexane
   - (4) octyne

39. Which compound has the structural formula shown below?

   - (1) Hexane
   - (2) 2,3-dimethyl butane
   - (3) 2,2-dimethyl butane
   - (4) Ethyl butane

Base your answers to questions 40 and 41 on the information below and on your knowledge of chemistry.

Natural gas and coal are two fuels burned to produce energy. Natural gas consists of approximately 80% methane, 10% ethane, 4% propane, 2% butane, and other components.

40. Draw a structural formula for the hydrocarbon that is approximately 2% of natural gas.

41. Write the general formula for the homologous series that includes the components of the natural gas listed in this passage.

Base your answers to questions 42 and 43 on the information below.

Two hydrocarbons that are isomers of each other are represented by the structural formulas and molecular formulas below.

Hydrocarbon 1　　　　　　Hydrocarbon 2

C_5H_8　　　　　　　　　C_5H_8

42. Explain, in terms of bonds, why these hydrocarbons are unsaturated.

43. What is the IUPAC name for Hydrocarbon 2?

Base your answers to questions 44 and 45 on the information below.

Many esters have distinctive odors, which lead to their widespread use as artificial flavorings and fragrances. For example, methyl butanoate has an odor like pineapple and ethyl methanoate has an odor like raspberry. Esters are produced by reacting an organic acid with an alcohol. Methyl butanoate is produced by reacting methanol with butanoic acid.

44. Draw a structural formula for the ester that has an odor like pineapple.

45. Draw a structural formula for the acid that produce methyl butanoate.

Lesson 3: Isomers: *Same molecular formula, different structural formulas*

Isomers are organic compounds with the same molecular formula but different structural formulas. For example:

CH_3CH_2OH and CH_3OCH_3 are isomers

- same molecular formula: C_2H_5O
- same number of atoms: 2C 5H 1O
- same percent composition
- same number of covalent bonds

- different structural formulas
- different chemical and physical properties
- different substances

All hydrocarbons with four or more carbon atoms have isomers. The higher the number of carbon atoms, the greater the number of possible isomers.

Hydrocarbon Isomers

Alkane isomers usually have different arrangements of the carbon chain so the structures would have one or more side chains (alkyl groups).

IUPAC names	pentane	*is an isomer of*	2,2–dimethyl propane
Structural formulas	H H H H H | | | | | H–C–C–C–C–C–H | | | | | H H H H H		H CH₃ H | | | H–C–**C**–C–H | | | H CH₃ H
Condensed formulas	$CH_3CH_2CH_2CH_2CH_3$		$CH_3 (CH_3)\mathbf{C}(CH_3)CH_3$
Molecular formulas	C_5H_{12}		C_5H_{12}

Alkene and alkyne isomers typically have the multiple (double or triple) bonds placed between different carbon atoms in the structure.

IUPAC names	1-butene	2-butene
Structural formulas	H H | | H –**C**=**C**–C–C–H | | | | H H H H	H H | | H–C–**C**=**C**–C–H | | | | H H H H
Condensed formulas	$CH_2CHCH_2CH_3$	$CH_3CHCHCH_3$
Molecular formula	C_4H_8	C_4H_8

IUPAC names	1-pentyne	2-pentyne
Structural formulas	H H H | | | H–C–C–C–**C**≡**C**–H | | | H H H	H H H | | | H–C–C–**C**≡**C**–C–H | | | H H H
Condensed formulas	$CH_3CH_2CH_2\mathbf{CCH}$	$CH_3CH_2\mathbf{CCC}H_3$
Molecular formula	C_5H_8	C_5H_8

     E3chemistry.com

Functional Group Isomers

Functional group compounds that are isomers usually have the functional group attached to different carbon atoms. In some cases, a compound from two different functional group classes may be isomers of each other.

Halide Isomers	1-bromopropane	2-bromopropane
	$\begin{array}{ccc} H & H & H \\ | & | & | \\ H-C-C-C-H \\ | & | & | \\ Br & H & H \end{array}$	$\begin{array}{ccc} H & H & H \\ | & | & | \\ H-C-C-C-H \\ | & | & | \\ H & Br & H \end{array}$
	$CH_2BrCH_2CH_3$	$CH_3CHBrCH_3$
	C_3H_7Br	C_3H_7Br
Alcohol Isomers	1-butanol	2-butanol
	$\begin{array}{cccc} H & H & H & H \\ | & | & | & | \\ H-C-C-C-C-OH \\ | & | & | & | \\ H & H & H & H \end{array}$	$\begin{array}{cccc} H & H & H & H \\ | & | & | & | \\ H-C-C-C-C-H \\ | & | & | & | \\ H & H & OH & H \end{array}$
	$CH_3CH_2CH_2CH_2OH$	$CH_3CH_2CH(OH)CH_3$
	C_4H_9OH	C_4H_9OH
Ether and Alcohol Isomers *An ether and a monohydroxy alcohol of the same number of C atoms are always isomers.*	methyl methyl ether	ethanol
	$\begin{array}{cc} H & H \\ | & | \\ H-C-O-C-H \\ | & | \\ H & H \end{array}$	$\begin{array}{cc} H & H \\ | & | \\ H-C-C-OH \\ | & | \\ H & H \end{array}$
	CH_3OCH_3	CH_3CH_2OH
	C_2H_6O	C_2H_6O
Ketone and Aldehyde Isomers *A ketone and an aldehyde of the same number of C atoms are always isomers.*	propanone	propanal
	$\begin{array}{ccc} H & O & H \\ | & \| & | \\ H-C-C-C-H \\ | & & | \\ H & & H \end{array}$	$\begin{array}{ccc} H & H & O \\ | & | & \| \\ H-C-C-C-H \\ | & | \\ H & H \end{array}$
	CH_3COCH_3	CH_3CH_2CHO
	C_3H_6O	C_3H_6O

Ester and Organic acid Isomers	methyl propanoate	ethyl ethanoate	butanoic acid
	$CH_3CH_2COOCH_3$	$CH_3COOCH_2CH_3$	$CH_3CH_2CH_2COOH$

Review Questions: Isomers

Vocabulary: Briefly define the following term.

46. Isomer

47. Two isomers must have the same
    (1) percent composition
    (2) arrangement of atoms
    (3) physical properties
    (4) chemical properties

48. 2-methyl pentane and 2,3-dimethyl butane are isomers. Molecules of these two compounds have different
    (1) numbers of covalent bonds
    (2) structural formulas
    (3) molecular formulas
    (4) number of carbon

49. Which hydrocarbon has the least number of isomers?
    (1) C_5H_8
    (2) C_4H_6
    (3) C_6H_{10}
    (4) C_7H_{12}

50. Which compound is an isomer of butanoic acid, $CH_3CH_2CH_2COOH$?
    (1) $CH_3CH_2CH_2CH_2OH$
    (2) $CH_3CH_2COOCH_3$
    (3) $CH_3CH_2CH_2CH_2COOH$
    (4) $CH_3CH_2OCH_3$

51. Which IUPAC name is an isomer of 3-hexene?
    (1) 3-heptyne
    (2) 3-heptene
    (3) 2-methyl hexene
    (4) 2-hexene

52. Given a formula representing a compound below:

Which formula represents an isomer of this compound?

Base your answers to questions 53 through 55 on the information below.

The equation below represents a reaction between propene and hydrogen bromide.

53. Draw and name a structural formula for an isomer of the product.

54. How many electrons are shared in the propene molecule?

55. Identify the class of organic compounds to which the product of this reaction belongs.

Base your answer to question 56 on the information below.

Cyclobutane, an isomer of butene, has a boiling point of 12.5°C at standard pressure and is represented by the formula below.

56. Explain, in terms of molecular formulas and structural formulas, why cyclobutane is an isomer of butene.

Lesson 4: Organic Reactions

An organic compound can react with another organic compound or with an inorganic compound to form one or products. Organic reactions can be slow because strong covalent bonds within the molecules must first be broken.

In this lesson, you'll learn about the different types of organic reactions.

A summary of these reactions is given in the table below. On the next page, each reaction is defined with an example given.

Organic Reactions: Summary Table

Reactions	Reactants		Products	
1. Substitution	Alkane (saturated)	Halogen	1 – Halide (one halogen)	Acid (inorganic)
2. Addition				
Hydrogenation	Alkene (unsaturated)	Hydrogen	Alkane	
Halogenation	Alkene	Halogen	1,2 – Halide (a-two halogen halide)	
3. Saponification	Fat	Base	1,2,3-propanetriol (glycerol)	Soap
4. Fermentation	$C_6H_{12}O_6$ (sugar)		C_2H_5OH (ethanol)	CO_2
5. Combustion	Hydrocarbon	O_2	Carbon dioxide	Water
6. Esterification	Organic acid	Alcohol	Ester	Water
7. Polymerization				
Condensation Polymerization	Alcohol Alcohol (monomers)		Ether (a polymer)	Water
Addition Polymerization	$n(CH_2=CH_2)$ (ethene monomers)		$(-CH_2-CH_2-)_n$ (polyethylene polymer)	
8. Cracking	$C_{14}H_{30}$ (large long chain)		C_7H_{16} C_7H_{14} (small shorter chains)	

Organic Reactions:

Substitution: *Replacing a hydrogen atom of an alkane with a halogen*

Alkane   +   Halogen   →   Halide   +   Acid

```
  H  H  H                              H  H  H
  |  |  |                              |  |  |
H-C--C--C-H   +   F-F   →   H-C--C--C-F   +   H-F
  |  |  |                              |  |  |
  H  H  H                              H  H  H
```

    propane   fluorine   fluoropropane   hydrogen fluoride

Addition: Hydrogenation - *Adding H atoms to the double bond of an alkene*

Alkene   +   Hydrogen   →   Alkane
(unsaturated)   (saturated)

C_3H_6 + H_2 → C_3H_8

```
  H  H  H                           H  H  H
  |  |  |                           |  |  |
H-C=C--C-H   +   H-H   →   H-C--C--C-H
     |                              |  |  |
     H                              H  H  H
```

    propene   hydrogen   propane

Addition: Halogenation - *Adding halogens to the double bond of an alkene*

Alkene   +   Halogen   →   Halide

C_3H_6 + Br_2 → $C_3H_6Br_2$

```
  H  H  H                             H  H  H
  |  |  |                             |  |  |
H-C=C--C-H   +   Br-Br   →   H-C--C--C-H
     |                                |  |  |
     H                                Br Br H
```

    propene   bromine   1,2-dibromopropane

Esterification: *Reacting an organic acid with an alcohol to make an ester*

Organic acid   +   Alcohol   →   Ester   +   Water

CH_3COOH + $HOCH_2CH_2CH_3$ → $CH_3COOCH_2CH_2CH_3$ + H_2O

```
  H  O                     H  H  H          H  O          H  H  H
  |  ||                    |  |  |          |  ||         |  |  |
H-C--C-OH   +   HO-C--C--C-H   →   H-C--C-O-C--C--C-H   +   H2O
  |                       |  |  |          |             |  |  |
  H                       H  H  H          H             H  H  H
```

  ethanoic acid   propanol   propyl ethanoate

Condensation Polymerization: *Joining small molecules by removing water*

Monomer	+	Monomer	→	Polymer	+	water
CH_3OH	+	$HOCH_2CH_3$	→	$CH_3OCH_2CH_3$	+	H_2O

$$
\begin{array}{cccccc}
& H & & H\ \ H & & \\
& | & & |\ \ \ | & & \\
H-C-OH & + & HO-C-C-H & \rightarrow & H-C-O-C-C-H & + \quad H_2O \\
& | & & |\ \ \ | & & \\
& H & & H\ \ H & & \\
\end{array}
$$

methanol   ethanol   methyl ethyl ether   water

Addition Polymerization: *Joining small unsaturated molecules together*

$$n(\text{-}CH_2=CH_2) \rightarrow (\text{-}CH_2\text{-}CH_2\text{-})_n$$

monomers   polymer

n represent several repeated units of the monomer.

Fermentation: *Making ethanol (alcohol) from sugar*

Sugar   ethanol   carbon dioxide

$$C_6H_{12}O_6 \xrightarrow{\ \ zymase\ \ } 2C_2H_5OH \quad + \quad CO_2$$

$$
\begin{array}{c}
\ \ H\ \ \ H \\
\ \ |\ \ \ \ | \\
H-C-C-OH \\
\ \ |\ \ \ \ | \\
\ \ H\ \ \ H \\
\end{array}
$$

Saponification: *Making soap from fat and base*

Fat   +   Base   →   Soap   +   Glycerol (an alcohol)

$$
\begin{array}{c}
H\ \ \ \ \ H\ \ \ \ \ H \\
|\ \ \ \ \ \ |\ \ \ \ \ \ | \\
H-C\ -\ C\ -\ C-H \\
|\ \ \ \ \ \ |\ \ \ \ \ \ | \\
OH\ \ \ OH\ \ \ OH \\
\end{array}
$$

1,2,3-propanetriol (glycerol)

Combustion: *Burning organic substance with oxygen*

Organic compound   +   Oxygen   →   Carbon dioxide   +   water

$$2C_8H_{18} \quad + \quad 25O_2 \quad \rightarrow \quad 16CO_2 \quad + \quad 18H_2O$$

Octane (car fuel)

Review Questions: Organic Reactions

Vocabulary: Briefly define each of the following terms.

57. Substitution   58. Addition   59. Fermentation   60. Saponification
61. Combustion   62. Esterification   63. Polymerization
64. Addition polymerization   65. Condensation polymerization

66. Carbon dioxide and water are two products formed from which organic reaction?
    (1) Combustion   (3) Fermentation
    (2) Esterification   (4) Saponification

67. Unsaturated hydrocarbons can become saturated through which organic reaction?
    (1) Esterification   (3) Addition
    (2) Fermentation   (4) Substitution

68. An alcohol and an organic acid are combined to form water and a compound with a pleasant odor. This reaction is an example of
    (1) esterification   (3) polymerization
    (2) fermentation   (4) saponification

69. A compound of which formula is likely formed from an addition reaction?
    (1) C_2H_5Cl (3) $C_2H_4Cl_2$
    (2) C_2H_5OH (4) CH_3OCH_3

70. Which compound is likely formed from a substitution reaction?
    (1) C_4H_6 (3) C_4H_9Br
    (2) $C_4H_8Br_2$ (4) C_4H_8

71. Which organic product is likely to form from addition polymerization of alkene monomers?
    (1) Glycerol   (3) Dichloromethane
    (2) Polyethylene   (4) Ethanol

72. A structure of which organic compound likely formed from a reaction between an organic acid and alcohol?

73. The reaction below
$$CH_3COOH \ + \ CH_3OH \ \rightarrow \ CH_3COOCH_3 \ + \ H_2O$$
    is best classified as
    (1) esterification   (3) combustion
    (2) polymerization   (4) saponification

74. Given an organic reaction below:
$$C_5H_{12} \ + \ Cl_2 \ \rightarrow \ C_5H_{11}Cl \ + \ HCl$$
    This reaction can be best classified as
    (1) addition   (3) polymerization
    (2) substitution   (4) hydrogenation

75. Given the equation: $C_2H_6 \ + \ F_2 \ \rightarrow \ X \ + \ HF$
    What is the name of compound X produced?
    (1) Ethene   (3) 1,2-difluoroethane
    (2) Fluoroethane   (4) Fluoropropane

Base your answers to questions 76 through 78 on the information below.

A reaction between bromine and a hydrocarbon is represented by the balanced equation below.

$$Br_2 + H-\overset{\displaystyle H}{\underset{\displaystyle H}{C}}=\overset{\displaystyle H}{\underset{\displaystyle H}{C}}-\overset{\displaystyle H}{\underset{\displaystyle H}{C}}-H \longrightarrow H-\overset{\displaystyle H}{\underset{\displaystyle Br}{C}}-\overset{\displaystyle H}{\underset{\displaystyle Br}{C}}-\overset{\displaystyle H}{\underset{\displaystyle H}{C}}-H$$

76. Write the name of the homologous series to which the hydrocarbon belongs.

77. Write the name of the product.

78. Identify the type of organic reaction represented by the equation.

Base your answers to questions 79 through 83 on the information below and on your knowledge of chemistry.

The unique odors and flavors of many fruits are primarily due to small quantities of a certain class of organic compounds. The equation below represents the production of one of these compounds.

$$H-\overset{\displaystyle H}{\underset{\displaystyle H}{C}}-\overset{\displaystyle H}{\underset{\displaystyle H}{C}}-OH + H-\overset{\displaystyle O}{C}-O-H \longrightarrow H-\overset{\displaystyle O}{C}-O-\overset{\displaystyle H}{\underset{\displaystyle H}{C}}-\overset{\displaystyle H}{\underset{\displaystyle H}{C}}-H + HOH$$

| Reactant 1 | Reactant 2 | Product 1 | Product 2 |

79. State the class of organic compounds to which Reactant 2 belongs.

80. Identify the type of organic reaction represented by the equation.

81. What is the IUPAC name of Product 1.

82. Draw and name a structural formula for an isomer of Product 1.

Base your answers to questions 83 and 84 on the information below.

One type of soap is produced when ethyl stearate and sodium hydroxide react. The soap produced by this reaction is called sodium stearate. The other product of the reaction is ethanol. This reaction is represented by the balanced equation below.

$$C_{17}H_{35}-\overset{\displaystyle O}{C}-O-C_2H_5 + NaOH \longrightarrow C_{17}H_{35}-\overset{\displaystyle O}{C}-O^- Na^+ + C_2H_5OH$$

| Ethyl stearate | Sodium hydroxide | Sodium stearate | Ethanol |

83. To which class of organic compounds does ethyl stearate belong?

84. Identify the type of organic reaction used to make soap.

Lesson 1 : Oxidation Numbers (States)

Certain chemical reactions involve the transfer of electrons between species (molecules, atoms, or ions) in the reaction.

Oxidation is the **loss** of electrons in a reaction.

Reduction is the **gain** of electrons in a reaction.

Redox is any chemical reaction that involves both oxidation and reduction.

Species that gain and lose electrons undergo changes in their oxidation numbers.

In this lesson, you will learn about oxidation numbers, which are important in determining the oxidized and reduced species in redox reactions.

Oxidation Number: *Charge of an Atom*

An oxidation number is the charge of an atom when it has lost or gained electrons. Rules for assigning oxidation numbers to elements in formulas are given on the next page.

The oxidation number of an element can be 0, negative(-) or positive(+).

For example:

K atom has an oxidation number of **0**.

O^{2-} ion has an oxidation number of **-2**.

Al^{3+} ion has an oxidation number of **+3**.

In all compounds, the sum of all oxidation numbers is equal to **zero**.

In polyatomic ions (Table E), the sum of all oxidation numbers is equal to the **charge** of the ion.

In the compound Na_2SO_4 , the sum of oxidation numbers of Na, S and O is Zero (0).

In the polyatomic ion CO_3^{2-}, the sum of oxidation numbers of C and O is equal to **-2**.

Determining Oxidation Numbers

When an atom in a formula has a few possible positive oxidation numbers, the actual oxidation number of the atom in that formula can be determined using simple math.

Example 1: What is the oxidation number of **S** in the compound Na_2SO_4?

Note: The sum of charges must be equal to **zero (0)**.

Na = +1 charge: 2Na = 2(+1) = +2 total positive charge

O = -2 charge: 4O = 4(-2) = - 8 total negative charge

S oxidation number must be a **+6** for all charges to equal 0   (+2 − 8 +6 = 0)

Example 2: What is the oxidation number of **C** in the polyatomic ion CO_3^{2-} ?

Note: The sum of charges must be equal to **-2**.

$$1C + 3O = -2$$
$$C + 3(-2) = -2$$
$$C = -2 + 6 = +4$$

Oxidation Number Rules

In redox equations, oxidation numbers are assigned to the elements to help determine the oxidized and reduced species, as well as the number of electrons that are lost and gained. A few simple rules must be followed to correctly assign oxidation numbers to all elements in a reaction equation.

1. The oxidation number of a free element is always zero (0). Ex. Na, O_2, S_8.

2. The oxidation number of a monatomic ion is the charge of the ion. Ex. Na^+, O^{2-}

3. The sum of all the oxidation numbers in a neutral compound is zero.

4. The sum of all the oxidation numbers in a polyatomic ion is the charge of the ion.

5. The common oxidation state of an element in a compound can be found on the Periodic Table. The table below lists categories of elements and their common oxidation states, as well as exceptions in which the charge of the element is different.

Table of Rules for Assigning Oxidation Numbers

Element	Common Oxidation State	Exceptions
Group 1 metals	always +1	
Group 2 metals	always +2	
Oxygen	usually -2	In peroxides (ex. N_2O_2), it's a -1. In a compound with fluorine (OF_2), it's a +2.
Hydrogen	usually +1	In metal hydrides (ex. NaH, CaH_2), it's a -1.
Fluorine	always -1	
Chlorine Bromine Iodine	usually -1	In compounds and polyatomic ions with O (ex. NaClO, $LiBrO_3$), it can be one of a few positive values. The actual +charge value of Cl, Br, or I can be determined as shown on page 181.

Review Questions: Oxidation Numbers

Vocabulary: Briefly define the following term.

1. Oxidation number

2. What is the oxidation number of oxygen in ozone, O_3,
   (1) +1   (2) 0   (3) -2   (4) -6

3. The oxidation number of hydrogen in BeH_2 is
   (1) +1   (2) -1   (3) 0   (4) +2

4. What is the oxidation number of Pt in K_2PtCl_6?
   (1) +4   (2) -4   (3) +2   (4) -2

5. What are the two oxidation states of nitrogen in the compound NH_4NO_3?
   (1) -3 and +5   (3) +3 and +5
   (2) -3 and -5   (4) +3 and -5

6. Below, two compounds of chlorine are given:
        Compound A: Cl_2O Compound B: HClO
   Which is true of the oxidation number of chlorine in compounds A and B?
   (1) Chlorine's oxidation number is +2 in A, but +1 in B.
   (2) Chlorine's oxidation number is +1 in A, but +2 in B.
   (3) Chlorine's oxidation number is +2 in both A and B.
   (4) Chlorine's oxidation number is +1 in both A and B.

7. What is the oxidation number of Cr in the polyatomic ion, $Cr_2O_7{}^{2-}$?
   (1) +7   (2) +6   (3) -2   (4) +2

8. In which substance does bromine have an oxidation number of +3?
   (1) KBrO   (3) $KBrO_2$
   (2) $KBrO_3$ (4) $KBrO_4$

9. Sulfur has an oxidation number of +6 in which two formulas?
   (1) SO_3 and $SO_4{}^{2-}$ (3) SO_2 and $SO_4{}^{2-}$
   (2) H_2SO_4 and SO_2 (4) $HSO_4{}^-$ and $S_2O_3{}^{2-}$

Base your answers to questions 10 and 11 on the information below.

     Litharge, PbO, is an ore that can be roasted (heated) in the presence of carbon monoxide, CO, to produce elemental lead. The reaction that takes place during this roasting process is represented by the balanced equation below.
$$PbO(s) + CO(g) \rightarrow Pb(s) + CO_2(g)$$

10. Determine the oxidation number of lead in litharge.

11. In which compound does carbon have the greater oxidation number?

Base your answers to questions 12 and 13 on the information below.

     The head of matches contains an oxidizing agent such as potassium chlorate, $KClO_3$, together with tetraphosphorus trisulfide, P_4S_3, glass and binder. When struck either by an object or on the side of a box of matches, the phosphorus sulfide compound is easily ignited, causing the potassium chlorate to decompose into potassium chloride and oxygen. The oxygen in turn causes the phosphorus sulfide to burn more vigorously.

12. Determine the oxidation number of chlorine in potassium chlorate.

13. In terms of charges, explain why potassium chloride, KCl, is neutral.

Lesson 2: Redox: Oxidation and Reduction Reactions

In **redox** reactions, **electrons** are lost (oxidation) and gained (reduction).
The number of moles of electrons lost and gained must be the same (equal).
Species that lose and gain electrons undergo a change in their oxidation numbers.

Redox Reactions: *Involve Transfer of Electrons*

Single replacement, synthesis and decomposition are generally redox reactions.
• In these reactions, electrons are lost and gained simultaneously.
Examples of these reactions are shown below. They were also covered in Topic 5.

Synthesis	$N_2 + O_2 \rightarrow 2NO$	
Decomposition	$2H_2O_2 \rightarrow 2H_2O + O_2$	
Single replacement	$Cu + 2AgNO_3 \rightarrow Cu(NO_3)_2 + 2Ag$	
Simplified redox	$Cu^0 + 2Ag^+ \rightarrow Cu^{2+} + 2Ag^0$	

These and similar reactions are redox because:
• Two species in each equation have a change of oxidation number.
• Therefore, electrons are both lost and gained.

Non-redox Reactions
Double replacement reactions are *not* redox reactions.
• In these reactions, electrons are neither lost nor gained.
Examples of non-redox reactions are given below.

Double replacement	$KI + AgNO_3 \rightarrow AgI + KNO_3$	
Ions combining	$Na^+ + Cl^- \rightarrow NaCl$	
Ionization	$H_2O \rightarrow H^+ + OH^-$	

These and similar reactions are *NOT* redox because:
• None of the elements in the equations has a change of oxidation number.
• Therefore, electrons are neither lost nor gained.

Oxidation: *Loss of Electrons is Oxidation* **(LEO).**
In redox reactions, the **oxidized substance** is the substance or ion that is losing or transferring its electrons. The oxidized substance is also the *reducing agent* because it will cause another substance in the reaction to gain electrons.
• Oxidation number of the oxidized substance always increases (becomes more positive) because the substance has lost negative particles (electrons).

Reduction: *Gain of Electrons is Reduction* **(GER).**
In redox reactions, the **reduced substance** is the substance or ion that is gaining or accepting electrons. The reduced substance is also the *oxidizing agent* because it will cause another substance in the reaction to lose electrons.
• Oxidation number of the reduced substance always decreases (becomes more negative) because the substance has gained negative particles (electrons).

Half-reactions: *Written for Oxidation or Reduction*

A **half-reaction** shows either the oxidation or reduction portion of a redox reaction. A correct half-reaction must show conservation of atoms and charge. Consider the redox reaction below:

$$2Na + Cl_2 \rightarrow 2NaCl$$

An **oxidation half-reaction** shows the loss of electrons by a species in a redox reaction. In the above redox reaction, sodium is the species that is losing electrons.
• The electrons that are lost are always shown on the *right* side of the half-reaction equation as represented below.

$$2Na^0 \rightarrow 2Na^+ + 2e^- \quad \textbf{oxidation half-reaction}$$

A **reduction half-reaction** shows the gain of electrons by a substance in a redox reaction. In the above redox reaction, chlorine is the species that is gaining electrons.
• The electrons that are gained are always shown on the *left* side of the half-reaction equation as represented below.

$$Cl_2^0 + 2e^- \rightarrow 2Cl^- \quad \textbf{reduction half-reaction}$$

Note: Both half-reaction equations demonstrate conservation of atoms and charge. All half-reaction equations must be balanced.

Interpreting Half-reaction Equations

A half-reaction equation provides information about the change a species undergoes in a redox reaction. Two half-reaction equations are given below. One has electrons on the left and the other has electrons on the right. Each half-reaction is interpreted by describing changes the substance is going through.

Reduction Half-reaction *Equation with Electrons on the LEFT*	Oxidation Half-reaction *Equation with Electrons on the RIGHT*
$$C^0 + 4e^- \rightarrow C^{4-}$$	$$Sb^{3+} \rightarrow Sb^{5+} + 2e^-$$
C^0 atom gains 4 electrons to become C^{4-}.	Sb^{3+} loses 2 electrons to become Sb^{5+}.
C^0 oxidation number decreases from 0 to -4.	Sb^{3+} oxidation number increases from +3 to +5.
C^0 is the reduced substance, and also the oxidizing agent.	Sb^{3+} is the oxidized substance, and also the reducing agent.
The number of electrons gained (4) is the difference in the two oxidation states. $$0 - (-4) = 4$$	The number of electrons lost (2) is the difference in the two oxidation states. $$+5 - +3 = 2$$

Interpreting Oxidation Number Changes

Oxidation number change can be used to determine if oxidation or reduction has occurred.

Oxidation or Loss of Electrons:

An increase in oxidation number represents oxidation.

$$0 \longrightarrow +1$$

This change indicates 1 e- is lost.

$$+3 \longrightarrow +5$$

This change indicates 2 e- are lost.

Reduction or Gain of Electrons:

A decrease in oxidation number represents reduction.

$$0 \longrightarrow -4$$

This change indicates 4 e- are gained.

$$+4 \longrightarrow +2$$

This change indicates 2 e- are gained.

number of electrons gained or lost = difference in two oxidation numbers.

Making a scale like the one on the right can also help you determine the number of electrons that are gained or lost.

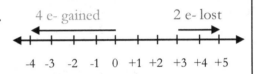

4 e- gained   2 e- lost

-4 -3 -2 -1 0 +1 +2 +3 +4 +5

Redox Reaction Equations

A redox equation can be given in one of two forms as shown below.

Redox equation 1 $Mg^0 + Al^{3+} \rightarrow Mg^{2+} + Al^0$

Redox equation 2 $Ca + H_2SO_4 \rightarrow CaSO_4 + H_2$

Note the difference between the equations. Equation 1 has oxidation numbers clearly noted for the elements. For equation 2, oxidation numbers must first be assigned to the elements before changes in oxidation numbers can be considered and used to answer questions.

For any redox equation that is given, you should be able to answer these questions:

1. What is the oxidation number change of a substance?
2. Which substance is oxidized or lost electrons?
3. Which substance is reduced or gained electrons?
4. Which substance is the reducing agent?
5. Which substance is the oxidizing agent?
6. How many electrons are lost or gained?
7. What is the correct oxidation half-reaction?
8. What is the correct reduction half-reaction?

To answer these questions correctly, oxidation numbers must be correctly assigned, and changes in oxidation numbers correctly considered.

Interpreting Redox Reaction Equations

The two equations given on the previous page are interpreted below:

TIP: When determining oxidized and reduced substances in a reaction, consider the following about the equation given.

Oxidized substance: The substance *left* of the arrow with the *smaller charge.*

Reduced substance: The substance *left* of the arrow with the *greater charge.*

$$3Mg^0 \quad + \quad 2Al^{3+} \longrightarrow \quad 3Mg^{2+} \quad + \quad 2Al^0$$

Mg^0 has a *smaller* charge than Al^{3+}. Therefore: Mg^0 is oxidized. Mg^0 loses 2 electrons. Mg^0 is also the reducing agent. Mg^0 oxidation number increases from 0 to +2. *Oxidation half-reaction:* $Mg^0 \rightarrow Mg^{2+} + 2e\text{-}$	Al^{3+} has a *larger* charge than Mg^0 Therefore: Al^{3+} is reduced. Al^{3+} gains 3 electrons . Al^{3+} is also the oxidizing agent. Al^{3+} oxidation number decreases from +3 to 0 . *Reduction half-reaction:* $Al^{3+} + 3e\text{-} \rightarrow Al^0$	Species to the *right* of the arrow in redox equations (ex. Mg^{2+} and Al^0) are the results of species on the *left* losing and gaining electrons. Therefore, species on the *right* are neither oxidized nor reduced.

Note: For the equation below, oxidation numbers are ***correctly assigned*** (according to rules) to elements before it can be interpreted.

$$Ca \quad + \quad H_2SO_4 \longrightarrow \quad CaSO_4 \quad + \quad H_2$$
$$0 \qquad\qquad +1 +6 -2 \qquad\qquad +2 +6 -2 \qquad 0$$
$$Ca \quad + \quad H_2SO_4 \longrightarrow \quad CaSO_4 \quad + \quad H_2$$

Ca^0 has a *smaller* charge than H^+. Therefore: Ca^0 is oxidized. Ca^0 loses 2 electrons. Ca^0 is also the reducing agent. Ca^0 oxidation number increases from 0 to +2. *Oxidation half-reaction:* $Ca^0 \rightarrow Ca^{2+} + 2e\text{-}$	H^+ has a *greater* charge than Ca^0. Therefore: H^+ is reduced. H^+ gains 1 electron. H^+ is also the oxidizing agent. H^+ oxidation number decreases from +1 to 0. *Reduction half-reaction:* $2H^+ + 2e\text{-} \rightarrow H_2^0$	Species to the *right* of the arrow in redox equations (ex. Ca^{2+} and H_2^0) are the results of species on the *left* losing and gaining electrons. Therefore, species on the *right* are neither oxidized nor reduced. The oxidation numbers of S and O did not change. Therefore, S and O are neither oxidized nor reduced .

Review Questions: Oxidation and Reduction Reactions

Vocabulary: Briefly define each of the following terms.

14. Redox   15. Oxidation   16. Reduction   17. Oxidized substance
18. Reduced substance   19. Oxidizing agent   20. Reducing agent
21. Half-reaction

22. Oxidation in a redox reaction involves a
    (1) gain of protons   (3) gain of electrons
    (2) loss of protons   (4) loss of electrons

23. A reduced substance in oxidation and reduction reactions
    (1) gains electrons and has a decrease in oxidation number.
    (2) gains electrons and has an increase in oxidation number.
    (3) loses electrons and has a decrease in oxidation number.
    (4) loses electrons and has an increase in oxidation number.

24. Which equation represents an oxidation – reduction reaction?
    (1) $SO_2 + H_2O \rightarrow H_2SO_3$ (3) $O_2 + 2H_2 \rightarrow 2H_2O$
    (2) $SO_3^{2-} + 2H^+ \rightarrow H_2SO_4$ (4) $OH^- + H^+ \rightarrow H_2O$

25. Given the four equations below.
    I: $AgNO_3 + NaCl \rightarrow AgCl + NaNO_3$
    II: $Cl_2 + H_2O \rightarrow HClO + HCl$
    III: $CuO + CO \rightarrow CO_2 + Cu$
    IV: $LiOH + HCl \rightarrow LiCl + H_2O$

    Which two equations represent redox reactions?
    (1) I and II   (3) III and I
    (2) II and III   (4) IV and II

26. Which of the following oxidation number changes represents oxidation?
    (1) 0 to +1   (3) 0 to -1
    (2) -2 to -3   (4) +1 to 0

27. Which oxidation number change indicates the most number of electrons gained
    by a species in a redox reaction?
    (1) +3 to +7   (3) 0 to +4
    (2) +6 to +3   (4) +3 to -1

28. Which half-reaction correctly shows reduction?
    (1) $Sn^{2+} \rightarrow Sn^{4+} + 2e^-$ (3) $Sn^{2+} + 2e^- \rightarrow Sn^0$
    (2) $Sn^{2+} \rightarrow Sn^0 + 2e^-$ (4) $Sn^{2+} + 2e^- \rightarrow Sn^{4+}$

29. Which half-reaction correctly represents oxidation?
    (1) $Ag + e^- \rightarrow Ag^-$ (3) $Au^{3+} + 3e^- \rightarrow Au$
    (2) $Ag \rightarrow Ag^+ + e^-$ (4) $Au^{3+} \rightarrow Au + 3e^-$

30. Which change occurs when an Sn^{2+} ion is oxidized to Sn^{4+}?
    (1) Two electrons are lost .   (3) Two protons are lost.
    (2) Two electrons are gained.   (4) Two protons are gained.

31. Which change occurs when N^{3+} is changed to an N atom?
    (1) Three neutrons are lost.   (3) Three protons are gained.
    (2) Three electrons are lost.   (4) Three electrons are gained.

E3chemistry.com

32. In the half-reaction equation:
    $$Mn^{3+} \rightarrow Mn^{7+} + 4e^-$$
    Which is true of the Mn^{3+} ion?
    (1) It is oxidized by gaining 4 electrons.   (3) It is reduced by gaining 4 electrons.
    (2) It is oxidized by losing 4 electrons.   (4) It is reduced by losing 4 electrons.

33. Consider the oxidation-reduction reaction:
    $$Co^0 + Cu^{2+} \rightarrow Co^{2+} + Cu$$
    Which species is reduced?
    (1) Co^0 (3) Co^{2+}
    (2) Cu^0 (4) Cu^{2+}

34. Given the balanced equation representing a reaction:
    $$Fe_2O_3 + 2Al \rightarrow Al_2O_3 + 2Fe$$
    During this reaction, the oxidation number of Fe changes from
    (1) +2 to 0 as electrons are transferred.   (3) +3 to 0 as electrons are transferred.
    (2) +2 to 0 as protons are transferred.   (4) +3 to 0 as protons are transferred.

35. Given the oxidation-reduction reaction:
    $$Co(s) + PbCl_2(aq) \rightarrow CoCl_2(aq) + Pb(s)$$
    Which statement correctly describes the oxidation and reduction that occur?
    (1) Co(s) is oxidized and Cl^-(aq) is reduced.
    (2) Co(s) is oxidized and Pb^{2+}(aq) is reduced.
    (3) Co(s) is reduced and Cl^-(aq) is oxidized.
    (4) Co(s) is reduced and Pb^{2+}(aq) is oxidized.

36. Consider the redox reaction:
    $$Mn^0 + O_2 \rightarrow Mn^{4+} + 2O^{2-}$$
    Which half-reaction is correct for the reduction that occurs?
    (1) $O_2 \rightarrow 2O^{2-} + 4e^-$ (3) $Mn^0 + 4e^- \rightarrow Mn^{4+}$
    (2) $O_2 + 4e^- \rightarrow 2O^{2-}$ (4) $Mn^0 \rightarrow Mn^{4+} + 4e^-$

37. Complete the equation: $2N^{3-} \rightarrow N_2{}^0 + $ _____

38. Complete the equation: _____ $+ 4e^- \rightarrow Cr^{2+}$

Base your answers to questions 39 and 40 on the following redox reaction, which occurs spontaneously.
$$Zn + Fe^{3+} \rightarrow Zn^{2+} + Fe$$

39. State what happens to the number of protons in a Zn atom when it changes to Zn^{2+} as the redox reaction occurs.

40. Which species in this reaction is losing electrons?

Base your answers to questions 41 and 42 on the information below.

In a laboratory investigation, magnesium reacts with hydrochloric acid to produce hydrogen gas and magnesium chloride. This reaction is represented by the unbalanced equation below.

$$Mg(s) + HCl(aq) \rightarrow H_2(g) + MgCl_2(aq)$$

41. Write a balanced half-reaction equation for the reduction that occurs.

42. Compare the number of electrons lost and gained by species in this reaction.

Lesson 3: Electrochemistry

Electrochemistry is the study of relationships between redox chemical reactions and electrical energy. When a substance in a redox reaction is oxidized, the electrons that are lost are gained by the reduced substance. If a redox reaction system is set up so that there are paths for the electrons and ions to flow, electrical current can be produced. A *battery* is a good example of a system that is set up to produce electrical energy from a redox reaction.

In this lesson of topic 11, you will learn about redox reactions that produce electrical energy and those that use electrical energy.

Electrochemical Cells: *Voltaic and Electrolytic Cells*

An **electrochemical cell** is a device or system that can either produce electrical energy from a chemical reaction or use electrical energy to force a chemical reaction. Voltaic and electrolytic cells are types of electrochemical cells.

Voltaic Cells: *Chemical to Electrical Energy*

A **voltaic cell** is a type of cell in which a spontaneous redox reaction occurs to produce electrical energy. In voltaic cells:
• **Chemical energy is converted to electrical energy.**
• Reaction is spontaneous and exothermic.
• Oxidation and reduction occur in two separate cells.
• A salt bridge connects the two half-cells and provides a path for ions to flow between cells.
• A battery is an example of a voltaic cell.

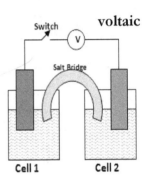

Electrolytic Cells: *Electrical to Chemical Energy*

An **electrolytic cell** is a type of cell in which electrical energy is used to force a nonspontaneous redox reaction to occur. In electrolytic cells:
• **Electrical energy is converted to chemical energy.**
• External energy source (such as a battery) provides the energy needed to force the reaction.
• Reaction is nonspontaneous and endothermic.
• Both oxidation and reduction occur in one cell.
• Electrolytic reduction, electroplating of metals, and electrolysis of water use electrolytic cell processes.

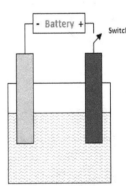

E3chemistry.com

Anode, Cathode, Wire, Salt Bridge, and Battery

Oxidation and reduction reactions that occur in electrochemical cells take place at specific sites called electrodes.

Electrodes are sites on electrochemical cells where oxidation and reduction take place. The anode and cathode are the two electrodes in all electrochemical cells. The anode and cathode on electrochemical cells are labeled with a positive(+) or a negative(-) sign. The type of cell determines which electrode is positive and which electrode is negative.

Anode: *Oxidation Site. Where Electrons are Lost.*
The anode is the electrode where oxidation occurs in both voltaic and electrolytic cells. The anode, therefore, is the site on any electrochemical cell where *electrons are lost*.
Signs for anode on voltaic and electrolytic cells are as follows:

> Voltaic cells: **A**node is **N**egative **(–)**.
> Electrolytic cells: **An**ode is **P**ositive **(+)**.

Cathode: *Reduction Site. Where Electrons are Gained.*
The cathode is the electrode where reduction occurs in both voltaic and electrolytic cells. The cathode, therefore, is the site on any electrochemical cell where *electrons are gained*.
Signs for cathode on voltaic and electrolytic cells are as follows:

> Voltaic cells: **C**athode is **P**ositive **(+)**.
> Electrolytic cells: **C**athode is **N**egative **(–)**.

External Conduit (Wire): *Permits Flow of Electrons from Anode to Cathode.*
Electrons that are lost at the anode flow to the cathode via the external conduit, which is usually any electrical wire that connects the two electrodes. The external conduit is present in both voltaic and electrolytic cells.

Salt Bridge: *Permits Flow of Ions (Voltaic only)*
The salt bridge is any porous substance that connects the solutions in the two half-cells of a voltaic cell. The positive and negative ions in the solutions flow or migrate between the two cells via the salt bridge. The flow of ions is necessary to keep the two half-cells neutral, and for the appropriate functioning of a voltaic cell. A salt bridge is not present in electrolytic cells.

Battery or Power Source: *Provides Energy (Electrolytic only).*
In electrolytic cell processes, energy is needed to force the nonspontaneous redox reaction to occur. Without an external energy source, half-reactions will not occur in an electrolytic cell.

Codes to Remembering Key Redox and Electrochemistry Information:

LEO : **L**oss of **E**lectrons is **O**xidation	**GER**: **G**ain of **E**lectrons is **R**eduction.
An Ox: **An**ode is for **Ox**idation	**Red Cat**: **Red**uction is at **Cat**hode
APE: **A**node is **P**ositive in **E**lectrolytic	**VCP**: **V**oltaic **C**athode is **P**ositive
VAN: **V**oltaic **A**node is **N**egative	**CEN**: **C**athode in **E**lectrolytic is **N**egative

Voltaic Cell Diagram: *Anode, Cathode, Salt bridge, Voltmeter, Wire, Beakers, Switch*

Below is a diagram representing a voltaic cell. The components of the cell are labeled on the diagram. All components must be present and correctly connected for a voltaic cell to operate. The redox equation representing the reaction taking place in this cell is given at the bottom of the diagram.

Volatic Cell Diagram

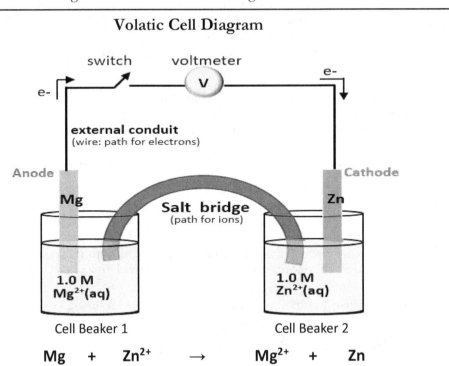

switch   **voltmeter**

external conduit
(wire: path for electrons)

Anode   Cathode

Mg   **Zn**

Salt bridge
(path for ions)

1.0 M
Mg²⁺(aq)   **1.0 M**
Zn²⁺(aq)

Cell Beaker 1   Cell Beaker 2

$$Mg \;+\; Zn^{2+} \;\longrightarrow\; Mg^{2+} \;+\; Zn$$

The equation of the redox reaction taking place in the cell is sometimes given.
The equation can be used to determine oxidized and reduced substances.

For voltaic cells, TABLE J can be used to determine the anode and cathode.

According to Table J	Table J	According to TABLE J
	Metals	

According to Table J

Mg is more active than Zn.

Therefore

Mg is the **anode** (oxidation site).
Mg is the **negative(-)** electrode.
Mg is **oxidized** (lost electrons).
Mg will lose mass.

Oxidation half-reaction

$$Mg \;\rightarrow\; Mg^{2+} \;+\; 2e\text{-}$$

Table J

Metals

Li
Rb
K
Cs
Ba
Sr
Ca
Na
Mg
Al
Ti
Mn
Zn
Cr

According to TABLE J

Zn is less active than Mg.

Therefore

Zn is the **cathode** (reduction site).
Zn is the **positive(+)** electrode.
Zn will gain mass.

However

Zn²⁺ is **reduced** (gained electrons)

Reduction half-reaction

$$Zn^{2+} \;+\; 2e\text{-} \;\rightarrow\; Zn$$

Electrolytic Cell Diagrams: *Anode, Cathode, Battery, Wire, Beaker, Switch*

An electrolytic cell is set up to use electrical energy (from battery or other external energy source) to force a nonspontaneous chemical reaction to occur. The setup of the cell depends on what needs to be accomplished in the process. Three common electrolytic processes are described below.

Electrolysis of water is a process that splits water molecules to produce oxygen and hydrogen.

$$2H_2O(l) \;+\; electricity \;\rightarrow\; 2H_2(g) \;+\; O_2(g)$$

Electrolytic reduction is used to obtain a reactive metal from its fused salt. Elements in Group 1 and Group 2 of the Periodic Table, because of their high reactivity, are generally obtained from this process.

$$2NaBr(l) \;+\; electricity \;\rightarrow\; 2Na(s) \;+\; Br_2(g)$$

fused salt   *a highly reactive*
element is obtained

Electroplating is a process in which the ion of a desired metal is reduced to produce the metal. The metal that is produced is coated onto the surface of another object.

$$Au^+(aq) \;+\; e^- \;\rightarrow\; Au(s)$$

Electrolytic Reduction Cell Diagram   **Electroplating Cell Diagram**

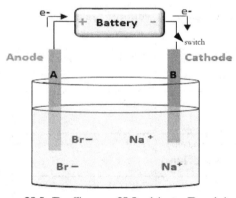

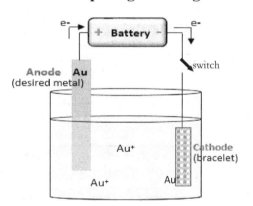

$$2NaBr(l) \;\rightarrow\; 2Na(s) + Br_2(g)$$ $$Au^+(aq) \;+\; e^- \;\rightarrow\; Au(s)$$

Rod at the positive end (**A**)	**Anode**	Metal at the positive end (**Au**) *(will lose mass)*
Rod at the negative end (**B**)	**Cathode**	Object at the negative end (**bracelet**) *(will gain mass)*
The negative ion (**Br⁻**) $2Br^- \rightarrow Br_2 + 2e^-$	**Oxidized** Half-reaction	The metal element (**Au**) $Au \rightarrow Au^+ + e^-$
The positive ion (**Na⁺**) $2Na^+ + 2e^- \rightarrow 2Na$	**Reduced** Half-reaction	The metal ion (**Au⁺**) $Au^+ + e^- \rightarrow Au$

Summary of the Two Electrochemical Cells

Below is a summary of voltaic and electrolytic cells. Use this table for a quick review and comparisons of the two electrochemical cells.

		Voltaic	Electrolytic
	Diagrams		
D i f f e r e n c e s	*Example redox equation*	$Pb + Cu^{2+} \longrightarrow Pb^{2+} + Cu$	$H_2O + electricity \longrightarrow H_2 + O_2$
	Type of reaction	Spontaneous redox Exothermic	Non-spontaneous redox Endothermic
	Energy conversion	Chemical to electrical energy	Electrical to chemical energy
	Anode (site for oxidation)	Negative (-) electrode	Positive (+) electrode
	Cathode (site for reduction)	Positive (+) electrode	Negative (-) electrode
	Half-Reactions occur in	Two separate cells	One cell
	Salt bridge present?	Yes (connects the two cells) (permits the flow of ions)	No
	Usages and examples	Battery	Electroplating Electrolytic reduction Electrolysis
S i m i l a r i t i e s	*Oxidation (losing of electrons) at*	Anode (-) (loses mass)	Anode (+) (loses mass)
	Reduction (gaining of electrons) at	Cathode (+) (gains mass)	Cathode (-) (gains mass)
	Direction of electron flow (through the wire)	Anode to Cathode	Anode to Cathode

Review Questions: Electrochemistry

Vocabulary: Briefly define each of the following terms.
43. Electrochemical cell   44. Electrode   45. Anode   46. Cathode
47. Voltaic cell   48. Electrolytic cell   49. Electroplating   50. Electrolytic reduction
51. Electrolysis   52. Salt Bridge   53. Battery

54. What kind of reaction occurs in an operating electrolytic cell?
(1) Non-spontaneous oxidation-reduction   (3) Non-spontaneous oxidation, only
(2) Spontaneous oxidation-reduction   (4) Spontaneous reduction, only

55. An electrochemical cell setup consists of two half cells connected by an external
conductor and a salt bridge. The function of the salt bridge is to
(1) block a path for the flow of electrons
(2) block a path for the flow of ions
(3) provide a path for the flow of electrons
(4) provide a path for the flow of ions

56. In both the voltaic and the electrolytic cell, the anode is the electrode at which
(1) reduction occurs and electrons are lost
(2) reduction occurs and electrons are gained
(3) oxidation occurs and electrons are lost
(4) oxidation occurs and electrons are gained

57. In an electrolytic cell, the positive electrode is the
(1) anode, at which reduction occurs   (3) cathode, at which reduction occurs
(2) anode, at which oxidation occurs   (4) cathode, at which oxidation occurs

58. Given the reaction:
$$Mg(s) + FeSO_4(aq) \rightarrow Fe(s) + MgSO_4(aq)$$
The reaction would most likely occur in
(1) a voltaic cell, and will produce energy
(2) an electrolytic cell, and will produce energy
(3) a voltaic cell, and will absorb energy
(4) an electrolytic cell, and will absorb energy

59. Which energy conversion occurs during the operation of a voltaic cell?
(1) Chemical energy is spontaneously converted to electrical energy.
(2) Chemical energy is converted to electrical energy only when an external power
source is provided.
(3) Electrical energy is spontaneously converted to chemical energy.
(4) Electrical energy is converted to chemical energy only when an external power
source is provided.

Base your answers to questions 60 and 61 on the diagram below.

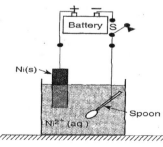

60. In this cell diagram, which is reduced?
(1) Ni atoms   (3) Ni^{2+} ions
(2) The battery   (4) The spoon

61. Which statement best describes the spoon in this diagram?
(1) It acts as the anode, and is negative.
(2) It acts as the cathode, and is negative.
(3) It acts as the anode, and is positive.
(4) It acts as the cathode, and is positive.

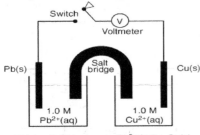

$$Pb(s) + Cu^{2+}(aq) \longrightarrow Pb^{2+}(aq) + Cu(s)$$

62. When the switch is closed, the species oxidized is
   (1) $Cu^{2+}(aq)$ (3) $Pb(s)$
   (2) $Pb^{2+}(aq)$ (4) $Cu(s)$

63. The salt bridge in the electrochemical diagram will connect
   (1) Pb atoms to Cu atoms
   (2) Pb^{2+} ions to Cu^{2+} ions
   (3) Pb^{2+} ions to Cu atoms
   (4) Cu^{2+} ions to Pb atoms

64. The anode in this electrochemical cell is the
   (1) Cu atom, which is the positive electrode.
   (2) Pb atom, which is the positive electrode.
   (3) Cu atom, which is the negative electrode.
   (4) Pb atom, which is the negative electrode.

Base your answers to questions 65 through 68 on the information below and on your knowledge of chemistry.

A small digital clock can be powered by a battery made from two potatoes and some household materials. The "potato clock" battery consists of two cells connected in a way to produce enough electricity to allow the clock to operate. In each cell, zinc atoms react to form zinc ions. Hydrogen ions from phosphoric acid in the potatoes react to form hydrogen gas. The labeled diagram and balanced ionic equation below show the reaction, the materials, and connections necessary to make a "potato clock" battery.

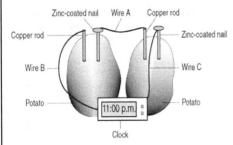

$$Zn(s) + 2H^+(aq) \rightarrow Zn^{2+}(aq) + H_2(g)$$

65. What type of an electrochemical cell is a "potato clock" battery?

66. State the direction of electron flow in wire A as the two cells operate.

67. Write a balanced half-reaction equation for the oxidation that occurs in the "potato clock" battery.

68. Explain why phosphoric acid is needed for the battery to operate.

Base your answers to questions 69 and 70 on the information below.

Metallic elements are obtained from their ores by reduction. Some metals, such as zinc, lead, iron, and copper, can be obtained by heating their oxides with carbon.

More active metals, such as aluminum, magnesium, and sodium, cannot be reduced by carbon. These metals can be obtained by the electrolysis of their molten (melted) ores. The diagram below represents an incomplete cell for the electrolysis of molten NaCl. The equation below represents the reaction that occurs when the completed cell operates.

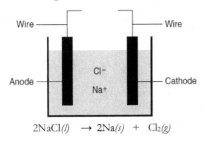

$$2NaCl(l) \rightarrow 2Na(s) + Cl_2(g)$$

69. Identify the component required for the electrolysis of molten NaCl that is missing from the cell diagram.

70. Write a balanced half-reaction equation for the reduction that will occur when the completed cell operates.

       E3chemistry.com

Lesson 4: Spontaneous Reactions and The Activity Series

A **spontaneous reaction** is a reaction that will take place or occur on its own under a specific set of conditions. The **Activity Series (Table J)** can be used to predict if a reaction is spontaneous or nonspontaneous.

In general, a single replacement reaction will be spontaneous if the free element reactant is more reactive than the similar element in the compound reactant.

Spontaneous reaction 1

$$Zn \quad + \quad FeCl_2 \quad \rightarrow \quad ZnCl_2 \; + \; Fe$$

free element   similar element
reactant   in a compound

According to the equation, Zn replaces Fe to form $ZnCl_2$.
The reaction is *spontaneous* because Zn is more reactive (higher up on Table J) than Fe.

Spontaneous reaction 2

$$Cl_2 \quad + \quad SnBr_2 \quad \rightarrow \quad SnCl_2 \; + \; Br_2$$

free element   similar element
reactant   in a compound

According to the equation, Cl replaces Br to form $SnCl_2$.
The reaction is *spontaneous* because Cl is more reactive (higher up on Table J) than Br.

Nonspontaneous reaction

$$Pb \quad + \quad NiCl_2 \quad \rightarrow \quad PbCl_2 \; + \; Ni$$

free element   similar element
reactant   in a compound

According to the equation, Pb replaces Ni to form $PbCl_2$.
The reaction is *nonspontaneous* (will not occur on its own) because Pb is less reactive (lower down on Table J) than Ni.

Table J
Activity Series**

Most Active	Metals	Nonmetals	Most Active
	Li	F_2	
	Rb	Cl_2 ◇	
	K	Br_2 ◇	
	Cs	I_2	
	Ba		
	Sr		
	Ca		
	Na		
	Mg		
	Al		
	Ti		
	Mn		
	Zn ●		
	Cr		
	Fe ●		
	Co		
	Ni □		
	Sn		
	Pb □		
	H_2		
	Cu		
	Ag		
Least Active	Au		Least Active

Some elements are more easily oxidized; others are more easily reduced.

Metals
Most easily oxidized: The metal closest to the top of Table J (Li).

Most easily reduced: Ion of the metal closest to the bottom (Au^+).

- An element on the top will react spontaneously with an ion of an element below it. For an example: Zn will react spontaneously with Fe^{2+}. When the reaction occurs:
  Zn will cause Fe^{2+} to be reduced to Fe atoms.
  Fe^{2+} will cause Zn to be oxidized to Zn^{2+}.

Nonmetals
Most easily oxidized: Ion of the nonmetal closest to the bottom (I^-).

Most easily reduced: Nonmetal closest to the top (F_2).

Review Questions: Spontaneous Reactions and the Activity Series

71. Based on Reference Table J, which metal is most easily oxidized?
    (1) Ni   (2) Zn   (3) Cr   (4) Co

72. Based on Reference Table J, which ion is most easily reduced?
    (1) Sr^{2+} (2) Ba^{2+} (3) Ca^{2+} (4) Mg^{2+}

73. Which metal will reduce Zn^{2+} to Zn?
    (1) Mn   (2) Cr   (3) H_2 (4) Ag

74. Which metal, according to Table J, will react spontaneously with Al^{3+}?
    (1) Co(s)   (2) Cr(s)   (3) Cu(s)   (4) Ca(s)

75. According to information from Reference Table J, which redox reaction occurs spontaneously?
    (1) $Cu(s)$ + $2H^+(aq)$ $\rightarrow$ $Cu^{2+}(aq)$ + $H_2(g)$
    (2) $Mg(s)$ + $2H^+(aq)$ $\rightarrow$ $Mg^{2+}(aq)$ + $H_2(g)$
    (3) $2Ag(s)$ + $2H^+(aq)$ $\rightarrow$ $2Ag^+(aq)$ + $H_2(g)$
    (4) $2Au(s)$ + $2H^+(aq)$ $\rightarrow$ $2Au^+(aq)$ + $H_2(g)$

76. Based on Reference Table J, which redox reaction will occur spontaneously?
    (1) Br_2 +   2KI $\rightarrow$ 2KBr   + I_2
    (2) I_2 +   2KCl $\rightarrow$ 2KI   + Cl_2
    (3) Cl_2 +   2KF $\rightarrow$ 2KCl   + F_2
    (4) I_2 +   2KBr $\rightarrow$ 2KI   + Br_2

Base your answers to questions 77 and 78 on the information below.

The outer structure of the Statue of Liberty is made of copper metal. The framework is made of iron. Over time, a thin green layer (patina) forms on the copper surface. When copper oxidized to form this patina layer, the copper atoms became copper(II) ions (Cu^{2+}).

77. Write a balanced half-reaction for this oxidation of copper.

78. Where the iron framework came in contact with the copper surface, a reaction occurred in which iron was oxidized. Using information from Reference Table *J*, explain why the iron was oxidized.

Base your answer to the following question on the information below.

Because tap water is slightly acidic, water pipes made of iron corrode over time, as shown by the balanced ionic equation below:

     $2Fe$ + $6H^+$ $\rightarrow$ $2Fe^{3+}$ + $3H_2$

79. Explain, in terms of chemical reactivity, why copper pipes are *less* likely to corrode than iron pipes.

Base your answers to questions 80 through 82 on the voltaic cell diagram below.

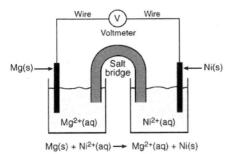

80. Identify *one* metal from your Reference Tables that is more easily oxidized than Mg(s).

81. Identify one piece of information in the diagram that indicates this system is a voltaic cell.

82. Compare the number of moles of electrons lost to the number of moles of electrons gained during the reaction in the cell.

Additional Materials

Reduction Potentials and Calculation of Cell Potentials

In voltaic cells, electrons flow from the anode (oxidation-half cell) to the cathode (reduction-half cell) as a redox reaction occurs. It is the flow of electrons that generates the electrical potential energy in voltaic cells. A voltmeter placed between the anode and cathode of a voltaic cell will measure the electrical potential difference, **voltage**, resulting from the two half-reactions of the cell.

Every half-reaction has a known potential, E^0, associated with it. The Standard Reduction Potential Table on the next page shows some common reduction half-reactions and their standard potentials, E^0. Each reduction potential on the table is given in comparison to a hydrogen cell, which has E^0 of 0.00 V at standard conditions (1 M solution, 1 atm, 298 K). For any cell, voltaic or electrolytic, potentials for the two half-reactions occurring in the cell can be added to get the net reaction potential of the cell, E^0_{cell}.

Reading E⁰ Values from the Table of Potentials

Reduction Potential (E^0 value as written) $Cu^{2+} + 2e^- \rightarrow Cu$ $E^0_{red} = +0.34$ V

Oxidation Potential (E^0 sign is reversed) $Cu \rightarrow Cu^{2+} + 2e^-$ $E^0_{oxi} = -0.34$ V

Comparing Species on the Table of Potentials

A species on the left of the table will cause any species on the right and above it to be oxidized.   *Example:* Cu^{2+} will cause Zn to be oxidized to Zn^{2+}.

A species on the right of the table will cause any species on the left and below it to be reduced.   *Example:* Zn will cause Cu^{2+} to be reduced to Cu.

Comparing Half-reactions on the Table of Potentials

Given any two half-reactions:

The *half-reaction with the highest E^0 value* will proceed forward as *reduction*.

The *half-reaction with the lowest E^0* value will proceed in reverse as *oxidation*.

Calculating the Net Cell Reaction Potential, E⁰cell.

$$E^0_{cell} = E^0_{oxidation} + E^0_{reduction}$$

Example 3: Calculate the net cell potential for:

$$Zn + Cu^{2+} \rightarrow Zn^{2+} + Cu$$

Step 1: Write the two half-reactions. Make a note of their E^0 values from the Table.

   Reduction half: $Cu^{2+} + 2e^- \rightarrow Cu$ $E^0_{reduction} = +0.34$ V   (Sign as is)

   Oxidation half: $Zn \rightarrow Zn^{2+} + 2e^-$ $E^0_{oxidation} = +0.76$ V   (The sign is reversed)

Step 2: Calculate the net cell potential, **E^0_{cell}**, by adding the two potentials

   $E^0_{cell} = 0.76$ V $+ 0.34$ V $= $ **+1.10V**
   (Never multiply E^0 by the coefficient)

Interpreting the Net Cell Reaction Potential, E⁰cell

$E^0_{cell} > 0$ The redox reaction is spontaneous. (*Example 3 reaction is spontaneous.*)
$E^0_{cell} < 0$ The redox reaction is nonspontaneous.
$E^0_{cell} = 0$ The reaction in the cell is at equilibrium.

Table of Standard Reduction Potentials
in 1 M water solution at 298 K and 1 atm

Least
easily reduced →

Most
easily oxidized

Cathode (Reduction) Half-Reaction	Standard Potential E° (volts, V)
$Li^+(aq)\ +\ e^-\ \rightarrow\ Li(s)$	-3.04
$K^+(aq)\ +\ e^-\ \rightarrow\ K(s)$	-2.92
$Ca^{2+}(aq)\ +\ 2e^-\ \rightarrow\ Ca(s)$	-2.76
$Na^+(aq)\ +\ e^-\ \rightarrow\ Na(s)$	-2.71
$Mg^{2+}(aq)\ +\ 2e^-\ \rightarrow\ Mg(s)$	-2.37
$Ac^{3+}(aq)\ +\ 3e^-\ \rightarrow\ Ac(s)$	-2.20
$Be^{2+}(aq)\ +\ 2e^-\ \rightarrow\ Be(s)$	-1.85
$Al^{3+}(aq)\ +\ 3e^-\ \rightarrow\ Al(s)$	-1.66
$Zn^{2+}(aq)\ +\ 2e^-\ \rightarrow\ Zn(s)$	-0.76
$Cr^{3+}(aq)\ +\ 3e^-\ \rightarrow\ Cr(s)$	-0.74
$Fe^{2+}(aq)\ +\ 2e^-\ \rightarrow\ Fe(s)$	-0.41
$Cd^{2+}(aq)\ +\ 2e^-\ \rightarrow\ Cd(s)$	-0.40
$Co^{2+}(aq\ +\ 2e^-\ \rightarrow\ Co(s)$	-0.28
$Ni^{2+}(aq)\ +\ 2e^-\ \rightarrow\ Ni(s)$	-0.23
$Sn^{2+}(aq)\ +\ 2e^-\ \rightarrow\ Sn(s)$	-0.14
$Pb^{2+}(aq)\ +\ 2e^-\ \rightarrow\ Pb(s)$	-0.13
$Fe^{3+}(aq)\ +\ 3e^-\ \rightarrow\ Fe(s)$	-0.04
$2H^+(aq)\ +\ 2e^-\ \rightarrow\ H_2(g)$	0.00
$Sn^{4+}(aq)\ +\ 2e^-\ \rightarrow\ Sn^{2+}(aq)$	0.15
$Cu^{2+}(aq)\ +\ e^-\ \rightarrow\ Cu^+(aq)$	0.16
$Bi^{3+}(aq)\ +\ 3e^-\ \rightarrow\ Bi(s)$	0.31
$Cu^{2+}(aq)\ +\ 2e^-\ \rightarrow\ Cu(s)$	0.34
$Cu^+(aq)\ +\ e^-\ \rightarrow\ Cu(s)$	0.52
$I_2(s)\ +\ 2e^-\ \rightarrow\ 2I^-(aq)$	0.54
$Fe^{3+}(aq)\ +\ e^-\ \rightarrow\ Fe^{2+}(aq)$	0.77
$Hg_2^{2+}(aq)\ +\ 2e^-\ \rightarrow\ 2Hg(\ell)$	0.80
$Ag^+(aq)\ +\ e^-\ \rightarrow\ Ag(s)$	0.80
$Hg^{2+}(aq)\ +\ 2e^-\ \rightarrow\ Hg(\ell)$	0.85
$2Hg^{2+}(aq)\ +\ 2e^-\ \rightarrow\ Hg_2^{2+}(aq)$	0.90
$Br_2(\ell)\ +\ 2e^-\ \rightarrow\ 2Br^-(aq)$	1.07
$Cl_2(g)\ +\ 2e^-\ \rightarrow\ 2Cl^-(aq)$	1.36
$Ce^{4+}(aq)\ +\ e^-\ \rightarrow\ Ce^{3+}(aq)$	1.44
$Au^{3+}(aq)\ +\ 3e^-\ \rightarrow\ Au(s)$	1.52
$Co^{3+}(aq\ +\ e^-\ \rightarrow\ Co^{2+}(aq)$	1.82
$F_2(g)\ +\ 2e^-\ \rightarrow\ 2F^-(aq)$	2.87

Increased Strength of Oxidizing Agent

Increased Strength of Reducing Agent

Most
easily reduced →

Least
easily oxidized

E3chemistry.com

Review Questions: Additional Materials

Use the Table of Standard Reduction Potentials to answer questions 93 to 100.

83. What is the standard electrode potential, E^0, for the oxidation of gold to gold(III) ion?
    (1) +1.52 V   (2) +0.80 V   (3) -0.80 V   (4) -1.52 V

84. Which ion can be both an oxidizing agent and a reducing agent?
    (1) Sn^{2+} (2) Fe^{3+} (3) Al^{3+} (4) Cu^{2+}

85. Which half-cell has a lower electrode potential than the standard hydrogen cell?
    (1) $Au^{3+} + 3e- \rightarrow Au$ (3) $Cu^+ + e- \rightarrow Cu$
    (2) $Hg^{2+} + 2e- \rightarrow Hg$ (4) $Pb^{2+} + 2e- \rightarrow Pb$

86. Given the redox reaction : $Mg(s) + 2Ag^+(aq) \rightarrow Mg^{2+}(aq) + 2Ag(s)$
    What is the cell voltage, $E^0{}_{cell}$, for the overall reaction?
    (1) +1.57 V   (2) +2.37 V   (3) +3.17 V   (4) +3.97 V

87. Given the reaction: $Zn(s) + Br_2(\ell) \rightarrow Zn^{2+}(aq) + 2Br^-(aq)$.
    What is the net cell potential, $E^0{}_{cell}$, for the overall reaction?
    (1) +0.76 V   (2) -1.09 V   (3) +1.83 V   (4) 0.00 V

88. Given the reaction: $2NaCl(\ell) \rightarrow 2Na(\ell) + Cl_2(g)$
    What is the net cell potential, $E^0{}_{cell}$, for the overall reaction?
    (1) - 4.07 V   (2) +4.07 V   (3) +0.35 V   (4) - 0.35 V

89. Which overall reaction in a chemical cell has the highest net potential, $E^0{}_{cell}$?
    (1) $Zn(s) + 2H^+ \rightarrow Zn^{2+} + H_2(g)$ (3) $Mg(s) + 2H^+ \rightarrow Mg^{2+} + H_2(g)$
    (2) $Ni(s) + 2H^+ \rightarrow Ni^{2+} + H_2(g)$ (4) $Sn(s) + 2H^+ \rightarrow Sn^{2+} + H_2(g)$

90. A chemical cell is composed of two separate beakers connected by a salt bridge.

    In Beaker 1: A piece of $Ag(s)$ is placed in a 1.0 M $AgNO_3(aq)$ solution.

    In Beaker 2: A piece of $Fe(s)$ is placed in a 1.0 M $Fe(NO_3)_2(aq)$ solution.

    a) Which electrode of the cell is the anode? Which is the cathode?

    b) Write the overall balanced redox equation for the reaction that will occur in the cell.

    c) Write the balanced oxidation-half and reduction-half reactions that will occur.

    d) Calculate the net cell potential, $E^0{}_{cell}$, for the overall reaction that will occur.

    e) Indicate if the reaction will be spontaneous or nonspontaneous.

Lesson 1: Nuclear Particles and Stability of the Nucleus

Nuclear chemistry is the study of changes that occur in the nucleus of an atom. The nucleus and nuclear particles of an atom were discussed in Topic 3: The Atomic Structure.

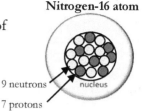
Nitrogen-16 atom

9 neutrons / nucleus

7 protons

- Protons and neutrons are found in the nucleus of atoms.
- The number of protons (atomic number) identifies each element.
- The number of neutrons plus protons determines the mass number of an atom.

Any change to the nucleus of an atom likely involves a change in the number of protons and/or neutrons. Any change to the nucleus of an atom will change that atom to a different atom.

Nuclear reactions lead to changes in the nucleus contents of one or more atoms. *Transmutation, fission* and *fusion* are types of nuclear reactions. These reactions are discussed in lesson 2.

Nuclear Equations

A **nuclear equation** is used to show changes that are taking place during a nuclear reaction. Three types of equations are shown below. There is a clear difference between the nuclear reaction equation and chemical and physical change equations.

Nuclear change equation: $^{90}_{38}Sr \longrightarrow {}^{86}_{36}Rn + {}^{4}_{2}He$

Chemical change equation: $2KClO_3(s) \longrightarrow 2KCl(s) + 3O_2(g)$

Physical change equation: $CO_2(s) \longrightarrow CO_2(g)$

Stability of a Nucleus: *Depends on Neutron to Proton Ratio*

Most atoms, especially those found in nature, have stable nuclei.

The ratio of neutrons to protons determines the stability of an atom.

- *Stable nuclei* generally have *equal* number of neutrons and protons (1 : 1 ratio). Stable nuclei are not radioactive and do not spontaneously decay.

- *Unstable nuclei* generally have *unequal* number of neutrons to protons. Unstable nuclei are radioactive and spontaneously decay in their natural state.

- Radioactive atoms of small atomic numbers are "proton rich," meaning they have more protons than neutrons.

- Radioactive atoms of high atomic numbers are "neutron rich," meaning they have more neutrons than protons.

- **Elements with atomic number 84 and above have no stable isotopes.**
  Nuclei of these elements contain many more neutrons than protons.
  For example: Francium (atomic number 87) has no stable isotopes.
          All 33 known isotopes of francium are radioactive.

Particles and Radiations in Nuclear Chemistry

During nuclear transmutations and radioactivity, particles are absorbed and/or released by the nucleus. The change or transmutation depends on the type of particles that are absorbed and/or released.

Particles and radiation commonly involved in nuclear reactions are given below.

Alpha particles are similar to helium nuclei. They have a mass of 4 and a charge of +2.

Beta particles are produced when neutrons are converted to protons. A beta particle is similar to a high-speed electron. Beta particles have a mass of 0 and a charge of -1.

Positrons are produced when protons are converted to neutrons. They have a mass of 0 and a charge of +1.

Gamma radiation is similar to high energy x-rays. They have a mass of 0 and a charge of 0.

Protons are found in the nucleus of atoms. They have a mass of 1 and a charge of +1.

Neutrons are found in the nucleus of atoms. They have a mass of 1 and a charge of 0.

More information about nuclear particles is listed on the table below and on **Reference Table O.**

An **accelerator** is a device that moves charged particles to a high speed. Only charged particles (*alpha, beta, and positron*) can be accelerated.

Penetrating power refers to the strength of a particle to go through a given object. See diagram below.

- Alpha particles have the weakest penetrating power. They can be stopped by a piece of paper.

- Gamma radiation has the strongest penetrating power. It can be stopped only by a high-density metal, like lead.

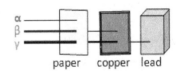

Summary Table of Common Nuclear Particles and Radiations

Nuclear Particle	Symbol	Mass	Charge	Penetrating power	Able to be accelerated
Alpha	$^{4}_{2}He$, α	4 amu	+2	Low (weakest)	Yes
Beta	$^{0}_{-1}e$, $-\beta$	0 amu	-1	Medium	Yes
Positron	$^{0}_{+1}e$, $+\beta$	0 amu	+1	Medium	Yes
Proton	$^{1}_{1}p$	1 amu	1	Medium	Yes
Gamma	$^{0}_{0}\gamma$	0 amu	0	High (strongest)	No
Neutron	$^{1}_{0}n$	1 amu	0	------	No

Note: **On Reference Table O,** you can find name, notation, and symbol of each particle

Separation of Nuclear Particles: *Opposites Attract*

An *electric* or a *magnetic field* can be used to separate particles and radiation that are released from a radioactive source during a nuclear decay.

An electric field contains two charged plates, a positively and negatively charged plate as shown below. The path of each radiation from a radioactive source is shown below.

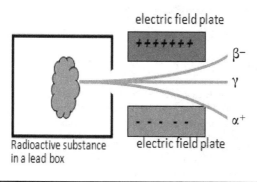

electric field plate

Radioactive substance in a lead box

electric field plate

As particles are released:

- **Negative particles (β-)** will attract or deflect toward the positive plate(+) of the electric field.

- **Particles with no charge (γ)** will be unaffected by the electric field, and will go straight through.

- **Positive particles (α+)** will attract or deflect toward the negative plate(-) of the electric field.

Radioisotopes and Decay Modes: *Reference Table N*

Decay mode refers to the type of particle that a radioisotope will release as it decays. *Reference Table N* lists selected radioisotopes and their decay modes.

Table N
Selected Radioisotopes

Nuclide	Half-Life	Decay Mode	Nuclide Name	
^{53}Fe	8.51 min	β^+	iron-53	*positron emitter*
^{220}Fr	27.4 s	α	francium-220	*alpha emitter*
^{3}H	12.31 y	β^-	hydrogen-3	*beta emitter*

A **radioisotope** is any radioactive isotope of an element. A radioisotope can be described as one of the following depending on its decay mode.

An **alpha emitter** is a radioisotope that releases *alpha particles* (α^+) as it decays. Radioisotopes with atomic number 84 and above tend to be alpha emitters.

  Ex. Francium–220 and uranium–238 are alpha emitters.

A **beta emitter** is a radioisotope that releases *beta particles* (β^-) as it decays.

  Ex. Hydrogen–3 and strontium–90 are beta emitters.

A **positron emitter** is a radioisotope that releases *positrons* (β^+) as it decays.

  Ex. Iron–53 and neon–19 are positron emitters.

Radioisotopes of small atomic numbers tend to be beta and positron emitters.

Review Questions: Nuclear Particles and Stability of the Nucleus

Vocabulary: Briefly define each of the following terms.
1. Alpha particle   2. Beta particle   3. Positron   4. Gamma ray   5. Accelerator
6. Radioisotope

7. Spontaneous decay of certain elements in nature occurs because these elements have
   (1) disproportionate ratios of electrons to protons
   (2) disproportionate ratios of neutrons to protons
   (3) high reactivity with oxygen
   (4) low reactivity with oxygen

8. Which statement describes the relative masses of two different particles?
   (1) A neutron has less mass than a positron.
   (2) A beta particle has less mass than a neutron.
   (3) An alpha particle has less mass than a positron.
   (4) An alpha particle has less mass than a beta particle.

9. Which list is showing the particles arranged in order of increasing penetrating power?
   (1) Gamma → Beta → Alpha   (3) Alpha → Beta → Gamma
   (2) Beta → Gamma → Alpha   (4) Gamma → Alpha → Beta

10. Which nuclear radiation is similar to high energy X-rays?
    (1) Beta   (3) Gamma
    (2) Alpha   (4) Neutron

11. Alpha particles and beta particles differ in
    (1) mass only   (3) both mass and charge
    (2) charge only   (4) neither mass and charge

12. In which list can all particles be accelerated by an electric field?
    (1) Alpha, beta, and neutrons   (3) Alpha, protons, and neutrons
    (2) Alpha, beta, and protons   (4) Beta, protons, and neutrons

13. Which notation of a radioisotope is correctly paired with the notation of its emission particle?
    (1) $^{37}_{19}K$ and $^{0}_{-1}e$ (3) $^{222}_{86}Rn$ and $^{4}_{2}He$
    (2) $^{16}_{7}N$ and $^{1}_{1}p$ (4) $^{99}_{43}Tc$ and $^{0}_{+1}e$

14. Atoms of I-131 spontaneously decay when the
    (1) stable nuclei emit alpha particles   (3) unstable nuclei emit alpha particles
    (2) stable nuclei emit beta particles   (4) unstable nuclei emit beta particles

15. Which Group 18 element is naturally radioactive and has no known stable isotope?
    (1) Ar   (3) Xe
    (2) Po   (4) Kr

16. Explain why it is more difficult to cause an artificial transmutation with an alpha particle than with a neutron.

17. Explain, in terms of atomic particles, why S-32 is a stable nuclide.

Lesson 2 – Nuclear Reactions

Transmutation, fission and fusion are types of nuclear reactions.
High amounts of energy and radiation are released during a nuclear reaction.

Transmutation: *Converts One Atom to Another*

Transmutation is a nuclear reaction that changes or converts one atom to a different atom. A nuclear transmutation can be natural or artificial.

Natural transmutation occurs when a single unstable radioactive nucleus spontaneously decays by breaking down and emitting particles.
• Alpha decay, beta decay, and positron emission are natural transmutation.

Artificial transmutation occurs when an atom is intentionally hit (bombarded) with high speed particles and is changed to another atom.

Alpha Decay: *A Natural Transmutation*

Alpha decay occurs when a radioactive nucleus spontaneously breaks down to emit an alpha particle. The equation below shows the decay of uranium-238, an alpha emitter.

$$^{238}_{92}\text{U} \longrightarrow \ ^{4}_{2}\text{He} \ + \ ^{234}_{90}\text{Th}$$

alpha emitter   alpha particle   new atom
(radioactive atom)   emitted

When a radioactive nucleus emits an alpha particle, the nucleus of the new atom will have different amounts of particles from the radioactive atom. The table below compares the number of particles in the two atoms.

	Radioactive Atom $^{238}_{92}\text{U}$	New Atom $^{234}_{90}\text{Th}$
Mass number	238	234 (decreases by 4)
Number of protons (atomic number)	92	90 (decreases by 2)
Number of neutrons (mass number - atomic number)	146	144 (decreases by 2)

Beta Decay: *A Natural Transmutation*

Beta decay occurs when a radioactive nucleus converts a neutron to a proton and an electron. The electron is then released from the nucleus. The equation below shows the decay of carbon-14, a beta emitter.

$$^{14}_{6}C \longrightarrow \ ^{0}_{-1}e \ + \ ^{14}_{7}N$$

beta emitter   beta particle   new atom
(radioactive atom)   emitted

When a radioactive nucleus emits a beta particle, the nucleus of the new atom will have different amounts of particles from the radioactive atom. The table below compares the number of particles in the two atoms.

	Radioactive atom $^{14}_{6}C$	New atom $^{14}_{7}N$
Mass number	14	14 (stays the same)
Number of protons (atomic number)	6	7 (increases by 1)
Number of neutrons (mass number - atomic number)	8	7 (decreases by 1)

Positron Emission: *A Natural Transmutation*

Positron emission occurs when a radioactive nucleus converts a proton to a neutron and positron. The positron is then released from the nucleus. The equation below shows the decay of calcium-37, a positron emitter.

$$^{37}_{20}Ca \longrightarrow \ ^{0}_{+1}e \ + \ ^{37}_{19}K$$

positron emitter   positron emitted   new atom

When a radioactive nucleus emits a positron, the nucleus of the new atom will have different amounts of particles from the radioactive atom. The table below compares the number of particles in the two atoms.

	Radioactive atom $^{37}_{20}Ca$	New atom $^{37}_{19}K$
Mass number	37	37 (stays the same)
Number of protons (atomic number)	20	19 (decreases by 1)
Number of neutrons (mass number - atomic number)	17	18 (increases by 1)

                                E3chemistry.com

Decay Series: *Ends with a Stable Isotope*

A decay series is a chain of decays of one radioactive element after another until a stable isotope, usually lead, is produced. The graph to the right shows the decay series of Th-230. Each disintegration or decay by alpha (↙) or beta (→) leads to a new radioisotope until a stable Pb-206 isotope is produced.

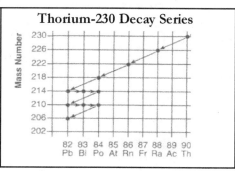

Thorium-230 Decay Series

Artificial Transmutation: *A Stable Nucleus is Hit by a High-Speed Particle*

Artificial transmutation occurs when an atom is *intentionally* bombarded (hit) with particles to change it to a different atom. An artificial transmutation is done in a particle accelerator because the particles must move at the speed of light to be able to penetrate the nucleus of the atom. The equation below shows an artificial transmutation of beryllium-9 nuclide through alpha bombardment.

$$_2^4 He \quad + \quad _4^9 Be \quad \longrightarrow \quad _6^{12}C \quad + \quad _0^1 n$$

accelerated high speed alpha particle   *nuclide to be hit*   *new atom*   *neutron released*

Fission and Fusion: *Convert Mass to Energy*

Fission and *fusion* reactions are two types of nuclear reactions that produce tremendous amounts of energy and radiations. During these nuclear processes, it is known that the mass of the new atom is slightly less than that of the reactants. The result of this is called the **mass defect.** The relationship between the missing mass and the tremendous amounts of energy produced from nuclear reactions is given by this well-known equation:

$$E = mc^2$$

Where **E** is energy produced
m is the mass defect (missing mass)
c is the speed of light

According to the above equation, it can be concluded that during a nuclear reaction:

• **Energy is converted from mass (or mass is converted to energy).**

The amount of energy that is released is much higher in comparison to that of an ordinary chemical reaction.

Fission: *A Large Nucleus Splits into Fragments. Mass is Converted to Energy.*

Fission is a nuclear reaction in which a large nucleus is split into smaller nuclei. The diagram and equation below show nuclear fission of uranium-235. In the reaction, a neutron hits a uranium nucleus, causing it to break into two smaller fragments. Three neutrons and a tremendous amount of energy and radiation are also produced in the reaction.

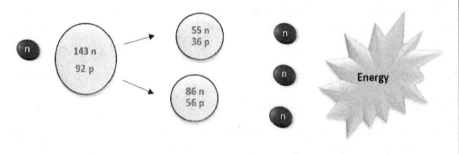

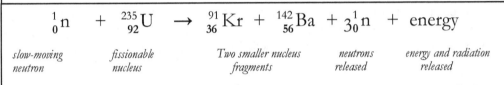

$$\underset{0}{^{1}}n \; + \; \underset{92}{^{235}}U \; \rightarrow \; \underset{36}{^{91}}Kr \; + \; \underset{56}{^{142}}Ba \; + \; 3\underset{0}{^{1}}n \; + \; energy$$

| *slow-moving neutron* | *fissionable nucleus* | *Two smaller nucleus fragments* | *neutrons released* | *energy and radiation released* |

In a fission reaction:

• A large fissionable nucleus absorbs a slow-moving neutron.
  The large nucleus is split into smaller fragments, with the release of more neutrons.

• Tons of nuclear energy is released. Energy is converted from mass.
  The energy that is released is less than that of a fusion reaction.

• In nuclear power plants, the fission process is well controlled.
  The energy is used to produce electricity, which benefits us.

• In nuclear bombs, the fission process is uncontrolled.
  Energy and radiation released are used to cause destruction.

• Dangerous nuclear waste is also produced.
  Nuclear wastes must be stored and disposed of properly.

Fusion: *Two Small Nuclei Join. Mass is Converted to Energy.*

Fusion is a nuclear reaction in which small nuclei are joined (fused) to create a larger nucleus. Only small atoms like those of hydrogen and helium can be fused in a nuclear fusion reaction.

The diagram and equation below show a nuclear fusion reaction. In the reaction, two small hydrogen nuclei join to produce a larger helium nucleus. A tremendous amount of energy is also produced.

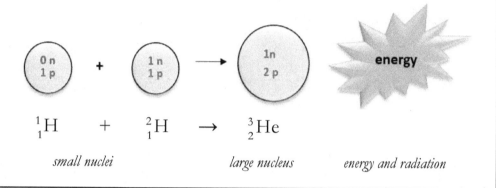

$$^{1}_{1}H \quad + \quad ^{2}_{1}H \quad \rightarrow \quad ^{3}_{2}He$$

    small nuclei   *large nucleus*   *energy and radiation*

In a fusion reaction:

• Two small nuclei are brought together under extremely high temperature and pressure.
   The two nuclei join to create a slightly larger nucleus.

• Tons of nuclear energy is released. Energy is converted from mass.
   Energy released is much greater than that of a fission or chemical reaction.

• No nuclear waste, unlike fission.

• Energy from the sun is due to fusion reactions that occur in the core of the sun.

• High temperature and high pressure are required for a fusion reaction to occur in order to overcome the repelling force of the two positive nuclei that are to be fused.

Nuclear Equations: Summary Table

Below is a summary of the five types of nuclear processes discussed in the last few pages.

Use this table for a quick study and comparison of the five nuclear reactions.

Nuclear process and equation	Mass number *after decay*	Protons (atomic number) *after decay*	Neutrons *after decay*
Alpha decay (natural transmutation) $$_{88}^{226}\text{Ra} \rightarrow {}_{86}^{222}\text{Rn} + {}_{2}^{4}\text{He}$$	$\downarrow 4$	$\downarrow 2$	$\downarrow 2$
Beta decay (natural transmutation) $$_{6}^{14}\text{C} \rightarrow {}_{7}^{14}\text{N} + {}_{-1}^{0}\text{e}$$	same	$\uparrow 1$	$\downarrow 1$
Positron emission (natural transmutation) $$_{88}^{226}\text{Ra} \rightarrow {}_{87}^{226}\text{Fr} + {}_{+1}^{0}\text{e}$$	same	$\downarrow 1$	$\uparrow 1$
Artificial transmutation $$_{18}^{40}\text{Ar} + {}_{1}^{1}\text{H} \rightarrow {}_{19}^{40}\text{K} + {}_{0}^{1}\text{n}$$	Bombarding nucleus with high speed particles.		
Fission (nuclear energy) $$_{92}^{235}\text{U} + {}_{0}^{1}\text{n} \rightarrow {}_{56}^{142}\text{Ba} + {}_{36}^{91}\text{Kr} + 3{}_{0}^{1}\text{n}$$	Nucleus splits into smaller nuclei. Mass is converted to energy. More energy than chemical reaction. *Problem:* Produces dangerous radioactive wastes.		
Fusion (nuclear energy) $$_{1}^{2}\text{H} + {}_{1}^{2}\text{H} \rightarrow {}_{2}^{4}\text{He} + \text{energy}$$	Nuclei join to make a larger nucleus. Mass is converted to energy. Energy is more than that of fission. Produces no radioactive waste. *Problem:* High temperature and pressure are needed to overcome repelling nuclei.		

Balancing Nuclear Equations

A nuclear equation is balanced when the **top numbers (mass numbers)** and **bottom numbers (charges)** are equal on both sides as in the equation below.

$$^{222}_{86}\text{Rn} \rightarrow {}^{4}_{2}\text{He} + {}^{218}_{84}\text{Po}$$

An incomplete equation typically contains an X or a blank as in Example 1. The X or blank represents the missing particle in the equation.

Top and bottom numbers for X can be determined mathematically.

Example 1

Which particle is represented by the X in the equation below?

$$X + {}^{0}_{-1}e \rightarrow {}^{37}_{17}\text{Cl}$$

$$\overbrace{{}^{37}_{18}X + {}^{0}_{-1}e}^{37} \rightarrow {}^{37}_{17}\text{Cl}$$

Top number for X must be **37**

Bottom number for X must be **18**

The symbol for X can be determined from the **Periodic Table** (if X is an element) or **Table O** (if X is a particle).

$$X \text{ is } {}^{37}_{18}\text{Ar}$$

Writing a Balanced Nuclear Equation

This is generally done by piecing together information from Reference Tables N and O, and the Periodic Table.

Below are steps for writing balanced nuclear equations for two radioisotopes from Table N. Study the steps below to learn how to do the same for any radioisotope whose decay mode is known.

Example 2

Write nuclear equations for the decay of plutonium-239 and iodine-131.

Step 1: Write Nuclide symbol (Use Table N)	*Step 2: Write* Decay mode symbol (Use Table N and O)	*Step 3 : Determine the missing* Top #, bottom #, and atom's symbol (numbers must make for a balanced equation)
$^{239}_{94}\text{Pu}$ $\rightarrow$	$^{4}_{2}\text{He}$ +	$^{235}_{92}\text{U}$
$^{131}_{53}\text{I}$ $\rightarrow$	$^{0}_{-1}e$ +	$^{131}_{54}\text{Xe}$

Review Questions: Transmutation and Nuclear Reactions

Vocabulary: Briefly define each of the following terms.

18. Transmutation   19. Artificial transmutation   20. Natural transmutation
21. Alpha decay   22. Beta decay   23. Positron emission
24. Fission   25. Fusion

26. The greatest amount of energy released per gram of reactants occurs during a
    (1) redox reaction   (3) fusion reaction
    (2) fission reaction   (4) combustion reaction

27. What is one benefit associated with a nuclear fission reaction?
    (1) The products are not radioactive.
    (2) Stable isotopes are used as reactants.
    (3) There is no chance of biological exposure.
    (4) A large amount of energy is produced.

28. Radioactive cobalt-60 is used in radiation therapy treatment. Cobalt-60 undergoes beta decay. This type of nuclear reaction is called
    (1) natural transmutation   (3) nuclear fusion
    (2) artificial transmutation   (4) nuclear fission

29. Given the balanced equation representing a nuclear reaction:

$$^{2}_{1}H \; + \; ^{3}_{1}H \; \rightarrow \; ^{4}_{2}He \; + \; ^{1}_{0}n$$

    Which phrase identifies and describes this reaction?
    (1) fission, mass converted to energy
    (2) fission, energy converted to mass
    (3) fusion, mass converted to energy
    (4) fusion, energy converted to mass

30. When an atom of the unstable isotope Na-24 decays, it becomes an atom of Mg-24 because the Na-24 atom spontaneously releases
    (1) an alpha particle   (3) a neutron
    (2) a beta particle   (4) a positron

31. A nuclear change resulting in a release of an alpha particle is shown in which equation?
    (1) $^{252}_{98}Cf \; \rightarrow \; ^{248}_{96}Cm \; + \; ^{4}_{2}He$

    (2) $^{19}_{10}Ne \; \rightarrow \; ^{19}_{11}Na \; + \; ^{0}_{-1}e$

    (3) $^{220}_{87}Fr \; + \; ^{4}_{2}He \; \rightarrow \; ^{224}_{89}Ac$

    (4) $^{228}_{89}Ac \; \rightarrow \; ^{228}_{88}Ra \; + \; ^{1}_{1}p$

32. Artificial transmutation is represented by which nuclear equation?
    (1) $^{2}_{1}H \; + \; ^{1}_{1}H \; \rightarrow \; ^{3}_{2}He$

    (2) $^{235}_{92}U \; + \; ^{1}_{0}n \; \rightarrow \; ^{87}_{35}Br \; + \; ^{146}_{57}La \; + \; 3\,^{1}_{0}n$

    (3) $^{210}_{84}Po \; + \; \rightarrow \; ^{206}_{82}Pb \; + \; ^{4}_{2}He$

    (4) $^{238}_{92}U \; + \; ^{4}_{2}He \; \rightarrow \; ^{241}_{94}Pu \; + \; ^{1}_{0}n$

E3chemistry.com

33. Given the nuclear reaction

$$^{60}_{27}Co \rightarrow \,^{0}_{-1}e + \,^{60}_{28}Ni$$

the reaction is an example of
(1) fission
(3) fusion
(2) natural transmutation
(4) artificial transmutation

34. In the nuclear equation:

$$^{234}_{91}Pa \rightarrow X + \,^{0}_{-1}e$$

Which particle is represented by the X ?
(1) $^{234}_{92}U$
(2) $^{234}_{93}Np$
(3) $^{235}_{92}U$
(4) $^{235}_{93}Np$

Base your answers to questions 35 through 38 on the information below.

A breeder reactor is one type of nuclear reactor. In a breeder reactor, uranium-238 is transformed in a series of nuclear reactions into plutonium-239.

The plutonium-239 can undergo fission as shown in the equation below. The *X* represents a missing product in the equation.

$$^{1}_{0}n + \,^{239}_{94}Pu \rightarrow X + \,^{94}_{36}Kr + 2\,^{1}_{0}n$$

35. Write a notation for the nuclide represented by missing product *X* in this equation.

36. Compare the amount of energy released by 1 mole of completely fissioned plutonium-239 to the amount of energy released by the complete combustion of 1 mole of methane.

37. Based on Table *N*, identify the decay mode of the plutonium radioisotope produced in the breeder reactor.

38. Determine the number of neutrons in an atom of the uranium isotope used in the breeder reactor.

Base your answers to questions 39 through 41 on in the diagram and information below.

A U-238 atom decays to a Pb-206 atom through a series of steps. Each point on the graph below represents a nuclide and each arrow represents a nuclear decay mode.

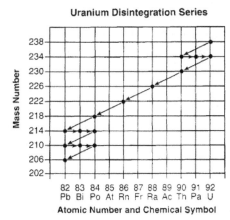

Uranium Disintegration Series

Mass Number

238
234
230
226
222
218
214
210
206
202

82 83 84 85 86 87 88 89 90 91 92
Pb Bi Po At Rn Fr Ra Ac Th Pa U

Atomic Number and Chemical Symbol

39. Explain why the U-238 disintegration series ends with the nuclide Pb-206.

40. Based on this graph, what particle is emitted during the nuclear decay of a Po-218 atom?

41. Based on this graph, what is the mass of the particle emitted during the nuclear decay of Bi-214?

Lesson 3: Half-life

Half-life is the length of time it takes for a sample of a radioactive element to decay to half of its original mass. During a radioactive decay, the radioisotope is converted to a different element. Over time, less and less of the radioactive element remains as a new element is formed. At a certain time in the decay process, exactly half of the original mass (or atoms) of the radioactive element will remain unchanged. The time (seconds, minutes, hours, or years) it takes the substance to decay to half its original mass is the half-life of that element.

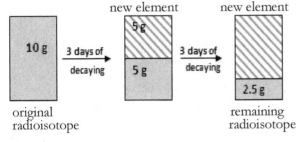

This diagram shows a 10-gram sample of a radioisotope decaying to 5 grams after 3 days, and to 2.5 grams in another 3 days.

- The half-life of the radioisotope is 3 days.

- The number of half-life periods (how many half-lives) is 2.

- The total length of time is 6 days.

- The decaying of a radioisotope is at a constant rate. Therefore, the half-life of a radioisotope is constant.

- Temperature, pressure, or amount does not change the half-life of a radioisotope.

Reference Table N lists selected radioisotopes and their half-life and decay mode.

Comparing Decay of Radioisotopes

If a 20-gram sample of Au-198 and a 20-gram sample of I-131 were left to decay for 100 days:

Decays to greatest extent (Au-198)
Smallest remaining % (Au-198)
 - Shortest half-life

Decays to least extent (I-131)
Greatest remaining % (I-131)
 - Longest half-life

Table N
Selected Radioisotopes

Nuclide	Half-Life	Decay Mode	Nuclide Name
^{198}Au	2.69 d	β^-	gold-198
^{14}C	5730 y	β^-	carbon-14
^{37}Ca	175 ms	β^+	calcium-37
^{60}Co	5.26 y	β^-	cobalt-60
^{137}Cs	30.23 y	β^-	cesium-137
^{53}Fe	8.51 min	β^+	iron-53
^{220}Fr	27.5 s	α	francium-220
^{3}H	12.26 y	β^-	hydrogen-3
^{131}I	8.07 d	β^-	iodine-131
^{37}K	1.23 s	β^+	potassium-37
^{42}K	12.4 h	β^-	potassium-42
^{85}Kr	10.76 y	β^-	krypton-85
^{16}N	7.2 s	β^-	nitrogen-16
^{19}Ne	17.2 s	β^+	neon-19
^{32}P	14.3 d	β^-	phosphorus-32
^{239}Pu	2.44×10^4 y	α	plutonium-239
^{226}Ra	1600 y	α	radium-226
^{222}Rn	3.82 d	α	radon-222
^{90}Sr	28.1 y	β^-	strontium-90
^{99}Tc	2.13×10^5 y	β^-	technetium-99
^{232}Th	1.4×10^{10} y	α	thorium-232
^{233}U	1.62×10^5 y	α	uranium-233
^{235}U	7.1×10^8 y	α	uranium-235
^{238}U	4.51×10^9 y	α	uranium-238

ms = milliseconds; s = seconds; min = minutes;
h = hours; d = days; y = years

E3chemistry.com

Number of Half-life Periods: *How Many Times a Radioisotope Decays in Half*

Solving a half-life problem quickly, easily and correctly depends on your understanding of the half-life concept. Most half-life problems can be solved with little or no set up if you have a clear understanding of the concept. When solving any half-life problem, the one key piece of information that must be known is the number of half-life periods.

Half-life period is the number of times a radioactive sample decays in half.

If it is not given in a question, it can be calculated from length of time and half-life (*Example 3*) or from original and remaining mass (*Example 4*).

In the next few pages, several examples of half-life problems are given and solved. The number of half-life periods is directly or indirectly used in solving the problem in each example.

Example 3: *Half-life Periods from Length of Time and Half-life*

The radioisotope C-14 (half-life of 5715 years) decays for 22860 years. What is the number of half-life periods?

$$\text{Half-life Periods (n)} \quad = \quad \frac{\textbf{Length of Time (t)}}{\textbf{Half-life (T)}}$$

$$\text{Half-life Periods (n)} \quad = \quad \frac{22860 \text{ years}}{5715 \text{ years}} = \textbf{4 half-life periods}$$

Example 4: *Half-life Periods from Original Mass (OM) and Remaining Mass (RM)*

In how many half-life periods would a 60-gram sample of a radioisotope decay to 7.5 grams?

From original mass to remaining mass:
Cut the original mass in ***half*** or divide it by 2. The **number of times** you do this to get to the remaining mass is the **number of half-life periods**.

$$\underset{\text{OM}}{\textbf{60 g}} \rightarrow 30 \rightarrow 15 \rightarrow \underset{\text{RM}}{\textbf{7.5 g}}$$

3 arrows = **3 half-life periods**

From remaining mass to original mass:
Reverse the above process by doubling (multiplying by 2) the remaining mass as many times as needed to get to the original mass.

$$\underset{\text{RM}}{\textbf{7.5 g}} \rightarrow 15 \rightarrow 30 \rightarrow \underset{\text{OM}}{\textbf{60 g}}$$

3 arrows = **3 half-life periods**

Note: No formula is given in the Reference Table for half-life problems.

Length of Time: *The Total Time of a Decay*

The length of time of a decaying process is the total time it takes for a radioisotope sample to decay from one mass to another. It can be calculated from half-life and half-life periods (*Example 5*) or from original and remaining masses (*Example 6*).

Example 5: *Length of Time from Half-life and Half-life Periods*
What is the total number of years it takes for a sample of C-14 (half-life of 5715 years) to undergo 6 half-life periods?

Length of Time = Half-life x Half-life periods

Length of Time = 5715 x 6 = **34,290 years**

Example 6: *Length of Time from Original and Remaining Masses*
How long will it take for a 12-gram sample of carbon-14 to decay to just 3 grams?

1st: Find **half-life period (n)** from original and remaining masses as shown on the previous page.

$12\,g \rightarrow 6\,g \rightarrow 3\,g$
n = 2 (2 arrows)

2nd: Calculate **length of time (t)** using the above equation.

Length of Time = Half-life x Half-life Periods
Length of Time = 5715 x 2 = **11,430 yrs.**

Half-life: *The Time for Half of a Radioisotope to Decay*

Half-life of a radioisotope can be determined if it is not listed on Table N. Half-life can be calculated from length of time and half-life periods (*Example 7*), or from original and remaining masses.

Example 7: *Half-life from Length of Time and Number of Half-life Periods*
Radioisotope X takes 60 years to undergo 4 half-life periods. What is the half-life of X?

$$\textbf{Half-life} = \frac{\text{Length of Time}}{\text{Half-life Periods}} = \frac{60 \text{ yrs.}}{4} = \textbf{15 yrs.}$$

Half-life from masses can be calculated in two steps.

1st : Determine the number of half-life periods from masses as shown on page 217.
2nd : Calculate half-life using the above equation.

Original Mass *(before)* and Remaining Mass *(after)* of a Decay

When the number of half-life periods (n) or half-life (T) and length of time (t) of a decaying process is given, the original or remaining mass can be determined.
To determine original mass: *Double* remaining mass as many times as **n.**
To determine remaining mass: *Cut* original mass ***in half*** as many times as **n.**

Example 8: *Remaining Mass from Length of Time and Half-life*
In approximately 4800 years, how many grams of a 100-gram sample of radon-226 will remain unchanged? The half-life of radon-226 is 1599 years (see Table N).

n = 4800 / 1599 = 3   Remaining mass = $100\,g \rightarrow 50 \rightarrow 25 \rightarrow$ **12.5 g**

Fraction Remaining

Fraction remaining expresses the remaining mass of a radioisotope as a ratio. It can be calculated from the number of half-life periods (*Example 9*) or from length of time and half-life (*Example 10*).

***Example 9**: Fraction Remaining from Number of Half-life Periods (n)*
What fraction of a sample of C-14 remains unchanged after 3 half-life periods?

$$\text{Fraction Remaining} = \frac{1}{2^n} = \frac{1}{2^3} = \frac{1}{2 \times 2 \times 2} = \frac{1}{8}$$

***Example 10**: Fraction Remaining from Length of Time (t) and Half-life (T)*
What fraction of iodine-131 (half-life of 8.021 days) will remain unchanged after 32 days?

$$\text{Fraction Remaining} = \frac{1}{(2)^{t/T}} = \frac{1}{(2)^{32/8.021}} = \frac{1}{2^4} = \frac{1}{16}$$

$$t/T = n$$

Half-life Data and Graphs

The decaying process of a radioisotope can be represented on a data table or graph. Examples of such representations are given below.

Time (days)	Mass of radioisotope sample remaining (g)
0	160
4	120
8	80 (half original mass)
12	60
16	40
20	30
24	20
28	15
32	10

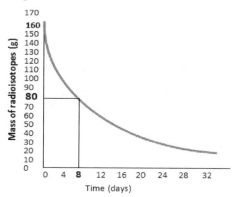

The half-life of the radioisotope is 8 days.
This is when half (80 g) of the original (160 g) remains unchanged.

The radioisotope is likely iodine-131.
According to Reference Table N, the half-life of I-131 is 8.021 days.

Common Uses and Benefits of Selected Radioisotopes and Tracers

Radioactive isotopes have many useful and beneficial applications to us. Radioisotopes are used in the field of medicine for diagnosis and treatment of diseases. They are used in the field of science for research. They are used in the food industry to kill harmful bacteria in our food. In geological and archeological fields, radioisotopes are used in determining the age of rocks and fossils.

Tracers are radioisotopes that are used to follow the course or progress of a chemical reaction, medical diagnosis or treatment.
Tracers for diagnosis and treatments must have *short half-lives* and be *quickly eliminated* from the body.
Radioisotopes for dating usually have very long half-lives.

The table below lists selected radioisotopes and their common beneficial applications.

Radioisotope Name	Radioisotope Symbol	Common Application	Field of Application
Iodine-131	^{131}I	Thyroid disorder diagnosis and treatments	Medical
Technetium-99	^{99}Tc	Cancer tumor diagnosis	Medical
Cobalt-60	^{60}Co	Cancer treatments	Medical
Iron-56	^{56}Fe	Blood disorder treatments	Medical
Carbon-14 *(alone)*	^{14}C	Tracer for chemical reactions	Research
Carbon-14 *with* **Carbon-12**	^{14}C ^{12}C	Fossil dating	Archeological dating
Uranium – 238 *with* **Lead - 206**	^{238}U ^{206}Pb	Rock dating	Geological dating

Radioactive Wastes and Radiation

Wastes and radiation that are produced from nuclear reactors are very dangerous and pose a threat to life on earth. Prolonged and high dose exposures to radiation can cause serious health issues and sometimes death.

- *Radiation* from nuclear power plants must be well contained to protect humans and other living things.

- *Nuclear wastes* are equally dangerous because they are highly radioactive

- *Nuclear wastes* have to be stored in safe areas to protect the public from being exposed to them.

Solid Wastes (highly radioactive): Sr-90   Cs-137

Gaseous Wastes: Rn-222   Kr-85   N-16

Review Questions: Half-life

Vocabulary: Briefly define each of the following terms.
42. Half-life   43. Tracer

44. The course of a chemical reaction can be traced by using a
    (1) polar molecule   (3) stable isotope
    (2) diatomic molecule   (4) radioisotope

45. A radioisotope is called a tracer when it is used to
    (1) determine the age of animal skeletal remains
    (2) kill cancerous tissue
    (3) determine the course of a chemical reaction
    (4) kill bacteria in food

46. Which procedure is based on the half-life of a radioisotope?
    (1) Accelerating to increase kinetic energy
    (2) Dating to determine age
    (3) Counting to determine a level of radioactivity
    (4) Radiating to kill cancer cells

47. Diagnostic injections of radioisotopes used in medicine normally have
    (1) short half-lives and are quickly eliminated from the body
    (2) short half-lives and are slowly eliminated from the body
    (3) long half-lives and are quickly eliminated from the body
    (4) long half-lives and are slowly eliminated from the body

48. What is the half-life of potassium – 42?
    (1) 1.23 s   (3) 14.28 d
    (2) 12.36 h   (4) 27.4 s

49. Which radioisotope has a half-life that is more than 1 minute?
    (1) K – 37   (3) K – 42
    (2) Ca – 37   (4) Ne – 19

50. Compared to uranium – 238, uranium – 235 has a
    (1) shorter half-life and the same decay mode
    (2) shorter half-life and a different decay mode
    (3) longer half-life and the same decay mode
    (4) longer half-life and a different decay mode

51. Which radioisotope has the slowest rate of decay?
    (1) gold-198   (3) iodine-131
    (2) phosphorus-32   (4) radon-222

52. How many days are required for a 200-gram sample of radon-222 to decay to 50.0 grams?
    (1) 1.912   (3) 7.646
    (2) 3.823   (4) 11.464

53. After decaying for 34.5 minutes, $1/8$ of the original mass of krypton-74 remains unchanged. What is the half-life of this radioisotope?
    (1) 11.5 min   (3) 34.5 min
    (2) 23.0 min   (4) 46.0 min

54. What is the half-life of sodium-25 if 1.00 gram of a 16.00-gram sample of the radioisotope remains unchanged after 237 seconds?
    (1) 47.4 s   (3) 79.0 s
    (2) 59.3 s   (4) 118 s

55. Based on Reference Table N, what fraction of a 10-g sample of gold-198 remains radioactive after 5.4 days?
   (1) ¼
   (2) ½
   (3) ¾
   (4) ⁷/₈

56. The radioisotope I-131 is used to
   (1) control nuclear reactors
   (2) determine the age of fossils
   (3) diagnose thyroid disorders
   (4) trigger fission reactors

57. Which isotopic ratio needs to be determined when studying the geological age of a rock formation?
   (1) lead-208 to uranium-238
   (2) hydrogen-2 to hydrogen-3
   (3) nitrogen-16 to nitrogen-14
   (4) carbon-14 to carbon-12

Base your answers to questions 58 through 59 on the information below and your knowledge of chemistry.

The radioisotopes carbon-14 and nitrogen-16 are present in a living organism. Carbon-14 is commonly used to date a once-living organism.

58. A sample of wood is found to contain $1/8$ as much C-14 as is present in the wood of a living tree. What is the approximate age, in years, of this sample of wood?

59. Explain why N-16 is a poor choice for radioactive dating of a bone.

60. Complete the nuclear equation for the decay of C-14. Include *both* the atomic number and the mass number of the missing particle.

$$^{14}_{6}C \rightarrow {}^{0}_{-1}e + \underline{\hspace{3cm}}$$

Base your answers to questions 61 through 63 on the information below and your knowledge of chemistry.

Radioactivity and radioactive isotopes have the potential for both benefiting and harming living organisms. One use of radioactive isotopes is in radiation therapy as a treatment for cancer. Cesium-137 is sometimes used in radiation therapy. A sample of cesium-137 was left in an abandoned clinic in Brazil in 1987. Cesium-137 gives off a blue glow because of its radioactivity. The people who discovered the sample were attracted by the blue glow and had no idea of any danger. Hundreds of people were treated for overexposure to radiation, and four people died.

61. State one benefit or useful application of radioactivity *not* mentioned in this article.

62. Suppose a 40-gram sample of iodine-131 and a 40-gram sample of cesium-137 were both abandoned at the clinic in 1987.
    Explain why the sample of iodine-131 would not pose as great a radiation risk to people as the sample of cesium-137 would.

63. If 12.5 grams of the original sample of cesium-137 remained after 90.6 years, what was the mass of the original sample?

Lab Safety: *Always follow the instructions of your teacher.*

During a lab experiment, appropriate safety guidelines must be followed.

Safety Precautions
- Wear protective goggles at all times.
- Tie back long hair.
- Roll up long sleeves.
- No eating or drinking in the lab, or out of lab equipment.
- No running in the lab.

Safe Procedures
- When lighting a Bunsen burner, strike a match first, then turn on the gas.
- When diluting an acid, pour the acid slowly into water while stirring. Never add water to acid.

In Case of an Accident: *Report all accidents to your teacher immediately*
- Know the locations of all lab safety equipment and procedures for using them.
- Rinse skin with water if any chemical spills on your skin.
- Rinse eyes with water for 15 minutes if any chemical splashes in your eyes.
- A spilled acid or base should be neutralized first before cleaning it up.

Laboratory Equipment

	Beaker	Measuring volume of a liquid.
	Test Tube	Placing a substance for observation or to conduct experiment.
	Evaporating dish	Heating a substance.
	Crucible	Heating a substance.
	Watch glass	Drying a wet solid. Covering up glassware while heating.
	Tongs	Holding an object over heat, or removing heated glassware from heat.
	Buret	Dispensing an exact volume of a liquid. Often used in titration experiments.
	Erlenmeyer flask	Measuring volume of a liquid.
hottest part of a flame	**Bunsen burner**	A heat source for laboratory experiments. Requires natural gas such as propane.

Significant Figures

Significant figures in a number include all digits that are known for certain plus one estimated digit.

Rules for Determining Number of Significant Figures

Significant figures in a number can be determined using Atlantic – Pacific rule.	**405** has **3** significant figures
If a decimal is <u>Absent</u> in a number (whole number) • Start counting with the first nonzero from the **A**tlantic (right) side of the number.	**405**0 has **3** significant figures
• Count toward the Pacific (left).	**2**00 has **1** significant figure
• Stop counting with the last nonzero digit. How many you counted is the number of significant figures in that number.	0**2** has **1** significant figure
If a decimal is <u>Present</u> in a number (decimal fraction) • Start counting with the first nonzero from the **Pacific** (left) side of the number.	0.00**36** has **2** significant figures
• Count toward the Atlantic (right), and count all numbers (including zeros) once you've started counting.	0.0**936** has **3** significant figures
How many you counted is the number of significant figures in that number.	0.0**9360** has **4** significant figures
	200. has 3 significant figures
In Summary: *All zeros to start a number* are never counted as significant.	**0.013** has **2** significant figures
All zeros between two real numbers are always counted as significant.	**104**0 has **3** significant figures
Zeros at the end of a number are significant only if the number contains a decimal point.	**1.040** has **4** significant figures

E3chemistry.com

Significant Figures in Calculations

When Multiplying or Dividing

The answer should be limited or rounded to the same number of significant figures as the factor with the **least number** of significant figures.

Example 1

How much heat is absorbed by a 17-gram sample of ice to melt? Answer must have the correct number of significant figures.

Heat = (mass)(H_f)

Heat = (17)(334)

Heat = 5678 J

Heat = **5700 J**

17 is the factor with the least number of significant figures: 2

5678 (calculated result) has 4 significant figures. It MUST be rounded and limited to 2 significant figures.

5700 (answer) is rounded and limited to 2 significant figures.

Example 2

What is the density of an unknown substance if a 42.6 cm³ sample has a mass of 22.43 g?

$$Density = \frac{mass}{volume}$$

$$Density = \frac{22.43 \text{ g}}{42.6 \text{ cm}^3} = \textbf{0.527 g/cm}^3$$

42.6 is the factor with the least number of significant figures: 3

0.527 (answer) also has 3 significant figures

When Adding or Subtracting

The answer should be limited or rounded to the same number of decimal places as the factor with the *least number of decimal places*.

Example 3

What is the sum of 0.31, 1.310 and 1.3205 to the correct number of significant figures?

0.31 + 1.310 + 1.3205 = 2.9405 = **2.94**

0.31 is the factor with the least number of decimal places: **2**

2.**9405** (calculated result) has **4** decimal places. It must be rounded and limited to 2 decimal places.

2.**94** (answer) has **2** decimal places.

Reading Measuring Equipment

- All laboratory measurements should include a value and unit.
- Measurements should be given to the correct number of significant figures.
- A measurement has the correct number of significant figures when it includes all digits known with certainty, and one estimated digit determined between two of the smallest unit markings on the measuring equipment.

Mass Measurement

Triple-Beam Balance	An equipment for measuring the mass of a substance.
Grams (g)	A unit of measurement for mass.

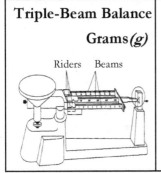

Riders   Beams

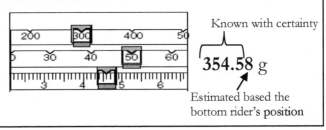

Known with certainty

354.58 g

Estimated based the
bottom rider's position

Volume Measurement

Graduated Cylinder	An equipment for measuring the volume of a liquid.
Milliliters (mL)	A unit of measurement for volume.
Meniscus	The curve surface of a liquid in a graduated cylinder. • Accurate volume of a liquid should be read at eye level with the bottom of the meniscus.

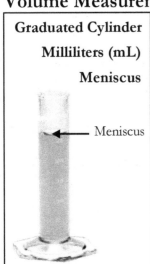

← Meniscus

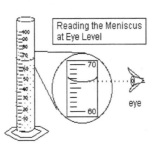

Reading the Meniscus
at Eye Level

eye

Known with certainty

66.1°C

Estimated based on the
bottom of the meniscus level.

Temperature Measurement

Thermometer	An equipment for measuring temperature.
Celsius	A unit of measurement for temperature. • Accurate reading should be at the eye level with the top of the red liquid inside the thermometer.

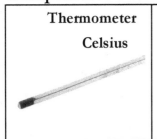

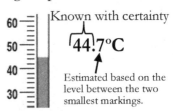

Known with certainty

44.7°C

Estimated based on the
level between the two
smallest markings.

60
50
40
30

Accuracy, Precision, and Uncertainty in Measurements

Accuracy describes the closeness of a measured value to the known or true measurement.

Precision describes the closeness of several measurements of the same substance or material.

For example: If the temperature of a sample of water is known to be 42.3°C, accurate and precise measurements of the same water sample are given below:

Accurate temperature measurement: 42.4°C
Accurate and precise measurements: 42.4°C, 42.6°C, 42.2°C.

Inaccurate temperature measurement: 45.3°C
Inaccurate but precise measurements: 45.3°C, 45.4°C, 45.0°C
Inaccurate and imprecise measurements: 45.3°C, 49.8°C, 37.9°C

Uncertainty describes the best estimate of how far a measured quantity is from the true or known value. All measuring devices have an allowable level of uncertainty.

- $\pm$ value (usually half the measuring unit) is used to represent the uncertainty of a measuring device.
- The smaller the $\pm$ of a measuring device, the higher its precision.

Example:
If the thermometer used in measuring the above water sample is scaled at 1.0°C interval:

- The estimated uncertainty of the thermometer will be $\pm$0.5°C.
- The known temperature of the water can be recorded as 42.3 $\pm$0.5°C.
- All temperature measurements that are 0.5°C lower or greater than 42.3°C can be claimed as accurate.

Percent Error

An expression of the difference (in percent) between the experimental (measured) and actual (accepted) values. The percent error equation is given on **Table T.**

- Percent error should always be positive.
- The smaller the percent error, the more accurate the measured value.
- Human errors and imprecision of measuring equipment are the common causes of high percent errors in a lab experiment.

$$\% \text{ error} = \frac{\text{measured value} - \text{accepted value}}{\text{accepted value}} \times 100$$

Example 4
A student calculated the percent by mass of water in a hydrate sample as 16.2%. What is the student's percent error if the actual percent of water is 14.7%?

$$\% \text{ Error} = \frac{16.2 - 14.7}{14.7} \times 100$$

$$\% \textbf{ Error} = \frac{1.5}{14.7} \times 100 = \textbf{10\%}$$

Review Questions: Lab Safety, Measurements and Significant Figures

1. Which of the following statements in a student's laboratory report is an observation?
   (1) Metal A will also react with an acid.   (3) Metal A is an alkali metal.
   (2) Metal A has luster.   (4) Metal A will conduct electricity.

2. A student investigated the physical and chemical properties of a sample of an unknown gas and then identified the gas. Which statement represents a conclusion rather than an experimental observation?
   (1) The gas is carbon dioxide.
   (2) The gas is colorless.
   (3) When the gas is bubbled into limewater, the liquid becomes cloudy.
   (4) When placed in the gas, a flaming splint stops burning.

3. A student wishes to prepare approximately 100 mL of an aqueous solution of 6 M HCl using 12 M HCl. Which procedure is correct?
   (1) Adding 50 mL of 12 M HCl to 50 mL of water while stirring the mixture steadily
   (2) Adding 50 mL of 12 M HCl to 50 mL of water, and then stirring the mixture steadily
   (3) Adding 50 mL of water to 50 mL of 12 M HCl while stirring the mixture steadily
   (4) Adding 50 mL of water to 50 mL of 12 M HCl, and then stirring the mixture steadily

4. A student determined in the laboratory that the percent by mass of water in $CuSO_4 \cdot 5H_2O$ is 40.0%. If the accepted value is 36%, what is the percent error?
   (1) 0.11%   (2) 1.1%   (3) 11%   (4) 4.0%

5. A student found the boiling point of a liquid to be 80.4°C . If the liquid's actual boiling point is 80.6°C, the experimental percent error is equal to

   (1) $\dfrac{80.6 - 80.4}{80.6} \times 100$ (3) $\dfrac{80.5 - 80.4}{80.5} \times 100$

   (2) $\dfrac{80.6 - 80.4}{80.4} \times 100$ (4) $\dfrac{80.5 - 80.4}{80.4} \times 100$

6.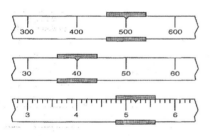

   What is the total mass reading of the triple beam balance?

   (1) 540.20 g   (3) 540.52 g
   (2) 545.20 g   (4) 545.52 g

7.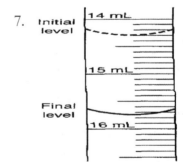

   According to the reading of the buret, what is the total volume of the liquid used?
   (1) 1.10 mL   (3) 1.30 mL
   (2) 1.40 mL   (4) 1.45 mL

E3chemistry.com

8. Which volume measurement is expressed to two significant figures?
   (1) 20 mL   (2) 202 mL   (3) 220 mL   (4) 0.2 mL

9. The volume of a gas sample is 22 L at STP. The density of the gas is 1.35 g/L. What is the mass of the gas sample, expressed to the correct number of significant figures?
   (1) 30. g   (2) 30.0 g   (3) 16.7 g   (4) 2.56 g

10. The density of a solid is 1.235 g/mL and its volume is 40.2 mL. A student calculating the mass of the solid should have how many significant figures in the final answer?
    (1) 1   (2) 2   (3) 3   (4) 4

11. Which set of laboratory equipment would most likely be used with a crucible?

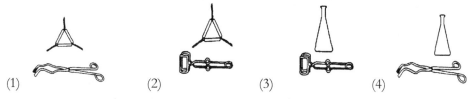

(1)   (2)   (3)   (4)

12. The two pieces of lab equipment shown below are

   (1) Round bottom flask and a crucible   (3) Evaporating dish and a beaker
   (2) Round bottom flask and a watch glass   (4) Evaporating dish and a watch glass

Base your answers to questions 13 through 15 on the information below.

During a laboratory activity, a student places 25.0 mL of HCl(aq) of unknown concentration into a flask. The student adds four drops of phenolphthalein to the solution in the flask. The solution is titrated with 0.150 M KOH(aq) until the solution appears faint pink. The volume of KOH(aq) added is 18.5 mL.

13. Describe *one* laboratory safety procedure that should be used if a drop of the KOH(aq) is spilled on the arm of the student.

14. What number of significant figures is used to express the concentration of the KOH(aq)?

15. Calculate the concentration of the HCl solution in the flask that was titrated.
    Your response must include a correct numerical setup and the calculated result.

Base your answers to questions 16 and 17 on the information below.

A method used by ancient Egyptians to obtain copper metal from copper(I) sulfide ore was heating the ore in the presence of air. Later, copper was mixed with tin to produce a useful alloy called bronze. Archaeologists recently discovered a 129.5-gram piece of bronze artifact.

16. Calculate the density of the bronze artifact if its volume is 14.8 cubic centimeters.
    Your response must include a correct numerical setup and the calculated result.

17. A careful study of the 129.5-gram bronze artifact reveals that it is composed of approximately 110.0 grams of copper, and the rest tin. Calculate the percent composition of tin in the artifact.

Regents Practice

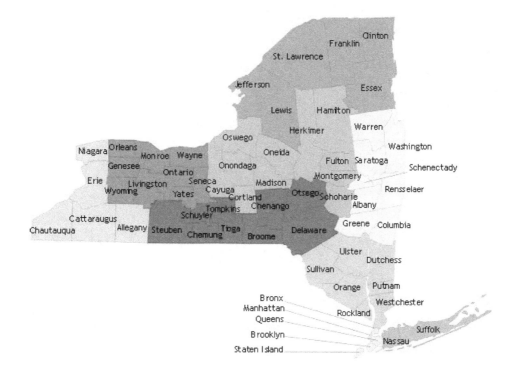

12 Topics of Regents Practice Questions

3 Most Recent Regents Exams

for

NYS Regents Chemistry
The Physical Setting
Exam

1 Which sample of matter represents a mixture?
   (1) aqueous ammonia (3) liquid mercury
   (2) gaseous ethane   (4) solid iodine

2 Which type of matter is composed of two or more elements that are chemically combined in a fixed proportion?

   (1) solution
   (2) compound
   (3) homogeneous mixture
   (4) heterogeneous mixture

3 The ratio of chromium to iron to carbon varies among the different types of stainless steel. Therefore, stainless steel is classified as

   (1) a compound   (3) a mixture
   (2) an element   (4) a substance

4 Which statement defines the temperature of a sample of matter?

   (1) Temperature is a measure of the total electromagnetic energy of the particles.
   (2) Temperature is a measure of the total thermal energy of the particles.
   (3) Temperature is a measure of the average potential energy of the particles.
   (4) Temperature is a measure of the average kinetic energy of a particles.

5 According to the kinetic molecular theory for an ideal gas, all gas particles

   (1) are in random, constant, straight-line motion
   (2) are separated by very small distances relative to their sizes
   (3) have strong intermolecular forces
   (4) have collisions that decrease the total energy of the system

6 Equal amounts of ethanol and water are mixed at room temperature and at 101.3 kPa. Which process is used to separate ethanol from the mixture?

   (1) distillation   (3) filtration
   (2) reduction   (4) ionization

7 Which statement explains why water is classified as a compound?

   (1) Water can be broken down by chemical means.
   (2) Water is a liquid at room temperature.
   (3) Water has a heat of fusion of 334 J/g.
   (4) Water is a poor conductor of electricity.

8 Given four particle models:

Key
◯ = an atom of element T
◉ = an atom of element X
◍ = an atom of element Z

  I   II   III   IV

Which two models can be classified as elements?

   (1) I and II   (3) II and III
   (2) I and IV   (4) II and IV

9 A sample of chlorine gas is at 300. K and 1.00 atmosphere. At which temperature and pressure would the sample behave more like an ideal gas?

   (1) 0 K and 1.00 atm
   (2) 150. K and 0.50 atm
   (3) 273 K and 1.00 atm
   (4) 600. K and 0.50 atm

10 Which rigid cylinder contains the same number of gas molecules at STP as a 2.0-liter rigid cylinder containing $H_2(g)$ at STP?

   (1) 1.0-L cylinder of $O_2(g)$
   (2) 2.0-L cylinder of $CH_4(g)$
   (3) 1.5-L cylinder of $NH_3(g)$
   (4) 4.0-L cylinder of $He(g)$

11 A rigid cylinder with a movable piston contains a sample of gas. At 300. K, this sample has a pressure of 240. kilopascals and a volume of 70.0 milliliters. What is the volume of this sample when the temperature is changed to 150. K and the pressure is changed to 160. kilopascals?

(1) 35.0 mL   (3) 70.0 mL
(2) 52.5 mL   (4) 105 mL

12 Which processes represent one chemical change and one physical change?

(1) freezing and melting
(2) freezing and vaporization
(3) decomposition and melting
(4) decomposition and combustion

13 Which equation represents sublimation?

(1) $Hg(\ell) \rightarrow Hg(s)$
(2) $H_2O(s) \rightarrow H_2O(g)$
(3) $NH_3(g) \rightarrow NH_3(\ell)$
(4) $CH_4(\ell) \rightarrow CH_4(g)$

14 What is the minimum amount of heat required to completely melt 20.0 grams of ice at its melting point?

(1) 20.0 J   (3) 6,680 J
(2) 83.6 J   (4) 45,200 J

15 Given the balanced particle-diagram equation:

Key	
O	= an atom of an element
●	= an atom of a different element

 + 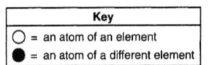 ⟶

Which statement describes the type of change and the chemical properties of the product and reactants?

(1) The equation represents a physical change, with the product and reactants having different chemical properties.
(2) The equation represents a physical change, with the product and reactants having identical chemical properties.
(3) The equation represents a chemical change, with the product and reactants having different chemical properties.
(4) The equation represents a chemical change, with the product and reactants having identical chemical properties.

Base your answers to questions **16** and **17** on the information below and on your knowledge of chemistry.

A few pieces of dry ice, $CO_2(s)$, at $-78°C$ are placed in a flask that contains air at $21°C$. The flask is sealed by placing an uninflated balloon over the mouth of the flask. As the balloon inflates, the dry ice disappears and no liquid is observed in the flask.

16 Write the name of the process that occurs as the dry ice undergoes a phase change in the flask.

17 State the direction of heat flow that occurs between the dry ice and the air in the flask.

Base your answers to questions **18** through **20** on the information below and on your knowledge of chemistry.

Cylinder A has a movable piston and contains hydrogen gas. An identical cylinder, B, contains methane gas. The diagram below represents these cylinders and the conditions of pressure, volume, and temperature of the gas in each cylinder.

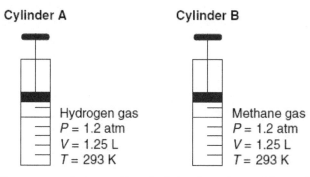

Cylinder A

Hydrogen gas
$P = 1.2$ atm
$V = 1.25$ L
$T = 293$ K

Cylinder B

Methane gas
$P = 1.2$ atm
$V = 1.25$ L
$T = 293$ K

18 Show a numerical setup for calculating the volume of the gas in cylinder B at STP.

19 State a change in temperature and a change in pressure that will cause the gas in cylinder A to behave more like an ideal gas.

20 Compare the total number of gas molecules in cylinder A to the total number of gas molecules in cylinder B.

Base your answers to questions **21** through **23** on the information below.

A student investigated heat transfer using a bottle of water. The student placed the bottle in a room at 20.5°C. The student measured the temperature of the water in the bottle at 7 a.m. and again at 3 p.m. The data from the investigation are shown in the table below.

Water Bottle Investigation Data

7 a.m.		3 p.m.	
Mass of Water (g)	Temperature (°C)	Mass of Water (g)	Temperature (°C)
800.	12.5	800.	20.5

21 Show a numerical setup for calculating the change in the thermal energy of the water in the bottle from 7 a.m. to 3 p.m.

22 State the direction of heat transfer between the surroundings and the water in the bottle from 7 a.m. to 3 p.m.

23 Compare the average kinetic energy of the water molecules in the bottle at 7 a.m. to the average kinetic energy of the water molecules in the bottle at 3 p.m.

_____

Base your answers to questions **24** and **25** on the information below.

Starting as a gas at 206°C, a sample of a substance is allowed to cool for 16 minutes. This process is represented by the cooling curve below.

Cooling Curve for a Substance

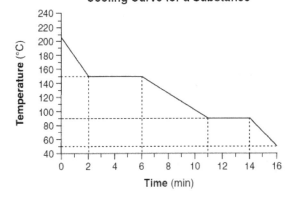

24 At what time do the particles of this sample have the *lowest* average kinetic energy?

25 What is the melting point of this substance?

1 The elements on the Periodic Table are arranged in order of increasing

(1) mass number
(2) atomic number
(3) number of isotopes
(4) number of valence electrons

2 Which phrase describes the molecular structure and properties of two solid forms of carbon, diamond and graphite?

(1) the same molecular structures and the same properties
(2) the same molecular structures and different properties
(3) different molecular structures and the same properties
(4) different molecular structures and different properties

3 Which property can be defined as the ability of a substance to be hammered into thin sheets?

(1) conductivity   (3) melting point
(2) malleability   (4) solubility

4 The number of valence electrons in each atom of an element affects the element's

(1) chemical properties
(2) number of isotopes
(3) decay mode
(4) half-life

5 A solid element that is malleable, a good conductor of electricity, and reacts with oxygen is classified as a

(1) metal   (3) noble gas
(2) metalloid   (4) nonmetal

6 As the elements is Period 3 are considered in order of increasing atomic number, there is a general *decrease* in

(1) atomic mass
(2) atomic radius
(3) electronegativity
(4) first ionization energy

7 What is the total number of valence electrons in a germanium atom in the ground state?

(1) 22   (2) 2   (3) 32   (4) 4

8 Which term represents the attraction one atom has for the electrons in a bond with another atom?

(1) electronegativity
(2) electrical conductivity
(3) first ionization energy
(4) mechanical energy

9 In the ground state, an atom of each of the elements in Group 2 has a different

(1) oxidation state
(2) first ionization energy
(3) number of valence electrons
(4) number of electrons in the first shell

10 Which statement explains why neon is a Group 18 element?

(1) Neon is a gas at STP.
(2) Neon has a low melting point.
(3) Neon atoms have a stable valence electron configuration.
(4) Neon atoms have two electrons in the first shell.

11 Which elements have the most similar chemical properties?

(1) Si, As, and Te   (3) Mg, Sr, and Ba
(2) N_2, O_2, and F_2 (4) Ca, Cs, and Cu

12 Which list of elements contains a metal, a metalloid, and a nonmetal?

(1) B, Si, I_2 (3) Li, Mn, F_2
(2) Hg, Te, Ne   (4) H_2, Si, C

13 Which element is a liquid at STP?

(1) bromine   (3) francium
(2) cesium   (4) iodine

14 Which element is malleable and a good conductor of electricity at STP?

(1) argon   (3) iodine
(2) carbon   (4) silver

15 Which element has the highest melting point?

(1) tantalum   (3) osmium

(2) rhenium   (4) hafnium

16 Which element has the greatest density at STP?

(1) calcium   (3) chlorine

(2) carbon   (4) copper

17 Which atom has the largest atomic radius?

(1) potassium   (3) francium

(2) rubidium   (4) cesium

18 Which atom has the *weakest* attraction for electrons in a chemical bond?

(1) a boron atom   (3) a fluorine atom

(2) a calcium atom   (4) a nitrogen atom

19 Which atom in the ground state requires the *least amount of energy to remove its valence electron?*

(1) lithium atom   (3) rubidium atom

(2) potassium atom   (4) sodium atom

Base your answers to questions **20** and **21** on the information below and on your knowledge of chemistry.

There are six elements in Group 14 on the Periodic Table. One of these elements has the symbol Uuq, which is a temporary, systematic symbol. This element is now known as flerovium.

20 State the expected number of valence electrons in an atom of the element flerovium in the ground state.

21 Explain, in terms of electron shells, why each successive element in Group 14 has a larger atomic radius, as the elements are considered in order of increasing atomic number.

Base your answers to questions **22** through **25** on the information below and on your knowledge of chemistry.

The diagram below represents three elements in Group 13 and three elements in Period 3 and their relative positions on the Periodic Table.

Some elements in the solid phase exist in different forms that vary in their physical properties. For example, at room temperature, red phosphorus has a density of 2.16 g/cm^3 and white phosphorus has a density of 1.823 g/cm^3.

22 Identify *one* element from the diagram that will combine with phosphorus in the same ratio of atoms as the ratio in aluminum phosphide.

23 Compare the number of atoms per cubic centimeter in red phosphorus with the number of atoms per cubic centimeter in white phosphorus.

24 Consider the Period 3 elements in the diagram in order of increasing atomic number. State the trend in electronegativity for these elements.

25 Identify the element from the diagram that will react with chlorine to form a compound with the general formula XCl_4.

1 Which statement describes the distribution of charge in an atom?

(1) A neutral nucleus is surrounded by one or more negatively charged electrons.
(2) A neutral nucleus is surrounded by one or more positively charged electrons.
(3) A positively charged nucleus is surrounded by one or more negatively charged electrons.
(4) A positively charged nucleus is surrounded by one or more positively charged electrons.

2 In the wave-mechanical model of the atom, an orbital is defined as

(1) a region of the most probable proton location
(2) a region of the most probable electron location
(3) a circular path traveled by a proton around the nucleus
(4) a circular path traveled by an electron around the nucleus

3 Which phrase describes the charge and mass of a neutron?

(1) a charge of +1 and no mass
(2) a charge of +1 and an approximate mass of 1 u
(3) no charge and no mass
(4) no charge and an approximate mass of 1 u

4 Which quantity represents the number of protons in an atom?

(1) atomic number
(2) oxidation number
(3) number of neutrons
(4) number of valence electrons

5 The atomic mass of magnesium is the weighted average of the atomic masses of

(1) all of the artificially produced isotopes of Mg
(2) all of the naturally occurring isotopes of Mg
(3) the two most abundant artificially produced isotopes of Mg
(4) the two most abundant naturally occurring isotopes of Mg

6 A specific amount of energy is emitted when excited electrons in an atom in a sample of an element return to the ground state. This emitted energy can be used to determine the

(1) mass of the sample
(2) volume of the sample
(3) identity of the element
(4) number of moles of the element

7 Which particle has the *least mass?*

(1) alpha particle   (3) neutron
(2) beta particle   (4) proton

8 Which conclusion was a direct result of the gold foil experiment?

(1) An atom is mostly empty space with a dense, positively charged nucleus.
(2) An atom is composed of at least three types of subatomic particles.
(3) An electron has a positive charge and is located inside the nucleus.
(4) An electron has properties of both waves and particles.

9 An electron in a sodium atom gains enough energy to move from the second shell to the third shell. The sodium atom becomes

(1) a positive ion
(2) a negative ion
(3) an atom in an excited state
(4) an atom in the ground state

10 Which statement about one atom of an element identifies the element?

(1) The atom has 1 proton.
(2) The atom has 2 neutrons.
(3) The sum of the number of protons and neutrons in the atom is 3.
(4) The difference between the number of neutrons and protons in the atom is 1.

11 What is the charge of the nucleus of an oxygen atom?

(1) 0   (2) −2   (3) +8   (4) +16

12 The nuclides I-131 and I-133 are classified as

(1) isomers of the same element   (3) isotopes of the same element
(2) isomers of Xe-131 and Cs-133   (4) isotopes of Xe-131 and Cs-133

13 Given the particle diagram:

Which substance at STP can be represented by this particle diagram?

(1) N_2 (2) H_2 (3) Mg   (4) Kr

14 Which two notations represent different isotopes of the same element?

(1) $^{6}_{4}Be$ and $^{9}_{4}Be$ (2) $^{7}_{3}Li$ and $^{7}_{3}Li$ (3) $^{14}_{7}N$ and $^{14}_{6}C$ (4) $^{32}_{15}P$ and $^{32}_{16}S$

15 The table below gives the atomic mass and the abundance of the two naturally occurring isotopes of chlorine.

Naturally Occuring Isotopes of Chlorine

Isotopes	AtomicMassof theIsotopes (u)	Natural Abundance (%)
^{35}Cl	34.97	75.76
^{37}Cl	36.97	24.24

Which numerical setup can be used to calculate the atomic mass of the element chlorine?

(1) (34.97 u)(75.76) + (36.97 u)(24.24)   (3) (34.97 u)(0.7576) + (36.97 u)(0.2424)
(2) (34.97 u)(0.2424) + (36.97 u)(0.7576)   (4) (34.97 u)(24.24) + (36.97 u)(75.76)

16 Which electron configuration represents the electrons of an atom in an excited state?

(1) 2-1   (3) 2-8-7
(2) 2-7-4   (4) 2-4

17 A bromine atom in an excited state could have an electron configuration of

(1) 2-8-18-6   (3) 2-8-17-7
(2) 2-8-18-7   (4) 2-8-17-8

18 A sample of matter must be copper if

(1) each atom in the sample has 29 protons
(2) atoms in the sample react with oxygen
(3) the sample melts at 1768 K
(4) the sample can conduct electricity

19 Which atom in the ground state has an outermost electron with the most energy?

(1) Cs   (2) K   (3) Li   (4) Na

Base your answers to questions **20** through **22** on the information below and on your knowledge of chemistry.

The bright-line spectra observed in a spectroscope for three elements and a mixture of two of these elements are represented in the diagram below.

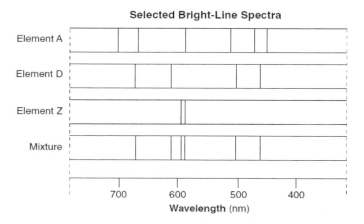

20 Describe, in terms of *both* electrons and energy state, how the light represented by the spectral lines is produced.

21 Explain why the spectrum produced by a 1-gram sample of element Z would have the same spectral lines at the same wavelengths as the spectrum produced by a 2-gram sample of element Z.

22 State evidence from the bright-line spectra that indicates element *A* is *not* present in the mixture.

_____

23 Explain, in terms of electron configuration, why arsenic and antimony are chemically similar.

_____

24 Copper has two naturally occurring isotopes. Information about the two isotopes is shown in the table below.

Naturally Occurring Isotopes of Copper

Isotope	Atomic Mass (atomic mass units, u)	Percent Natural Abundance (%)
Cu-63	62.93	69.17
Cu-65	64.93	30.83

In the space *in your answer booklet*, show a numerical setup for calculating the atomic mass of copper.

_____

25 In the box below, draw a Lewis electron-dot diagram for an atom of boron.

1 Given the balanced equation representing a reaction:

$$O_2 \rightarrow O + O$$

What occurs during this reaction?

(1) Energy is absorbed as bonds are broken.
(2) Energy is absorbed as bonds are formed.
(3) Energy is released as bonds are broken.
(4) Energy is released as bonds are formed.

2 What occurs as two atoms of fluorine combine to become a molecule of fluorine?

(1) A bond is formed as energy is absorbed.
(2) A bond is formed as energy is released.
(3) A bond is broken as energy is absorbed.
(4) A bond is broken as energy is released.

3 Which term indicates how strongly an atom attracts the electrons in a chemical bond?

(1) alkalinity   (3) electronegativity
(2) atomic mass   (4) activation energy

4 Which type of bond results when one or more valence electrons are transferred from one atom to another?

(1) a hydrogen bond
(2) an ionic bond
(3) a nonpolar covalent bond
(4) a polar covalent bond

5 A solid substance is an excellent conductor of electricity. The chemical bonds in this substance are most likely

(1) ionic, because the valence electrons are shared between atoms
(2) ionic, because the valence electrons are mobile
(3) metallic, because the valence electrons are stationary
(4) metallic, because the valence electrons are mobile

6 Conductivity in a metal results from the metal atoms having

(1) high electronegativity
(2) high ionization energy
(3) highly mobile protons in the nucleus
(4) highly mobile electrons in the valence shell

7 Which element reacts with oxygen to form ionic bonds?

(1) calcium   (3) chlorine
(2) hydrogen   (4) nitrogen

8 Which formulas represent one ionic compound and one molecular compound?

(1) N_2 and SO_2 (3) $BaCl_2$ and N_2O_4
(2) Cl_2 and H_2S (4) $NaOH$ and $BaSO_4$

9 A sample of a substance has these characteristics:

• melting point of 984 K
• hard, brittle solid at room temperature
• poor conductor of heat and electricity as a solid
• good conductor of electricity as a liquid or in an aqueous solution

This sample is classified as

(1) a metallic element
(2) a radioactive element
(3) a molecular compound
(4) an ionic compound

10 Metallic bonding occurs between atoms of

(1) sulfur   (3) fluorine
(2) copper   (4) carbon

11 The electronegativity difference between the atoms in a molecule of HCl can be used to determine

(1) the entropy of the atoms
(2) the atomic number of the atoms
(3) the first ionization energy of the atoms
(4) the polarity of the bond between the two atoms

12 Which formula represents a molecule with the most polar bond?

(1) CO (2) NO (3) HI (4) HCl

13 Which molecule has a nonpolar covalent bond?

(1) H−H   (3) H∕O∖H

(2) H∕N∖H   (4) H−Cl
    |
    H

14 Which phrase describes a molecule of CH_4, in terms of molecular polarity and distribution of charge?

(1) polar with an asymmetrical distribution of charge
(2) polar with a symmetrical distribution of charge
(3) nonpolar with an asymmetrical distribution of charge
(4) nonpolar with a symmetrical distribution of charge

15 Which symbol represents an atom in the ground state with the most stable valence electron configuration?

(1) B   (2) O   (3) Li   (4) Ne

16 Which element has the *lowest* electronegativity value?

(1) F   (2) Fr   (3) Cl   (4) Cr

17 Given the Lewis electron-dot diagram:

   H
   ••
H : C : H
   ••
   H

Which electrons are represented by all of the dots?

(1) the carbon valence electrons, only
(2) the hydrogen valence electrons, only
(3) the carbon and hydrogen valence electrons
(4) all of the carbon and hydrogen electrons

18 Which Lewis electron-dot diagram represents a nitrogen atom in the ground state?

(1) N̈   (3) ·N̈·

(2) ·N·   (4) :N̈:

19 Which Lewis electron-dot diagram represents a molecule having a nonpolar covalent bond?

(1) :C̈l:C̈l: (3) K⁺[:B̈r:]⁻

(2) H:C̈l: (4) H:S̈:
             H

20 Which Lewis electron-dot diagram is correct for CO_2?

(1) :Ö·
   ××
  ×C̈×Ö·

(2) :Ö:C̈:Ö:
      ××

(3) :O××C××O:

(4) ·Ö·
   ××
  ×C̈:Ö:

21 At standard pressure, CH_4 boils at 112 K and H_2O boils at 373 K. What accounts for the higher boiling point of H_2O at standard pressure?

(1) covalent bonding
(2) ionic bonding
(3) hydrogen bonding
(4) metallic bonding

22 Hydrogen bonding is a type of

(1) strong covalent bond
(2) weak ionic bond
(3) strong intermolecular force
(4) weak intermolecular force

23 An ionic bond can be formed when one or more electrons are

(1) equally shared by two atoms
(2) unequally shared by two atoms
(3) transferred from the nucleus of one atom to the nucleus of another atom
(4) transferred from the valence shell of one atom to the valence shell of another atom

Base your answers to questions **24** and **25** on the information below.

Physical Properties of CF$_4$ and NH$_3$
at Standard Pressure

Compound	Melting Point (°C)	Boiling Point (°C)	Solubility in Water at 20.0°C
CF$_4$	−183.6	−127.8	insoluble
NH$_3$	−77.7	−33.3	soluble

24 In the space *in your answer booklet*, draw a Lewis electron-dot diagram for CF₄.

25 State evidence that indicates NH₃ has stronger intermolecular forces than CF₄.

———————————————————————

Base your answers to questions **26** through **28** on the information below and on your knowledge of chemistry.

Rubbing alcohol is a product available at most pharmacies and supermarkets. One rubbing alcohol solution contains 2-propanol and water. The boiling point of 2-propanol is 82.3°C at standard pressure.

26 Explain, in term of charge distribution, why a molecule of the 2-propanol is a polar molecule.

27 Identify a strong intermolecular force of attraction between an alcohol molecule and a water molecule in the solution.

28 Explain in terms of electronegativity differences, why a C–O bond is more polar than a C–H bond.

1 Which list includes three type of chemical formulas for organic compounds?

(1) covalent, metallic, isotopic
(2) covalent, metallic, molecular
(3) empirical, structural, isotopic
(4) empirical, structural, molecular

2 Which type of formula represents the simplest whole-number ratio of atoms of the elements in a compound?

(1) molecular formula
(2) condensed formula
(3) empirical formula
(4) structural formula

3 The coefficients in a balanced chemical equation represent

(1) the mass ratios of the substances in the reaction
(2) the mole ratios of the substances in the reaction
(3) the total number of electrons in the reaction
(4) the total number of elements in the reaction

4 A balanced equation representing a chemical reaction can be written using

(1) chemical formulas and mass numbers
(2) chemical formulas and coefficients
(3) first ionization energies and mass numbers
(4) first ionization energies and coefficients

5 Given the balanced equation representing a reaction:
$H^+(aq) + OH^-(aq) \rightarrow H_2O(\ell) + 55.8$ kJ
In this reaction there is conservation of

(1) mass, only
(2) mass and charge, only
(3) mass and energy, only
(4) mass, charge, and energy

6 Which formula is both a molecular and an empirical formula?

(1) $C_6H_{12}O_6$ (3) C_3H_8O
(2) $C_2H_4O_2$ (4) C_4H_8

7 Given the formula for a compound:

Which molecular formula and empirical formula represent this compound?

(1) C_2HNO_2 and CHNO
(2) C_2HNO_2 and C_2HNO_2
(3) $C_4H_2N_2O_4$ and CHNO
(4) $C_4H_2N_2O_4$ and C_2HNO_2

8 What is the empirical formula for a compound with the molecular formula $C_6H_{12}Cl_2O_2$?

(1) CHClO   (3) C_3H_6ClO
(2) CH_2ClO (4) $C_6H_{12}C_{12}O_2$

9 Which equation shows a conservation of mass?

(1) $Na + Cl_2 \rightarrow NaCl$
(2) $Al + Br_2 \rightarrow AlBr_3$
(3) $H_2O \rightarrow H_2 + O_2$
(4) $PCl_5 \rightarrow PCl_3 + Cl_2$

10 Which terms identify types of chemical reactions?

(1) decomposition and sublimation
(2) decomposition and synthesis
(3) deposition and sublimation
(4) deposition and synthesis

11 Which formula represents strontium phosphate?

(1) $SrPO_4$ (3) $Sr_2(PO_4)_3$
(2) Sr_3PO_8 (4) $Sr_3(PO_4)_2$

12 What is the IUPAC name for the compound ZnO?

(1) zinc oxide   (3) zinc peroxide
(2) zinc oxalate   (4) zinc hydroxide

13 What is the chemical formula of iron(III) sulfide?

(1) FeS   (3) $FeSO_3$
(2) Fe_2S_3 (4) $Fe_2(SO_3)_3$

14 Which formula represents copper(I) oxide?

(1) CuO   (3) Cu_2O
(2) CuO_2 (4) Cu_2O_2

15 In the formula X_2SO_4, the symbol X could represent the element

(1) Al   (2) Ar   (3) Mg   (4) Li

16 Given the incomplete equation representing a reaction:

$$2C_6H_{14} + \underline{\hspace{2cm}} O_2 \rightarrow 12CO_2 + 14H_2O$$

What is the coefficient of O_2 when the equation is completely balanced using the smallest whole-number coefficients?

(1) 13   (2) 14   (3) 19   (4) 26

17 Given the balanced equations representing two chemical reactions:

$$Cl_2 + 2NaBr \rightarrow 2NaCl + Br_2$$
$$2NaCl \rightarrow 2Na + Cl_2$$

Which type of chemical reactions are represented by these equations?

(1) single replacement and decomposition
(2) single replacement and double replacement
(3) synthesis and decomposition
(4) synthesis and double replacement

18 Which balanced equation represents a double replacement reaction?

(1) $Mg + 2AgNO_3 \rightarrow Mg(NO_3)_2 + 2Ag$
(2) $2Mg + O_2 \rightarrow 2MgO$
(3) $MgCO_3 \rightarrow MgO + CO_2$
(4) $MgCl_2 + 2AgNO_3 \rightarrow 2AgCl + Mg(NO_3)_2$

Base your answers to questions 19 through 22 on the information below.

The reaction between aluminum and an aqueous solution of copper(II) sulfate is represented by the unbalanced equation below.

$$Al(s) + CuSO_4(aq) \rightarrow Al_2(SO_4)_3(aq) + Cu(s)$$

19 Explain why the equation represents a chemical change.

20 Balance the equation below, using the smallest whole-number coefficients.

    ____Al(s) + ____CuSO4(aq) → ____Al2(SO4)3(aq) + ____Cu(s)

21 Identify the type of chemical reaction represented by the equation.

22 Determine the total mass of Cu produced when 1.08 grams of Al reacts completely with 9.58 grams of CuSO4 to produce 6.85 grams of Al2(SO4)3.

---

23 Base your answer to the following question on the information below.

In an experiment, 2.54 grams of copper completely reacts with sulfur, producing 3.18 grams of copper(I) sulfide.

Write the chemical formula of the compound produced.

248

1 The sum of the atomic masses of the atoms in one molecule of $C_3H_6Br_2$ is called the

   (1) formula mass
   (2) isotopic mass
   (3) percent abundance
   (4) percent composition

2 The gram-formula mass of NO_2 is defined as the mass of

   (1) one mole of NO_2
   (2) one molecule of NO_2
   (3) two moles of NO
   (4) two molecules of NO

3 Which sample contains a mole of atoms?

   (1) 23 g Na   (3) 42 g Kr
   (2) 24 g C   (4) 78 g K

4 What is the gram-formula mass of $(NH_4)_3PO_4$?

   (1) 112 g/mol   (3) 149 g/mol
   (2) 121 g/mol   (4) 242 g/mol

5 What is the mass of 1.5 moles of CO_2?

   (1) 66 g   (2) 44 g   (3) 33 g   (4) 29 g

6 The molar mass of $Ba(OH)_2$ is

   (1) 154.3 g   (3) 171.3 g
   (2) 155.3 g   (4) 308.6 g

7 Which compound has the greatest percent composition by mass of sulfur?

   (1) BaS   (2) CaS   (3) MgS   (4) SrS

8 What is the percent composition by mass of sulfur in the compound $MgSO_4$ (gram-formula mass = 120. grams per mole)?

   (1) 20%   (2) 27%   (3) 46%   (4) 53%

9 Given the balanced equation representing a reaction:

$$4NH_3(g) + 5O_2(g) \rightarrow 4NO(g) + 6H_2O(g)$$

What is the number of moles of $H_2O(g)$ formed when 2.0 moles of $NH_3(g)$ react completely?

   (1) 6.0 mol   (3) 3.0 mol
   (2) 2.0 mol   (4) 4.0 mol

10 Given the balanced equation representing the reaction between methane and oxygen:

$$CH_4 + 2O_2 \rightarrow CO_2 + 2H_2O$$

According to this equation, what is the mole ratio of oxygen to methane?

   (1) $\frac{1 \text{ gram } O_2}{2 \text{ grams } CH_4}$ (3) $\frac{2 \text{ grams } O_2}{1 \text{ gram } CH_4}$
   (2) $\frac{1 \text{ mole } O_2}{2 \text{ moles } CH_4}$ (4) $\frac{2 \text{ moles } O_2}{1 \text{ mole } CH_4}$

11 Given the balanced equation representing a reaction:

$$Al_2(SO_4)_3 + 6NaOH \rightarrow 2Al(OH)_3 + 3Na_2SO_4$$

The mole ratio of NaOH to $Al(OH)_3$ is

   (1) 1:1   (2) 1:3   (3) 3:1   (4) 3:7

Base your answers to questions **12** and **13** on the information below.

Vitamin C, also known as ascorbic acid, is water soluble and cannot be produced by the human body. Each day, a person's diet should include a source of vitamin C, such as orange juice. Ascorbic acid has a molecular formula of $C_6H_8O_6$ and a gram-formula mass of 176 grams per mole.

12 Show a numerical setup for calculating the percent composition by mass of oxygen in ascorbic acid.

13 Determine the number of moles of vitamin C in an orange that contains 0.071 gram of vitamin C.

Base your answers to questions **14** and **15** on the information below.

A tablet of one antacid contains citric acid, $H_3C_6H_5O_7$, and sodium hydrogen carbonate, $NaHCO_3$. When the tablet dissolves in water, bubbles of CO_2 are produced. This reaction is represented by the incomplete equation below.

$H_3C_6H_5O_7(aq) + 3NaHCO_3(aq) \rightarrow Na_3C_6H_5O_7(aq) + 3CO_2(g) + 3$_____ ($\ell$)

14 Determine the total number of moles of sodium hydrogen carbonate that will completely react with 0.010 mole of citric acid.

15 Write the formula of the missing product.

Base your answers to questions **16** through **18** on the information below.

Hydrogen peroxide, H_2O_2, is a water-soluble compound. The concentration of an aqueous hydrogen peroxide solution that is 3% by mass H_2O_2 is used as an antiseptic. When the solution is poured on a small cut in the skin, H_2O_2 reacts according to the balanced equation below.

$$2H_2O_2 \rightarrow 2H_2O + O_2$$

16 Determine the gram-formula mass of H_2O_2.

17 Calculate the total mass of H_2O_2 in 20.0 grams of an aqueous H_2O_2 solution that is used as an antiseptic. Your response must include both a numerical setup and the calculated result.

18 Identify the type of chemical reaction represented by the balanced equation.

---

1 Which property of an unsaturated solution of sodium chloride in water remains the same when more water is added to the solution?

(1) density of the solution
(2) boiling point of the solution
(3) mass of sodium chloride in the solution
(4) percent by mass of water in the solution

2 Under which conditions of temperature and pressure is a gas most soluble in water?

(1) high temperature and low pressure
(2) high temperature and high pressure
(3) low temperature and low pressure
(4) low temperature and high pressure

3 A change in pressure would have the greatest effect on the solubility of a

(1) solid in a liquid   (3) liquid in a liquid
(2) gas in a liquid   (4) liquid in a solid

4 Which phrase describes the molarity of a solution?

(1) liters of solute per mole of solution
(2) liters of solution per mole of solution
(3) moles of solute per liter of solution
(4) moles of solution per liter of solution

5 The concentration of a solution can be expressed in

(1) milliliters per minute
(2) parts per million
(3) grams per kelvin
(4) joules per gram

6 Two substances in a mixture differ in density and particle size. These properties can be used to

(1) separate the substances
(2) chemically combine the substances
(3) determine the freezing point of the mixture
(4) predict the electrical conductivity of the mixture

7 A solution consists of 0.50 mole of $CaCl_2$ dissolved in 100. grams of H_2O at 25°C. Compared to the boiling point and freezing point of 100. grams of H_2O at standard pressure, the solution at standard pressure has

(1) a lower boiling point and a lower freezing point
(2) a lower boiling point and a higher freezing point
(3) a higher boiling point and a lower freezing point
(4) a higher boiling point and a higher freezing point

8 According to Reference Table F, which of these compounds is most soluble at 298 K and 1 atm?

(1) $AgNO_3$ (3) $PbCrO_4$
(2) $AgCl$ (4) $PbCO_3$

9 Which ion, when combined with chloride ions, Cl^-, forms an insoluble substance in water?

(1) Fe^{2+} (3) Pb^{2+}
(2) Mg^{2+} (4) Zn^{2+}

10 Which substance is most soluble in water?

(1) $(NH_4)_3PO_4$ (3) Ag_2SO_4
(2) $Cu(OH)_2$ (4) $CaCO_3$

11 At standard pressure, which substance becomes *less* soluble in water as temperature increases from 10.°C to 80.°C?

(1) HCl (3) $NaCl$
(2) KCl (4) NH_4Cl

12 An unsaturated aqueous solution of NH_3 is at 90°C in 100. grams of water. According to Reference Table G, how many grams of NH_3 could this unsaturated solution contain?

(1) 5 g   (3) 15 g
(2) 10. g   (4) 20. g

13 What is the total mass of KNO_3 that must be dissolved in 50. grams of H_2O at 60.°C to make a saturated solution?

(1) 32 g   (3) 64 g
(2) 53 g   (4) 106 g

14 A 2400.-gram sample of an aqueous solution contains 0.012 gram of NH_3. What is the concentration of NH_3 in the solution, expressed as parts per million?

(1) 5.0 ppm   (3) 20. ppm
(2) 15 ppm   (4) 50. ppm

15 Which solution has the highest boiling point at standard pressure?

(1) 0.10 M KCl(aq)
(2) 0.10 M K_2SO_4(aq)
(3) 0.10 M K_3PO_4(aq)
(4) 0.10 M KNO_3(aq)

16 Which sample, when dissolved in 1.0 liter of water, produces a solution with the highest boiling point?

(1) 0.1 mole KI   (3) 0.1 mole $MgCl_2$
(2) 0.2 mole KI   (4) 0.2 mole $MgCl_2$

17 A student prepares four aqueous solutions, each with a different solute. The mass of each dissolved solute is shown in the table below.

Mass of Dissolved Solute
for Four Aqueous Solutions

Solution Number	Solute	Mass of Dissolved Solute (per 100. g of H_2O at 20.°C)
1	KI	120. g
2	$NaNO_3$	88 g
3	KCl	25 g
4	$KClO_3$	5 g

Which solution is saturated?

(1) 1   (2) 2   (3) 3   (4) 4

18 Base your answer to the following question on the information below and on your knowledge of chemistry.

Ethane, C_2H_6, has a boiling point of $-89°C$ at standard pressure. Ethanol, C_2H_5OH, has a much higher boiling point than ethane at standard pressure. At STP, ethane is a gas and ethanol is a liquid.

A liquid boils when the vapor pressure of the liquid equals the atmospheric pressure on the surface of the liquid. Based on Table H, what is the boiling point of ethanol at standard pressure?

19 Base your answer to the following question on the information below and on your knowledge of chemistry.

A 2.50-liter aqueous solution contains 1.25 moles of dissolved sodium chloride. The dissolving of NaCl(s) in water is represented by the equation below.

$$NaCl(s) \xrightarrow{H_2O} Na^+(aq) + Cl^-(aq)$$

Compare the freezing point of this solution to the freezing point of a solution containing 0.75 mole NaCl per 2.50 liters of solution.

20 Base your answer to the following question on the information below.

A scientist makes a solution that contains 44.0 grams of hydrogen chloride gas, HCl(g), in 200. grams of water, $H_2O(\ell)$, at 20. °C. This process is represented by the balanced equation below.

$$HCl(g) \xrightarrow{H_2O} H^+(aq) + Cl^-(aq)$$

Based on Reference Table G, identify, in terms of saturation, the type of solution made by the scientist.

Base your answers to questions 21 through 23 on the information below.

The compounds $NH_4Br(s)$ and $NH_3(g)$ are soluble in water. Solubility data for $NH_4Br(s)$ in water are listed in the table below.

Solubility of NH$_4$Br in H$_2$O

Temperature (°C)	Mass of NH$_4$Br per 100. g of H$_2$O (g)
0	60.
20.	75
40.	90.
60.	105
80.	120.
100.	135

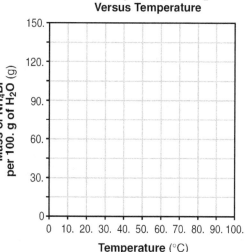

Solubility of NH$_4$Br in H$_2$O Versus Temperature

21. On the grid above, plot the data from the data table. Circle and connect the points.

22. Compare the solubilities of $NH_4Br(s)$ and $NH_3(g)$, each in 100. grams of H_2O, as temperature increases at standard pressure. Your response must include both $NH_4Br(s)$ and $NH_3(g)$.

23. Determine the total mass of $NH_4Br(s)$ that must be dissolved in 200. grams of H_2O at 60.°C to produce a saturated solution.

1 What can be explained by the Arrhenius theory?

(1) the behavior of many acids and bases
(2) the effect of stress on a phase equilibrium
(3) the operation of an electrochemical cell
(4) the spontaneous decay of some nuclei

2 Which statement describes one acid-base theory?

(1) An acid is an H^+ acceptor, and a base is an H^+ donor.
(2) An acid is an H^+ donor, and a base is an H^+ acceptor.
(3) An acid is an H^- acceptor, and a base is an H^- donor.
(4) An acid is an H^- donor, and a base is an H^- acceptor.

3 The reaction of an Arrhenius acid with an Arrhenius base produces water and

(1) a salt   (3) an aldehyde
(2) an ester   (4) a halocarbon

4 Potassium hydroxide is classified as an Arrhenius base because KOH contains

(1) OH^- ions   (3) K^+ ions
(2) O^{2-} ions   (4) H^+ ions

5 According to the Arrhenius theory, an acid is a substance that

(1) changes litmus from red to blue
(2) changes phenolphthalein from colorless to pink
(3) produces hydronium ions as the only positive ions in an aqueous solution
(4) produces hydroxide ions as the only negative ions in an aqueous solution

6 Which compounds are classified as Arrhenius acids?

(1) HCl and NaOH   (3) NH_3 and H_2CO_3
(2) HNO_3 and NaCl (4) HBr and H_2SO_4

7 The pH of a solution is 7. When acid is added to the solution, the hydronium ion concentration becomes 100 times greater. What is the pH of the new solution?

(1) 1   (2) 5   (3) 9   (4) 14

8 When the pH of an aqueous solution is changed from 1 to 2, the concentration of hydronium ions in the solution is

(1) decreased by a factor of 2
(2) decreased by a factor of 10
(3) increased by a factor of 2
(4) increased by a factor of 10

9 Three samples of the same solution are tested, each with a different indicator. All three indicators, bromthymol blue, bromcresol green and thymol blue, appear blue if the pH of the solution is

(1) 4.7   (2) 6.0   (3) 7.8   (4) 9.9

10 What is the color of the indicator thymol blue in a solution that has a pH of 11?

(1) red   (3) pink
(2) blue   (4) yellow

11 Which solution reacts with LiOH(aq) to produce a salt and water?

(1) KCl(aq)   (3) NaOH(aq)
(2) CaO(aq)   (4) H_2SO_4(aq)

12 What are the products when potassium hydroxide reacts with hydrochloric acid?

(1) KH(s), Cl^+(aq), and OH^-(aq)
(2) K(s), Cl_2(g), and $H_2O(\ell)$
(3) KCl(aq) and $H_2O(\ell)$
(4) KOH(aq) and Cl_2(g)

13 Which process is used to determine the concentration of an acid?

(1) chromatography   (3) electrolysis
(2) distillation   (4) titration

14 Given the balanced equation representing a reaction:

$$HSO_4^-(aq) + H_2O(l) \rightarrow H_3O^+(aq) + SO_4^{2-}(aq)$$

According to one acid-base theory, the $H_2O(l)$ molecules act as

(1) a base because they accept H^+ ions   (3) an acid because they accept H^+ ions
(2) a base because they donate H^+ ions   (4) an acid because they donate H^+ ions

15 In a titration, 20.0 milliliters of a 0.150 M NaOH(aq) solution exactly neutralizes 24.0 milliliters of an HCl(aq) solution. What is the concentration of the HCl(aq) solution?

(1) 0.125 M   (3) 0.250 M
(2) 0.180 M   (4) 0.360 M

16 Which laboratory test result can be used to determine if KCl(s) is an electrolyte?

(1) pH of KCl(aq)
(2) pH of KCl(s)
(3) electrical conductivity of KCl(aq)
(4) electrical conductivity of KCl(s)

17 Which compound is an electrolyte?

(1) H_2O (3) H_3PO_4
(2) C_2H_6 (4) CH_3OH

18 Which substance is an electrolyte?

(1) O_2 (3) C_3H_8
(2) Xe   (4) KNO_3

Base your answers to questions 19 and 20 on the information below and on your knowledge of chemistry.

The pH of various aqueous solutions are shown in the table below.

pH of Various Aqueous Solutions

Aqueous Solution	pH
HCl(aq)	2
$HC_2H_3O_2$(aq)	3
NaCl(aq)	7
NaOH(aq)	12

19 State how many times greater the hydronium ion concentration in the HCl(aq) is than the hydronium ion concentration in the $HC_2H_3O_2$(aq).

20 Complete the table by writing the color of thymol blue in the NaCl(aq) and in the NaOH(aq) solutions.

Aqueous Solution	Color of Thymol Blue
NaCl(aq)	
NaOH(aq)	

Base your answers to questions 21 and 22 on the information below and on your knowledge of chemistry.

In a titration, 50.0 milliliters of 0.026 M HCl(aq) is neutralized by 38.5 milliliters of KOH(aq).

21 Complete the equation for the neutralization by writing the formula of the missing product.

$KOH(aq) + HCl(aq) \rightarrow$ _____ $(aq) + H_2O(\ell)$

22 Show a numerical setup for calculating the molarity of the KOH(aq).

1 A chemical reaction between iron atoms and oxygen molecules can only occur if

(1) the particles are heated
(2) the atmospheric pressure decreases
(3) there is a catalyst present
(4) there are effective collisions between the particle

2 A reaction is most likely to occur when reactant particles collide with

(1) proper energy, only
(2) proper orientation, only
(3) both proper energy and proper orientation
(4) neither proper energy nor proper orientation

3 The energy needed to start a chemical reaction is called

(1) potential energy   (3) activation energy
(2) kinetic energy   (4) ionization energy

4 Which factors have the greatest effect on the rate of a chemical reaction between $AgNO_3$(aq) and Cu(s)?

(1) solution concentration and temperature
(2) solution concentration and pressure
(3) molar mass and temperature
(4) molar mass and pressure

5 A catalyst lowers the activation energy of a reaction by

(1) providing an alternate reaction pathway
(2) decreasing the heat of reaction
(3) increasing the mass of the reactants
(4) changing the mole ratio of the reactants

6 Entropy is a measure of the

(1) acidity of a sample
(2) disorder of a system
(3) concentration of a solution
(4) chemical activity of an element

7 Which expression represents the heat of reaction for a chemical change in terms of potential energy, PE?

(1) $(PE_{products}) + (PE_{reactants})$
(2) $(PE_{products}) - (PE_{reactants})$
(3) $(PE_{products}) \times (PE_{reactants})$
(4) $(PE_{products}) \div (PE_{reactants})$

8 Which statement describes a reversible reaction at equilibrium?

(1) The activation energy of the forward reaction must equal the activation energy of the reverse reaction.
(2) The rate of the forward reaction must equal the rate of the reverse reaction.
(3) The concentration of the reactants must equal the concentration of the products.
(4) The potential energy of the reactants must equal the potential energy of the products.

9 Systems in nature tend to undergo changes toward

(1) lower energy and higher entropy
(2) lower energy and lower entropy
(3) higher energy and higher entropy
(4) higher energy and lower entropy

10 The entropy of a sample of CO_2 increases as the CO_2 changes from

(1) gas to liquid   (3) liquid to solid
(2) gas to solid   (4) solid to gas

11 At 101.3 kPa and 298 K, a 1.0-mole sample of which compound absorbs the greatest amount of heat as the entire sample dissolves in water?

(1) LiBr   (3) NaOH
(2) NaCl   (4) NH_4Cl

12 Which compound is formed from its elements by an exothermic reaction at 298 K and 101.3 kPa?

(1) C_2H_4(g)   (3) H_2O(g)
(2) HI(g)   (4) NO_2(g)

13 Given the balanced equation representing a reaction:

$$Fe(s) + 2HCl(aq) \rightarrow FeCl_2\ (aq) + H_2(g)$$

This reaction occurs more quickly when powdered iron is used instead of a single piece of iron of the same mass because the powdered iron

(1) acts as a better catalyst than the single piece of iron
(2) absorbs less energy than the single piece of iron
(3) has a greater surface area than the single piece of iron
(4) is more metallic than the single piece of iron

14 Given the potential energy diagram for a reaction:

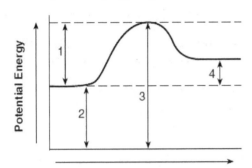

Reaction Coordinate

Which intervals are affected by the addition of a catalyst?

(1) 1 and 2   (3) 2 and 4
(2) 1 and 3   (4) 3 and 4

15 For a given chemical reaction, the addition of a catalyst provides a different reaction pathway that

(1) decreases the reaction rate and has a higher activation energy
(2) decreases the reaction rate and has a lower activation energy
(3) increases the reaction rate and has a higher activation energy
(4) increases the reaction rate and has a lower activation energy

16 Given the equation and potential energy diagram representing a reaction:

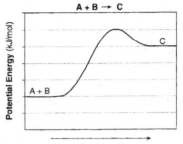

Reaction Coordinate

If each interval on the axis labeled "Potential Energy (kJ/mol)" represents 10. kJ/mol, what is the heat of reaction?

(1) +60. kJ/mol   (3) +30. kJ/mol
(2) +20. kJ/mol   (4) +40. kJ/mol

17 Given the equation representing a system at equilibrium:

$$AgCl(s) \overset{H_2O}{\rightleftharpoons} Ag^+(aq) + Cl^-(aq)$$

When the concentration of Cl^- (aq) is increased, the concentration of Ag^+ (aq)

(1) decreases, and the amount of AgCl(s) increases
(2) decreases, and the amount of AgCl(s) decreases
(3) increases, and the amount of AgCl(s) increases
(4) increases, and the amount of AgCl(s) decreases

18 Given the equation representing a reaction at equilibrium:

$$2SO_2(g) + O_2(g) \rightleftharpoons 2SO_3(g) + heat$$

Which change causes the equilibrium to shift to the right?

(1) adding a catalyst
(2) adding more $O_2(g)$
(3) decreasing the pressure
(4) increasing the temperature

19 Given the equation representing a system at equilibrium:

$N_2(g) + 3H_2(g) \leftrightarrow 2NH_3(g) + energy$

Which changes occur when the temperature of this system is *decreased*?

(1) The concentration of $H_2(g)$ increases and the concentration of $N_2(g)$ increases.
(2) The concentration of $H_2(g)$ decreases and the concentration of $N_2(g)$ increases.
(3) The concentration of $H_2(g)$ decreases and the concentration of $NH_3(g)$ decreases
(4) The concentration of $H_2(g)$ decreases and the concentration of $NH_3(g)$ increases.

Base your answers to questions **20** and **21** on the information below.

The chemical reaction between methane and oxygen is represented by the potential energy diagram and balanced equation below.

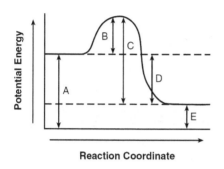

$CH_4(g) + 2O_2(g) \rightarrow CO_2(g) + 2H_2O(\ell) + 890.4 \text{ kJ}$

20 Explain, in terms of collision theory, why a lower concentration of oxygen gas *decreases* the rate of this reaction.

21 Which potential energy interval in the diagram represents the activation energy of the forward reaction?

Base your answers to questions **22** and **23** on the information below and on your knowledge of chemistry.

Carbon monoxide, $CO(g)$, is a toxic gas found in automobile exhaust. The concentration of $CO(g)$ can be decreased by using a catalyst in the reaction between $CO(g)$ and $O_2(g)$. This reaction is represented by the balanced equation below.

$2CO(g) + O_2 \xrightarrow{catalyst} 2CO_2(g) + energy$

22 On the labeled axes below, draw the potential energy curve for the reaction represented by this equation.

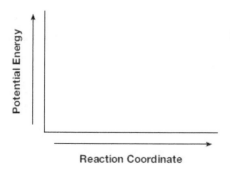

23 Explain, in terms of collision theory, why an increase in temperature increases the rate of the reaction.

Base your answers to questions **24** through **26** on the information below and on your knowledge of chemistry.

Common household bleach is an aqueous solution containing hypochlorite ions. A closed container of bleach is an equilibrium system represented by the equation below.

$$Cl_2(g) + 2OH^-(aq) \rightleftharpoons ClO^-(aq) + Cl^-(aq) + H_2O(\ell)$$

24 State the effect on the concentration of the ClO^- ion when there is a *decrease* in the concentration of the OH^- ion.

25 Explain why the container must be closed to maintain equilibrium.

26 Compare the rate of the forward reaction to the rate of the reverse reaction for this system.

1 Hydrocarbons are compounds that contain

(1) carbon, only
(2) carbon and hydrogen, only
(3) carbon, hydrogen, and oxygen, only
(4) carbon, hydrogen, oxygen, and nitrogen, only

2 A molecule of an unsaturated hydrocarbon must have

(1) at least one single carbon-carbon bond
(2) at least one multiple carbon-carbon bond
(3) two or more single carbon-carbon bonds
(4) two or more multiple carbon-carbon bonds

3 Which element is present in all organic compounds?

(1) nitrogen   (3) carbon
(2) oxygen   (4) sulfur

4 Two types of organic reactions are

(1) deposition and saponification
(2) deposition and transmutation
(3) polymerization and saponification
(4) polymerization and transmutation

5 Which reaction produces ethanol?

(1) combustion   (3) fermentation
(2) esterification   (4) polymerization

6 When butane burns in an excess of oxygen, the principal products are

(1) CO_2 and H_2O (3) CO and H_2O
(2) CO_2 and H_2 (4) CO and H_2

7 Which compound is a saturated hydrocarbon?

(1) propanal   (3) propene
(2) propane   (4) propyne

8 Which formula represents an unsaturated hydrocarbon?

(1) C_2H_4 (3) C_4H_{10}
(2) C_3H_8 (4) C_5H_{12}

9 Which term identifies a type of organic reaction?

(1) deposition   (3) esterification
(2) distillation   (4) sublimation

10 Given the formula representing a compound:

$$H-\overset{\overset{\displaystyle H}{|}}{\underset{\underset{\displaystyle H}{|}}{C}}-\overset{\overset{\displaystyle H}{|}}{\underset{\underset{\displaystyle H}{|}}{C}}-\overset{\overset{\displaystyle H}{|}}{C}=\overset{}{\underset{\underset{\displaystyle H}{|}}{C}}-\overset{\overset{\displaystyle H}{|}}{\underset{\underset{\displaystyle H}{|}}{C}}-H$$

What is a chemical name of this compound?

(1) 2-pentene   (3) 3-pentene
(2) 2-pentyne   (4) 3-pentyne

11 Which compound is classified as a hydrocarbon?

(1) butanal   (3) 2-butanol
(2) butyne   (4) 2-butanone

12 A carbon-carbon triple bond is found in a molecule of

(1) butane   (3) butene
(2) butanone   (4) butyne

13 Functional groups are used to classify

(1) organic compounds
(2) inorganic compounds
(3) heterogeneous mixtures
(4) homogeneous mixtures

14 The two isomers of butane have different

(1) formula masses
(2) empirical formulas
(3) molecular formulas
(4) structural formulas

15 Given a formula of a functional group:

$$-\overset{\overset{\displaystyle O}{\|}}{C}-OH$$

An organic compound that has this functional group is classified as

(1) an acid   (3) an ester
(2) an aldehyde   (4) a ketone

16 Which class of organic compounds has molecules that contain nitrogen atoms?

(1) alcohol   (3) ether
(2) amine   (4) ketone

17 Given a formula representing a compound:

$$\begin{array}{ccccc} & O & H & H & H \\ & \parallel & | & | & | \\ H-&C-&C-&C-&C-H \\ & & | & | & | \\ & & H & H & H \end{array}$$

Which formula represents an isomer of this compound?

(1)
$$\begin{array}{ccccc} & H & H & H & O \\ & | & | & | & \parallel \\ H-&C-&C-&C-&C-H \\ & | & | & | & \\ & H & H & H & \end{array}$$

(2)
$$\begin{array}{ccccc} & H & O & H & H \\ & | & \parallel & | & | \\ H-&C-&C-&C-&C-H \\ & | & & | & | \\ & H & & H & H \end{array}$$

(3)
$$\begin{array}{ccccc} & H & H & H & O \\ & | & | & | & \parallel \\ H-&C-&C-&C-&C-OH \\ & | & | & | & \\ & H & H & H & \end{array}$$

(4)
$$\begin{array}{cccccc} & H & H & O & & H \\ & | & | & \parallel & & | \\ H-&C-&C-&C-&O-&C-H \\ & | & | & & & | \\ & H & H & & & H \end{array}$$

18 Given the formula for a compound:

$$\begin{array}{cccccc} & H & H & & H \\ & | & | & & | \\ H-&C-&C-& C-&C-H \\ & | & | & \parallel & | \\ & H & H & O & H \end{array}$$

A chemical name for this compound is

(1) butanal   (3) butanone
(2) butanol   (4) butanoic acid

19 Which class of compounds contains *at least one* element from Group 17 of the Periodic Table?

(1) aldehyde   (3) ester
(2) amine   (4) halide

20 Which formula represents the product of the addition reaction between ethene and chlorine, Cl_2?

(1)
$$\begin{array}{ccc} & Cl & Cl \\ & | & | \\ Cl-&C-&C-Cl \\ & | & | \\ & H & H \end{array}$$

(2)
$$\begin{array}{ccc} & Cl & Cl \\ & | & | \\ H-&C-&C-H \\ & | & | \\ & H & H \end{array}$$

(3)
$$\begin{array}{ccc} & Cl & Cl \\ & | & | \\ H-&C=&C-H \\ & | & | \\ & H & H \end{array}$$

(4)
$$\begin{array}{ccc} & Cl & H \\ & | & | \\ H-&C-&C-H \\ & | & | \\ & H & H \end{array}$$

21 Which equation represents fermentation?

(1) $C_2H_6 + Cl_2 \rightarrow C_2H_6Cl + HCl$
(2) $C_6H_{12}O_6 \rightarrow 2\ C_2H_5OH + 2\ CO_2$
(3) $CH_3COOH + CH_3OH \rightarrow CH_3COOCH_3 + H_2O$
(4) $nC_2H_4 \rightarrow (C_2H_4)n$

Base your answers to questions **22** through **24** on the information below and on your knowledge of chemistry.

The diagrams below represent ball-and-stick models of two molecules. In a ball-and-stick model, each ball represents an atom, and the sticks between balls represent chemical bonds.

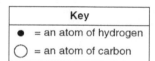

Key
● = an atom of hydrogen
○ = an atom of carbon

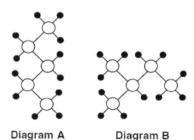

Diagram A   Diagram B

22 Explain why the molecules in diagrams A and B are isomers of each other.

23 Explain, in terms of carbon-carbon bonds, why the hydrocarbon represented in diagram B is saturated.

24 Draw a Lewis electron-dot diagram for an atom of the element present in all organic compounds.

Base your answers to questions **25** through **27** on information below.

One type of soap is produced when ethyl stearate and sodium hydroxide react. The soap produced by this reaction is called sodium stearate. The other product of the reaction is ethanol. This reaction is represented by the balanced equation below.

$$C_{17}H_{35}-\overset{\overset{\displaystyle O}{\|}}{C}-O-C_2H_5 \;+\; NaOH \;\longrightarrow\; C_{17}H_{35}-\overset{\overset{\displaystyle O}{\|}}{C}-O^-\,Na^+ \;+\; C_2H_5OH$$

Ethyl stearate   Sodium hydroxide   Sodium stearate   Ethanol

25 Identify the *two* types of bonds in the compound sodium stearate.

26 To which class of organic compounds does ethyl stearate belong?

27 Identify the type of organic reaction used to make soap.

Base your answers to questions **28** and **29** on the information below.

A reaction between bromine and a hydrocarbon is represented by the balanced equation below.

$$Br_2 \;+\; H-\overset{\overset{\displaystyle }{\underset{\underset{\displaystyle H}{|}}{|}}}{C}=\overset{\overset{\displaystyle H}{|}}{\underset{\underset{\displaystyle H}{|}}{C}}-\overset{\overset{\displaystyle H}{|}}{\underset{\underset{\displaystyle H}{|}}{C}}-H \;\longrightarrow\; H-\overset{\overset{\displaystyle H}{|}}{\underset{\underset{\displaystyle Br}{|}}{C}}-\overset{\overset{\displaystyle H}{|}}{\underset{\underset{\displaystyle Br}{|}}{C}}-\overset{\overset{\displaystyle H}{|}}{\underset{\underset{\displaystyle H}{|}}{C}}-H$$

28 Write the name of the homologous series to which the hydrocarbon belongs.

29 Identify the type of organic reaction.

1 In an oxidation-reduction reaction, the number of electrons lost is

(1) equal to the number of electrons gained
(2) equal to the number of protons gained
(3) less than the number of electrons gained
(4) less than the number of protons gained

2 The chemical process in which electrons are gained by an atom or an ion is called

(1) addition
(2) oxidation
(3) reduction
(4) substitution

3 Which process occurs in an operating voltaic cell?

(1) Electrical energy is converted to chemical energy.
(2) Chemical energy is converted to electrical energy.
(3) Oxidation takes place at the cathode.
(4) Reduction takes place at the anode.

4 Which energy conversion must occur in an operating electrolytic cell?

(1) electrical energy to chemical energy
(2) electrical energy to nuclear energy
(3) chemical energy to electrical energy
(4) chemical energy to nuclear energy

5 Which term identifies the half-reaction that occurs at the anode of an operating electrochemical cell?

(1) oxidation
(2) reduction
(3) neutralization
(4) transmutation

6 Which reaction occurs at the cathode in an electrochemical cell?

(1) combustion
(2) neutralization
(3) oxidation
(4) reduction

7 When a voltaic cell operates, ions move through the

(1) anode
(2) cathode
(3) salt bridge
(4) external circuit

8 What is the oxidation state of nitrogen in the compound NH_4Br?

(1) -1 (2) $+2$ (3) -3 (4) $+4$

9 Reduction occurs at the cathode in

(1) electrolytic cells, only
(2) voltaic cells, only
(3) both electrolytic cells and voltaic cells
(4) neither electrolytic cells nor voltaic cells

10 What is the oxidation number of manganese in $KMnO_4$?

(1) $+7$ (2) $+2$ (3) $+3$ (4) $+4$

11 Which half-reaction correctly represents oxidation?

(1) $Mn^{4+} \rightarrow Mn^{3+} + e^-$
(2) $Mn^{4+} \rightarrow Mn^{7+} + 3e^-$
(3) $Mn^{4+} + e^- \rightarrow Mn^{3+}$
(4) $Mn^{4+} + 3e^- \rightarrow Mn^{7+}$

12 Given the balanced ionic equation below:

$$2Al(s) + 3Cu^{2+}(aq) \rightarrow 2Al^{3+}(aq) + 3Cu(s)$$

Which half-reaction represents the reduction that occurs?

(1) $Al \rightarrow Al^{3+} + 3e$
(2) $Al^{3+} + 3e \rightarrow Al$
(3) $Cu \rightarrow Cu^{2+} + 2e$
(4) $Cu^{2+} + 2e \rightarrow Cu$

13 Which metal will spontaneously react with Zn^{2+} (aq), but will *not* spontaneously react with Mg^{2+} (aq)?

(1) Mn(s)
(2) Cu(s)
(3) Ni(s)
(4) Ba(s)

14 Given the balanced equation representing a reaction:

$$2Al(s) + 3Cu^{2+}(aq) \rightarrow 2Al^{3+}(aq) + 3Cu(s)$$

Which particles are transferred in this reaction?

(1) electrons
(2) neutrons
(3) positrons
(4) protons

Base your answers to questions **15** through **17** on the information below and on your knowledge of chemistry.

An operating voltaic cell has zinc and iron electrodes. The cell and the unbalanced ionic equation representing the reaction that occurs in the cell are shown below.

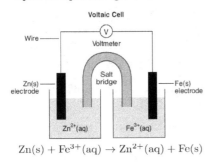

$$Zn(s) + Fe^{3+}(aq) \rightarrow Zn^{2+}(aq) + Fe(s)$$

15 Explain, in terms of Zn atoms and Zn ions, why the mass of the Zn electrode *decreases* as the cell operates.

16 Describe the direction of electron flow in the external circuit in this operating cell.

17 State the purpose of the salt bridge in this voltaic cell.

Base your answers to questions **18** through **20** on the information below.

The diagram below represents an operating electrolytic cell used to plate silver onto a nickel key. As the cell operates, oxidation occurs at the silver electrode and the mass of the silver electrode decreases.

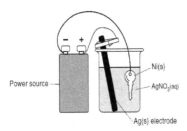

18 Explain, in terms of Ag atoms and $Ag^+(aq)$ ions, why the mass of the silver electrode *decreases* as the cell operates.

19 State the purpose of the power source in the cell.

20 Identify the cathode in the cell.

Base your answers to questions **21** through **24** on the information below.

In a laboratory investigation, a student constructs a voltaic cell with iron and copper electrodes. Another student constructs a voltaic cell with zinc and iron electrodes. Testing the cells during operation enables the students to write the balanced ionic equations below.

Cell with iron and copper electrodes: $Cu^{2+}(aq) + Fe(s) \rightarrow Cu(s) + Fe^{2+}(aq)$

Cell with zinc and iron electrodes: $Fe^{2+}(aq) + Zn(s) \rightarrow Fe(s) + Zn^{2+}(aq)$

21 State the relative activity of the three metals used in these two voltaic cells.

22 Write a balanced half-reaction equation for the reduction that takes place in the cell with zinc and iron electrodes.

23 Identify the particles transferred between Fe^{2+} and Zn during the reaction in the cell with zinc and iron electrodes.

24 State evidence from the balanced equation for the cell with iron and copper electrodes that indicates the reaction in the cell is an oxidation-reduction reaction.

25 Explain, in terms of activity, why HCl(aq) reacts with Mg(s), but HCl(aq) does *not* react with Cu(s).

1 Which nuclear emission is negatively charged?

(1) an alpha particle   (3) a neutron
(2) a beta particle   (4) a positron

2 Positrons and beta particles have

(1) the same charge and the same mass
(2) the same charge and different masses
(3) different charges and the same mass
(4) different charges and different masses

3 Compared to the mass and the penetrating power of an alpha particle, a beta particle has

(1) less mass and greater penetrating power
(2) less mass and less penetrating power
(3) more mass and greater penetrating power
(4) more mass and less penetrating power

4 The dating of geological formations is an example of a beneficial use of

(1) isomers
(2) electrolytes
(3) organic compounds
(4) radioactive nuclides

5 Which term identifies a type of nuclear reaction?

(1) transmutation   (3) deposition
(2) neutralization   (4) reduction

6 What occurs in both fusion and fission reactions?

(1) Small amounts of energy are converted into large amounts of matter.
(2) Small amounts of matter are converted into large amounts of energy.
(3) Heavy nuclei are split into lighter nuclei.
(4) Light nuclei are combined into heavier nuclei.

7 Which reaction releases the greatest amount of energy per mole of reactant?

(1) decomposition   (3) fermentation
(2) esterification   (4) fission

8 The energy released by a nuclear reaction results primarily from the

(1) breaking of bonds between atoms
(2) formation of bonds between atoms
(3) conversion of mass into energy
(4) conversion of energy into mass

9 Which radioisotope is used in dating geological formations?

(1) I-131   (3) Ca-37
(2) U-238   (4) Fr-220

10 Which nuclides are used to date the remains of a once-living organism?

(1) C-14 and C-12
(2) Co-60 and Co-59
(3) I-131 and Xe-131
(4) U-238 and Pb-206

11 Which radioisotope is used for diagnosing thyroid disorders?

(1) U-238   (3) I-131
(2) Pb-206   (4) Co-60

12 Which risk is associated with using nuclear fission to produce energy in a power plant?

(1) depletion of hydrocarbons
(2) depletion of atmospheric oxygen
(3) exposure of workers to radiation
(4) exposure of workers to sulfur dioxide

13 Given the equation representing a nuclear reaction in which X represents a nuclide:

$$^{232}_{90}\text{Th} \rightarrow {}^{4}_{2}\text{He} + X$$

Which nuclide is represented by X?

(1) $^{236}_{92}\text{Ra}$ (3) $^{236}_{92}\text{U}$
(2) $^{228}_{88}\text{Ra}$ (4) $^{228}_{88}\text{U}$

14 Which balanced equation represents a spontaneous radioactive decay?

(1) $14\text{C} + \text{Ca}_3(\text{PO}_4)_2 \rightarrow 3\text{CaC}_2 + 2\text{P} + 8\text{CO}$
(2) $^{14}_{7}\text{N} + {}^{1}_{0}\text{n} \rightarrow {}^{14}_{6}\text{C} + {}^{1}_{1}\text{P}$
(3) $\text{H}_2\text{CO}_3 \rightarrow \text{H}_2\text{O} + \text{CO}_2$
(4) $^{14}_{6}\text{C} \rightarrow {}^{14}_{7}\text{N} + {}^{0}_{-1}\text{e}$

15 Which nuclear emission has the greatest penetrating power?

(1) proton   (3) gamma radiation

(2) beta particle   (4) positron

16 In which reaction is mass converted to energy by the process of fission?

(1) $^{14}_{7}\text{N} + ^{1}_{0}\text{n} \rightarrow ^{14}_{6}\text{C} + ^{1}_{1}\text{H}$

(2) $^{235}_{92}\text{U} + ^{1}_{0}\text{n} \rightarrow ^{87}_{35}\text{Br} + ^{146}_{57}\text{La} + 3\,^{1}_{0}\text{n}$

(3) $^{226}_{88}\text{Ra} \rightarrow ^{222}_{86}\text{Ra} + ^{4}_{2}\text{He}$

(4) $^{2}_{1}\text{H} + ^{2}_{1}\text{H} \rightarrow ^{4}_{2}\text{He}$

17 Which balanced equation represents nuclear fusion?

(1) $^{3}_{1}\text{H} \rightarrow ^{3}_{2}\text{He} + ^{0}_{-1}\text{e}$

(2) $^{235}_{92}\text{U} \rightarrow ^{231}_{90}\text{Th} + ^{4}_{2}\text{He}$

(3) $^{2}_{1}\text{H} + ^{2}_{1}\text{H} \rightarrow ^{4}_{2}\text{He}$

(4) $^{235}_{92}\text{U} + ^{1}_{0}\text{n} \rightarrow ^{90}_{38}\text{Sr} + ^{143}_{54}\text{Xe} + 3\,^{1}_{0}\text{n}$

18 Given the equation representing a reaction where the masses are expressed in atomic mass units:

hydrogen-2 + hydrogen-1 $\rightarrow$ helium-3 + 8.814 × 10^{-16} kJ
2.014 102 u   1.007 825 u   3.016 029 u

Which phrase describes this reaction?

(1) a chemical reaction and mass being converted to energy

(2) a chemical reaction and energy being converted to mass

(3) a nuclear reaction and mass being converted to energy

(4) a nuclear reaction and energy being converted to mass

19 What fraction of a Sr-90 sample remains unchanged after 87.3 years?

(1) 1/2   (3) 1/4

(2) 1/3   (4) 1/8

20 After decaying for 48 hours, $\frac{1}{16}$ of the original mass of a radioisotope sample remains unchanged. What is the half-life of this radioisotope?

(1) 3.0 h   (3) 12 h

(2) 9.6 h   (4) 24 h

Base your answers to questions **21** through **24** on the information below.

Nuclear fission has been used to produce electricity. However, nuclear fusion for electricity production is still under development. The notations of some nuclides used in nuclear reactions are shown in the table below.

Some Nuclides Used in Nuclear Reactions

Reaction	Nuclides
nuclear fission	$^{233}_{92}\text{U}$, $^{235}_{92}\text{U}$
nuclear fusion	$^{1}_{1}\text{H}$, $^{3}_{1}\text{H}$

21 State *one* potential benefit of using nuclear fusion instead of the current use of nuclear fission to produce electricity.

22 Complete the table below that compares the total number of protons and the total number of neutrons for the hydrogen nuclides used for fusion.

Nuclide	Total Number of Protons	Total Number of Neutrons
$^{1}_{1}\text{H}$		
$^{3}_{1}\text{H}$		

23 Compare the atomic masses of nuclides used in fusion to the atomic masses of nuclides used in fission

24 Complete the nuclear equation below for the fission of $^{235}_{92}\text{U}$ by writing the notation of the missing product.

$^{235}_{92}\text{U} + ^{1}_{0}\text{n} \rightarrow ^{142}_{56}\text{Ba} + ^{91}_{36}\text{Kr} + 3\underline{\hspace{2cm}} + \text{energy}$

Base your answers to questions **25** through **27** on the information below.

Nuclear radiation is harmful to living cells, particularly to fast-growing cells, such as cancer cells and blood cells. An external beam of the radiation emitted from a radioisotope can be directed on a small area of a person to destroy cancer cells within the body.

Cobalt-60 is an artificially produced radioisotope that emits gamma rays and beta particles. One hospital keeps a 100.0-gram sample of cobalt-60 in an appropriate, secure storage container for future cancer treatment.

25 Determine the total time that will have elapsed when 12.5 grams of the original Co-60 sample at the hospital remains unchanged.

26 Compare the penetrating power of the two emissions from the Co-60.

27 State *one* risk to human tissue associated with the use of radioisotopes to treat cancer.

Base your answers to questions **28** through **30** on the information below.

Polonium-210 occurs naturally, but is scarce. Polonium-210 is primarily used in devices designed to eliminate static electricity in machinery. It is also used in brushes to remove dust from camera lenses.

Polonium-210 can be created in the laboratory by bombarding bismuth-209 with neutrons to create bismuth-210. The bismuth-210 undergoes beta decay to produce polonium-210. Polonium-210 has a half-life of 138 days and undergoes alpha decay.

28 Determine the total mass of an original 28.0-milligram sample of Po-210 that remains unchanged after 414 days.

29 Complete the nuclear equation for the decay of Po-210, by writing a notation for the missing product.

$$^{210}_{84}\text{Po} \rightarrow {}^{4}_{2}\text{He} + \underline{\hspace{3cm}}$$

30 State *one beneficial use of Po-210.*

Base your answers to questions **31** and **32** on the information below.

Some radioisotopes used as tracers make it possible for doctors to see the images of internal body parts and observe their functions. The table below lists information about three radioisotopes and the body part each radioisotope is used to study.

Medical Uses of Some Radioisotopes

Radioisotope	Half-life	Decay Mode	Body Part
^{24}Na	15 hours	beta	circulatory system
^{59}Fe	44.5 days	beta	red blood cells
^{131}I	8.1 days	beta	thyroid

32 It could take up to 60. hours for a radioisotope to be delivered to the hospital from the laboratory where it is produced. What fraction of an original sample of ^{24}Na remains unchanged after 60. hours?

31 Write the equation for the nuclear decay of the radioisotope used to study red blood cells. Include *both* the atomic number and the mass number for *each* missing particle.

$$^{59}\text{Fe} \rightarrow \underline{\hspace{1.5cm}} + \underline{\hspace{1.5cm}} + \text{energy}$$

269

Physical Setting/Chemistry
Regents Exam - January 2017

Part A

Answer all questions in this part.

Directions (1–30): For *each* statement or question, record on your separate answer sheet the *number* of the word or expression that, of those given, best completes the statement or answers the question. Some questions may require the use of the *2011 Edition Reference Tables for Physical Setting/Chemistry*.

1 Which statement describes the location of two types of subatomic particles in a helium atom?

(1) Protons and neutrons are located in the nucleus.
(2) Protons and neutrons are located outside the nucleus.
(3) Protons and electrons are located in the nucleus.
(4) Protons and electrons are located outside the nucleus.

2 An atom that contains six protons, six neutrons, and six electrons has a mass of approximately

(1) 12 u   (3) 18 u
(2) 12 g   (4) 18 g

3 Which term identifies the most probable location of an electron in the wave-mechanical model of the atom?

(1) anode   (3) nucleus
(2) orbital   (4) cathode

4 Which element has atoms in the ground state with the greatest number of valence electrons?

(1) tin   (3) arsenic
(2) sulfur   (4) fluorine

5 Which group on the Periodic Table has two elements that exist as gases at STP?

(1) Group 1   (3) Group 16
(2) Group 2   (4) Group 17

6 Which list of elements contains a metal, a metalloid, and a nonmetal?

(1) Ag, Si, I_2 (3) K, Cu, Br_2
(2) Ge, As, Ne   (4) S, Cl_2, Ar

7 What is the charge of the nucleus of a copper atom?

(1) +1   (3) +29
(2) +2   (4) +64

8 At STP, $O_2(g)$ and $O_3(g)$ have different properties because $O_3(g)$ has

(1) more dense nuclei than in $O_2(g)$
(2) more protons per atom than in $O_2(g)$
(3) molecules with a different structure than in $O_2(g)$
(4) molecules with fewer covalent bonds than in $O_2(g)$

9 A compound is a substance composed of two or more elements that are

(1) physically mixed in a fixed proportion
(2) physically mixed in a variable proportion
(3) chemically combined in a fixed proportion
(4) chemically combined in a variable proportion

10 Which element has the highest boiling point at standard pressure?

(1) Mg   (3) Rb
(2) Na   (4) Sr

11 How many pairs of electrons are shared between the nitrogen atoms in a molecule of N_2?

(1) 5   (3) 3
(2) 2   (4) 6

12 A molecule must be nonpolar if the molecule

(1) is linear
(2) is neutral
(3) has ionic and covalent bonding
(4) has a symmetrical charge distribution

13 Which property is used to determine the degree of polarity between two bonded atoms?

(1) density
(2) electronegativity
(3) pressure
(4) temperature

14 In a chemical reaction, a catalyst provides an alternate reaction pathway that

(1) decreases the concentration of the products
(2) increases the concentration of the reactants
(3) has a lower activation energy
(4) has a higher activation energy

15 Which substance can be decomposed by chemical means?

(1) cobalt
(2) krypton
(3) methane
(4) zirconium

16 Which sample of matter represents a mixture?

(1) aqueous ammonia
(2) gaseous ethane
(3) liquid mercury
(4) solid iodine

17 Differences in which property allow the separation of a sample of sand and seawater by filtration?

(1) concentration of ions
(2) volume of sample
(3) mass of sample
(4) particle size

18 Which process is a chemical change?

(1) evaporating an alcohol
(2) subliming of iodine
(3) melting an ice cube
(4) rusting of iron

19 Which term represents an intermolecular force in a sample of water?

(1) hydrogen bonding
(2) covalent bonding
(3) metallic bonding
(4) ionic bonding

20 Which sample of matter has particles arranged in a crystalline structure?

(1) $Ne(g)$
(2) $Br_2(\ell)$
(3) $NaCl(aq)$
(4) $CuSO_4(s)$

21 Which term is defined as a measure of the randomness of a system?

(1) heat
(2) entropy
(3) pressure
(4) temperature

22 Which formula represents an alkane?

(1) C_2H_2
(2) C_2H_4
(3) C_3H_4
(4) C_3H_8

23 Which term represents a chemical reaction?

(1) deposition
(2) combustion
(3) sublimation
(4) vaporization

24 Which type of reaction includes esterification and polymerization?

(1) decomposition
(2) neutralization
(3) organic
(4) nuclear

25 In a redox reaction, the total number of electrons lost is

(1) less than the total number of electrons gained
(2) greater than the total number of electrons gained
(3) equal to the total number of electrons gained
(4) unrelated to the total number of electrons gained

26 Which type of equation can represent the oxidation occurring in a reaction?

(1) a double-replacement reaction equation
(2) a half-reaction equation
(3) a neutralization reaction equation
(4) a transmutation reaction equation

27 The electrical conductivity of an aqueous solution depends on the concentration of which particles in the solution?

(1) molecules
(2) electrons
(3) atoms
(4) ions

28 An electrolytic cell differs from a voltaic cell because an electrolytic cell

(1) generates its own energy from a spontaneous physical reaction

(2) generates its own energy from a nonspontaneous physical reaction

(3) requires an outside energy source for a spontaneous chemical reaction to occur

(4) requires an outside energy source for a nonspontaneous chemical reaction to occur

29 A sample of which radioisotope emits particles having the greatest mass?

(1) ^{137}Cs (3) ^{220}Fr
(2) ^{53}Fe (4) ^{3}H

30 Which term represents a nuclear reaction?

(1) combustion   (3) transmutation
(2) fermentation   (4) saponification

Part B–1

Answer all questions in this part.

Directions (31–50): For *each* statement or question, record on your separate answer sheet the *number* of the word or expression that, of those given, best completes the statement or answers the question. Some questions may require the use of the *2011 Edition Reference Tables for Physical Setting/Chemistry*.

31 Which electron configuration represents the distribution of electrons in a potassium atom in the ground state?

(1) 2-8-8-1   (3) 2-8-5
(2) 2-8-7-2   (4) 2-7-6

32 At STP, which element is malleable and a good conductor of electricity?

(1) xenon   (3) platinum
(2) silicon   (4) hydrogen

33 Which general trends in atomic radius and electronegativity are observed as the elements in Period 3 are considered in order of increasing atomic number?

(1) Atomic radius decreases and electronegativity increases.
(2) Atomic radius increases and electronegativity decreases.
(3) Both atomic radius and electronegativity increase.
(4) Both atomic radius and electronegativity decrease.

34 What is the chemical name for Na_2SO_3?

(1) sodium sulfite   (3) sodium sulfide
(2) sodium sulfate   (4) sodium thiosulfate

35 Which molecular formula is also an empirical formula?

(1) C_6H_6 (3) N_2H_4
(2) H_2O_2 (4) N_2O_5

36 Given the balanced equation representing a reaction:

$$2H_2 + O_2 \rightarrow 2H_2O + energy$$

Which mass of oxygen completely reacts with 4.0 grams of hydrogen to produce 36.0 grams of water?

(1) 8.0 g   (3) 32.0 g
(2) 16.0 g   (4) 40.0 g

37 What is the gram-formula mass of $Ca(OH)_2$?

(1) 29 g/mol   (3) 57 g/mol
(2) 54 g/mol   (4) 74 g/mol

38 Given the equation representing a reaction:

$$H_2(g) + I_2(g) \rightarrow 2HI(g)$$

Which statement describes the energy changes that occur in this reaction?

(1) Energy is absorbed as bonds are formed, only.
(2) Energy is released as bonds are broken, only.
(3) Energy is absorbed as bonds are formed, and energy is released as bonds are broken.
(4) Energy is absorbed as bonds are broken, and energy is released as bonds are formed.

39 Based on Table *F*, which compound is *least* soluble in water?

(1) $AlPO_4$ (3) $Ca(OH)_2$
(2) Li_2SO_4 (4) $AgC_2H_3O_2$

40 How many joules of heat are absorbed to raise the temperature of 435 grams of water at 1 atm from 25°C to its boiling point, 100.°C?

(1) 4.5×10^4 J   (3) 2.5×10^7 J
(2) 1.4×10^5 J   (4) 7.4×10^7 J

41 Which temperature represents the highest average kinetic energy of the particles in a sample of matter?

(1) 298 K   (3) 27°C
(2) 267 K   (4) 12°C

42 Which change in the H^+ ion concentration of an aqueous solution represents a *decrease* of one unit on the pH scale?

(1) a tenfold increase
(2) a tenfold decrease
(3) a hundredfold increase
(4) a hundredfold decrease

43 Which particle diagram represents a mixture of three substances?

Key
= an atom of one element
● = an atom of a different element

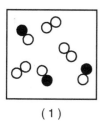

(1)

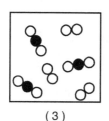

(3)

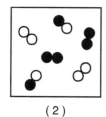

(2)

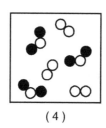

(4)

44 Given the equation representing a system at equilibrium:

$$PCl_5(g) \rightleftharpoons PCl_3(g) + Cl_2(g)$$

Which statement describes this system?

(1) The concentration of $PCl_5(g)$ is increasing.
(2) The concentration of $PCl_5(g)$ is decreasing.
(3) The concentrations of $PCl_5(g)$ and $PCl_3(g)$ are equal.
(4) The concentrations of $PCl_5(g)$ and $PCl_3(g)$ are constant.

45 Given the formula representing a compound:

$$H-\underset{\underset{H}{|}}{\overset{\overset{H}{|}}{C}}-\underset{\underset{H}{|}}{\overset{\overset{H}{|}}{C}}-\underset{\underset{H}{|}}{\overset{\overset{H}{|}}{C}}-\underset{\underset{H}{|}}{\overset{\overset{H}{|}}{C}}-\underset{\underset{H}{|}}{\overset{\overset{H}{|}}{C}}-\underset{\underset{Cl}{|}}{\overset{\overset{Cl}{|}}{C}}-\underset{\underset{H}{|}}{\overset{\overset{H}{|}}{C}}-H$$

What is the IUPAC name of this compound?

(1) 2-chloroheptane
(2) 6-chloroheptane
(3) 2,2-dichloroheptane
(4) 6,6-dichloroheptane

46 Given the equation representing a reaction:

$$Sn^{4+}(aq) + 2e^- \rightarrow Sn^{2+}(aq)$$

Which term best describes this reaction?

(1) ionization   (3) oxidation
(2) neutralization   (4) reduction

47 Which ionic equation represents a spontaneous reaction that can occur in a voltaic cell?

(1) $Cu(s) + Zn(s) \rightarrow Cu^{2+}(aq) + Zn^{2+}(aq)$
(2) $Cu(s) + Zn^{2+}(aq) \rightarrow Cu^{2+}(aq) + Zn(s)$
(3) $Cu^{2+}(aq) + Zn(s) \rightarrow Cu(s) + Zn^{2+}(aq)$
(4) $Cu^{2+}(aq) + Zn^{2+}(aq) \rightarrow Cu(s) + Zn(s)$

48 Given the formulas representing two compounds at standard pressure:

$$H-\overset{\overset{\displaystyle H}{|}}{\underset{\underset{\displaystyle H}{|}}{C}}-\overset{\overset{\displaystyle H}{|}}{\underset{\underset{\displaystyle H}{|}}{C}}-\overset{\overset{\displaystyle H}{|}}{\underset{\underset{\displaystyle H}{|}}{C}}-O-H$$

1 – propanol

$$H-\overset{\overset{\displaystyle H}{|}}{\underset{\underset{\displaystyle H}{|}}{C}}-O-\overset{\overset{\displaystyle H}{|}}{\underset{\underset{\displaystyle H}{|}}{C}}-\overset{\overset{\displaystyle H}{|}}{\underset{\underset{\displaystyle H}{|}}{C}}-H$$

methyl ethyl ether

The compounds can be differentiated by their

(1) boiling points
(2) gram-formula masses
(3) numbers of hydrogen atoms
(4) percent compositions by mass of carbon

49 The table below shows the atomic mass and natural abundance of the two naturally occurring isotopes of lithium.

Naturally Occurring Isotopes of Lithium

Isotope	Atomic Mass (u)	Natural Abundance (%)
Li-6	6.015	7.6
Li-7	7.016	92.4

Which numerical setup can be used to determine the atomic mass of naturally occurring lithium?

(1) $(7.6)(6.015 \text{ u}) + (92.4)(7.016 \text{ u})$

(2) $(0.076)(6.015 \text{ u}) + (0.924)(7.016 \text{ u})$

(3) $\dfrac{(7.6)(6.015 \text{ u}) + (92.4)(7.016 \text{ u})}{2}$

(4) $\dfrac{(0.076)(6.015 \text{ u}) + (0.924)(7.016 \text{ u})}{2}$

50 Given the equation representing a reaction at equilibrium:

$$H_2S(aq) + CH_3NH_2(aq) \rightleftharpoons HS^-(aq) + CH_3NH_3^+(aq)$$

According to one acid-base theory, the forward reaction is classified as an acid-base reaction because

(1) H_2S is a H^+ donor and CH_3NH_2 is a H^+ acceptor
(2) CH_3NH_2 is a H^+ donor and H_2S is a H^+ acceptor
(3) HS^- and $CH_3NH_3^+$ are both H^+ donors
(4) $CH_3NH_3^+$ and HS^- are both H^+ acceptors

Part B–2

Answer all questions in this part.

Directions (51–65): Record your answers in the spaces provided in your answer booklet. Some questions may require the use of the *2011 Edition Reference Tables for Physical Setting/Chemistry.*

51 Explain, in terms of electron configuration, why arsenic and antimony are chemically similar. [1]

52 Identify the element in Period 3 that is an unreactive gas at STP. [1]

53 Compare the energy of an electron in the first shell of a cadmium atom to the energy of an electron in the third shell of the same atom. [1]

Base your answers to questions 54 and 55 on the information below and on your knowledge of chemistry.

The densities for two forms of carbon at room temperature are listed in the table below.

Densities of Two Forms of Carbon

Element Form	Density (g/cm^3)
carbon (graphite)	2.2
carbon (diamond)	3.513

54 Compare the number of carbon atoms in a 0.30-cm^3 sample of graphite and a 0.30-cm^3 sample of diamond. [1]

55 A student calculated the density of a sample of graphite to be 2.3 g/cm^3. Show a numerical setup for calculating the student's percent error for the density of graphite. [1]

Base your answers to questions 56 and 57 on the information below and on your knowledge of chemistry.

A sample of calcium carbonate, $CaCO_3$, has a mass of 42.2 grams. Calcium carbonate has a gram-formula mass of 100. g/mol.

56 Show a numerical setup for calculating the number of moles in the sample of $CaCO_3$. [1]

57 Determine the percent composition by mass of oxygen in the $CaCO_3$. [1]

Base your answers to questions 58 and 59 on the information below and on your knowledge of chemistry.

Carbon monoxide, CO(g), is a toxic gas found in automobile exhaust. The concentration of CO(g) can be decreased by using a catalyst in the reaction between CO(g) and $O_2(g)$. This reaction is represented by the balanced equation below.

$$2CO(g) + O_2(g) \xrightarrow{\text{catalyst}} 2CO_2(g) + \text{energy}$$

58 Explain, in terms of collision theory, why an increase in temperature increases the rate of the reaction. [1]

59 On the labeled axes *in your answer booklet*, draw the potential energy curve for the reaction represented by this equation. [1]

Base your answers to questions 60 and 61 on the information below and on your knowledge of chemistry.

The diagram and data below represent a gas and the conditions of pressure, volume, and temperature of the gas in a rigid cylinder with a moveable piston.

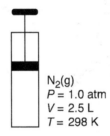

$N_2(g)$
$P = 1.0$ atm
$V = 2.5$ L
$T = 298$ K

60 Determine the volume of the gas in the cylinder at STP. [1]

61 State *one* change in temperature and *one* change in pressure that will cause the gas in the cylinder to behave more like an ideal gas. [1]

Base your answers to questions 62 through 65 on the information below and on your knowledge of chemistry.

During a titration, 10.00 mL of acetic acid, $HC_2H_3O_2(aq)$, is completely neutralized by adding 12.50 mL of 0.64 M sodium hydroxide, $NaOH(aq)$.

62 Identify the only positive ion in the $HC_2H_3O_2(aq)$. [1]

63 State the number of significant figures used to express the volume of the acetic acid. [1]

64 Determine the molarity of the acetic acid. [1]

65 Explain why it is better to use data from multiple trials to determine the molarity of acetic acid, rather than data from a single trial. [1]

Part C

Answer all questions in this part.

Directions (66–85): Record your answers in the spaces provided in your answer booklet. Some questions may require the use of the *2011 Edition Reference Tables for Physical Setting/Chemistry*.

Base your answers to questions 66 through 68 on the information below and on your knowledge of chemistry.

Carbon dioxide, CO_2, changes from the solid phase to the gas phase at 1 atm and 194.5 K. In the solid phase, CO_2 is often called dry ice. When dry ice sublimes in air at 298 K, the water vapor in the air can condense, forming a fog of small water droplets. This fog is often used for special effects at concerts and in movie-making.

66 State the direction of heat flow between the dry ice and the water vapor in the air. [1]

67 At 1 atm and 298 K, compare the potential energies of the water molecules before and after the water vapor condenses. [1]

68 At 1 atm and 190. K, compare the amount of thermal energy in a 1.0-kilogram block of dry ice to the amount of thermal energy in a 2.0-kilogram block of dry ice. [1]

[OVER]

Base your answers to questions 69 through 72 on the information below and on your knowledge of chemistry.

A solution of ethylene glycol and water can be used as the coolant in an engine-cooling system. The ethylene glycol concentration in a coolant solution is often given as percent by volume. For example, 100. mL of a coolant solution that is 40.% ethylene glycol by volume contains 40. mL of ethylene glycol diluted with enough water to produce a total volume of 100. mL. The graph below shows the freezing point of coolants that have different ethylene glycol concentrations.

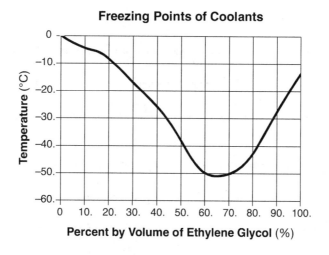

Freezing Points of Coolants

69 Explain, in terms of particle distribution, why a coolant solution is a homogeneous mixture. [1]

70 Explain, in terms of the molecular polarity, why ethylene glycol dissolves in water to form a solution. [1]

71 Identify the percent by volume of ethylene glycol in a solution that freezes at −10.°C. [1]

72 One engine-cooling system has a volume of 6400 mL. Determine the volume of ethylene glycol in the completely filled engine-cooling system when the concentration of ethylene glycol is 50.% by volume. [1]

Base your answers to questions 73 through 77 on the information below and on your knowledge of chemistry.

Molecules containing two carbon atoms and a functional group have many home and industrial uses. These compounds can be produced by a variety of reactions, as shown by the equations below.

Equation 1: $C_2H_4 + H_2O \rightarrow CH_3CH_2OH$

Equation 2: $2CH_3CH_2OH + O_2 \rightarrow 2CH_3CHO + 2H_2O$

Equation 3: $2CH_3CHO + O_2 \rightarrow 2CH_3COOH$

73 Explain, in terms of bonding, why the hydrocarbon reactant in equation 1 is unsaturated. [1]

74 Draw a structural formula of the ethanal molecule in equation 2. [1]

75 Explain, in terms of atoms, why CH_3CH_2OH and CH_3CHO are *not* isomers of each other. [1]

76 Identify the class of organic compounds to which the product in equation 3 belongs. [1]

77 Determine the number of moles of oxygen required to completely react with six moles of CH_3CHO in equation 3. [1]

Base your answers to questions 78 and 79 on the information below and on your knowledge of chemistry.

The hydrangea is a flowering plant. The color of the flowers it produces can change depending on the pH value of the soil in which the plant grows. Adding aluminum sulfate makes the soil more acidic and adding calcium hydroxide makes the soil more basic.

A student performed an experiment by varying soil pH and recording the color of the flowers. The following table summarizes the results of the experiment.

Hydrangea Soil pH and Flower Color

Soil pH	Flower Color
5.5 and below	blue
between 5.5 and 6.5	purple
6.5 and above	pink

78 Identify the independent variable in this experiment. [1]

79 Hydrangea plants can be grown in soil that turns litmus red. What color are the flowers of the plants grown in this soil? [1]

Base your answers to questions 80 through 82 on the information below and on your knowledge of chemistry.

The diagram and balanced ionic equation below represent two half-cells connected to produce an operating voltaic cell in a laboratory investigation. The half-cells are connected by a salt bridge.

Voltaic Cell

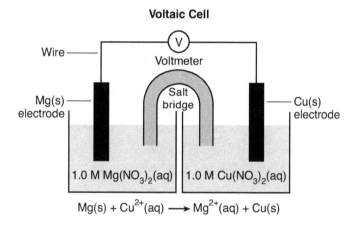

$$Mg(s) + Cu^{2+}(aq) \longrightarrow Mg^{2+}(aq) + Cu(s)$$

80 Determine the oxidation number of nitrogen in the negative ion in the aqueous solutions. [1]

81 State the purpose of the salt bridge in this voltaic cell. [1]

82 Explain, in terms of atoms and ions, why the mass of the Mg(s) electrode decreases as the cell operates. [1]

Base your answers to questions 83 through 85 on the information below and on your knowledge of chemistry.

The radioisotope Mo-99 naturally decays to produce the metastable isotope Tc-99m, which is used in medical diagnosis. A doctor can obtain images of organs and bones by injecting a patient with a solution of Tc-99m. The half-life of the metastable Tc-99m is six hours.

83 Complete the nuclear equation *in your answer booklet* for the nuclear decay of Mo-99. [1]

84 State *both* the number of protons and the number of neutrons in a Tc-99 nuclide. [1]

85 Determine the fraction of an original sample of metastable Tc-99m that remains unchanged after 24 hours. [1]

The University of the State of New York

REGENTS HIGH SCHOOL EXAMINATION

PHYSICAL SETTING
CHEMISTRY

Wednesday, January 25, 2017 — 9:15 a.m. to 12:15 p.m., only

ANSWER BOOKLET

☐ Male

Student . . . . Sex: ☐ Female

Teacher . . . .

School . . . . Grade . . . .

Record your answers for Part B–2 and Part C in this booklet.

Part B–2
51
52
53
54

55

56

57 _____ %

58 ____

____

____

59

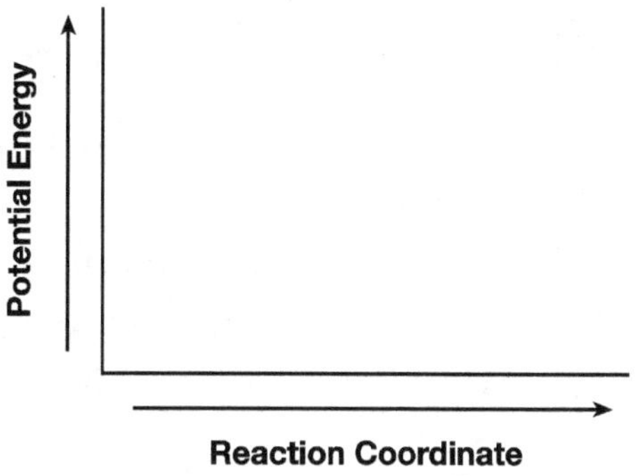
Potential Energy
Reaction Coordinate

60 ____________ L

61 Temperature: ____

Pressure: ____

62 _____

63 _____

64 _____ M

65 _____

_____

_____

Part C

66 From _____ to _____

67 _____

_____

_____

68 _____

_____

_____

69 _____

_____

_____

70 _____

_____

_____

71 _____ %

72 _____ mL

73 _____

_____

_____

74

75 _____

_____

_____

76 _____

77 _____ **mol**

78 _____

79 _____

80 _____

81 _____

_____

_____

82 _____

_____

_____

83 $^{99}_{42}\text{Mo} \rightarrow$ _____ $+ \, ^{99m}_{43}\text{Tc}$

84 Protons: _____

Neutrons: _____

85 _____

Physical Setting/Chemistry
Regents Exam - August 2016

Part A

Answer all questions in this part.

Directions (1–30): For *each* statement or question, record on your separate answer sheet the *number* of the word or expression that, of those given, best completes the statement or answers the question. Some questions may require the use of the *2011 Edition Reference Tables for Physical Setting/Chemistry*.

1 Which change occurs when an atom in an excited state returns to the ground state?

(1) Energy is emitted.
(2) Energy is absorbed.
(3) The number of electrons decreases.
(4) The number of electrons increases.

2 The valence electrons in an atom of phosphorus in the ground state are all found in

(1) the first shell   (3) the third shell
(2) the second shell   (4) the fourth shell

3 Which two elements have the most similar chemical properties?

(1) beryllium and magnesium
(2) hydrogen and helium
(3) phosphorus and sulfur
(4) potassium and strontium

4 Which phrase describes a compound that consists of two elements?

(1) a mixture in which the elements are in a variable proportion

(2) a mixture in which the elements are in a fixed proportion

(3) a substance in which the elements are chemically combined in a variable proportion

(4) a substance in which the elements are chemically combined in a fixed proportion

5 The formula mass of a compound is the

(1) sum of the atomic masses of its atoms
(2) sum of the atomic numbers of its atoms
(3) product of the atomic masses of its atoms
(4) product of the atomic numbers of its atoms

6 The arrangement of the elements from left to right in Period 4 on the Periodic Table is based on

(1) atomic mass
(2) atomic number
(3) the number of electron shells
(4) the number of oxidation states

7 Which diatomic molecule is formed when the two atoms share six electrons?

(1) H_2 (3) O_2
(2) N_2 (4) F_2

8 Which formula represents a polar molecule?

(1) O_2 (3) NH_3
(2) CO_2 (4) CH_4

9 Which element is *least* likely to undergo a chemical reaction?

(1) lithium   (3) fluorine
(2) carbon   (4) neon

10 Which element has a melting point higher than the melting point of rhenium?

(1) iridium   (3) tantalum
(2) osmium   (4) tungsten

11 Which property can be defined as the ability of a substance to be hammered into thin sheets?

(1) conductivity   (3) melting point
(2) malleability   (4) solubility

12 Which list of elements consists of a metal, a metalloid, and a noble gas?

(1) aluminum, sulfur, argon
(2) magnesium, sodium, sulfur
(3) sodium, silicon, argon
(4) silicon, phosphorus, chlorine

13 Which sample of matter has a crystal structure?

(1) $Hg(\ell)$　　　　　(3) $NaCl(s)$
(2) $H_2O(\ell)$　　　　(4) $CH_4(g)$

14 One mole of liquid water and one mole of solid water have *different*

(1) masses
(2) properties
(3) empirical formulas
(4) gram-formula masses

15 Which substance can *not* be broken down by a chemical change?

(1) butanal　　　　(3) gold
(2) propene　　　　(4) water

16 Which statement describes particles of an ideal gas, based on the kinetic molecular theory?

(1) Gas particles are separated by distances smaller than the size of the gas particles.
(2) Gas particles do not transfer energy to each other when they collide.
(3) Gas particles have no attractive forces between them.
(4) Gas particles move in predictable, circular motion.

17 Which expression could represent the concentration of a solution?

(1) 3.5 g　　　　(3) 3.5 mL
(2) 3.5 M　　　　(4) 3.5 mol

18 Which form of energy is associated with the random motion of the particles in a sample of water?

(1) chemical energy　　(3) nuclear energy
(2) electrical energy　　(4) thermal energy

19 Which change is most likely to occur when a molecule of H_2 and a molecule of I_2 collide with proper orientation and sufficient energy?

(1) a chemical change, because a compound is formed
(2) a chemical change, because an element is formed
(3) a physical change, because a compound is formed
(4) a physical change, because an element is formed

20 Which changes can reach dynamic equilibrium?

(1) nuclear changes, only
(2) chemical changes, only
(3) nuclear and physical changes
(4) chemical and physical changes

21 What occurs when a reaction reaches equilibrium?

(1) The concentration of the reactants increases.
(2) The concentration of the products increases.
(3) The rate of the forward reaction is equal to the rate of the reverse reaction.
(4) The rate of the forward reaction is slower than the rate of the reverse reaction.

22 In terms of potential energy, *PE*, which expression defines the heat of reaction for a chemical change?

(1) $PE_{products} - PE_{reactants}$

(2) $PE_{reactants} - PE_{products}$

(3) $\dfrac{PE_{products}}{PE_{reactants}}$

(4) $\dfrac{PE_{reactants}}{PE_{products}}$

23 Systems in nature tend to undergo changes that result in

(1) lower energy and lower entropy
(2) lower energy and higher entropy
(3) higher energy and lower entropy
(4) higher energy and higher entropy

24 What occurs when Cr^{3+} ions are reduced to Cr^{2+} ions?

(1) Electrons are lost and the oxidation number of chromium increases.
(2) Electrons are lost and the oxidation number of chromium decreases.
(3) Electrons are gained and the oxidation number of chromium increases.
(4) Electrons are gained and the oxidation number of chromium decreases.

25 Where do reduction and oxidation occur in an electrolytic cell?

(1) Both occur at the anode.
(2) Both occur at the cathode.
(3) Reduction occurs at the anode, and oxidation occurs at the cathode.
(4) Reduction occurs at the cathode, and oxidation occurs at the anode.

26 Which compound is an electrolyte?

(1) H_2O
(2) C_2H_6
(3) H_3PO_4
(4) CH_3OH

27 When the hydronium ion concentration of an aqueous solution is increased by a factor of 10, the pH value of the solution

(1) decreases by 1
(2) increases by 1
(3) decreases by 10
(4) increases by 10

28 The stability of isotopes is related to the ratio of which particles in the atoms?

(1) electrons and protons
(2) electrons and positrons
(3) neutrons and protons
(4) neutrons and positrons

29 Which radioisotope has the fastest rate of decay?

(1) ^{14}C
(2) ^{37}Ca
(3) ^{53}Fe
(4) ^{42}K

30 The atomic mass of an element is the weighted average of the atomic masses of

(1) the least abundant isotopes of the element
(2) the naturally occurring isotopes of the element
(3) the artificially produced isotopes of the element
(4) the natural and artificial isotopes of the element

Part B–1

Answer all questions in this part.

Directions (31–50): For *each* statement or question, record on your separate answer sheet the *number* of the word or expression that, of those given, best completes the statement or answers the question. Some questions may require the use of the *2011 Edition Reference Tables for Physical Setting/Chemistry*.

31 Which list of elements is arranged in order of increasing electronegativity?

(1) Be, Mg, Ca   (3) K, Ca, Sc
(2) F, Cl, Br   (4) Li, Na, K

32 The table below gives the masses of two different subatomic particles found in an atom.

Subatomic Particles and Their Masses

Subatomic Particle	Mass (g)
X	1.67×10^{-24}
Z	9.11×10^{-28}

Which of the subatomic particles are each paired with their corresponding name?

(1) X, proton and Z, electron
(2) X, proton and Z, neutron
(3) X, neutron and Z, proton
(4) X, electron and Z, proton

33 Which electron configuration represents an excited state for an atom of calcium?

(1) 2-8-7-1   (3) 2-8-7-3
(2) 2-8-7-2   (4) 2-8-8-2

34 At STP, graphite and diamond are two solid forms of carbon. Which statement explains why these two forms of carbon differ in hardness?

(1) Graphite and diamond have different ionic radii.
(2) Graphite and diamond have different molecular structures.
(3) Graphite is a metal, but diamond is a nonmetal.
(4) Graphite is a good conductor of electricity, but diamond is a poor conductor of electricity.

35 Which equation shows conservation of charge?

(1) $Cu + Ag^+ \rightarrow Cu^{2+} + Ag$
(2) $Mg + Zn^{2+} \rightarrow 2Mg^{2+} + Zn$
(3) $2F_2 + Br^- \rightarrow 2F^- + Br_2$
(4) $2I^- + Cl_2 \rightarrow I_2 + 2Cl^-$

36 What occurs when potassium reacts with chlorine to form potassium chloride?

(1) Electrons are shared and the bonding is ionic.
(2) Electrons are shared and the bonding is covalent.
(3) Electrons are transferred and the bonding is ionic.
(4) Electrons are transferred and the bonding is covalent.

37 Given the balanced equation representing a reaction:

$$H_2 + energy \rightarrow H + H$$

What occurs as bonds are broken in one mole of H_2 molecules during this reaction?

(1) Energy is absorbed and one mole of unbonded hydrogen atoms is produced.
(2) Energy is absorbed and two moles of unbonded hydrogen atoms are produced.
(3) Energy is released and one mole of unbonded hydrogen atoms is produced.
(4) Energy is released and two moles of unbonded hydrogen atoms are produced.

38 Which pair of atoms has the most polar bond?

(1) H–Br   (3) I–Br
(2) H–Cl   (4) I–Cl

39 Which two notations represent isotopes of the same element?

(1) $^{14}_{7}N$ and $^{18}_{9}N$ (3) $^{14}_{7}N$ and $^{17}_{10}Ne$

(2) $^{20}_{7}N$ and $^{20}_{10}Ne$ (4) $^{19}_{7}N$ and $^{16}_{10}Ne$

40 The graph below shows the volume and the mass of four different substances at STP.

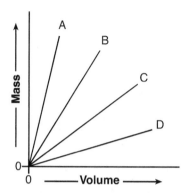

Which of the four substances has the *lowest* density?

(1) A (3) C

(2) B (4) D

41 What is the total amount of heat required to completely melt 347 grams of ice at its melting point?

(1) 334 J   (3) 116 000 J

(2) 1450 J   (4) 784 000 J

42 As the temperature of a reaction increases, it is expected that the reacting particles collide

(1) more often and with greater force
(2) more often and with less force
(3) less often and with greater force
(4) less often and with less force

43 Given the formula representing a compound:

$$\begin{array}{c} \text{H} \quad \text{H} \quad \text{H} \quad \text{O} \quad \text{H} \quad \text{H} \\ | \quad | \quad | \quad || \quad | \quad | \\ \text{H}-\text{C}-\text{C}-\text{C}-\text{C}-\text{C}-\text{C}-\text{H} \\ | \quad | \quad | \quad \quad | \quad | \\ \text{H} \quad \text{H} \quad \text{H} \quad \quad \text{H} \quad \text{H} \end{array}$$

What is an IUPAC name for this compound?

(1) ethyl propanoate   (3) 3-hexanone
(2) propyl ethanoate   (4) 4-hexanone

44 A voltaic cell converts chemical energy to

(1) electrical energy with an external power source
(2) nuclear energy with an external power source
(3) electrical energy without an external power source
(4) nuclear energy without an external power source

45 Which acid and base react to form water and sodium sulfate?

(1) sulfuric acid and sodium hydroxide
(2) sulfuric acid and potassium hydroxide
(3) sulfurous acid and sodium hydroxide
(4) sulfurous acid and potassium hydroxide

46 Given the equation representing a reaction:

$$H_2CO_3 + NH_3 \rightarrow NH_4^+ + HCO_3^-$$

According to one acid-base theory, the compound NH_3 acts as a base because it

(1) accepts a hydrogen ion
(2) donates a hydrogen ion
(3) accepts a hydroxide ion
(4) donates a hydroxide ion

47 Which statement describes characteristics of a 0.01 M KOH(aq) solution?

(1) The solution is acidic with a pH less than 7.
(2) The solution is acidic with a pH greater than 7.
(3) The solution is basic with a pH less than 7.
(4) The solution is basic with a pH greater than 7.

48 Four statements about the development of the atomic model are shown below.

A: Electrons have wavelike properties.
B: Atoms have small, negatively charged particles.
C: The center of an atom is a small, dense nucleus.
D: Atoms are hard, indivisible spheres.

Which order of statements represents the historical development of the atomic model?

(1) $C \to D \to A \to B$
(2) $C \to D \to B \to A$
(3) $D \to B \to A \to C$
(4) $D \to B \to C \to A$

49 Five cubes of iron are tested in a laboratory. The tests and the results are shown in the table below.

Iron Tests and the Results

Test	Procedure	Result
1	A cube of Fe is hit with a hammer.	The cube is flattened.
2	A cube of Fe is placed in 3 M HCl(aq).	Bubbles of gas form.
3	A cube of Fe is heated to 1811 K.	The cube melts.
4	A cube of Fe is left in damp air.	The cube rusts.
5	A cube of Fe is placed in water.	The cube sinks.

Which tests demonstrate chemical properties?

(1) 1, 3, and 4   (3) 2 and 4
(2) 1, 3, and 5   (4) 2 and 5

50 A rigid cylinder with a movable piston contains a sample of helium gas. The temperature of the gas is held constant as the piston is pulled outward. Which graph represents the relationship between the volume of the gas and the pressure of the gas?

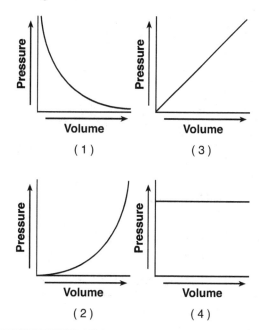

Part B–2

Answer all questions in this part.

Directions (51–65): Record your answers in the spaces provided in your answer booklet. Some questions may require the use of the *2011 Edition Reference Tables for Physical Setting/Chemistry.*

51 What is the empirical formula for C_6H_{12}? [1]

52 Using Table G, determine the minimum mass of NaCl that must be dissolved in 200. grams of water to produce a saturated solution at 90.°C. [1]

53 State the physical property that makes it possible to separate a solution by distillation. [1]

Base your answers to questions 54 and 55 on the information below and on your knowledge of chemistry.

A beaker contains a liquid sample of a molecular substance. Both the beaker and the liquid are at 194 K. The graph below represents the relationship between temperature and time as the beaker and its contents are cooled for 12 minutes in a refrigerated chamber.

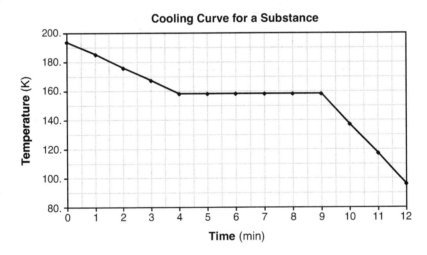

Cooling Curve for a Substance

54 State what happens to the average kinetic energy of the molecules in the sample during the first 3 minutes. [1]

55 Identify the physical change occurring during the time interval, minute 4 to minute 9. [1]

[OVER]

Base your answers to questions 56 through 59 on the information below and on your knowledge of chemistry.

The equation below represents a reaction between propene and hydrogen bromide.

$$
\begin{array}{c}
\text{H\ \ H} \\
\ \ |\ \ \ | \\
\text{H}-\text{C}-\text{C}=\text{C}-\text{H} \\
\ \ |\ \ \ \ \ \ \ \ | \\
\text{H\ \ \ \ \ \ \ H}
\end{array}
\ +\ \text{H}-\text{Br}\ \longrightarrow\
\begin{array}{c}
\text{H\ \ H\ \ H} \\
\ \ |\ \ \ |\ \ \ | \\
\text{H}-\text{C}-\text{C}-\text{C}-\text{H} \\
\ \ |\ \ \ |\ \ \ | \\
\text{H\ \ Br\ H}
\end{array}
$$

Cyclopropane, an isomer of propene, has a boiling point of –33°C at standard pressure and is represented by the formula below.

$$
\begin{array}{c}
\text{H}\diagdown\ \diagup\text{H} \\
\text{C} \\
\diagup\ \ \diagdown \\
\text{H}\diagdown\ \ \ \ \diagup\text{H} \\
\text{C}-\text{C} \\
\diagup\ \ \ \ \diagdown \\
\text{H}\ \ \ \ \ \text{H}
\end{array}
$$

56 Explain why this reaction can be classified as a synthesis reaction. [1]

57 Identify the class of organic compounds to which the product of this reaction belongs. [1]

58 Explain, in terms of molecular formulas and structural formulas, why cyclopropane is an isomer of propene. [1]

59 Convert the boiling point of cyclopropane at standard pressure to kelvins. [1]

Base your answers to questions 60 through 63 on the information below and on your knowledge of chemistry.

The radius of a lithium atom is 130. picometers, and the radius of a fluorine atom is 60. picometers. The radius of a lithium ion, Li^+, is 59 picometers, and the radius of a fluoride ion, F^-, is 133 picometers.

60 Compare the radius of a fluoride ion to the radius of a fluorine atom. [1]

61 Explain, in terms of subatomic particles, why the radius of a lithium ion is smaller than the radius of a lithium atom. [1]

62 In the space *in your answer booklet*, draw a Lewis electron-dot diagram for a fluoride ion. [1]

63 Describe the general trend in atomic radius as each element in Period 2 is considered in order from left to right. [1]

Base your answers to questions 64 and 65 on the information below and on your knowledge of chemistry.

Nuclear fission reactions can produce different radioisotopes. One of these radioisotopes is Te-137, which has a half-life of 2.5 seconds. The diagram below represents one of the many nuclear fission reactions.

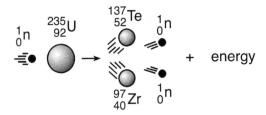

64 State evidence that this nuclear reaction represents transmutation. [1]

65 Complete the nuclear equation *in your answer booklet* for the beta decay of Zr-97, by writing an isotopic notation for the missing product. [1]

Part C

Answer all questions in this part.

Directions (66–85): Record your answers in the spaces provided in your answer booklet. Some questions may require the use of the *2011 Edition Reference Tables for Physical Setting/Chemistry*.

Base your answers to questions 66 through 69 on the information below and on your knowledge of chemistry.

      Stamping an identification number into the steel frame of a bicycle compresses the crystal structure of the metal. If the number is filed off, there are scientific ways to reveal the number.

      One method is to apply aqueous copper(II) chloride to the number area. The Cu^{2+} ions react with some iron atoms in the steel frame, producing copper atoms that show the pattern of the number. The ionic equation below represents this reaction.

$$Fe(s) + Cu^{2+}(aq) \rightarrow Fe^{2+}(aq) + Cu(s)$$

      Another method is to apply hydrochloric acid to the number area. The acid reacts with the iron, producing bubbles of hydrogen gas. The bubbles form faster where the metal was compressed, so the number becomes visible. The equation below represents this reaction.

$$2HCl(aq) + Fe(s) \rightarrow FeCl_2(aq) + H_2(g)$$

66 Explain why the Fe atoms in the bicycle frame react with the Cu^{2+} ions. [1]

67 Determine the number of moles of hydrogen gas produced when 0.001 mole of HCl(aq) reacts completely with the iron metal. [1]

68 Write a balanced half-reaction equation for the reduction of the hydrogen ions to hydrogen gas. [1]

69 Describe *one* change in the HCl(aq) that will increase the rate at which hydrogen bubbles are produced when the acid is applied to the steel frame. [1]

Base your answers to questions 70 through 73 on the information below and on your knowledge of chemistry.

In an investigation, aqueous solutions are prepared by completely dissolving a different amount of $NaCl(s)$ in each of four beakers containing 100.00 grams of $H_2O(\ell)$ at room temperature. Each solution is heated and the temperature at which boiling occurred is measured. The data are recorded in the table below.

Boiling Point Data for Four NaCl(aq) Solutions

Beaker Number	Mass of $H_2O(\ell)$ (g)	Mass of NaCl(s) Dissolved (g)	Boiling Point of Solution (°C)
1	100.00	8.76	101.5
2	100.00	17.52	103.1
3	100.00	26.28	104.6
4	100.00	35.04	106.1

70 Identify the solute and the solvent used in this investigation. [1]

71 Show a numerical setup for calculating the percent by mass of NaCl in the solution in beaker 4. [1]

72 Explain, in terms of ions, why the ability to conduct an electric current is greater for the solution in beaker 4 than for the solution in beaker 1. [1]

73 State the relationship between the concentration of ions and the boiling point for these solutions. [1]

Base your answers to questions 74 through 76 on the information below and on your knowledge of chemistry.

One type of voltaic cell, called a mercury battery, uses zinc and mercury(II) oxide to generate an electric current. Mercury batteries were used because of their miniature size, even though mercury is toxic. The overall reaction for a mercury battery is given in the equation below.

$$Zn(s) + HgO(s) \rightarrow ZnO(s) + Hg(\ell)$$

74 Determine the change in the oxidation number of zinc during the operation of the cell. [1]

75 Compare the number of moles of electrons lost to the number of moles of electrons gained during the reaction. [1]

76 Using information in the passage, state *one* risk and *one* benefit of using a mercury battery. [1]

Base your answers to questions 77 through 80 on the information below and on your knowledge of chemistry.

A company produces a colorless vinegar that is 5.0% $HC_2H_3O_2$ in water. Using thymol blue as an indicator, a student titrates a 15.0-milliliter sample of the vinegar with 43.1 milliliters of a 0.30 M NaOH(aq) solution until the acid is neutralized.

77 Based on Table *M*, what is the color of the indicator in the vinegar solution before any base is added? [1]

78 Identify the negative ion in the NaOH(aq) used in this titration. [1]

79 The concentration of the base used in this titration is expressed to what number of significant figures? [1]

80 Determine the molarity of the $HC_2H_3O_2$ in the vinegar sample, using the titration data. [1]

Base your answers to questions 81 through 85 on the information below and on your knowledge of chemistry.

In industry, ethanol is primarily produced by two different reactions. One process involves the reaction of glucose in the presence of an enzyme that acts as a catalyst. The equation below represents this reaction.

$$\text{Equation 1: } C_6H_{12}O_6 \xrightarrow{\text{enzyme}} 2CH_3CH_2OH + 2CO_2$$
$$\underset{\text{glucose}}{} \qquad\qquad \underset{\text{ethanol}}{}$$

In another reaction, ethanol is produced from ethene and water. The equation below represents this reaction in which H_2SO_4 is a catalyst.

$$\text{Equation 2: } CH_2CH_2 + H_2O \xrightarrow{H_2SO_4} CH_3CH_2OH$$

Industrial ethanol can be oxidized using a catalyst to produce ethanal. The equation representing this oxidation is shown below.

$$\text{Equation 3: } CH_3CH_2OH \xrightarrow{\text{catalyst}} CH_3CHO + H_2$$

81 Identify the element that causes the reactant in equation 1 to be classified as an organic compound. [1]

82 Identify the type of organic reaction represented by equation 1. [1]

83 Explain why the hydrocarbon in equation 2 is unsaturated. [1]

84 Explain, in terms of intermolecular forces, why ethanol has a much higher boiling point than ethene, at standard pressure. [1]

85 Draw a structural formula for the organic product in equation 3. [1]

_____

The University of the State of New York

REGENTS HIGH SCHOOL EXAMINATION

PHYSICAL SETTING
CHEMISTRY

Wednesday, August 17, 2016 — 8:30 to 11:30 a.m., only

ANSWER BOOKLET

☐ Male

Student . . . . Sex: ☐ Female

Teacher . . . .

School . . . . Grade . . . .

Record your answers for Part B–2 and Part C in this booklet.

Part B–2
51 _____
52 _____ g
53 _____
54 _____
_____
_____
55 _____

56 _____

_____

_____

57 _____

58 _____

_____

_____

59 _____ **K**

60 _____

_____

_____

61 _____

_____

_____

62

63 _____

_____

_____

64 _____

_____

_____

65 $_{40}^{97}\text{Zr} \rightarrow \,_{-1}^{0}\text{e} + $ _____

Part C

66 _____

_____

_____

67 _____ **mol**

68 _____

69 _____

_____

_____

70 Solute: _____

Solvent: _____

71

72 _____

_____

_____

73 _____

_____

_____

74 From _____ to _____

75 _____

_____

_____

76 Risk: _____

Benefit: _____

77 _____

78 _____

79 _____

80 _____ **M**

P.S./Chem. Answer Booklet–Aug. '16   [OVER]

311

81 _____

82 _____

83 _____

_____

_____

84 _____

_____

_____

85

Physical Setting/Chemistry
Regents Exam - June 2016

Part A

Answer all questions in this part.

Directions (1–30): For *each* statement or question, record on your separate answer sheet the *number* of the word or expression that, of those given, best completes the statement or answers the question. Some questions may require the use of the *2011 Edition Reference Tables for Physical Setting/Chemistry.*

1 Which statement describes the charge of an electron and the charge of a proton?

  (1) An electron and a proton both have a charge of +1.

  (2) An electron and a proton both have a charge of −1.

  (3) An electron has a charge of +1, and a proton has a charge of −1.

  (4) An electron has a charge of −1, and a proton has a charge of +1.

2 Which subatomic particles are found in the nucleus of an atom of beryllium?

  (1) electrons and protons

  (2) electrons and positrons

  (3) neutrons and protons

  (4) neutrons and electrons

3 The elements in Period 4 on the Periodic Table are arranged in order of increasing

  (1) atomic radius

  (2) atomic number

  (3) number of valence electrons

  (4) number of occupied shells of electrons

4 Which phrase describes two forms of solid carbon, diamond and graphite, at STP?

  (1) the same crystal structure and the same properties

  (2) the same crystal structure and different properties

  (3) different crystal structures and the same properties

  (4) different crystal structures and different properties

5 Which element has six valence electrons in each of its atoms in the ground state?

  (1) Se   (3) Kr

  (2) As   (4) Ga

6 What is the chemical name for $H_2SO_3(aq)$?

  (1) sulfuric acid

  (2) sulfurous acid

  (3) hydrosulfuric acid

  (4) hydrosulfurous acid

7 Which substance is most soluble in water?

  (1) $(NH_4)_3PO_4$ (3) Ag_2SO_4

  (2) $Cu(OH)_2$ (4) $CaCO_3$

8 Which type of bonding is present in a sample of an element that is malleable?

  (1) ionic   (3) nonpolar covalent

  (2) metallic   (4) polar covalent

9 Which atom has the greatest attraction for the electrons in a chemical bond?

  (1) hydrogen   (3) silicon

  (2) oxygen   (4) sulfur

10 Which type of reaction involves the transfer of electrons?

  (1) alpha decay

  (2) double replacement

  (3) neutralization

  (4) oxidation-reduction

11 A 10.0-gram sample of nitrogen is at STP. Which property will increase when the sample is cooled to 72 K at standard pressure?

  (1) mass   (3) density

  (2) volume   (4) temperature

12 Which element is a gas at STP?

  (1) sulfur   (3) potassium

  (2) xenon   (4) phosphorus

13 A 5.0-gram sample of Fe(s) is to be placed in 100. milliliters of HCl(aq). Which changes will result in the fastest rate of reaction?

(1) increasing the surface area of Fe(s) and increasing the concentration of HCl(aq)

(2) increasing the surface area of Fe(s) and decreasing the concentration of HCl(aq)

(3) decreasing the surface area of Fe(s) and increasing the concentration of HCl(aq)

(4) decreasing the surface area of Fe(s) and decreasing the concentration of HCl(aq)

14 Which process is commonly used to separate a mixture of ethanol and water?

(1) distillation   (3) filtration

(2) ionization   (4) titration

15 A sample of hydrogen gas will behave most like an ideal gas under the conditions of

(1) low pressure and low temperature

(2) low pressure and high temperature

(3) high pressure and low temperature

(4) high pressure and high temperature

16 The collision theory states that a reaction is most likely to occur when the reactant particles collide with the proper

(1) formula masses

(2) molecular masses

(3) density and volume

(4) energy and orientation

17 At STP, which sample contains the same number of molecules as 3.0 liters of $H_2(g)$?

(1) 1.5 L of $NH_3(g)$ (3) 3.0 L of $CH_4(g)$

(2) 2.0 L of $CO_2(g)$ (4) 6.0 L of $N_2(g)$

18 The addition of a catalyst to a chemical reaction provides an alternate pathway that

(1) increases the potential energy of reactants

(2) decreases the potential energy of reactants

(3) increases the activation energy

(4) decreases the activation energy

19 A sample of water is boiling as heat is added at a constant rate. Which statement describes the potential energy and the average kinetic energy of the water molecules in this sample?

(1) The potential energy decreases and the average kinetic energy remains the same.

(2) The potential energy decreases and the average kinetic energy increases.

(3) The potential energy increases and the average kinetic energy remains the same.

(4) The potential energy increases and the average kinetic energy increases.

20 Entropy is a measure of the

(1) acidity of a sample

(2) disorder of a system

(3) concentration of a solution

(4) chemical activity of an element

21 Which element has atoms that can bond with each other to form ring, chain, and network structures?

(1) aluminum   (3) carbon

(2) calcium   (4) argon

22 What is the number of electrons shared in the multiple carbon-carbon bond in one molecule of 1-pentyne?

(1) 6   (3) 3

(2) 2   (4) 8

23 Butanal, butanone, and diethyl ether have different properties because the molecules of each compound differ in their

(1) numbers of carbon atoms

(2) numbers of oxygen atoms

(3) types of functional groups

(4) types of radioactive isotopes

24 What occurs when a magnesium atom becomes a magnesium ion?

(1) Electrons are gained and the oxidation number increases.
(2) Electrons are gained and the oxidation number decreases.
(3) Electrons are lost and the oxidation number increases.
(4) Electrons are lost and the oxidation number decreases.

25 Energy is required to produce a chemical change during

(1) chromatography   (3) boiling
(2) electrolysis   (4) melting

26 The reaction of an Arrhenius acid with an Arrhenius base produces water and

(1) a salt   (3) an aldehyde
(2) an ester   (4) a halocarbon

27 One acid-base theory defines an acid as an

(1) H^- acceptor   (3) H^+ acceptor
(2) H^- donor   (4) H^+ donor

28 Which phrase describes the decay modes and the half-lives of K-37 and K-42?

(1) the same decay mode but different half-lives
(2) the same decay mode and the same half-life
(3) different decay modes and different half-lives
(4) different decay modes but the same half-life

29 Which particle has a mass that is approximately equal to the mass of a proton?

(1) an alpha particle   (3) a neutron
(2) a beta particle   (4) a positron

30 Which change occurs during a nuclear fission reaction?

(1) Covalent bonds are converted to ionic bonds.
(2) Isotopes are converted to isomers.
(3) Temperature is converted to mass.
(4) Matter is converted to energy.

Part B–1

Answer all questions in this part.

Directions (31–50): For *each* statement or question, record on your separate answer sheet the *number* of the word or expression that, of those given, best completes the statement or answers the question. Some questions may require the use of the *2011 Edition Reference Tables for Physical Setting/Chemistry.*

31 Which notations represent hydrogen isotopes?

(1) ^1_1H and ^2_1H

(2) ^1_1H and ^4_2H

(3) ^1_2H and ^1_3H

(4) ^2_1H and ^7_2H

32 Naturally occurring gallium is a mixture of isotopes that contains 60.11% of Ga-69 (atomic mass = 68.93 u) and 39.89% of Ga-71 (atomic mass = 70.92 u). Which numerical setup can be used to determine the atomic mass of naturally occurring gallium?

(1) $\dfrac{(68.93 \text{ u} + 70.92 \text{ u})}{2}$

(2) $\dfrac{(68.93 \text{ u})(0.6011)}{(70.92 \text{ u})(0.3989)}$

(3) $(68.93 \text{ u})(0.6011) + (70.92 \text{ u})(0.3989)$

(4) $(68.93 \text{ u})(39.89) + (70.92 \text{ u})(60.11)$

33 Which list of symbols represents nonmetals, only?

(1) B, Al, Ga

(2) Li, Be, B

(3) C, Si, Ge

(4) P, S, Cl

34 In the formula XSO_4, the symbol X could represent the element

(1) Al

(2) Ar

(3) Mg

(4) Na

35 What is the chemical formula for lead(IV) oxide?

(1) PbO_2

(2) PbO_4

(3) Pb_2O

(4) Pb_4O

36 Which statement describes the general trends in electronegativity and atomic radius as the elements in Period 2 are considered in order from left to right?

(1) Both electronegativity and atomic radius increase.

(2) Both electronegativity and atomic radius decrease.

(3) Electronegativity increases and atomic radius decreases.

(4) Electronegativity decreases and atomic radius increases.

37 What is the percent composition by mass of nitrogen in $(NH_4)_2CO_3$ (gram-formula mass = 96.0 g/mol)?

(1) 14.6%

(2) 29.2%

(3) 58.4%

(4) 87.5%

38 Given the balanced equation:

$$2KI + F_2 \rightarrow 2KF + I_2$$

Which type of chemical reaction does this equation represent?

(1) synthesis

(2) decomposition

(3) single replacement

(4) double replacement

W

H–H   O=C=O $\overset{\displaystyle N}{\underset{H \ \ H \ \ H}{|}}$ $\overset{\displaystyle O}{\underset{H \qquad H}{\diagup \diagdown}}$

(1)   (2)   (3)   (4)

40 A reaction reaches equilibrium at 100.°C. The equation and graph representing this reaction are shown below.

$$N_2O_4(g) \rightleftharpoons 2NO_2(g)$$

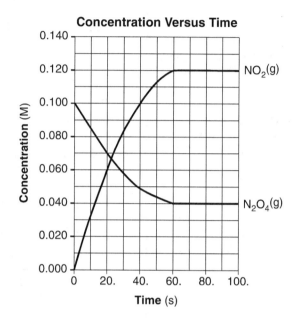

The graph shows that the reaction is at equilibrium after 60. seconds because the concentrations of both $NO_2(g)$ and $N_2O_4(g)$ are

(1) increasing
(2) decreasing

(3) constant
(4) zero

41 Given the balanced equation representing a reaction:

$$2H_2O + energy \rightarrow 2H_2 + O_2$$

Which statement describes the changes in energy and bonding for the reactant?

(1) Energy is absorbed as bonds in H_2O are formed.
(2) Energy is absorbed as bonds in H_2O are broken.
(3) Energy is released as bonds in H_2O are formed.
(4) Energy is released as bonds in H_2O are broken.

42 At standard pressure, what is the temperature at which a saturated solution of NH_4Cl has a concentration of 60. g $NH_4Cl/100.$ g H_2O?

(1) 66°C   (3) 22°C
(2) 57°C   (4) 17°C

43 Which aqueous solution has the highest boiling point at standard pressure?

(1) 1.0 M KCl(aq)   (3) 2.0 M KCl(aq)
(2) 1.0 M $CaCl_2$(aq)   (4) 2.0 M $CaCl_2$(aq)

44 Given the equation representing a system at equilibrium:

$$KNO_3(s) + energy \xrightleftharpoons{H_2O} K^+(aq) + NO_3^-(aq)$$

Which change causes the equilibrium to shift?

(1) increasing pressure
(2) increasing temperature
(3) adding a noble gas
(4) adding a catalyst

45 Which hydrocarbon is saturated?

(1) C_2H_2 (3) C_4H_6
(2) C_3H_4 (4) C_4H_{10}

46 Which volume of 0.600 M H_2SO_4(aq) exactly neutralizes 100. milliliters of 0.300 M $Ba(OH)_2$(aq)?

(1) 25.0 mL   (3) 100. mL
(2) 50.0 mL   (4) 200. mL

47 Given the formula for an organic compound:

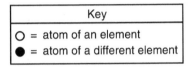

What is the name given to the group in the box?

(1) butyl   (3) methyl
(2) ethyl   (4) propyl

48 Given the particle diagram:

Key
O = atom of an element
● = atom of a different element

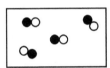

Which type of matter is represented by the particle diagram?

(1) an element
(2) a compound
(3) a homogeneous mixture
(4) a heterogeneous mixture

49 Which substance is an electrolyte?

(1) O_2 (3) C_3H_8
(2) Xe   (4) KNO_3

50 Which type of organic reaction produces both water and carbon dioxide?

(1) addition   (3) esterification
(2) combustion   (4) fermentation

Part B–2

Answer all questions in this part.

Directions (51–65): Record your answers in the spaces provided in your answer booklet. Some questions may require the use of the *2011 Edition Reference Tables for Physical Setting/Chemistry.*

51 Draw a Lewis electron-dot diagram for a chloride ion, Cl^-. [1]

Base your answers to questions 52 and 53 on the information below and on your knowledge of chemistry.

At STP, Cl_2 is a gas and I_2 is a solid. When hydrogen reacts with chlorine, the compound hydrogen chloride is formed. When hydrogen reacts with iodine, the compound hydrogen iodide is formed.

52 Balance the equation *in your answer booklet* for the reaction between hydrogen and chlorine, using the smallest whole-number coefficients. [1]

53 Explain, in terms of intermolecular forces, why iodine is a solid at STP but chlorine is a gas at STP. [1]

Base your answers to questions 54 and 55 on the information below and on your knowledge of chemistry.

Some properties of the element sodium are listed below.
- is a soft, silver-colored metal
- melts at a temperature of 371 K
- oxidizes easily in the presence of air
- forms compounds with nonmetallic elements in nature
- forms sodium chloride in the presence of chlorine gas

54 Identify *one* chemical property of sodium from this list. [1]

55 Convert the melting point of sodium to degrees Celsius. [1]

Base your answers to questions 56 through 58 on the information below and on your knowledge of chemistry.

At standard pressure, water has unusual properties that are due to both its molecular structure and intermolecular forces. For example, although most liquids contract when they freeze, water expands, making ice less dense than liquid water. Water has a much higher boiling point than most other molecular compounds having a similar gram-formula mass.

56 Explain why $H_2O(s)$ floats on $H_2O(\ell)$ when both are at 0°C. [1]

57 State the type of intermolecular force responsible for the unusual boiling point of $H_2O(\ell)$ at standard pressure. [1]

58 Determine the total amount of heat, in joules, required to completely vaporize a 50.0-gram sample of $H_2O(\ell)$ at its boiling point at standard pressure. [1]

Base your answers to questions 59 and 60 on the information below and on your knowledge of chemistry.

At 1023 K and 1 atm, a 3.00-gram sample of $SnO_2(s)$ (gram-formula mass = 151 g/mol) reacts with hydrogen gas to produce tin and water, as shown in the balanced equation below.

$$SnO_2(s) + 2H_2(g) \rightarrow Sn(\ell) + 2H_2O(g)$$

59 Show a numerical setup for calculating the number of moles of $SnO_2(s)$ in the 3.00-gram sample. [1]

60 Determine the number of moles of $Sn(\ell)$ produced when 4.0 moles of $H_2(g)$ is completely consumed. [1]

Base your answers to questions 61 and 62 on the information below and on your knowledge of chemistry.

The incomplete data table below shows the pH value of solutions A and B and the hydrogen ion concentration of solution A.

Hydrogen Ion and pH Data for HCl(aq) Solutions

HCl(aq) Solution	Hydrogen Ion Concentration (M)	pH
A	1.0×10^{-2}	2.0
B	?	5.0

61 State the color of methyl orange in a sample of solution A. [1]

62 Determine the hydrogen ion concentration of solution B. [1]

Base your answers to questions 63 through 65 on the information below and on your knowledge of chemistry.

A sample of helium gas is placed in a rigid cylinder that has a movable piston. The volume of the gas is varied by moving the piston, while the temperature is held constant at 273 K. The volumes and corresponding pressures for three trials are measured and recorded in the data table below. For each of these trials, the product of pressure and volume is also calculated and recorded. For a fourth trial, only the volume is recorded.

**Pressure and Volume Data for
a Sample of Helium Gas at 273 K**

Trial Number	Pressure (atm)	Volume (L)	P x V (L•atm)
1	1.000	0.412	0.412
2	0.750	0.549	0.412
3	0.600	0.687	0.412
4	?	1.373	?

63 State evidence found in the data table that allows the product of pressure and volume for the fourth trial to be predicted. [1]

64 Determine the pressure of the helium gas in trial 4. [1]

65 Compare the average distances between the helium atoms in trial 1 to the average distances between the helium atoms in trial 3. [1]

Part C

Answer all questions in this part.

Directions (66–85): Record your answers in the spaces provided in your answer booklet. Some questions may require the use of the *2011 Edition Reference Tables for Physical Setting/Chemistry*.

Base your answers to questions 66 through 69 on the information below and on your knowledge of chemistry.

Potassium phosphate, K_3PO_4, is a source of dietary potassium found in a popular cereal. According to the Nutrition-Facts label shown on the boxes of this brand of cereal, the accepted value for a one-cup serving of this cereal is 170. milligrams of potassium. The minimum daily requirement of potassium is 3500 milligrams for an adult human.

66 Identify *two* types of chemical bonding in the source of dietary potassium in this cereal. [1]

67 Identify the noble gas whose atoms have the same electron configuration as a potassium ion. [1]

68 Compare the radius of a potassium ion to the radius of a potassium atom. [1]

69 The mass of potassium in a one-cup serving of this cereal is determined to be 172 mg. Show a numerical setup for calculating the percent error for the mass of potassium in this serving. [1]

Base your answers to questions 70 and 71 on the information below and on your knowledge of chemistry.

During photosynthesis, plants use carbon dioxide, water, and light energy to produce glucose, $C_6H_{12}O_6$, and oxygen. The reaction for photosynthesis is represented by the balanced equation below.

$$6CO_2 + 6H_2O + \text{light energy} \rightarrow C_6H_{12}O_6 + 6O_2$$

70 Write the empirical formula for glucose. [1]

71 State evidence that indicates photosynthesis is an endothermic reaction. [1]

Base your answers to questions 72 through 74 on the information below and on your knowledge of chemistry.

Fireworks that contain metallic salts such as sodium, strontium, and barium can generate bright colors. A technician investigates what colors are produced by the metallic salts by performing flame tests. During a flame test, a metallic salt is heated in the flame of a gas burner. Each metallic salt emits a characteristic colored light in the flame.

72 Explain why the electron configuration of 2-7-1-1 represents a sodium atom in an excited state. [1]

73 Explain, in terms of electrons, how a strontium salt emits colored light. [1]

74 State how bright-line spectra viewed through a spectroscope can be used to identify the metal ions in the salts used in the flame tests. [1]

Base your answers to questions 75 through 77 on the information below and on your knowledge of chemistry.

The unique odors and flavors of many fruits are primarily due to small quantities of a certain class of organic compounds. The equation below represents the production of one of these compounds.

$$\underset{\text{Reactant 1}}{\text{H}-\overset{\overset{\text{H}}{|}}{\underset{\underset{\text{H}}{|}}{\text{C}}}-\overset{\overset{\text{H}}{|}}{\underset{\underset{\text{H}}{|}}{\text{C}}}-\text{OH}} \;+\; \underset{\text{Reactant 2}}{\text{H}-\overset{\overset{\text{O}}{\|}}{\text{C}}-\text{O}-\text{H}} \;\longrightarrow\; \underset{\text{Product 1}}{\text{H}-\overset{\overset{\text{O}}{\|}}{\text{C}}-\text{O}-\overset{\overset{\text{H}}{|}}{\underset{\underset{\text{H}}{|}}{\text{C}}}-\overset{\overset{\text{H}}{|}}{\underset{\underset{\text{H}}{|}}{\text{C}}}-\text{H}} \;+\; \underset{\text{Product 2}}{\text{HOH}}$$

75 Show a numerical setup for calculating the gram-formula mass for reactant 1. [1]

76 Explain, in terms of molecular polarity, why reactant 2 is soluble in water. [1]

77 State the class of organic compounds to which product 1 belongs. [1]

Base your answers to questions 78 through 81 on the information below and on your knowledge of chemistry.

A student develops the list shown below that includes laboratory equipment and materials for constructing a voltaic cell.

Laboratory Equipment and Materials
- a strip of zinc
- a strip of copper
- a 250-mL beaker containing 150 mL of 0.1 M zinc nitrate
- a 250-mL beaker containing 150 mL of 0.1 M copper(II) nitrate
- wires
- a voltmeter
- a switch
- a salt bridge

78 State the purpose of the salt bridge in the voltaic cell. [1]

79 Complete and balance the half-reaction equation *in your answer booklet* for the oxidation of the Zn(s) that occurs in the voltaic cell. [1]

80 Compare the activities of the two metals used by the student for constructing the voltaic cell. [1]

81 Identify *one* item of laboratory equipment required to build an electrolytic cell that is *not* included in the list. [1]

Base your answers to questions 82 through 85 on the information below and on your knowledge of chemistry.

In 1896, Antoine H. Becquerel discovered that a uranium compound could expose a photographic plate wrapped in heavy paper in the absence of light. It was shown that the uranium compound was spontaneously releasing particles and high-energy radiation. Further tests showed the emissions from the uranium that exposed the photographic plate were *not* deflected by charged plates.

82 Identify the highly penetrating radioactive emission that exposed the photographic plates. [1]

83 Complete the nuclear equation *in your answer booklet* for the alpha decay of U-238. [1]

84 Determine the number of neutrons in an atom of U-233. [1]

85 Identify the type of nuclear reaction that occurs when an alpha or a beta particle is spontaneously emitted by a radioactive isotope. [1]

The University of the State of New York

REGENTS HIGH SCHOOL EXAMINATION

PHYSICAL SETTING
CHEMISTRY

Tuesday, June 21, 2016 — 9:15 a.m. to 12:15 p.m., only

ANSWER BOOKLET

Student . . . .   Sex: ☐ Male ☐ Female

Teacher . . . .

School . . . .   Grade . . . .

Record your answers for Part B–2 and Part C in this booklet.

Part B–2

51

52 _____ $H_2(g)$ + _____ $Cl_2(g) \rightarrow$ _____ $HCl(g)$

53 _____

_____

_____

---

54 _____

_____

55 _____ °**C**

56 _____

_____

_____

57 _____

58 _____ **J**

59

60 _____ **mol**

61 _____

62 _____ **M**

63 _____

_____

_____

64 _____ **atm**

65 _____

_____

_____

Part C

66 _____ and _____

67 _____

68 _____

_____

69

70 _____

71 _____

_____

_____

72 _____

_____

_____

73 _____

_____

_____

74 _____

_____

_____

75

76 _____

_____

_____

77 _____

78 _____

_____

79 $Zn(s) \rightarrow$ _____ + _____

80 _____

_____

_____

81 _____

82 _____

83 $^{238}_{92}U \rightarrow ^{4}_{2}He + $ _____

84 _____

85 _____

Reference Tables for Physical Setting/CHEMISTRY
2011 Edition

Table A
Standard Temperature and Pressure

Name	Value	Unit
Standard Pressure	101.3 kPa 1 atm	kilopascal atmosphere
Standard Temperature	273 K 0°C	kelvin degree Celsius

Table B
Physical Constants for Water

Heat of Fusion	334 J/g
Heat of Vaporization	2260 J/g
Specific Heat Capacity of $H_2O(\ell)$	4.18 J/g•K

Table C
Selected Prefixes

Factor	Prefix	Symbol
10^3	kilo-	k
10^{-1}	deci-	d
10^{-2}	centi-	c
10^{-3}	milli-	m
10^{-6}	micro-	μ
10^{-9}	nano-	n
10^{-12}	pico-	p

Table D
Selected Units

Symbol	Name	Quantity
m	meter	length
g	gram	mass
Pa	pascal	pressure
K	kelvin	temperature
mol	mole	amount of substance
J	joule	energy, work, quantity of heat
s	second	time
min	minute	time
h	hour	time
d	day	time
y	year	time
L	liter	volume
ppm	parts per million	concentration
M	molarity	solution concentration
u	atomic mass unit	atomic mass

Table E
Selected Polyatomic Ions

Formula	Name	Formula	Name
H_3O^+	hydronium	CrO_4^{2-}	chromate
Hg_2^{2+}	mercury(I)	$Cr_2O_7^{2-}$	dichromate
NH_4^+	ammonium	MnO_4^-	permanganate
$C_2H_3O_2^-$ CH_3COO^- } acetate		NO_2^-	nitrite
		NO_3^-	nitrate
CN^-	cyanide	O_2^{2-}	peroxide
CO_3^{2-}	carbonate	OH^-	hydroxide
HCO_3^-	hydrogen carbonate	PO_4^{3-}	phosphate
$C_2O_4^{2-}$	oxalate	SCN^-	thiocyanate
ClO^-	hypochlorite	SO_3^{2-}	sulfite
ClO_2^-	chlorite	SO_4^{2-}	sulfate
ClO_3^-	chlorate	HSO_4^-	hydrogen sulfate
ClO_4^-	perchlorate	$S_2O_3^{2-}$	thiosulfate

Table F
Solubility Guidelines for Aqueous Solutions

Ions That Form Soluble Compounds	Exceptions	Ions That Form Insoluble Compounds*	Exceptions
Group 1 ions (Li^+, Na^+, etc.)		carbonate (CO_3^{2-})	when combined with Group 1 ions or ammonium (NH_4^+)
ammonium (NH_4^+)		chromate (CrO_4^{2-})	when combined with Group 1 ions, Ca^{2+}, Mg^{2+}, or ammonium (NH_4^+)
nitrate (NO_3^-)			
acetate ($C_2H_3O_2^-$ or CH_3COO^-)		phosphate (PO_4^{3-})	when combined with Group 1 ions or ammonium (NH_4^+)
hydrogen carbonate (HCO_3^-)		sulfide (S^{2-})	when combined with Group 1 ions or ammonium (NH_4^+)
chlorate (ClO_3^-)		hydroxide (OH^-)	when combined with Group 1 ions, Ca^{2+}, Ba^{2+}, Sr^{2+}, or ammonium (NH_4^+)
halides (Cl^-, Br^-, I^-)	when combined with Ag^+, Pb^{2+}, or Hg_2^{2+}		
sulfates (SO_4^{2-})	when combined with Ag^+, Ca^{2+}, Sr^{2+}, Ba^{2+}, or Pb^{2+}	*compounds having very low solubility in H_2O	

Table G
Solubility Curves at Standard Pressure

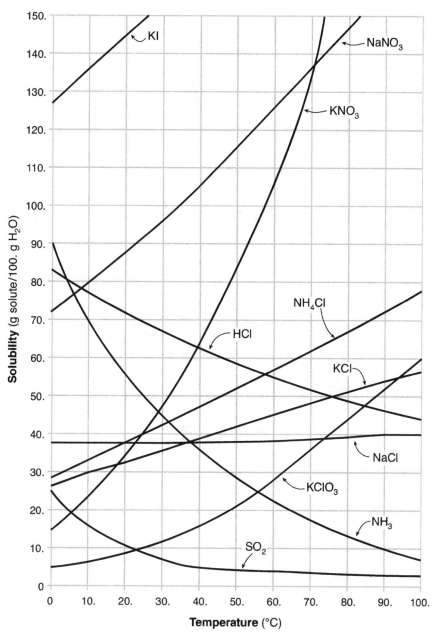

Table H
Vapor Pressure of Four Liquids

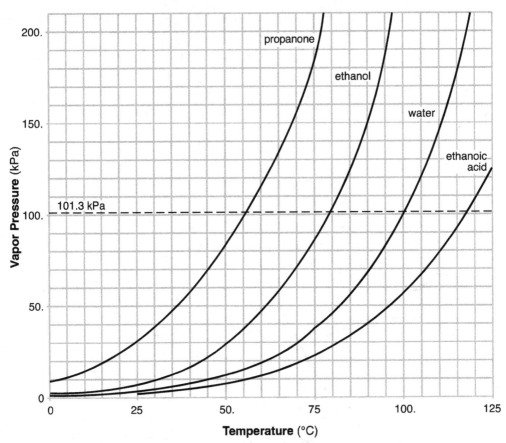

Table I
Heats of Reaction at 101.3 kPa and 298 K

Reaction	ΔH (kJ)*
$CH_4(g) + 2O_2(g) \longrightarrow CO_2(g) + 2H_2O(\ell)$	−890.4
$C_3H_8(g) + 5O_2(g) \longrightarrow 3CO_2(g) + 4H_2O(\ell)$	−2219.2
$2C_8H_{18}(\ell) + 25O_2(g) \longrightarrow 16CO_2(g) + 18H_2O(\ell)$	−10943
$2CH_3OH(\ell) + 3O_2(g) \longrightarrow 2CO_2(g) + 4H_2O(\ell)$	−1452
$C_2H_5OH(\ell) + 3O_2(g) \longrightarrow 2CO_2(g) + 3H_2O(\ell)$	−1367
$C_6H_{12}O_6(s) + 6O_2(g) \longrightarrow 6CO_2(g) + 6H_2O(\ell)$	−2804
$2CO(g) + O_2(g) \longrightarrow 2CO_2(g)$	−566.0
$C(s) + O_2(g) \longrightarrow CO_2(g)$	−393.5
$4Al(s) + 3O_2(g) \longrightarrow 2Al_2O_3(s)$	−3351
$N_2(g) + O_2(g) \longrightarrow 2NO(g)$	+182.6
$N_2(g) + 2O_2(g) \longrightarrow 2NO_2(g)$	+66.4
$2H_2(g) + O_2(g) \longrightarrow 2H_2O(g)$	−483.6
$2H_2(g) + O_2(g) \longrightarrow 2H_2O(\ell)$	−571.6
$N_2(g) + 3H_2(g) \longrightarrow 2NH_3(g)$	−91.8
$2C(s) + 3H_2(g) \longrightarrow C_2H_6(g)$	−84.0
$2C(s) + 2H_2(g) \longrightarrow C_2H_4(g)$	+52.4
$2C(s) + H_2(g) \longrightarrow C_2H_2(g)$	+227.4
$H_2(g) + I_2(g) \longrightarrow 2HI(g)$	+53.0
$KNO_3(s) \xrightarrow{H_2O} K^+(aq) + NO_3^-(aq)$	+34.89
$NaOH(s) \xrightarrow{H_2O} Na^+(aq) + OH^-(aq)$	−44.51
$NH_4Cl(s) \xrightarrow{H_2O} NH_4^+(aq) + Cl^-(aq)$	+14.78
$NH_4NO_3(s) \xrightarrow{H_2O} NH_4^+(aq) + NO_3^-(aq)$	+25.69
$NaCl(s) \xrightarrow{H_2O} Na^+(aq) + Cl^-(aq)$	+3.88
$LiBr(s) \xrightarrow{H_2O} Li^+(aq) + Br^-(aq)$	−48.83
$H^+(aq) + OH^-(aq) \longrightarrow H_2O(\ell)$	−55.8

*The ΔH values are based on molar quantities represented in the equations.
A minus sign indicates an exothermic reaction.

Most Active	Metals	Nonmetals	Most Active
	Li	F_2	
	Rb	Cl_2	
	K	Br_2	
	Cs	I_2	
	Ba		
	Sr		
	Ca		
	Na		
	Mg		
	Al		
	Ti		
	Mn		
	Zn		
	Cr		
	Fe		
	Co		
	Ni		
	Sn		
	Pb		
	H_2		
	Cu		
	Ag		
Least Active	Au		Least Active

**Activity Series is based on the hydrogen
standard. H_2 is *not* a metal.

Table K
Common Acids

Formula	Name
HCl(aq)	hydrochloric acid
HNO_2(aq)	nitrous acid
HNO_3(aq)	nitric acid
H_2SO_3(aq)	sulfurous acid
H_2SO_4(aq)	sulfuric acid
H_3PO_4(aq)	phosphoric acid
H_2CO_3(aq) or CO_2(aq)	carbonic acid
CH_3COOH(aq) or $HC_2H_3O_2$(aq)	ethanoic acid (acetic acid)

Table L
Common Bases

Formula	Name
NaOH(aq)	sodium hydroxide
KOH(aq)	potassium hydroxide
$Ca(OH)_2$(aq)	calcium hydroxide
NH_3(aq)	aqueous ammonia

Table M
Common Acid–Base Indicators

Indicator	Approximate pH Range for Color Change	Color Change
methyl orange	3.1–4.4	red to yellow
bromthymol blue	6.0–7.6	yellow to blue
phenolphthalein	8–9	colorless to pink
litmus	4.5–8.3	red to blue
bromcresol green	3.8–5.4	yellow to blue
thymol blue	8.0–9.6	yellow to blue

Source: *The Merck Index*, 14th ed., 2006, Merck Publishing Group

Table N
Selected Radioisotopes

Nuclide	Half-Life	Decay Mode	Nuclide Name
^{198}Au	2.695 d	β^-	gold-198
^{14}C	5715 y	β^-	carbon-14
^{37}Ca	182 ms	β^+	calcium-37
^{60}Co	5.271 y	β^-	cobalt-60
^{137}Cs	30.2 y	β^-	cesium-137
^{53}Fe	8.51 min	β^+	iron-53
^{220}Fr	27.4 s	α	francium-220
^{3}H	12.31 y	β^-	hydrogen-3
^{131}I	8.021 d	β^-	iodine-131
^{37}K	1.23 s	β^+	potassium-37
^{42}K	12.36 h	β^-	potassium-42
^{85}Kr	10.73 y	β^-	krypton-85
^{16}N	7.13 s	β^-	nitrogen-16
^{19}Ne	17.22 s	β^+	neon-19
^{32}P	14.28 d	β^-	phosphorus-32
^{239}Pu	2.410×10^4 y	α	plutonium-239
^{226}Ra	1599 y	α	radium-226
^{222}Rn	3.823 d	α	radon-222
^{90}Sr	29.1 y	β^-	strontium-90
^{99}Tc	2.13×10^5 y	β^-	technetium-99
^{232}Th	1.40×10^{10} y	α	thorium-232
^{233}U	1.592×10^5 y	α	uranium-233
^{235}U	7.04×10^8 y	α	uranium-235
^{238}U	4.47×10^9 y	α	uranium-238

Source: *CRC Handbook of Chemistry and Physics*, 91st ed., 2010–2011, CRC Press

Table O
Symbols Used in Nuclear Chemistry

Name	Notation	Symbol
alpha particle	^4_2He or $^4_2\alpha$	α
beta particle	$^{\ 0}_{-1}\text{e}$ or $^{\ 0}_{-1}$▬▬▬▬▬▬▬▬▬-	
gamma radiation	$^0_0\gamma$	γ
neutron	^1_0n	n
proton	^1_1H or ^1_1p	p
positron	$^{\ 0}_{+1}\text{e}$ or $^{\ 0}_{+1}\beta$	β^+

Table P
Organic Prefixes

Prefix	Number of Carbon Atoms
meth-	1
eth-	2
prop-	3
but-	4
pent-	5
hex-	6
hept-	7
oct-	8
non-	9
dec-	10

Table Q
Homologous Series of Hydrocarbons

Name	General Formula	Examples	
		Name	Structural Formula
alkanes	C_nH_{2n+2}	ethane	H H | | H—C—C—H | | H H
alkenes	C_nH_{2n}	ethene	H H \ / C=C / \ H H
alkynes	C_nH_{2n-2}	ethyne	H—C≡C—H

Note: n = number of carbon atoms

Table R
Organic Functional Groups

Class of Compound	Functional Group	General Formula	Example
halide (halocarbon)	—F (fluoro-) —Cl (chloro-) —Br (bromo-) —I (iodo-)	$R-X$ (X represents any halogen)	$CH_3CHClCH_3$ 2-chloropropane
alcohol	—OH	$R-OH$	$CH_3CH_2CH_2OH$ 1-propanol
ether	—O—	$R-O-R'$	$CH_3OCH_2CH_3$ methyl ethyl ether
aldehyde	$\overset{\displaystyle O}{\overset{\displaystyle \|}{-C}}-H$	$\overset{\displaystyle O}{\overset{\displaystyle \|}{R-C}}-H$	$CH_3CH_2\overset{\displaystyle O}{\overset{\displaystyle \|}{C}}-H$ propanal
ketone	$\overset{\displaystyle O}{\overset{\displaystyle \|}{-C}}-$	$\overset{\displaystyle O}{\overset{\displaystyle \|}{R-C}}-R'$	$CH_3\overset{\displaystyle O}{\overset{\displaystyle \|}{C}}CH_2CH_2CH_3$ 2-pentanone
organic acid	$\overset{\displaystyle O}{\overset{\displaystyle \|}{-C}}-OH$	$\overset{\displaystyle O}{\overset{\displaystyle \|}{R-C}}-OH$	$CH_3CH_2\overset{\displaystyle O}{\overset{\displaystyle \|}{C}}-OH$ propanoic acid
ester	$\overset{\displaystyle O}{\overset{\displaystyle \|}{-C}}-O-$	$\overset{\displaystyle O}{\overset{\displaystyle \|}{R-C}}-O-R'$	$CH_3CH_2\overset{\displaystyle O}{\overset{\displaystyle \|}{C}}OCH_3$ methyl propanoate
amine	$\overset{\displaystyle \|}{-N-}$	$\overset{\displaystyle R'}{\overset{\displaystyle \|}{R-N}}-R''$	$CH_3CH_2CH_2NH_2$ 1-propanamine
amide	$\overset{\displaystyle O}{\overset{\displaystyle \|}{-C}}-\overset{\displaystyle \|}{N}H$	$\overset{\displaystyle O}{\overset{\displaystyle \|}{R-C}}-\overset{\displaystyle R'}{\overset{\displaystyle \|}{N}}H$	$CH_3CH_2\overset{\displaystyle O}{\overset{\displaystyle \|}{C}}-NH_2$ propanamide

Note: R represents a bonded atom or group of atoms.

Periodic Table of the Elements

Reference Tables for Physical Setting/Chemistry – 2011 Edition

KEY

Atomic Mass → 12.011
Symbol → C
Atomic Number → 6
Electron Configuration → 2-4

-4, +2, +4 — Selected Oxidation States

Relative atomic masses are based on $^{12}C = 12$ (exact)

Note: Numbers in parentheses are mass numbers of the most stable or common isotope.

* denotes the presence of (2-8-) for elements 72 and above

** The systematic names and symbols for elements of atomic numbers 113 and above will be used until the approval of trivial names by IUPAC.

Source: *CRC Handbook of Chemistry and Physics*, 91st ed., 2010–2011, CRC Press

343

Table S
Properties of Selected Elements

Atomic Number	Symbol	Name	First Ionization Energy (kJ/mol)	Electro-negativity	Melting Point (K)	Boiling* Point (K)	Density** (g/cm³)	Atomic Radius (pm)
1	H	hydrogen	1312	2.2	14	20.	0.000082	32
2	He	helium	2372	—	—	4	0.000164	37
3	Li	lithium	520.	1.0	454	1615	0.534	130.
4	Be	beryllium	900.	1.6	1560.	2744	1.85	99
5	B	boron	801	2.0	2348	4273	2.34	84
6	C	carbon	1086	2.6	—	—	—	75
7	N	nitrogen	1402	3.0	63	77	0.001145	71
8	O	oxygen	1314	3.4	54	90.	0.001308	64
9	F	fluorine	1681	4.0	53	85	0.001553	60.
10	Ne	neon	2081	—	24	27	0.000825	62
11	Na	sodium	496	0.9	371	1156	0.97	160.
12	Mg	magnesium	738	1.3	923	1363	1.74	140.
13	Al	aluminum	578	1.6	933	2792	2.70	124
14	Si	silicon	787	1.9	1687	3538	2.3296	114
15	P	phosphorus (white)	1012	2.2	317	554	1.823	109
16	S	sulfur (monoclinic)	1000.	2.6	388	718	2.00	104
17	Cl	chlorine	1251	3.2	172	239	0.002898	100.
18	Ar	argon	1521	—	84	87	0.001633	101
19	K	potassium	419	0.8	337	1032	0.89	200.
20	Ca	calcium	590.	1.0	1115	1757	1.54	174
21	Sc	scandium	633	1.4	1814	3109	2.99	159
22	Ti	titanium	659	1.5	1941	3560.	4.506	148
23	V	vanadium	651	1.6	2183	3680.	6.0	144
24	Cr	chromium	653	1.7	2180.	2944	7.15	130.
25	Mn	manganese	717	1.6	1519	2334	7.3	129
26	Fe	iron	762	1.8	1811	3134	7.87	124
27	Co	cobalt	760.	1.9	1768	3200.	8.86	118
28	Ni	nickel	737	1.9	1728	3186	8.90	117
29	Cu	copper	745	1.9	1358	2835	8.96	122
30	Zn	zinc	906	1.7	693	1180.	7.134	120.
31	Ga	gallium	579	1.8	303	2477	5.91	123
32	Ge	germanium	762	2.0	1211	3106	5.3234	120.
33	As	arsenic (gray)	944	2.2	1090.	—	5.75	120.
34	Se	selenium (gray)	941	2.6	494	958	4.809	118
35	Br	bromine	1140.	3.0	266	332	3.1028	117
36	Kr	krypton	1351	—	116	120.	0.003425	116
37	Rb	rubidium	403	0.8	312	961	1.53	215
38	Sr	strontium	549	1.0	1050.	1655	2.64	190.
39	Y	yttrium	600.	1.2	1795	3618	4.47	176
40	Zr	zirconium	640.	1.3	2128	4682	6.52	164

Atomic Number	Symbol	Name	First Ionization Energy (kJ/mol)	Electro-negativity	Melting Point (K)	Boiling* Point (K)	Density** (g/cm³)	Atomic Radius (pm)
41	Nb	niobium	652	1.6	2750.	5017	8.57	156
42	Mo	molybdenum	684	2.2	2896.	4912	10.2	146
43	Tc	technetium	702	2.1	2430.	4538	11	138
44	Ru	ruthenium	710.	2.2	2606	4423	12.1	136
45	Rh	rhodium	720.	2.3	2237	3968	12.4	134
46	Pd	palladium	804	2.2	1828	3236	12.0	130.
47	Ag	silver	731	1.9	1235	2435	10.5	136
48	Cd	cadmium	868	1.7	594	1040.	8.69	140.
49	In	indium	558	1.8	430.	2345	7.31	142
50	Sn	tin (white)	709	2.0	505	2875	7.287	140.
51	Sb	antimony (gray)	831	2.1	904	1860.	6.68	140.
52	Te	tellurium	869	2.1	723	1261	6.232	137
53	I	iodine	1008	2.7	387	457	4.933	136
54	Xe	xenon	1170.	2.6	161	165	0.005366	136
55	Cs	cesium	376	0.8	302	944	1.873	238
56	Ba	barium	503	0.9	1000.	2170.	3.62	206
57	La	lanthanum	538	1.1	1193	3737	6.15	194
Elements 58–71 have been omitted.								
72	Hf	hafnium	659	1.3	2506	4876	13.3	164
73	Ta	tantalum	728	1.5	3290.	5731	16.4	158
74	W	tungsten	759	1.7	3695	5828	19.3	150.
75	Re	rhenium	756	1.9	3458	5869	20.8	141
76	Os	osmium	814	2.2	3306	5285	22.587	136
77	Ir	iridium	865	2.2	2719	4701	22.562	132
78	Pt	platinum	864	2.2	2041	4098	21.5	130.
79	Au	gold	890.	2.4	1337	3129	19.3	130.
80	Hg	mercury	1007	1.9	234	630.	13.5336	132
81	Tl	thallium	589	1.8	577	1746	11.8	144
82	Pb	lead	716	1.8	600.	2022	11.3	145
83	Bi	bismuth	703	1.9	544	1837	9.79	150.
84	Po	polonium	812	2.0	527	1235	9.20	142
85	At	astatine	—	2.2	575	—	—	148
86	Rn	radon	1037	—	202	211	0.009074	146
87	Fr	francium	393	0.7	300.	—	—	242
88	Ra	radium	509	0.9	969	—	5	211
89	Ac	actinium	499	1.1	1323	3471	10.	201
Elements 90 and above have been omitted.								

*boiling point at standard pressure
** density of solids and liquids at room temperature and density of gases at 298 K and 101.3 kPa
- no data available
Source: CRC Handbook for Chemistry and Physics 91st ed., 2010-2011, CRC Press

Table T
Important Formulas and Equations

Density	$d = \dfrac{m}{V}$	d = density m = mass V = volume
Mole Calculations	number of moles = $\dfrac{\text{given mass}}{\text{gram-formula mass}}$	
Percent Error	% error = $\dfrac{\text{measured value} - \text{accepted value}}{\text{accepted value}} \times 100$	
Percent Composition	% composition by mass = $\dfrac{\text{mass of part}}{\text{mass of whole}} \times 100$	
Concentration	parts per million = $\dfrac{\text{mass of solute}}{\text{mass of solution}} \times 1\,000\,000$	
	molarity = $\dfrac{\text{moles of solute}}{\text{liter of solution}}$	
Combined Gas Law	$\dfrac{P_1V_1}{T_1} = \dfrac{P_2V_2}{T_2}$	P = pressure V = volume T = temperature
Titration	$M_AV_A = M_BV_B$	M_A = molarity of H^+ M_B = molarity of OH^- V_A = volume of acid V_B = volume of base
Heat	$q = mC\Delta T$ $q = mH_f$ $q = mH_v$	q = heat H_f = heat of fusion m = mass H_v = heat of vaporization C = specific heat capacity ΔT = change in temperature
Temperature	$K = {}^\circ C + 273$	K = kelvin ${}^\circ C$ = degree Celsius

Glossary and Index

A

Absolute Zero (6)
0 K or -273°C; the temperature at which all molecular movements stop.

Accelerator (204)
a device which gives charged particles sufficient kinetic energy to penetrate the nucleus.

Acid, Arrhenius (126)
a substance that produces H^+ (hydrogen ion, proton) or H_3O^+ (hydronium) ion as the only positive ion in solutions.

Acid, Brönsted-Lowry (126)
a substance that donates a proton (H^+, hydrogen ion) in a reaction.

Activated complex (148)
a high energy substance formed during a chemical reaction.

Activation energy (142)
minimal amount of energy needed to start a reaction.

Addition reaction (175, 176)
organic reaction that involves the adding of hydrogen atoms (or halogen atoms) to a double or a triple bond.

Addition polymerization (175, 177)
the joining of monomers (small unit molecules) with double bonds to form a polymer (a larger unit) molecule.

Alcohol (166, 167)
an organic compound containing the hydroxyl group (-OH) as the functional group.

Aldehyde (168)
an organic compound containing $-\overset{\overset{\displaystyle O}{\|}}{C}-H$ as the functional group.

Alkali metal (28)
an element in Group 1 of the Periodic Table.

Alkaline Earth metal (28)
an element in Group 2 of the Periodic Table.

Alkane (164, 165)
a saturated hydrocarbon with all single bonds and a general formula of C_nH_{2n+2}.

Alkene (164, 165)
an unsaturated hydrocarbon with a double bond and a general formula of C_nH_{2n}.

Alkyl group
a hydrocarbon group (found as a side chain) that contains one less H atom than an alkane with the same number of C atoms.

Alkyne (164, 165)
an unsaturated hydrocarbon with a triple ($\equiv$) bond and a general formula of C_nH_{2n-2}.

Allotropes (22)
two or more different forms of the same element that have different formulas, structures, and properties.

Alpha decay (207, 212)
a nuclear decay that releases an alpha particle.

Alpha particle (204)
a helium nucleus, ^4_2He

Alternate acid-base theory (Bronsted-Lowry theory)
describes acids as H^+ donors and bases as H^+ acceptors in reactions.

Amide (168)
an organic compound formed from a reaction of an organic acid with an amine.

Amine (168)
an organic compound that has $-\overset{|}{N}-$ (nitrogen) as its functional group.

Anode (191)
an electrode (site) where oxidation occurs in electrochemical (voltaic and electrolytic) cells.
In voltaic cells, the anode is negative.
In electrolytic cells, the anode is positive.

Aqueous solution (105)
a homogeneous mixture made with water as the solvent.

Arrhenius theory (126)
describes acids as substances that produce H^+ ion and bases as substances that produce OH^- ion in solutions.

Artificial Transmutation (209)
converting (transforming) a stable element to a radioactive unstable element by bombarding (hitting) the stable nucleus with a high energy particle.

Asymmetrical molecule (63)
a molecule that has a polarized structure because of an uneven charge distribution.

Atom (37, 40)
the basic or the smallest unit of an element that can be involved in chemical reactions.

Atomic mass (44)
the weighted average mass of an element's naturally occurring isotopes.

Atomic mass unit (44)
one-twelfth $(1/12^{th})$ the mass of a carbon-12 atom.

Atomic number (41)
the number of protons in the nucleus of an atom.

Atomic radius (size) (24, 31)
half the distance between adjacent nuclei of identical bonded atoms.

Avogadro's law (13)
equal volumes of all gases under the same pressure and temperature contain equal numbers of molecules.

Glossary and Index

B

Base, Arrhenius (126)
a substance that produces OH⁻ (hydroxide ion) as the only negative ion in solutions.

Base, Brönsted-Lowry (126)
a substance that accepts a proton (H^+, hydrogen ion) in a reaction.

Beta decay (208, 212)
a nuclear decay that releases a beta particle.

Beta particle (204)
a high-speed electron , $_{-1}^{0}e$, released from an atomic nucleus during a nuclear decay.

Binary compound (62)
a chemical substance composed of two different elements chemically combined.

Boiling point (120)
the temperature of a liquid at which the vapor pressure of the liquid is equal to the atmospheric pressure. Boiling point of water = 100°C at 1 atm pressure.

Boyle's Law (14)
describes behavior of a gas at constant temperature: At constant temperature, volume of a gas varies indirectly with the pressure.

C

Calorimeter (9)
a device used in measuring heat energy change during a physical and a chemical process.

Catalyst (142)
a substance that speeds up a reaction by providing an alternate, lower activation energy pathway.

Cathode (191)
an electrode (site) where reduction occurs in electrochemical cells.
In voltaic cells, the cathode is positive. In electrolytic cells, the cathode is negative.

Charles' Law (14)
describes behavior of gases at constant pressure: At constant pressure, the volume of a gas is directly proportional to its Kelvin (absolute) temperature.

Chemical bonding (59)
the simultaneous attraction of two nuclei to electrons.

Chemical change (17)
the changing of composition of one or more substances during chemical reactions.

Chemical formula (77)
expression of qualitative and quantitative composition of pure substances.

Chemical property (17)
a characteristic of a substance based on its interaction with other substances.

Chemistry (1)
the study of the composition, properties, changes, and energy of matter.

Coefficient (85)
a number (usually a whole number) in front of a formula that indicates how many moles (or units) of that substance.

Collision Theory (141)
for a chemical reaction to occur, reacting particles must collide effectively.

Combined gas law (14) $\dfrac{P_1 V_1}{T_1} = \dfrac{P_2 V_2}{T_2}$

Combustion (86, 177)
an exothermic reaction of a substance with oxygen to produce H_2O, CO_2, and energy

Compound (1)
a substance composed of two or more different elements chemically combined in a definite ratio
a substance that can be separated (decomposed) only by chemical methods.

Concentrated solution (112)
a solution containing a large amount of dissolved solute relative to the amount of solvent.

Condensation (5)
exothermic phase change of a substance from gas (vapor) to a liquid.

Condensation polymerization (177, 177)
the joining of monomers (small unit molecules) into a polymer (a large unit molecule) by the removal of water.

Conductivity (24)
ability of an electrical current to flow through a substance.
Conductivity of electrolytes (soluble substances) in aqueous and liquid phase is due to mobile ions. Conductivity of metallic substances is due to mobile valence electrons.

Conjugate acid-base pair (137)
species in acid-base reactions that differ by just one hydrogen atom

Coordinate covalent bond (64)
a type of covalent bond in which one atom provides both shared electrons with H^+

Covalent bond (63, 65)
a bond formed by the sharing of electrons between nonmetal atoms.

Cracking (175)
the breaking of a large hydrocarbon molecule into smaller molecules.

Crystallization (2, 106)
a process of recovering a solute from a solution (mixture) by evaporation (or boiling).

D

Dalton's law of partial pressures (20)
total pressure of a gas mixture is the sum of all the individual gas pressures.

Decomposition (86)
chemical reaction in which a compound is broken down into simpler substances.

Density (33, 102)
mass per unit volume of a substance; $\text{Density} = \dfrac{\text{mass}}{\text{volume}}$

Deposition   (5)
an exothermic phase change by which a gas changes to a solid.

Diatomic molecule (28, 63)
a molecule consisting of two identical atoms. Examples: O_2 and H_2

Dihydroxy alcohol   (167)
an alcohol with two —OH groups

Dilute solution   (112)
a solution containing little dissolved solute in comparison to the amount of solvent.

Distillation   (2)
a process by which components of a homogeneous mixture can be separated by differences in boiling points.

Double covalent bond (=)   (63, 164)
the sharing of two pairs of electrons (four total electrons) between two atoms.

Double replacement   (80)
a chemical reaction that involves the exchange of ions.

Ductility   (24)
ability (property) of a metal to be drawn into a thin wire.

E

Effective collision   (141)
a collision in which the particles collide with sufficient kinetic energy and at appropriate angle.

Electrochemical cell   (190)
a system in which there is a flow of electrical current while a chemical reaction is taking place. Voltaic and electrolytic cells are the two most common types of electrochemical cells.

Electrode   (191)
a site at which oxidation or reduction can occur in electrochemical cells.
The anode (oxidation site) and cathode (reduction site) are the two electrodes of electrochemical cells.

Electrolysis (193)
a process by which electrical current forces a nonspontaneous redox reaction to occur.
Electrolysis of water: $2H_2O$ + electricity $\rightarrow$ $2\,H_2$ + O_2

Electrolyte   (134)
a substances that dissolves in water to produce an aqueous solution that conducts electricity. Conductivity of an electrolyte is due to mobile ions in solution.

Electrolytic cell   (190, 193, 194)
an electrochemical cell that requires an electrical current to cause a nonspontaneous redox reaction to occur.

Electron   (41, 42)
a negatively charged subatomic particle found surrounding the nucleus (in orbitals) of an atom.

Electron configuration   (46)
distribution of electrons in electron shells (energy levels) of an atom.

Electron-dot diagram   (47, 72)
a diagram showing the symbol of an atom and dots equal to the number of valence electrons.

Electronegativity   (24, 32)
a measure of an atom's ability (tendency) to attract electrons during chemical bonding.

Electrolytic reduction   (193)
the use of an electrolytic cell to force an ion to gain electrons and form a neutral atom.

Electroplating   (193)
use of an electrolytic cell to coat a thin layer of a metal onto another surface.

Element   (1)
a substance composed of atoms of the same atomic number.
a substance that cannot be decomposed (broken down) into simpler substances.

Empirical formula   (78)
a formula showing atoms combined in the simplest whole number ratio.

Empty space model   (37)
Rutherford's gold foil experimental conclusion that an atom is mostly empty space.

Endothermic   (5, 145, 146)
a process that absorbs energy.
The products of an endothermic reaction always have more energy than the reactants.

Energy   (9)
ability to do work; can be measured in joules or calories.

Entropy   (152)
a measure of the disorder or randomness of a system.
Entropy increases from solid to liquid to gas and with an increase in temperature.

Equilibrium   (153)
a state of a system when the rates (speeds) of opposing processes (reactions) are equal.

Equilibrium expression / Equilibrium constant (158)
the ratio of the molar concentrations of the products to reactants of an equilibrium reaction. Liquids and solids are excluded from equilibrium expressions.

Ester (168)
an organic compound with $-\overset{\displaystyle O}{\overset{\displaystyle \|}{C}}-O$ $(-COO-)$ as the functional group.

Esterification   (175, 176)
an organic reaction between an alcohol and organic acid to produce an ester.

Ether   (167)
an organic compound with $-O-$ as the functional group.

Ethene (164)
first member of the alkene hydrocarbons with a formula of C_2H_4

$$\begin{array}{ccc} H & & H \\ \diagdown & & \diagup \\ & C = C & \\ \diagup & & \diagdown \\ H & & H \end{array}$$

Ethyne (164)
first member of the alkyne hydrocarbons with a formula of C_2H_2 $H-C\equiv C-H$

Evaporation (5)
an endothermic phase change of a liquid to its gas phase at a constant boiling point. See also vaporization.

Excited state (44)
a state of an atom in which electrons are at higher electron shells (energy levels)

Exothermic (5, 145, 146)
a process that releases energy.
The products of an exothermic reaction always have less energy than the reactants.

F

Fermentation (86, 177)
an organic reaction in which sugar is converted to alcohol (ethanol, C_2H_5OH) and carbon dioxide.

Filtration (2, 106)
a process that is used to separate a heterogeneous liquid mixture that is composed of substances with different particle sizes.

Fission (210, 212)
the splitting of a large nucleus into smaller nuclei fragments in a nuclear reaction. Mass is converted to huge amounts of energy during fission.

Formula (77)
symbols and subscripts used to represent the composition of a substance.

Formula mass (92)
total mass of all the atoms in one unit of a formula.

Freezing (solidification) (5)
an exothermic phase change by which a liquid changes to a solid.

Freezing point (6)
the temperature that a liquid changes to a solid.
The freezing point and melting point of a substance are the same.

Functional group (166)
an atom or a group of atoms that replaces a hydrogen atom in a hydrocarbon.

Fusion (211, 212)
the joining of two small nuclei to make a larger nucleus in a nuclear reaction.

G

Gamma radiation (ray)   (204)
high-energy rays similar to X-rays that are released during nuclear decay.
A gamma ray has zero mass and zero charge, $^{0}_{0}\gamma$

Gas phase   (4)
a phase of matter with no definite shape and no definite volume.

Gay-Lussac's law   (14)
at constant volume, pressure of a gas varies directly with the Kelvin temperature

Geological dating   (220)
determining the age of a rock or mineral by comparing amounts of Uranium-238 to
Lead-206 in the sample.

Graham's Law of Effusion   (19)
the rates at which gases travel is inversely proportional to their molar masses

Gram-formula mass   (92)
the mass of one mole of a substance expressed in grams
The total mass of all atoms in one mole of a substance.

Ground state   (48)
a state of an atom in which all electrons of the atom occupy the lowest available levels.

Group (family)   (22)
the vertical column of the Periodic Table.
Elements in the same group have the same number of valence electrons and share
similar chemical properties.

H

Haber process (86)
a chemical reaction that produces ammonia from nitrogen and hydrogen.
$$N_2 \quad + \quad 3H_2 \rightarrow \quad 2NH_3 \quad (\text{Haber process equation}).$$

Half-life   (216)
the length of time it takes for a sample of a radioisotope to decay to half its original
mass (or atoms)

Half-reaction   (185)
a reaction that shows either the oxidation or the reduction part of a redox reaction.

Halide   (166)
a compound that contains a halogen (Group 17) atom.

Halogen   (28)
an element found in Group 17 of the Periodic Table.

Heat   (9)
a form of energy that can flow (or transfer) from one substance (or area) to another.
Joules and calories are two units commonly used to measure the quantity of heat.

Heat of fusion   (10)
the amount of heat needed to change a unit mass of a solid to a liquid at its melting
point. The heat of fusion for water is 334 Joules per gram.

Heat of reaction (ΔH)   (145)
amount of heat absorbed or released during a reaction.
The difference between the potential energy of the products and the potential energy
of the reactants.
$$\Delta H \; = \; \text{Potential energy of products} \; - \; \text{Potential energy of reactants}.$$

Glossary and Index

Heat of vaporization (10)
the amount of heat needed to change a unit mass of a liquid to vapor (gas) at its boiling point. Heat of vaporization for water is 2260 Joules per gram.

Heterogeneous (2)
a mixture in which substances in the mixture are not uniformly or evenly mixed.

Homogeneous (2)
a type of mixture in which substances in the mixture are uniformly and evenly mixed. Solutions are homogeneous mixtures.

Homologous series (164)
a group of related compounds in which one member differs from the next member by a set number of atoms.

Hydrate (94, 95)
an ionic compound containing a set number of water molecules within its crystal structure.
$CuSO_4 \cdot 5H_2O$ is a hydrate. It contains five moles of water.

Hydrocarbon (164)
an organic compound containing only hydrogen and carbon atoms.

Hydrogen bonding (70)
attraction of a hydrogen atom to an oxygen, nitrogen, or fluorine atom of another molecule. Hydrogen bonding exists (or is strongest) in H_2O (water), NH_3 (ammonia), and HF (hydrogen fluoride).

Hydrogen ion (H^+) (126)
a hydrogen atom that has lost its only electron. H^+ is a proton.
The only positive ion produced by all Arrhenius acids in solution.

Hydrolysis (137)
a reaction of a salt in water to produce either an acidic, basic, or neutral solution.

Hydronium ion (H_3O^+) (126)
a polyatomic ion formed when H_2O (a water molecule) combines with H^+ (hydrogen ion). Ion formed by all Arrhenius acids in solution.

Hydroxide ion (OH^-) (126)
the only negative ion produced by Arrhenius bases in solution.

Hydroxyl group (–OH) (166)
a functional group found in compounds of alcohols.
NOTE: Hydroxyl groups do not ionize.

I

Ideal gas (12)
a theoretical gas that has all the characteristics described by the kinetic molecular theory.

Ideal gas law (19)
$PV = nRT$. Describes ideal gas behavior by relating moles, pressure, volume and absolute temperature of the gas.

Immiscible (108)
two liquids that do not mix well with each other.

Indicator   (127)
any substance that changes color in the presence of another substance.
Acid-base indicators are used to determine if a substance is an acid or a base.

Insoluble   (108)
a solute substance with low solubility (doesn't dissolve well) in a given solvent.

Intermolecular forces   (69)
weak forces of attraction between molecules of molecular substances in the liquid and solid states

Ion   (52)
a charged (+ or -) particle.

Ionic bond   (62)
a bond formed by the transfer of one or more electrons from a metal to a nonmetal.
An ionic bond is formed by electrostatic attraction of a positive ion to a negative ion.

Ionic compound (substance)   (62)
compounds that are composed of positive and negative particles.
$NaCl$, $NaNO_3$, and NH_4Cl are examples of ionic substances.

Ionic radius   (24)
the size of an ion as measured from the nucleus to the outer energy level of that ion.

Ionization energy   (24, 32)
energy needed to remove the most loosely bound valence electron from an atom.

Isomers   (172)
organic compounds with the same molecular formula but different structural formulas.

Isotopes   (43)
atoms of the same element with the same number of protons but different numbers of neutrons. Isotopes have the same atomic number but different mass numbers.

J - K

Joules   (9)
a unit for measuring the amount of heat energy.

Kelvin (K)   (6)
a unit for measuring temperature. Temperature in Kelvin is always 273 higher than the equivalent temperature in Celsius. $K = {}^{\circ}C + 273$

Ketone   (168)
an organic compound containing $-\overset{\overset{\displaystyle O}{\|}}{C}-$ or $(-CO-)$, a carbonyl functional group.

Kinetic energy   (6)
energy due to motion or movement of particles in a substance.
Average kinetic energy of particles determines temperature of a substance.

Kinetic molecular theory   (12)
a theory that is used to explain behavior of gas particles.

Kinetics   (141)
the study of rate and mechanisms of reactions

Glossary and Index

L

Law of conservation (86)
In a chemical reaction, mass, atoms, charges, and energy are conserved (neither created nor destroyed).

Law of definite proportions (1)
atoms of a compound are in a fixed ratio.

Le Chatelier's principle (154)
a chemical or physical process will shift at equilibrium to compensate for added stress.

Lewis electron-dot diagram (47, 72)
a diagram showing the symbol of an atom and dots equal to the number of its valence electrons.

Liquid phase (4)
a phase of matter with definite volume but no definite shape (takes the shape of the container).

Luster (24)
a property that describes the shininess of a metallic element

M

Malleability (24)
ability (or property) of a metal to be hammered into a thin sheet.

Mass number (41)
the total number of protons and neutrons in the nucleus of an atom.

Matter (1)
anything that has mass and volume (occupied space).

Melting point (5)
the temperature at which a solid changes to a liquid.
The melting point of water, 0°C or 273 K, is the same as the freezing point.

Metal (21, 22, 23)
an element that tends to lose electrons and form a positive ion during chemical reactions. The majority of the elements (about 75%) are metals.

Metallic bond (59, 60)
bonding in metals described as "positive ions immersed in a sea of mobile electrons"

Metalloid (24, 25)
an element with both metallic and nonmetallic properties (characteristics).

Mixture (1)
a physical combination of two or more substances that can be homogeneous or heterogeneous. Mixtures can be separated by physical methods.

Molar mass (92)
mass in grams of one mole of a formula.

Molar volume (96)
volume of one mole of a gas at STP is equal to 22.4 liters.

Molarity (118)
concentration of a solution expressed in moles of solute per liter of solution.

$$\text{Molarity} = \frac{\text{moles of solute}}{\text{liter of solution}}$$

Mole   (91)

unit of quantity of particles (atoms, molecules, ions, electrons) in a substance
1 mole = 6.02 x 10^{23} particles.

Molecular formula   (74, 91)

a formula showing the actual composition (or ratio of atoms) in a substance.

Molecule   (63)

the smallest unit of a covalent (molecular) substance that has the same properties of
the substance.
A molecule could be one nonmetal atom (He, Ne) or a group of nonmetal atoms
($C_6H_{12}O_6$, HCl, H_2O) covalently bonded

Molecular substance   (63)

a substance composed of molecules
H_2O, CO_2, O_2, NH_3, and $C_6H_{12}O_6$ are examples of molecular substances.

Monomer   (175, 177)

an individual unit of a polymer.

Multiple covalent bond (63, 164)

a double or a triple covalent bond formed by the sharing of more than two electrons.

N

Network covalent bond   (64)

covalent bonding with absence of discrete particles; in network solid substances

Neutralization   (132)

a reaction of an acid with a base to produce water and a salt.

Neutron   (41, 204)

the subatomic particle with no charge, found in the nucleus of an atom.

Noble gas   (26, 28)

an element found in Group 18 of the Periodic Table.

Nonmetal   (25, 26)

an element that tends to gain electrons and forms negative ions, or shares electrons
to form a covalent bond.

Nonpolar covalent bond   (63, 65)

a bond formed by the equal sharing of electrons between two identical nonmetal
atoms (or of the same electronegativity).

Nonpolar substance   (63)

a substance whose molecules have a symmetrical shape and even charge distribution.

Nucleons   (41)

particles in the nucleus that include protons and neutrons.

Nucleus   (40)

the small, dense, positive core of an atom containing protons and neutrons.

O

Octet rule   (59)

when an atom has a stable configuration with eight electrons in the valence shell.

Orbital   (37, 46)

a region in an atom where electrons are likely to be found (or located).

Orbital notation   (56)

a diagram showing arrangements of electrons in orbitals of atoms.

Glossary and Index

Organic acid   (169)
a compound containing $-COOH$ or $-\overset{\displaystyle O}{\overset{\displaystyle \|}{C}}-OH$ as its functional group.

Organic chemistry   (161)
the study of carbon-based compounds.

Oxidation   (181, 184)
the loss of electrons by an atom during a redox reaction.
Oxidation leads to an increase in oxidation state (number) of a substance.

Oxidized substance (Reducing agent)   (184)
a substance that loses electrons in a redox reaction.
a substance whose oxidation number (state) increases after a redox reaction

Oxidizing agent (Reduced substance)   (184)
a substance that is reduced (gains electrons) in a redox reaction.
a substance whose oxidation number (state) decreases after a redox reaction

Oxidation number/ Oxidation state   (181, 182)
a charge an atom has or appears to have

Ozone   (22)
O_3, an allotrope (a different molecular form) of oxygen

P

Parts per million   (118)
concentration of a solution expressed as the ratio of mass of solute per million parts of a solution.

$$\text{Part per million (ppm)} = \frac{\text{mass of solute}}{\text{mass of solution}} \times 1\ 000\ 000$$

Percent composition   (94, 95)
composition of a compound as the percentage by mass of each element compared to the total mass of the compound.

$$\text{Percent composition} = \frac{\text{mass of part}}{\text{mass of whole}} \times 100$$

Period   (22)
the horizontal rows of the Periodic Table
Elements in a period have the same number of occupied electron shells (or energy levels).

Periodic law (22)
states that properties of elements are periodic functions of their atomic numbers.

pH (127, 128)
values that indicate the strength of an acid or a base. pH values range from $0-14$.
pH value is determined from how many H^+ ions are in a solution.

Phase change diagram   (7)
a diagram showing changes in a substance as it is being heated or cooled over time.

Phase equilibrium   (153)
a state of balance when the rates of two opposing (opposite) phase changes are equal.

Physical change (17)
a change that does not alter the composition of a substance.
Phase changes and dissolving are examples of physical changes.

Physical properties   (17)
characteristics of a substance that can be observed or measured without changing the chemical composition of the substance

Polar covalent bond (63, 65)
a bond formed by the unequal sharing of electrons between two different nonmetal atoms.

Polyatomic ion (76)
group of two or more atoms with excess positive or negative charges (See Table E).

Polymer (172, 174)
an organic compound composed of chains of monomers (smaller units).

Polymerization (62)
an organic reaction by which monomers (small units of molecules) are joined together to make a polymer (a larger unit molecule).

Positron (204)
a positively charged particle similar in mass to an electron. $^{0}_{+1}e$

Positron decay (emission) (208, 212)
a nuclear decay that releases a positron

Potential energy (146)
stored energy in chemical substances.
Amount of potential energy depends on composition and the structure of a substance.

Potential energy diagram (148, 149)
a diagram showing the changes in potential energy of substances during a reaction.

Precipitate (115)
a solid that forms out of a solution

Primary alcohol (167)
an alcohol with an –OH functional group attached to an end carbon.

Product (85, 148)
a substance that remains (or forms) after a chemical reaction is completed.
Products are placed to the right of an arrow in equations.

Proton (40, 204)
a subatomic particle with a positive charge found in the nucleus of an atom.
The number of protons in an atom is equal to the atomic number of the element.

Pure substance (1)
a type of matter with the same composition and properties in all samples.
Pure substances are also referred to as substances.
Elements and compounds are pure substances.

Q

Qualitative (77)
indicates the type of atom that is in a chemical formula.

Quantum theory (55)
describes location and behavior of electrons in sets of four quantum numbers

Quantitative (77)
indicates the number of each atom in a formula.

Glossary and Index

Solid   (4)
a phase of matter with definite shape and definite volume

Solubility   (108)
a measure of the extent to which a solute will dissolve in a given solvent at a specified temperature.

Soluble   (108, 110)
a substance with high solubility.

Solute   (105)
the substance that is being dissolved.
When a salt dissolves in water, the solute is the salt.

Solution   (105)
a homogeneous mixture of substances in the same physical state.

Solvent   (105)
the substance (usually a liquid) that is dissolving the solute.
Water is the solvent in all aqueous solutions.

Specific heat capacity   (9)
amount of heat needed to change the temperature of a one-gram sample of a substance by one °C or one K.

Spectral lines (bright-line spectrum)   (49)
band of colors produced as electrons go from excited (high) to ground (low) state.

Spontaneous reaction   (159, 197)
a reaction that will occur under a given set of conditions
a reaction that proceeds in the direction of lower energy and greater entropy

Stoichiometry   (91)
the study and calculations of relative quantities of substances in formulas and equations.

STP   (13)
standard temperature (0°C, 273 K) and pressure (1 atm, 101.3 kPa)

Stress   (154)
a change in temperature, pressure, or concentration in a reaction at equilibrium.

Sublimation   (5)
an endothermic phase change from solid to gas.

Subscript   (77)
a whole number written next to a chemical symbol to indicate the number of atoms.

Substitution reaction   (175, 176)
an organic reaction of an alkane with a halogen to produce a halide.
a reaction in which a halogen atom replaces a hydrogen atom of an alkane (saturated) hydrocarbon.

Supersaturated solution   (112)
a solution containing more solute than would normally dissolve at that given temperature.

Symmetrical molecule   (63)
a molecule that has a nonpolarized structure due to an even charge distribution.

Synthesis   (86)
a chemical reaction in which two or more substances combine to make one substance.

Glossary and Index

T

Temperature   (6)
the measure of the average kinetic energy of particles in a substance.
Temperature and average kinetic energy are directly related.

Tertiary alcohol   (167)
an alcohol in which the –OH is bonded to a carbon atom that is already bonded to
three other carbon atoms.

Thomson, J.J.   (37, 38)
conducted cathode ray experiment that led to the discovery of electrons

Titration   (132)
a process used in determining the concentration of an unknown solution by reacting it
with a solution of known concentration.

Tracer   (220)
a radioisotope used to track a chemical reaction.

Transition element   (26, 28)
an element found in Groups 3 – 12 of the Periodic Table.

Transmutation   (207)
the changing or converting of a nucleus of one atom into a nucleus of a different atom

Trihydroxy alcohol   (167)
an alcohol with three –OH (hydroxyl) groups.

Triple covalent bond   (63, 164)
a covalent bond resulting from the sharing of three pairs of electrons (six total
electrons).

U - W

Unsaturated hydrocarbon   (164)
organic compound containing double or triple bonded carbon atoms.

Unsaturated solution   (112)
a solution containing less dissolved solute than can be dissolved at a given temperature.

Valence electrons   (47, 72)
the electrons in the outermost electron shell (energy level) of an atom.

Vapor   (120)
a gas form of a substance that is normally a liquid at room temperature.

Vapor pressure   (120)
the pressure exerted by vapor (evaporated particles) on the surface of the liquid.

Vaporization   (120)
spontaneous change of a liquid to its vapor at the surface of the liquid.
Vaporization can occur at any temperature.

Voltaic cell   (190)
an electrochemical cell in which electrical energy is produced from a spontaneous
redox chemical reaction.

Wave-mechanical model (electron-cloud model)   (37)
the current model of an atom that places electrons in orbitals.
The orbital is described as the most probable region of finding electrons in an atom.

CPSIA information can be obtained
at www.ICGtesting.com
Printed in the USA
BVHW012000041118
532134BV00010B/174/P

9 781978 362291